ADVERTISING
CREATIVE

4TH EDITION

SAGE was founded in 1965 by Sara Miller McCune to support the dissemination of usable knowledge by publishing innovative and high-quality research and teaching content. Today, we publish over 900 journals, including those of more than 400 learned societies, more than 800 new books per year, and a growing range of library products including archives, data, case studies, reports, and video. SAGE remains majority-owned by our founder, and after Sara's lifetime will become owned by a charitable trust that secures our continued independence.

Los Angeles | London | New Delhi | Singapore | Washington DC

ADVERTISING CREATIVE
STRATEGY · COPY · DESIGN

TOM ALTSTIEL
PKA MARKETING

JEAN GROW
MARQUETTE UNIVERSITY

4TH EDITION

Los Angeles | London | New Delhi
Singapore | Washington DC

Los Angeles | London | New Delhi
Singapore | Washington DC

FOR INFORMATION:

SAGE Publications, Inc.
2455 Teller Road
Thousand Oaks, California 91320
E-mail: order@sagepub.com

SAGE Publications Ltd.
1 Oliver's Yard
55 City Road
London EC1Y 1SP
United Kingdom

SAGE Publications India Pvt. Ltd.
B 1/I 1 Mohan Cooperative Industrial Area
Mathura Road, New Delhi 110 044
India

SAGE Publications Asia-Pacific Pte. Ltd.
3 Church Street
#10-04 Samsung Hub
Singapore 049483

Acquisitions Editor: Matt Byrnie
Editorial Assistant: Janae Masnovi
eLearning Editor: Gabrielle Piccininni
Production Editor: Laura Barrett
Copy Editor: Jim Kelly
Typesetter: C&M Digitals (P) Ltd.
Proofreader: Dennis Webb
Indexer: Nancy Fulton
Cover Designer: Lauren Habermehl
Marketing Manager: Ashlee Blunk

Printed in the United States of America

Library of Congress Cataloging-in-Publication Data

Names: Altstiel, Tom, author. | Grow, Jean, author.

Title: Advertising creative : strategy, copy, and design / Tom Altstiel, Jean Grow.

Description: Fourth edition. | Los Angeles : SAGE, [2017] | Includes bibliographical references and index.

Identifiers: LCCN 2015035696 | ISBN 978-1-5063-1538-6 (pbk. : alk. paper)

Subjects: LCSH: Advertising.

Classification: LCC HF5823 .A758 2017 | DDC 659.1—dc23 LC record available at http://lccn.loc.gov/2015035696

This book is printed on acid-free paper.

15 16 17 18 19 10 9 8 7 6 5 4 3 2 1

Brief Contents

Detailed Contents

Chapter 3 Ethical and Legal Issues: Doing the Right Thing   54

Chapter 4 Evolving Audiences: The Times They Are A-Changin'   78

Chapter 5   International Advertising: It's a Global Marketplace   110

Chapter 7   Campaigns: Synergy and Integration   168

Chapter 9 Print: Writing for Reading

Chapter 10 Radio and Television: Interruptions That Sell

Chapter 11   Websites: Copy and Content   272

Chapter 12   Socially Mobile: Reaching Communities That Buy   296

Chapter 13   Support Media: Everyone Out of the Box 326

Chapter 14   Direct Marketing: Hitting the Bull's-Eye   354

Chapter 15   Business-to-Business: Selling Along the Supply Chain   376

Chapter 16   Survival Guide: Landing Your First Job and Thriving   398

Preface

Welcome to the first postdigital edition.

We started this series in 2005 with the dot-com bust fresh in our memories and innovations like Facebook, Twitter, and iPhones on the near horizon. We heard they were coming, but no one could have predicted their impact on marketing communications. In those days we spoke of silos—solid containers for "traditional" and "nontraditional" media. Another analogy was swim lanes—well-defined boundaries where different marketing communication elements competed. "Digital" was one of those swim lanes. As technology evolved, digital competed in more lanes. Now we can take out the lane markers. Everybody and everything is in one big digital pool, swimming for their lives. Welcome to the postdigital age.

Digital Disruption

Advertising Age summed it up nicely: "Traditional media found itself scrambling to stay relevant as digital media wreaked havoc with the guarantee that consumers were likely to see ad messages. Expensive journalism distributed free online amassed audience but not ad dollars and wiped out a whole generation of magazines and newspapers, while DVRs, podcasts, streaming video services like Netflix and Hulu challenged TV and radio models. Out of this massive shift, marketers and agencies got very innovative in turning these new tools to their advantage."[1]

Despite the disruptions in the marketing world, some basic truths still apply. Brands need to make friends. Consumers still have wants and needs that must be satisfied. People read and see what interests them. Sometimes it's advertising, but now it's delivered in ways never imagined 10 years ago. We still need to find that One Thing—probably more than ever since the market has been so fragmented.

The next edition of this book will most likely be arranged a lot differently to align with new ideas about marketing communication in this postdigital age. Perhaps we'll be in a new age with a new name—with new thinking about the best ways to reach an increasingly advertising-resistant world. However that world takes shape, we'll bet the Big Idea—that One Thing—will still be the center of it all.

But how do you leverage that One Thing in a world that is more and more globally connected, more and more diverse, yet more and more, well—dare we say similar? In past editions we talked about the need to embrace diversity because the world was changing, because it was becoming a global marketplace. The truth is, that global marketplace now lives in your backyard—and across the world. Yes, understanding diversity is more important than ever. You'll need to leverage that understanding whether you're working on a local campaign for Mom and Pop's Pizza, a regional campaign for T-Mobile, a national campaign for Target, or a global campaign for McDonald's.

Being a great advertising practitioner means understanding the content within this book and others like it, but it also means becoming a student of culture—local and global culture. In Chapters 3, 4, and 5 we attempt to explore the complex issues of an ever changing advertising landscape. At the same time we have tried to weave examples, which speak to an increasingly diverse world, throughout the entire text. However, you might also consider stretching your wings. None of us can afford to live in a bubble. So pop yours now. Start taking classes on world religions, ethnography, anthropology, social psychology, and racial and ethnic identity. Along the way, why not become fluent in another language? Build a cultural knowledge base that gives you an advantage.

---

1. "Top Ad Campaigns of the 21st Century," *Advertising Age*, http://adage.com/lp/top15/ (accessed August 11, 2015).

Beyond the Book

We've worked with Sage to develop a new website (study.sagepub.com/altstiel4e), as outlined below. There you will find a test bank, PowerPoint® presentations, discussion questions, chapter exercises, video links, and other web resources. The digital additions, new for the fourth edition, will link you directly to the advertising world. There are websites, blogs, and feeds that will help keep you up to date and ever wiser. You will also find links to some of the digital work discussed in the book.

You may also want to see what we are doing outside of the classroom. We invite you to follow us. Find Tom at LinkedIn. Find Jean at @jeangrow or follow her two blogs: Grow Cultural Geography (growculturalgeography.wordpress.com) and Ethical Action (ethicalaction.wordpress.com). And, of course, we want to hear your ideas. So, don't hesitate to share them with us through the "Contact the Authors" link on the Sage site.

Ancillaries

The password-protected Instructor Teaching Site at **study.sagepub.com/altstiel4e** gives instructors access to a full complement of resources to support and enhance their courses. The following assets are available on the site:

Test Bank: This Word test bank offers a diverse set of test questions and answers for each chapter of **the** book. Multiple-choice, true/false, short-answer, and essay questions for every chapter help instructors assess students' progress and understanding.

What Would You Do? This is a new feature, woven into each chapter and featuring case studies from fellow teachers, with questions that will allow students to apply lessons learned in class to real-world marketing problems. We invite submissions for this edition and the next and will be delighted to cite you, adding another line on your CV.

Discussion Questions: Chapter-specific questions help launch discussion by prompting students to engage with the material and by reinforcing important content.

Chapter Exercises and Activities: These lively and stimulating ideas, found at the end of each chapter, can be used in and out of class to reinforce active learning. The activities apply to individual and group projects.

PowerPoint® Slides: Chapter-specific slide presentations offer assistance with lecture and review preparation by highlighting essential content, features, and artwork from the book.

Video Links: Carefully selected web-based video resources feature relevant interviews, lectures, personal stories, inquiries, and other content for use in independent or classroom-based explorations of key topics.

Web Resources: These links to relevant websites direct both instructors and students to additional resources for further research on important chapter topics.

The open-access Student Study Site available at **study.sagepub.com/altstiel4e** is designed to maximize student comprehension of the material and to promote critical thinking and application. The following resources and study tools are available on the student portion of the book's website:

- Mobile-friendly **practice quizzes** allow for independent assessment by students of their mastery of course material

- Mobile-friendly **eFlashcards** strengthen understanding of key terms and concepts

- Carefully selected chapter-by-chapter **video and multimedia** content which enhance classroom-based explorations of key topics

Acknowledgments

We would never have completed this fourth edition without the help of some amazing folks. First, you wouldn't be reading this if our previous editions had not been so well accepted. Thanks to the teachers and advertising professionals around the world who have purchased past editions and adopted them for classes. We hope you like this one even more. Thanks to the creative practitioners who have shared their wisdom by contributing more detailed case histories, called Closer Looks. Your views of the inner workings of our business are invaluable. Thanks to the young people who shared their personal stories in the new Rising Stars sections. Your voices brought an insightful new dimension to this edition. Finally, thanks to our newest contributors, our fellow teachers. Your What Would You Do? case studies provide a valuable new teaching tool.

We are especially grateful to Lauren Habermehl, who designed the cover, the interior layout, and most of the infographics. Not only is she extraordinarily talented, she was a joy to work with. She captured our vision for this edition immediately and hit a home run with every component. Lauren, you made our job a lot easier, and we can't thank you enough. Temo Xopin from PKA Marketing also provided some excellent infographics and brought some tables to life. Thanks to Andrew Taylor, who helped track down new images for the book and did the first round of copyediting.

We are very appreciative of the entire SAGE team who have helped guide this book to completion: Matt Byrnie, Janae Masnovi, and Laura Barrett. We'd also like to thank copy editor Jim Kelly, who not only did a fantastic job correcting our many technical erors, but also added insight which improved the content. It continues to be a pleasure to work with such a helpful and personable group of professionals.

We would like to thank all the academic reviewers for this edition: Susan Westcott Alessandri, Suffolk University; Roberta Asahina, California State University, Fresno; Cristanna Cook, Husson University; Linda Goulet Crosby, Davenport University; Dick Fox, Belmont Abbey College; Klaus Gensheimer, Emerson College; Karie Hollerbach, Southeast Missouri State University; Ying Huang, University of West Florida; Joni Koegel, Cazenovia College; Art Novak, Savannah College of Art and Design; Ginger Rosenkrans, Pepperdine University; David Short, Texas State University; and Debbie Wideroe, Pepperdine University. We're especially grateful to the academic and industry reviewers who provided kind words for testimonials.

We'd also like to acknowledge the support of our coworkers, both on the academic and on the professional side, who allowed our passion for this book to encroach on our real jobs.

Finally, we thank our loved ones, who tolerated our late nights and weekends sitting at the keyboard instead of by their sides.

Tom and Jean

Chapter 1

Creativity
The Changing Nature of Our Business

Spoiler alert.

This book won't teach you how to be creative. No one can. But you may be surprised how creative you really are. You may not have been an A+ English student. But you may find you're an excellent copywriter. You may not be a great sketch artist. But you may discover you have a talent for logo design or ad layouts. You may not know much about ad copy. But you may have a knack for building communities online through social media. You may never have to write a broadcast TV commercial. But you may be able to create innovative online videos that go viral. If you think advertising today is a remnant of the *Mad Men* era, think again. It's an industry that keeps reinventing itself, and you will be part of that process.

What You Need to Learn

If you're lucky, you'll take classes that allow you to discover a lot about creative strategy and tactics, and probably a lot about yourself. At the very least you should learn:

- The correct format for writing copy for traditional and new media.

- The basic rules of copywriting and when to break them.

- How to put more sell into your copy.

- Design basics that apply to all media.

- Sensitivity of issues that affect consumers.

- Awareness of ethical and legal issues.

- How to connect the reader or viewer with the advertiser.

- How to keep continuity throughout a campaign.

- Knowing how to use emerging technology as a tool, not an idea.

- Understanding what endures in the face of a rapidly changing marketing environment.

- The importance of presenting your work.

"Properly practiced creativity can make one ad do the work of ten."[1]

Bill Bernbach,
copywriter and founding
partner, Doyle Dane Bernbach

Who Wants to Be a Creative?

At the beginning of each semester we ask students, "Who wants to be a copywriter?" We get a halfhearted response from about two or three. "Who wants to be an art director or a designer?" Usually a few more raise their hands. Then we get to creative director. Typically more than half the students covet that exalted title, and almost none of them realize you have to be a copywriter or an art director first.

These are the most common reasons advertising students don't want to become writers:

- "I think I want to be an account exec."

- "I might want to be an account planner."

- "I want to be a media director."

- "I want to work in social media."

- "Words are boring. I'm more of a picture person."

- "I'm not sure I can write."

- "I'm not sure I even want to be in advertising."

After McDonald's ended its investment in the company, Chipotle released an animated short called *The Scarecrow* with a companion mobile video game that criticized "industrial farming." Coincidence?

Creating and meeting a consumer's immediate need. That's what effective marketing communication is all about.

Those are legitimate reasons, but we can make a case for learning about creative strategy and tactics to answer every one of them.

- **Account executives** need to know how to evaluate creative work. Does it meet the objectives? What's the strategy? Why is it great or not so great? When account executives and account managers understand the creative process, they become more valuable to the client and their agency.

- **Account planners** have to understand consumers, their clients' products, market conditions, and many other factors that influence a brand preference or purchase. In essence they function as the voice of the consumer in strategy sessions. The skills required to develop creative strategy are key components in account planning.

- **Media folks** need to recognize the creative possibilities of each medium. They need to understand tone, positioning, resonance, and the other basics pounded into copywriters.

- **Bloggers** and **social media specialists** have to be able to merge their mastery of digital media with creative skills. Someone has to write all those blog posts and build those online communities with a few well-chosen words—even if they are limited to 140 characters.

- **Designers**, **art directors**, **producers**, and **graphic artists** should know how to write or at least how to defend their work. Why does it meet the strategies? Do the words and visuals work together? Does the font match the tone of the ad? Is the body copy too long? (It's *always* too long for art directors.) As we'll stress repeatedly throughout this book, writers also need to understand the basics of design. Design can't be separate from the concept.

There is English, and there is advertising copy. What you say is more important than how you write it. Ideas come first. Writing with style can follow.

Regaining Thought Leadership for the World's Most Iconic Whisky—Chivas Regal

©Chivas

Live With Chivalry

Chivas Regal is heavily outspent in the global whisky market by Johnnie Walker. In the face of such competition, we couldn't rely on just telling consumers a story about a product truth, we had to create a transformative idea and campaign.

Based on the global insight of *collective honour amongst modern gentlemen* (success but not at any cost), in 2008 we moved Chivas from a lifestyle positioning of 'The Chivas Life' to a competitive, relevant and modern expression of its DNA— the call to arms for modern gentlemen to 'Live With Chivalry.'

Using a series of international campaigns since 2009, we had successfully explained the core values underpinning chivalry—success with honour, brotherhood, freedom and gallantry.

Recruiting a New Generation of Drinkers

Recruiting new customers to the brand is crucial for Chivas. Generation Y (those born after 1980), are the biggest generation of all time. Not only are Gen Y a big group, but current trends show an opportunity to take share from other spirits and beer. The opportunity was big, but so was the challenge; this is an uncompromising group of consumers, with new expectations for both brand conduct and contact.

A New Definition of Shared Success

We knew (through extensive primary and secondary research we undertook across our global agency network) that Gen Y are not concerned with the notion of 'business as usual,' and the old self-indulgent codes of luxury. They want to be their own bosses, and they believe that businesses have a responsibility to use their financial success to improve the world, rather than just the balance sheet. The opportunity was to respond to the consumer desire for more ethical business practices by highlighting that success can and should be shared, rather than hoarded.

This plays to a historical brand truth of Chivas, a brand founded on doing good whilst doing well, with brothers James and John Chivas using proceeds from their business to support their local community infrastructure and secure employment and contracts for others in their community.

Live With Chivalry— Winning the Right Way

Win the Right Way is the latest installment of 'Live With Chivalry.' It is a movement based on people not just doing good, but doing well. Social enterprise is growing across the world, and the principles of social entrepreneurship align perfectly with Gen Y's desires for independence and responsible corporate behaviour.

We worked with Chivas to create a $1m seed capital fund for budding social entrepreneurs called The Venture, which we supported with a connected and interactive campaign split into two broad stages of provocation and enablement.

- *Provocation:* We used inspiring case studies and renowned global personalities like Chiwetel Ejiofor to exhort the values and potential impact of social enterprise.
- *Enablement:* We created TheVenture.com to allow social enterprises to submit their ideas, assisting the best of them through TheVenture.com.

The campaign launched globally in late 2014 to great acclaim and is a true behavioral manifestation of the brand's thought leadership idea—Live With Chivalry.

Russ Lidstone, CEO, Havas Worldwide, London

Creativity outside of advertising. You can put the skills learned through developing creative strategy and tactics to work in more fields than advertising. The ability to gather information, process it, prioritize the most important facts, and develop a persuasive message is useful in almost every occupation. Even if you don't aspire to be the next David Ogilvy, you might learn something about marketing, advertising, basic writing skills, and presenting your work. Who knows? You might even like it.

The Golden Age of Creativity

Every generation seems to have a Golden Age. Many people who built their careers in the post–*Mad Men* era look back to the 1950s through the early 1970s as the Golden Age of Advertising. This so-called Creative Revolution was one of many uprisings during turbulent times. Unlike any other era before or since, the focus was on youth, freedom, antiestablishment thinking. If you don't believe us check out Denis Leary's FX series *Sex & Drugs & Rock & Roll*. So it's not surprising that some of the world's most recognized ads (some of which are included in this book) were created during this time.

What made these ads revolutionary?

©Volkswagen

Think small.

Doyle Dane Bernbach turned the ad world on its head with its Volkswagen campaign. When other automakers were crowing about tail fins and chrome, VW took the opposite position with self-deprecating humor, a twist headline, white space, a small logo, and intelligent, yet friendly, copy.

- First, they began to shift focus to the brand, rather than the product. They developed a look, introduced memorable characters, and kept a consistent theme throughout years of long-running campaigns. All of these factors built brand awareness and acceptance.

- Second, they twisted conventional thinking. When most cars touted tail fins and chrome, Volkswagen told us to "Think small." When Hertz was bragging about being the top dog, Avis said it tried harder because it was number two. When Levy's advertised their Jewish rye bread, they used an Irish cop, an Asian man, and a Native American as models (although today, we'd say this is a blatant example of stereotyping).

- Third, they created new looks, using white space, asymmetrical layouts, minimal copy, and unique typography—all design elements that we take for granted in today's ads. The driving forces of this revolution included such giants as Leo Burnett, David Ogilvy, Mary Wells Lawrence, Howard Gossage, and Bill Bernbach, who are mentioned prominently in this text. First and foremost, they were copywriters. But they were also creative partners with some of the most influential designers of their era, such as George Lois, Helmut Krone, and Paul Rand. Even though these top creative talents went on to lead mega-agencies, their first love was writing and design.

Today we look to creative inspiration in the digital space from visionaries such as the late Steve Jobs, Mark Zuckerberg, and Biz Stone. In this brave new world where the "third screen" is rapidly becoming our primary window for communication, news, and entertainment, we may be entering a new Golden Age. Who knows? Maybe *you* could become a leader in the next creative revolution.

The Creative Team

Most copywriters do a lot more than just write ads. In fact, writing may be only a small part of their jobs. Although this section focuses on the copywriter, designers and art directors also handle many of these functions.

Co-Captain of the Creative Team

Traditionally a creative team has comprised a copywriter and an art director, with participation by web developers and broadcast producers. This team usually answers to a coach—the creative director.

Every player has his or her role, but in many cases the copywriter drives the creative process. However, once the art director understands the creative problem, he or she may become the idea leader. No matter who drives the process, the creative team needs to know the product frontward and backward, inside and out.

They have to understand who uses the product, how it compares with the competition, what's important to the consumer, and a million other facts. Sometimes art directors write the best headlines. Or writers come up with a killer visual. Sometimes the inspiration comes from a comment on Facebook or a tweet. The creative leaders need to be able to sift that nugget of an idea from all the white noise that surrounds it.

So, What Else Does a Writer Do?

In small shops, the writers wear so many hats, it's no wonder they develop big heads. Some of the responsibilities besides writing copy include:

- **Research**—primary and secondary.
- **Client contact**—getting the facts direct from the source rather than filtered through an account executive, presenting those ideas, and defending the work.
- **Broadcast producer**—finding the right director, talent, music, and postproduction house to make your vision come to life.
- **New business**—gathering data, organizing the creative, working on the pitch, and presenting the work.
- **Public relations**—some copywriters also write the news releases, plan promotional events, and even contact editors.
- **Internet content**—the Internet has become an integral part of a total marketing communication effort. A lot of "traditional" media writers are now writing websites, blogs, and social media content.
- **Creative management**—much has been written about whether copywriters or art directors make the best creative directors. The answer: yes.

Don (creative director): It's your job. I give you money. You give me ideas.

Peggy (copywriter): But you never say thank you.

Don: That's what the money is for![2]

Dialogue from *Mad Men*

Controlling the Creative Process

Step 1: Getting the facts. If you have a research department or account planners, take advantage of their knowledge. But don't settle for someone else's opinion. Talk to people who use the product, as well as those who don't. Talk to retailers who sell the product. Look at competitive advertising. In short, know as much as you can about the product, the competition, the market, and the people who buy it. Try to make the product part of your life.

Step 2: Brainstorming with a purpose. If you've done your homework, you can direct the free flow of creative ideas. Thanks to your knowledge, you can concentrate on finding a killer creative idea rather than floundering in a sea of pointless questions. But you must also be open to new ideas and independent thinking from your creative team members.

Step 3: Picking up a pencil before you reach for the mouse. This is critical, because it's all about the creative concept. Even if you can only draw stick people, that's okay. Where does the headline go? How much copy do you think you'll need? What's the main visual? How should the elements be arranged? Even though artists may ridicule your design, they will appreciate having the raw elements they can massage into a great-looking ad.

Step 4: Finding the reference/visuals. You may have a clear vision of the creative concept. Can you communicate that to your art director, creative director, account exec, or client? You can help your art

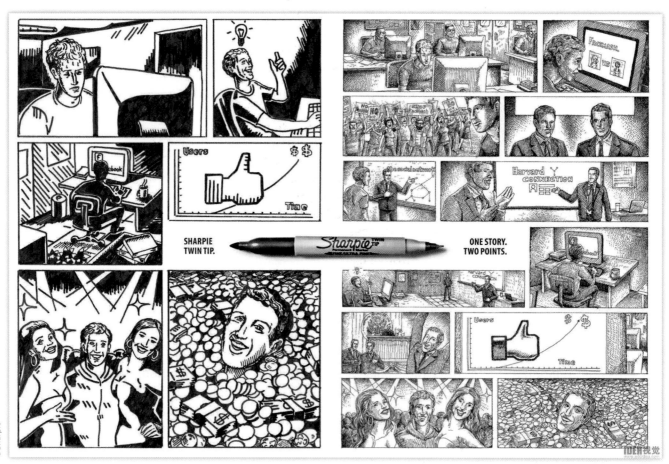

Product demonstrations are usually hard to show in a print ad, but Sharpie did it through thick and thin—with the same pen.

director by finding photos, artwork, or design elements, not to rip them off but to help you make your point. The finished piece may not look anything like your original vision, but at least you can start with a point of reference. Browse the web, stock photo books, and awards annuals. We can't emphasize this enough, especially for beginning writers—if you can't find what you want, it might trigger a new idea. The visual selection is a starting point, not the end game.

Step 5: Working with the rest of the team. For most creatives, the happiest and most productive years of their careers are spent collaborating with others. When two creative minds click, the whole really is greater than the sum of the parts. A great creative partnership, like any relationship, needs to be nurtured and will have its ups and downs. While one person may want to drive the whole process, it's best not to run over other teammates. They may come up with some ideas that will make you look like a genius.

Step 6: Preselling the creative director and account executive. Chances are you will not be working directly with the client, and even if you are, you probably won't be the sole contact. That's why you need the people who interface with the client to buy into your ideas. Maintaining a good relationship with the creative director not only protects your job; it also gives you an ally when you pitch your idea to the account executive and client. In many cases, the account executive represents the client in these discussions. He or she may try to poke holes in your logic or question your creative choices. That's why every creative choice must be backed with sound reasoning. In the end, if the account executive is sold, you have a much better chance of convincing the client.

Step 7: Selling the client. As the person who developed the idea, you have to be prepared to defend your work, using logic rather than emotion. Many times your brilliant reasoning will fail because clients usually think with their wallets. Over time you'll know how far you can push a client. The trick is to know when to retreat so you can fight another day. Most clients don't mind being challenged creatively, as long as there are sound reasons for taking chances.

The three things you *never* want to hear from a client:

- "That looks just like the competitor's ads. I want our ads to stand out."

- "I was looking for something a lot more creative. Take some risks."

- "You obviously don't understand our product or our market."

You won't hear those things if you take care of Steps 1 to 6.

Step 8: Getting it right. Okay, you've sold the client. Now what? You have to hand your creation to the production team, but your responsibilities don't end. Does the copy fit the way it should? If not, can you cut it? Can you change a word here and there to make it even better? Are the graphics what you envisioned? Your involvement is

"Our job is to read things that are not yet on the page."[3]

Steve Jobs, founder and former CEO, Apple

even more critical for broadcast. Did you have a specific talent in mind for voice or on-camera roles? Does the director understand and share your vision? Does the music fit?

If you remember nothing else, keep the following quote from the great Leo Burnett in mind and follow it through Step 10: "Nothing takes the guts out of a great idea like bad execution."

Step 9: Maintaining continuity. Almost everyone can come up with a great idea. Once. The hard part is extending that great idea in other media and repeating it, only differently, in a campaign. Over time, elements of a campaign tend to drift away from the original idea. Clients usually get tired of a look before the consumer. Art directors may want to "enhance" the campaign with new elements. Someone on the creative team needs to continually monitor the elements of an ongoing campaign to make sure they are true to the original idea.

Step 10: Discover what worked and why. If the ads in a campaign achieve their objectives, great! If they win awards, but the client loses market share, look out. Keep monitoring the efficacy of the campaign. What are the readership scores? What do the client's salespeople and retailers think? How are sales? If you had to make any midcourse corrections, what would you do? If you never stop learning, you'll never miss an opportunity to make the next project or campaign even better.

Where Do I Go From Here?

A lot of entry-level copywriters and art directors see themselves as senior creative directors after toiling in the trenches for two or three years. It usually doesn't happen that quickly, if at all. However, many junior writers or designers don't consider the other exciting possibilities.

Copywriter/art director for life: Many people are happy to hone their creative talents throughout their whole careers.

Account service: Many writers are drawn to the "dark side." It makes sense, especially if you like working with clients and thoroughly understand the product, market, and consumers. In some small shops, the copy-contact system gives account execs an opportunity to create and creative types a reason to wear a suit. Art directors also work directly with clients, and in many cases are the primary agency contacts.

one child dies from **water-related disease EVERY 15 SECONDS.**

Nearly 3.6 million people die every year from water-related disease, and 84% of them are children. Four will die in the next minute alone. Most of these deaths occur in the developing world, but we cannot ignore the fact that one in eight people worldwide lack access to safe water supplies. Water is the main ingredient in supporting life on earth. We must ensure its protection to ensure our survival.

WHY WATER?

Courtesy of Mike Bednar

Can advertising change the world? We keep hoping. This student-created ad was designed to raise awareness of waterborne illnesses around the world.

Account planner: A natural for many writers who like research and enjoy being the conduit between the account manager, the creative team, and the consumer. It involves thorough knowledge of research, marketing, creative, and media, as well as a lot of intuition. Most successful advertising copywriters already possess those skills.

Promotion director: Writers and art directors are idea people. So it makes sense to use that creativity to develop sales promotions, special events, sponsorships, specialty marketing programs, displays, and all the other marketing communication tools not included in "traditional advertising." This is a rapidly growing area with a lot of potential for creative people.

Public relations writer: Although most PR people won't admit it, it's easier to write a news release than an ad. Most advertising writers won't admit that editorial writing is usually more persuasive than advertising. PR writing involves much more than news releases, though. You may become an editor for a newsletter or an in-house magazine. You may produce video news releases or schedule events, press conferences, and any number of creative PR efforts.

Internal advertising or PR department: So far, we've outlined agency jobs, but other companies need talented creative people. In small companies, you may handle brochure writing or design, PR, trade shows, and media relations, in addition to advertising. In larger companies, you may handle promotional activities not covered by your ad agency. You may even write speeches for your CEO.

Creative people usually care about issues outside their jobs. In some cases, they can combine their creative talents with their passion for social causes to make a difference.

Web/interactive expert: The web is so integrated into most marketing communication programs that it seems ridiculous to consider it nontraditional media. Any writer or designer today should be web savvy. You should know the terminology and capabilities of the Internet—just as well as you understand magazines or television. You don't have to be a whiz at HTML, but having some technical expertise is a huge plus. As with any phase of advertising, creativity, not technology, is the most precious commodity.

Social media specialist: This job usually involves daily monitoring, posting, and content development. It can also mean developing social media advertising and creating friends for your brand online. You could moderate chats as well as initiate conversation through forums, tweets, and postings. Writing skills, creativity, and knowing when not to use social media are the keys to success.

Content provider: Content involves a wide variety of marketing communication activities from feature articles, lists, white papers, online newsletters, advertorial, and native advertising. You can provide content as part of an agency, in house, or as a freelancer. To succeed, you need a thorough understanding of that sweet spot where the wants of the target audience intersect with the brand message.

Freelance writer/designer: A lot of people like a flexible schedule and a variety of clients. Being a successful freelancer requires tremendous discipline and endless self-promotion, plus the mental toughness to endure the constant rejection, short deadlines, and long stretches between assignments.

Video and broadcast producer/director: Like to write video or radio commercials? Maybe you have the knack for writing scripts, selecting talent, editing, and other elements of audio and video production. As for web/interactive experts, creative talent and a logical mind are the keys. Technological expertise can be learned on the job.

Creative strategist: Some agencies take pride in providing only lofty strategic thinking—the view from 30,000 feet. Strategic recommendations should be derived from primary and secondary research, competitive and market analysis, and many other variables. Once the strategy is developed and sold, the strategic agency or consultant collects the money before anything is created. The people who actually make things—copywriters, designers, art directors, web developers, and the rest, have to wait for compensation when their work is completed.

Consultant: Some companies (and agencies) hire outside talent to provide a fresh point of view. Other times, consultants set the strategy that gives the creative their marching orders. Too often, "consultant" is another word for unemployed. A select few actually make a living as creative consultants. Sometimes they are no more than repackaged freelancers. Sometimes they are "rainmakers" who help with a new business pitch. Keeping current and connected are the keys to success.

Creativity and Online Media

While traditional media advertising usually rides up and down on the waves of economic conditions, many advertisers have shifted more money into social media and mobile. So what does this mean for the future of creative advertising? Many marketers will shift their emphasis to such "middle of the funnel" approaches as social media, in addition to paid search and email marketing. Creatives have to understand how to do business in the digital space and anticipate an increasingly faster pace to changes in technology, pop culture, and online viewing trends. That means you will have to know more than how to create a banner ad or post a tweet. You may have to develop entire online communities for very specific target audiences and find ways to keep them engaged . . . and oh, by the way, you still have to sell something. As the use of social media grows for business, we are discovering that it's great for building relationships and brand reputations, but not so great for generating direct sales.

Mobile technology such as iBanners makes it possible to engage users in real time in virtually any location, as this app for attendees at South by Southwest demonstrates.

What's in It for Me?

You might have discussed the role of advertising in society and explored ethical issues. You have probably reviewed theories of communication and might have even read about the greatest creative people of all time. That's all good, but let's be honest—if you want a creative career, you're interested in only three things: fame, fortune, and fun. Not necessarily in that order.

Let's look at each one in a little more detail.

Fame: Everyone wants recognition, especially Millennials. Since advertising is unsigned, there are only two ways to get recognized— awards and having people say, "You're *really* the person who did that?" While it's important for your fragile self-esteem, winning awards can also be the key to building your career. If there is a student section in your local advertising club's award competition, study it, and if your stuff is good, enter it. You will get noticed, and it could help you land that dream job right out of school. Continue entering and winning to build that reputation as a top-tier creative. Last time we looked, there are no books showcasing account execs and media buyers.

© Stone Selex. Inc.

Modern digital design has to take a "mobile first" approach to create sites that work seamlessly on smart phone, tablet, and desktop screens.

Fortune: Depending on experience, the economy, the results they generate, and a million other factors, creative people can make as much or more than any other people in advertising. Recent salary surveys show that salaries for top creatives and top account supervisors are pretty much the same. In many cases, senior creatives can actually earn more than some doctors—without years of postgraduate school, internships, and residency. All you need to know is how to sell toilet paper or health insurance versus how to save lives. As a writer or an art director, you get to earn a decent living and still wear jeans, have a tattoo, pierce your nose, and spike your hair. But only if you want to.

Fun: You can be famous and well compensated and still be unhappy in any business. You can still get a kick out of solving problems, even if you're not well known or a millionaire. It's still a treat to work with other creatives, interact with musicians and actors, win presentations, and travel to exotic locales. If the idea of persuading gullible consumers to buy things they don't need starts wearing thin, you might consider redirecting your talent toward more worthy causes. They need great creative ideas too. No matter how much you're earning, when it stops being meaningful, or if you lose your edge, you should probably consider getting out.

Knowing the Rules and When to Break Them

We will not dwell on too many of the rules of advertising writing and design, but we will look at some accepted practices. These are the tips and techniques that have proved successful over time.

One "rule" will always be true. Advertising is a business. A business populated by a lot of crazy people, but still a business. Although the slogan "It's not creative unless it sells" has lost its impact, we still have to persuade someone to buy something. This reality leads to something we call "creative schizophrenia"—the internal conflict between the stuff you want to do and the stuff clients make you do. For example, if you want to get a job, you need really cool, cutting-edge stuff in your portfolio, which is usually not usable in the real world. When you land that job, you'll probably be forced to do a lot of boring stuff that sells products but looks terrible in your book. So hold your nose and smile. Throughout your career, you're going to do a lot more crap than award-winning stuff.

You Don't Have to Be Crazy, but It Helps

Psychologists have spent years studying creativity. We know that creativity is not an isolated right-brained activity. Rather, it "reflects originality and appropriateness, intuition and logic. It requires both hemispheres."[5] The left side likes words, logic, and reasons. The right side likes pictures, emotions, and feelings. Bringing both hemispheres together in a mediated form is what Mihaly Csikszentmihalyi calls "flow . . . a phenomenon constructed through an interaction between producers and audience."[6]

Flow requires flexibility and "the capacity to adapt to the advances, opportunities, technologies, and changes that are a part of day-to-day living."[7] Advertising creativity is the end product of balancing logic with irrationality, artistic freedom with the constraints of the creative problem, and divergent thinking with convergent thinking.[8] It's about making strategy come to life.

What Does That Mean for You?

Daniel Pink, in his groundbreaking book *A Whole New Mind: Why Right-Brainers Will Rule the Future*, argues that we are moving away from left-brain leadership toward the attributes associated with the right brain. Pink describes right-brain thinking as holistic, big picture, intuitive, and nonlinear. He states, "The Information Age we all prepared for is ending. Rising in its place is what I call the Conceptual Age, an era in which mastery of abilities that we've often overlooked and undervalued marks the fault line between who gets ahead and who falls behind."[9] So we are moving from high tech to high concept and high touch. The Information Age was about knowledge workers. *The Conceptual Age is about creators and empathizers— in other words, right-brain thinking.*

The contradiction of increased reliance on big data is that left-brain thinking (cold, calculating technology) makes it more possible to create higher levels of empathy and engagement. Too often it creates a loss of privacy and crosses the creepiness line.

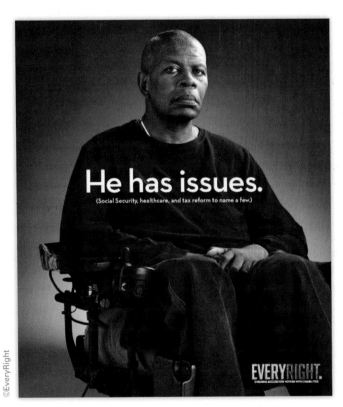

Creating an ad with a twist takes a reader in an unexpected direction, which strengthens the message. Here a handicapped man has issues, but they turn out to be the same as most other people his age. It's a way to create unity from diversity.

What Does This Mean for the Industry?

Pink's Conceptual Age is based on changing demographics as much as it is based on changing needs in the marketplace. Creative, empathic ideas do not come from a homogeneous group of individuals. Creative, empathic ideas come from a highly varied mix of individuals—a mix of people bringing diverse backgrounds and experiences to the creative process. Diversity of thought and experience will be the game changer. Diversity of thought and experience will be the driver of optimal flow.

Today too many ad agencies suffer from a lack of diversity, especially in their creative departments. FCB is one agency that acknowledges this issue. Under the leadership of global chief creative officer Susan Credle, FCB started the No 2 Six6 movement to help correct it. FCB's research shows that the ad industry won't achieve equality another 66 years at the current rate of hiring. Regardless of how workplace equality is defined, most people agree the advertising industry has a long way to go. As you'll see in subsequent chapters, diversity in advertising merits discussion. Like Csikszentmihalyi, Pink, and Credle, we too think diversity of thought and experience is at the heart of advertising's future.

Discovering Advertising

Courtesy of Nick Heiser

Advertising wasn't always my passion. I used to whine about commercial breaks and skip through them whenever I could. It wasn't even my passion when I chose it as a college major. For me, creative advertising became a way to channel my lifelong interests.

As a kid I was really into writing, drawing, and music, and early on I knew that a creative profession was the only route for me. During sophomore year of high school, I was lucky enough to take a course called graphic communication fundamentals, which was basically intro to graphic design with a conceptual focus. Our teacher pushed us to think about the *why* instead of just making stuff that looked cool. That idea of art with substance and thinking behind it really stuck with me, and by the end of high school I'd realized that advertising was essentially at the intersection of psychology, communication, and art. And that seemed pretty cool.

During college, I visited agencies and listened to ad club speakers, idolizing the creative directors who made a living by coming up with ideas and creating beautiful work. I wound up taking classes at the Milwaukee Institute of Art and Design to sharpen my design skills, while continuing advertising and psychology courses at Marquette. By senior year, it was clear that the key to landing an art director job out of school was a killer portfolio. The problem was, my art school peers were better designers than me. So, I created a portfolio that showcased my thinking, filling it with campaigns that were driven by concepts and supported by good design and writing. Somehow it worked, and I landed an internship at BVK my senior year, getting hired not long after graduation.

A year later, I'm concepting and designing for some of the strongest brands in tourism, health care, and education. Every day is a little different from the last. The biggest perk is getting to work on campaigns for Serve Marketing, BVK's nonprofit agency, on pro bono projects designed to tackle problems in the Milwaukee community. Last year, we covered teen pregnancy, animal abuse, and human trafficking. Working on campaigns that can truly change lives makes my whole pursuit of a job worth it, and I'm looking forward to whatever's next.

Nick Heiser, associate art director, BVK

nickheiser.com

Knowing What Makes the Consumer Tick

Consumer behavior is learning what makes people tick through a deep dive into how people buy, what they buy, when they buy, and why they buy. It blends elements from psychology, sociology, and marketing, and quite a bit of insight. Marketers attempt to dissect buyers' decision-making process, both for individuals and for groups.

They study demographics, psychographics, and lifestyles to understand what people want and how they want to get it. Billions of dollars are spent on research to test new products and the consumer's willingness to buy. But many times the most successful marketing concepts spring from some crazy idea no research could predict. Can you say Google?

Steve Jobs relied on his intuition instead of focus groups. He and the talented team that followed him developed products consumers didn't even know they wanted—the Macintosh, iMac, iTunes, iPod, iPhone, iPad, and Apple Watch—and in the process created the most valuable technology company in the world. We'll discuss some of the tools you can use to gauge consumer attitudes and opinions later in this book. However, at this point, suffice it to say that a successful creative practitioner writes and designs materials that appeal to a consumer's wants and needs. Unless you're the next Steve Jobs, you may need some research to guide you.

Creating From the Consumer's Point of View

If you remember nothing else from this chapter, remember this:

People do not buy things.
They buy satisfaction of their wants and needs.

You may have studied Abraham Maslow's theory of the hierarchy of needs. This model is usually depicted as a pyramid, ranging from the most basic needs to the most complex and sophisticated.

Collateral and direct mail often get overlooked in discussions about advertising writing and design, but a person who is able to create visually compelling and hard-selling marketing tools will always be in demand.

©Nissan

According to Maslow, the needs at each level must be met before one can progress to the next level. Maslow considered less than 1% of the population to be truly self-actualized.[11] Some communication theorists have expanded on Maslow's list. Some texts list more than 30 needs. To simplify matters, we can probably sum up wants and needs from a marketing communication standpoint as follows:

- Comfort (convenience, avoid pain and discomfort)
- Security (physical, financial)
- Stimulation (aesthetic, physical)
- Affiliation (esteem, respect)
- Fulfillment (self-satisfaction, status)

So how does all this talk about Maslow and wants and needs play in the ad business today? That's where account planning comes into play. The account planner is the connection between the business side and the creative side of a marketing campaign. The planner works with the account manager to understand what the client is looking for and then relates that to what the consumer wants. The planner also helps the creative team develop a more focused Creative Brief to lead them to that One Thing. Planners want to know what makes people tick—to bring the consumers' voice into the strategic process. They use that information to develop branding strategy for the campaign. It is the planner's job to take all this information, insight, and nuance and condense it into a form that the creative team can understand (preferably short sentences for the writers and pictures for the art directors). We provide more detail about account planning in Chapter 2.

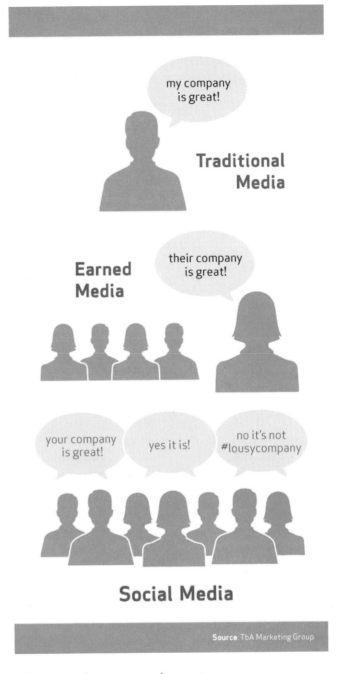

But what exactly do we do with all this? Once you have discovered consumers' sweet spot, you have to communicate in a way that convinces them your brand can satisfy their wants and needs. One of the best explanations of a consumer's wants and needs can be found in this simple declarative sentence: *Don't tell me about your grass seed; talk to me about my lawn.*

Think about that. People aren't really looking for seed. They need a play area for their kids. They want a calm green space for relaxing or a yard the neighbors will envy. Security. Comfort. Fulfillment. Wants and needs. A $30 Timex will probably tell the time just as well as a $3,000 Rolex. (Well, close enough for most folks.) What wants and needs are satisfied by spending 1,000% more? Hint: It's really not about telling time.

> "If you can't turn yourself into your customer, you probably shouldn't be in the ad writing business at all."[12]
>
> Leo Burnett,
> copywriter and founder,
> Leo Burnett

Green is part of the dream.

It gives our kids courage to leap.

Cushions their falls. Softens the edges of our lives.

Welcomes our visitors with open arms.

Green says we're committed to something.

Something the whole neighborhood believes in. Something good.

Something the world, even on its best days,

Could use more of.

For 75 years, Scotts® Turf Builder® has helped make millions of lawns greener. Because, better than any other fertilizer, Scotts Turf Builder feeds with the perfect blend of nutrients grass needs to flourish. And American dreams need to grow.

For help building your dream, go to scotts.com

Green is part of the dream.™

Don't tell me about your grass seed; talk to me about my lawn. Here's a classic example. While this ad isn't about grass seed, it's about a lot more than fertilizer.

Chapter 1

In this and future chapters, you'll see some Words of Wisdom floating around. Who are these wise guys and gals? At the end of most chapters we'll provide very brief bios on some of the best known voices in advertising, as well as other innovators whom we have cited in Words of Wisdom and Closer Look.

Leo Burnett

Founder of the agency that still bears his name, he established a new creative style of advertising, along with many memorable characters that are still working today, including Tony the Tiger, the Jolly Green Giant, the Keebler Elves, the Marlboro Man, and the Pillsbury Doughboy. Leo Burnett believed that creativity made an advertisement effective but, at the same time, that creativity required believability.

Steve Jobs

This legendary force drove Apple and Pixar to the top of their games. Complex, difficult to work and live with, impatient, and always outspoken, Steve Jobs controlled everything related to his products, including the copywriting for his ads. Biographer Walter Isaacson describes Jobs as "a creative entrepreneur whose passion for perfection and ferocious drive revolutionized six industries: personal computers, animated movies, music, phones, tablet computing and digital publishing."[13]

Mary Wells Lawrence

While CEO, chair, and president of the legendary Wells Rich Greene agency, Mary Wells was the highest paid, best known woman in American business. She was also the first female CEO of a *Fortune* 500 company. Her innovative campaigns for Braniff, Alka-Seltzer, Benson & Hedges, and American Motors brought a fresh new look to established brands. At age 40, she became the youngest person ever inducted into the Copywriters Hall of Fame.

Jon Steel

One of the early leaders in account planning, Jon Steel is well known for his innovative approach to focus groups, in which he elicits opinions from people where they live, work, and shop, rather than in sterile interview rooms. *Adweek* named Steel, head of Goodby, Silverstein & Partners' planning department, "West Coast Executive of the Year" in 2000. He also finds time to share his depth of knowledge at Stanford University's Graduate School of Business as a regular lecturer. His first book, *Truth, Lies, and Advertising: The Art of Account Planning*, has become a must-read for anyone interested in account planning.

Coffee and Conversation Gets Company in Hot Water

WHAT WOULD YOU DO?

Discussing hot topics like politics, race, religion and sexual orientation can freeze conversations. However, exchanging ideas about difficult issues is important to society. Fractured civic spaces surround us, and one marketer, the CEO of a multinational corporation that sells premium coffee, aimed to make a difference by using his business to start conversations that could potentially help customers see not only what divides them, but what unites them.

Long known for its commitment to social responsibility, the corporation has a history of making a positive impact on the communities it serves through its efforts to source products ethically, encourage sustainable farming practices that minimize the environmental footprint, hire veterans and military spouses, and celebrate diversity. Following in this tradition, the coffee chain wanted to make a difference by encouraging its customers to work through thorny social issues in discussions that respect and recognize different perspectives.

The Big Idea: A cup of coffee and a conversation worth having. What could be more natural? Convinced that the initiative to help citizens engage in civil conversations contributed to building the brand, the CEO endorsed his marketing team's campaign to invite customers into conversations about difference. Customers would receive their beverages with napkins imprinted with some provocative questions aimed at starting what might be difficult dialogues, such as these: When did you first remember thinking about race? Does your workplace favor one religious tradition over others? What does it mean to you when people say they don't see color/are colorblind with respect to race and ethnicity?

Nancy Mitchell, professor,
University of Nebraska

The campaign rolled out with much fanfare. The company took out full-page ads in the *New York Times* and *USA Today*. It attracted publicity during network morning talk shows. The coffee company sparked conversations, but it ignited a backlash that flamed into a media firestorm. Angry customers were insulted by the corporation, which tried to set the agenda for their conversations and intruded on their free time. Tweets and blogs were not kind to the corporation. Within a week, the coffee chain decided to abandon its controversial efforts to start conversations about difference.

1 Imagine that you are the brand manager for this coffee. Do you think that the CEO was wrong to approve this campaign? In what ways did the campaign help or hurt the brand image?

2 Where do you think this campaign went wrong? What went well?

3 A challenge of marketing in the midst of a communication environment teeming with social media is that corporations cannot control what people tweet or blog, as this case illustrates. What, if anything, could the marketer have done to prevent or mitigate the damage?

4 As brand manager, what steps would you take to prevent and/or manage situations like this in the future?

Exercises

1. No More Wonder Bread

Wonder Bread is bland, white bread. Sorry to insult any Wonder Bread lovers, but in advertising you can't be bland. You have to have flavor. Back in the 1940s Wonder Bread made the claim that it built "strong bodies in 12 ways." That's where we begin.

Below are 12 ways to build strong insights.

- Feel free to add and subtract as you see fit, making these experiences relevant to your environment. By semester break you must have experienced all 12.
- Keep a journal with an entry for each experience: who (alone or with friends), what (use brief detail, for instance, the title of a foreign film or name of a club), where (a no-brainer), when (another no-brainer), and why (your reaction, how it made you *feel*).

Use your six senses as you describe how each experience made you feel. That's where you'll find the insights.

1. Go to the local public market, where "slow" food is sold.
2. Watch a subtitled foreign film.
3. Hit the Latin dance floor.
4. Catch the week's news on BBC online: www.bbc.co.uk.
5. Check out live jazz or blues at a neighborhood club.
6. Attend an event sponsored by the Gay-Straight Alliance Network, the Muslim Students Association, the Black Student Council, or an international student organization—one for which you don't fit the demographics.
7. Attend a local Rotary function.
8. Dine on tofu.
9. Settle in for an afternoon of NASCAR racing or WWE (World Wrestling Entertainment).
10. Experience a meeting of the college Republican or Democratic student association—and it has to be the opposite of your political point of view.
11. Join in the fun at a bingo gathering.
12. Visit the local art museum and check out the current special exhibits.

2. Personal Branding Timeline

- Create a map moving across your life in 5-year increments. Begin with birth and end with your current age (which might be less than a 5-year gap). For each 5-year stage generate a list of the brands you associate with that time of your life.

- After each brand write a single sentence about what that brand meant to you at that time.

- Now extend this map out by 10-year increments: 30, 40, 50, 60, and 70. List brands you think will be a part of your life. Again write a single sentence about why you believe each brand will be relevant to you at that time.

- Now discuss what factors are influencing your choices: familiarity, aspiration, current use, personal or family associations, trends, and so on.

- Next see if there are any brands that were constant over a long period of time. Discuss what makes those brands have traction over time. What inherited qualities and brand messages enable brand loyalty?

3. AIDA in Action

Consider the buying process for the following product categories using the AIDA (attention, interest, desire, action) steps: hybrid cars, microbrews, running shoes, frozen vegetables, and cosmetics. Or create your own categories.

- Make a list based on the following questions: What gets your *attention*? What part of the brand messages within this category captures your *interest*? At what point and due to what circumstances do consumers feel a compelling *desire* for the product? What are common intended *actions* that might be relevant to this product category?

- Now find an ad for each category and discuss how the AIDA process works for that brand. How much influence do advertising and promotion have on the buying decision for that brand?

Review chapter content and study for exams. http://study.sagepub.com/altstiel4e.

- Interactive practice quizzes
- Mobile-friendly eFlashcards
- Carefully selected chapter-by-chapter video and multimedia content

Chapter 2

Strategy and Branding
Putting a Face on a Product

Congratulations! Your agency's request for proposal has been selected, and you've been invited to pitch the Garlowe Gizmo account to introduce their new line of Gizmos. Your job is to develop a creative strategy and build a marketing communication campaign that will knock the socks off the Garlowe management. You really need this account, because if you don't win, half of your agency will be laid off, including you. Right now, you know nothing about the company, its products, its customers, its competition, or its market. How will you develop something that differentiates Garlowe from the competition? Something no one else has done before. And something that might even win some creative awards. By the way, you've got two weeks until the presentation. Once again, congratulations!

Let's Review the Basics

The scenario in the introduction happens every day somewhere. The good news is you're invited to the dance. But there are very few "gimmes" when it comes to new business, and if you're lucky enough to win an account, the euphoria quickly dissolves into the daily grind of keeping the business.

Most texts will tell you that you just can't start creating an ad from scratch. Of course you can. And you just might get lucky the first time. But can you repeat that success? That's why we need to discuss the foundations of marketing communications. First, a few definitions.

Advertising, MarCom, IMC, or What?

Everyone knows what advertising is, right? George Orwell, author of *1984*, said it was "the rattling of a stick inside a swill bucket."[1] Science fiction author H. G. Wells claimed, "Advertising is legalized lying."[2] Humorist Will Rogers declared, "Advertising is the art of convincing people to spend money they don't have for something they don't need"[3] (and we could add "to impress people they don't like"). For a less cynical view, advertising professor Jef Richards said, "Advertising is the 'wonder' in Wonder Bread."[4]

You've probably learned that advertising is paid communication to promote a product, service, brand, or cause through the media. Is direct mail advertising? Well, if you consider mail a medium, yes. How about a brochure? Probably not; however, it can be mailed or inserted into a magazine as an ad. The Internet? Yes and no. A website by itself is not really advertising, although a banner ad on that site is. Social networks? They can be a platform for ads, but they are sometimes more effective when they influence consumer perceptions of a brand without advertising. Public relations? No, because the advertiser is not paying the editor to publish an article (at least not directly). PR professionals talk about **earned media**—where the quality of their content and relationship with editors earn mention of a product without a direct media payment. With earned media you're asking permission to share information, rather than hitting them over the head with a commercial. Then there's **native advertising**. When the ad message is blended with other content, does it also become PR, product placement, branded content, sales promotion, sponsorship, or something else? Confused? Don't feel alone. Many marketing professionals can't make the distinction between advertising and other forms of promotion.

Randall Rothenberg, CEO of the Interactive Advertising Bureau, described the dilemma of defining advertising: "Today's media landscape keeps getting more diverse—it's broadcast, cable and streaming; it's online, tablet and smartphone; it's video, rich media, social media, branded content, banners, apps, in-app advertising and interactive technology . . . it's physical interactive gear, like Nike + Fuelband . . . Google Chromecast dongle . . . and smart watches . . . ."[6]

> *"Our business is infested with idiots who try to impress by using pretentious jargon."*[5]
>
> David Ogilvy,
> copywriter and founder,
> Ogilvy & Mather

MarCom (Marketing Communications)

MarCom to some people takes in every form of marketing communication. Others describe MarCom as every form of promotion that's not traditional advertising. Traditional advertising usually covers print (newspapers, magazines), television, radio, and some forms of outdoor advertising. "Nontraditional" promotion includes direct marketing, sales promotion, point of sale, public relations, email, online advertising, search engine marketing, mobile, social networks, guerrilla marketing, viral, word of mouth, and everything else you can attach a logo, slogan, or message to. These divisions evolved as large agencies discovered they could make money beyond earning media commissions. So they created MarCom units or separate interactive, direct, and sales promotion divisions. Sometimes these are set up as separate entities under the corporate umbrella of a large agency.

IMC (Integrated Marketing Communications)

IMC unites the MarCom elements into a single campaign. *IMC* has become a buzzword, especially for agencies that set up MarCom divisions. Actually, IMC is nothing new. Smaller full-service agencies and in-house ad departments have been doing it for years under the banner of "doing whatever it takes to get the job done." With limited budgets, companies need to get the most mileage from their promotional dollar with a variety of tools, including advertising.

Advertising's Role in the Marketing Process

Many people describe the most common forms of advertising, such as a clever TV commercial or a slick catalog, as "good marketing." Actually, those forms of advertising and direct marketing are subsets of one of the four P's of marketing (promotion, place, product, and price). Unless a director of marketing can also control the product, distribution (place), and price, he or she is a glorified ad or promotion manager. And any director of marketing worth his or her salt also takes into account a fifth P—people. If you don't take the time to understand what motivates the people you are pitching your brand to, you may as well pick a new career.

Years ago advertisers were afraid to show minorities in mainstream ads. Recently gays and lesbians were subtly integrated. Today many brands openly embrace marriage equality and LGBT rights.

No matter how you slice it, Heinz has developed some very creative concepts, including eye-catching print ads and innovative digital sales promotion programs.

The buying process for some products may take a couple seconds, such as picking out a sandwich at the drive through, or it may take years, as with buying a multimillion dollar piece of industrial equipment. No matter the time frame, there is a process that starts with awareness and ends with the sale. One of the best ways to describe the process is using the acronym AIDA, which stands for *attention*, *interest*, *desire*, and *action*. Understanding AIDA helps you, as a creative person, guide a consumer from just recognizing your brand to demanding it.

Here's how AIDA works in advertising:

1. **Attention:** How do you get someone who is bombarded with hundreds if not thousands of messages a day to look at your ad or commercial? If you're a writer, one way is to use powerful words, or if you're an art director, you need a picture that will catch a person's eye.

2. **Interest:** Once you capture a person's attention, he or she will give you a little more time to make your point, but you must stay focused on the reader's or viewer's wants and needs. This means helping that person quickly sort out the relevant messages. In some cases, you might use bullet points and subheadings to make your points stand out.

3. **Desire:** The interest and desire parts of AIDA work together. Once people are interested, they need to really want the product. As you're building readers' interest, you also need to help them understand how what you're offering can help them in a real way. The main way of doing this is by appealing to their personal needs and wants. Another component of desire is conviction—the willingness to buy when the opportunity is right. So even if your message does not result in an immediate sale, keeping your messages on track and on time could eventually trigger a sale.

4. **Action:** Okay, they're hooked. Now what do you want them to do? Visit a website? Take a test drive? Call for information? Plunk down some cash now? You should be very clear about what action you want your readers or viewers to take.

Calling Consumers to Action

The fourth step in the AIDA process is the one that drives the bottom line. So let's take a moment to say a little more about the Call to Action. The Call to Action is the little voice you've planted in the consumer's head that keeps saying, "Go do it." But it's up to you to plant what the "it" is. Of course the "it" that gets a consumer is based on strategy, and we'll be talking a lot more about that. For now let's consider seven surefire ways to engage consumers in action[7]:

- Begin with a strong command verb
- Choose words that provoke emotion or enthusiasm
- Give the target a compelling reason to take action
- Build in a fear of missing out on something big
- Know the platform your message lives on or in and leverage it
- Spice it up with tantalizing details
- Add numbers that translate into a tangible value

A Call to Action that works is based on knowing what makes the consumer tick.

Objectives, Strategies, and Tactics

The difference between strategy and tactics stumps a lot of clients, their agencies, and, not surprisingly, students. Too often the first stab at the process looks like a tangled mess of what everyone would like to see happen—about as specific and realistic as wishing for world peace. Other than drafting a mission statement by committee, listing strategy and tactics can be the most confusing, thankless task in marketing, and without clear objectives, failure is guaranteed. Don't get us wrong. A creative person needs to follow a strategy. Otherwise you're working for the sake of creativity rather than solving a problem.

Consider this—your objective is to visit mid-America. Think of strategy development as picking the destination, such as "I want to go to Cleveland." The strategy is to make the trip. The tactics are how you get there. If I drive, which roads do I take? Should I fly? If so, which airlines have the best rates? Where will I stay? How long will I be there? And a bunch of other questions that deal with specific actions you must take to get to Cleveland and back. Another analogy comes from the military. The objective speaks to the big picture, like winning the war. Strategies deal with achieving objectives, like capturing specific cities, blocking their ports, and hacking into their power grids. Tactics are the means to achieve the strategy. In the case of taking a city, it might be tactics such as using a combination of close air support, flanking maneuvers from infantry, frontal assaults by tanks, and constant bombardment of artillery. So, it's objective, strategy, and tactics. Got it: one, two, and three.

Real men are comfortable in their own skin. The strategy for these Dove ads and TV commercials was to show men in a slightly different light. However, when you consider that women already love the Dove brand, and they buy the products for their men, it's a smart marketing move.

Account Planning—Solving the Client's Problem

Strategy often deals in long-term solutions such as building brand share. Strategy relates to continuity, growth, and return on investment. It should be specific, and measurable. It begins with account planning.

First, you have to know the target market and then develop a strategy to connect with it. Industrial tools like impact wrenches have to be made as tough as the people who use them.

If you were working on the Garlowe Gizmo account mentioned in the introduction to this chapter, where would *you* start? The first thing to do is ask, "What's their problem?" Every client has a problem. Otherwise they wouldn't need to promote their products. Some clients state the problem as a broad objective, such as to sell more Gizmos in the next fiscal year. That's not the problem. The problem is: What's going to make it difficult to sell more Gizmos, and how can we overcome those difficulties? The client may tell you, but these may not be the only problems. Often the client doesn't have an in-depth understanding of its target audience. An even more challenging situation emerges when the client can't even identify the problem.

Account planning is how agencies come up with the solutions that solve a client's problem. It's about finding consumers' sweet spot. So, even before you get to the strategies and tactics, account planning lays the foundation. All strategy documents and the subsequent strategies and tactics emerge from account planning.

Here's a little background on planning. It developed in Britain in the late 1960s and was based on the desire to create an environment where creativity flourished, but where the consumer's voice was a key part of strategic development. Coming into existence on the heels of the Creative Revolution of the 1960s, it's not surprising that planning also sought a modern, creative approach to replace irrelevant, inappropriate, and outmoded methodologies. Prior to the introduction of account planning, advertising research was highly marketing oriented, largely quantitative, and often detached from both the creative team and the consumer. At the heart of account planning is the need to understand consumers—to bring their voice into the strategic process. This often involves qualitative research as planners seek consumers' sweet spot and nail the key insight.

Stanley Pollitt, of London's Boase Massimi Pollitt, is credited with developing account planning. His goal was to put a trained researcher, representing the voice of the consumer, alongside every account person. In the 1980s Jay Chiat, of the original Chiat\Day in Los Angeles, brought account planning to North America. Jon Steel, of Goodby, Silverstein & Partners in San Francisco and a noted author on account planning, calls account planning an essential strategy tool. By the mid-1990s account planning was common practice in ad agencies across North America.

> "Brilliant creative isn't enough. You must be creative and effective. It's a time for the strategic thinker, not just the creative rebel."[8]
>
> Helayne Spivak,
> former global chief creative director, JWT, and head of VCU Brand Center

The One Thing about the Lexus GS—more standard horsepower than its German competitors. How do you make that point to a skeptical American reader? Run the headline in German. The traditional Lexus position has been luxury and quality first, not performance. TV ads also compared the performance of the GS directly with Audi, BMW, and Mercedes.

Marketing Tasks	What They Mean
Define the target audience	Who are we talking to?
Identify features and benefits	What makes this product better?
Clarify the current position	What do people think about the product?
Align wants and needs with the product	Why should people buy it?
Determine Call to Action	What do we want people to do?

Table 2.1   Defining Marketing Tasks

> "Some of the biggest advertising mistakes are made by people who imagine they know what the problem is . . . they're just coming up with that brilliant idea and trying to force the problem to fit it."[9]
>
> Mary Wells Lawrence, copywriter and founding partner, Wells Rich Greene

Get the Facts

The first step in planning for any type of research is gathering and organizing information. You have to answer the basic questions listed in Table 2.1.

Notice that the above creative development questions include some of the basic journalism questions, such as who, what, and why. Where and when are media questions, which may also influence your creative strategy. For example, if you want to reach gay men, a commercial on *Modern Family* might be smarter than a spot during the Super Bowl. Not to mention a whole lot less expensive.

Where to Look for Information

Research can be divided into two basic categories: primary, where you gather the facts directly, and secondary, where you assemble research done by others. We'll look at secondary research first, because it's usually more accessible.

Secondary Research

You can find a wealth of information about markets, products, and consumers. Most of it is quantitative, so learning how to read and understand stats benefits anyone going into advertising. You don't have to run the stats. You only need to be able to understand them. A lot of it is available for free on the Internet. However, most of the really good stuff comes from subscription services. Most university libraries offer the same information that costs companies thousands of dollars, although it is usually slightly out of date. Buying current data is often prohibitively expensive. Simmons Market Research Bureau and Mediamark Research & Intelligence are good places to begin.

Many universities will have one or the other, as they are commonly used by the industry. Learning how to navigate these databases will give you a leg up when you interview.

Primary Research

While most of the primary research you'll find is quantitative, a lot of the primary research that will help you as a planner is qualitative. Most people think of formal types of research such as focus groups or mail surveys, but primary research can be very informal and personal. Ethnography and projective techniques are hot right now and with good reason. With ethnography you'll find yourself immersed in consumers' world. There's no faster way to find consumers' sweet spot than spending time with them. With projective techniques you'll use psychological tools to find out how people feel about or perceive your product. This can help you define your insight and develop a strategy that really connects with consumers. Start thinking like an anthropologist or a psychologist, and you'll quickly learn how to identify consumers' sweet spot—the One Thing that links your consumers' desire with your product. As you might imagine, these kinds of techniques pose some ethical considerations. Not the least of which is, how far is too far? So before you begin your research take the time to know exactly how far is too far—and don't cross that line.

"The process begins with just filling my head with stuff. Devouring media, soaking up the world around me—words and image and music and life."[10]

Chris Adams,
creative director,
TBWA\Chiat\Day

- Check out the competition. Review ads and other promotional material for your product. Study their visual structure and symbolism. Study their claims. Where are they weaker or stronger compared with your product?

- Read the publications, pursue the online sites, and watch the TV shows your media department is considering. What do they tell you about your target and the competition?

- Talk to the people who buy, or might buy, your product. Why did they buy it or not buy it? Would they buy it again? If not, why not?

- Talk to people who considered, but did not buy, your product. Why didn't they? What would make them change their mind?

- Immerse yourself in the fine-grained details of your consumers' everyday life. Where do they live, work, and play? What makes them tick and why?

Ethnography—Immerse Yourself in Their World

- Visit a store and check how your product and its competitors are displayed. How does the shelf appeal of your product compare? While you're there, spend some time watching consumers interact with your brand and its competitors. What does that tell you about their expectations?

- Observe the salespeople who sell your product. Eavesdrop. What do they tell customers about it, and how do consumers respond?

- Sometimes it's helpful to take a factory tour. Observe with all your senses. Is there a key insight waiting to be shared with consumers?

- Hang out with the consumers. Go to their homes. Explore the rooms in which they will use your product and how they use it. Observe them at play. Where are they playing and who are they playing with? More important, what does their play look like? What do you observe that can help you successfully pitch this product?

The devil is in the details.

Projective Techniques—Eliciting Inner Feelings

- Provide some images or words related to the product and ask consumers to make associations. What can you learn about how they feel about your brand?

- Ask them to draw pictures or create collages that remind them of something related to your product or something you're trying to find out. What images begin to repeat themselves? What's happening inside your consumer?

- Give them sentences to complete based on what you want to find out. Do you notice any word patterns, and what do they tell you about the emotional state of consumers when they think of your brand?

- Show them a storyboard about the product and ask them to tell you what they think about the main character (the consumer) within the story. Do you think they might be projecting themselves into that story? Chances are you're right.

You can find subjects to observe or interview in a number of places—stores, malls, sporting events, chat rooms, online games, trade shows, basically anyplace where members of your target audience may gather. You might even consider conducting more traditional research, such as focus groups with members of the target audience. These groups, professionally moderated, can explore attitudes and opinions in depth. And of course, there are always the tried and true surveys. Whatever you decide on, the goal is to find the sweet spot—without crossing ethical boundaries.

Interpreting Research Findings

There's a funny thing about research—if it confirms the client's opinions, it wasn't really needed; if it contradicts the client's opinions, it's flawed. While the "facts" may be gathered and presented objectively, the interpretation is often subjective.

Migraine sufferers are looking for relief, not advertising claims. This microsite provides a lot of useful information, a link to mobile apps, and even an online coupon.

But remember the client hired you for that subjective knowledge of advertising and consumer behavior. So, as long as you keep your subjective knowledge balanced with an objective look at their consumers, you should be in good shape.

Sometimes research reveals information about something you're not even measuring. For example, a survey for a business-to-business client revealed a strong negative opinion of the brand in the Southeast. Why did they love them in Ohio but hate them in Georgia? The client considered running some image ads in the South to build a more favorable opinion. Further investigation revealed that the problem was not with the brand, but with the distributor representatives selling it. In this case, no amount of brilliant advertising could solve the problem. A quick realignment of the sales force did. Another observation we've seen from years of gathering information and testing concepts: Clients focus on verbatim comments rather than numbers. They pay attention to a few video interviews rather than a mountain of statistics. Clients, like consumers, want to see and hear real people. They may analyze all the facts and figures, but a few memorable quotes usually help them form an opinion. Knowing how clients respond to research can put the agency in the driver's seat.

No matter how much research you gather, always remember . . .

- Research does not replace insight.
- Facts are not always true.
- Objective research is evaluated subjectively.
- Data are perishable commodities.

Who Is the Target Audience?

Who are you talking to? Your client may tell you. Your account planner should tell you. Your secondary and primary research will tell you. If you're lucky, marketing objectives will be very specific, such as increasing brand recognition among 35- to 65-year-old married men, living in the top 10 markets, earning $100,000 or more. Usually, though, a client tells the creative team about the product. Period. It's up to the agency to find out who is most likely to buy it and why. *Why* is the key word. Unless you know *why* the consumer is buying the product—or not buying it—how they are using it and what their emotional connections with it are, your creative strategy is likely to fail.

Features and Benefits

The object of your effort may not be a tangible product at all. It may be something you can't hold in your hand, like the local bus company, an art museum, or a government agency. It may be about corporate image—a campaign that promotes the integrity or strength of a company, but doesn't highlight products. Good examples are utility and telephone companies and multinational megafirms like General Electric. You could also develop creative for an organization such as the American Cancer Society or Amnesty International. For the sake of simplicity, we will call the object of promotion the "product" no matter what it may really be.

"A core belief [is] that if you want to create anything new, you must always look outside your own work or industry for inspiration."[11]

Simon Mainwaring,
freelance creative director

From the Inside: Features

Products have characteristics and personality traits just like people. By themselves these features are not good or bad. They're just there. That's why listing product features without putting them in the context of a benefit to the customer usually wastes time and money. Sometimes the benefit is so obvious, the reader or viewer will make an instant connection. But other times, writers just include a list of features and hope someone will figure out why they're important. Sometimes the benefit is much more emotional and woven into a branded story. On a luxury car, for example, features can be technical, like collision avoidance; functional, like side curtain air bags; aesthetic, like brushed aluminum console trim; or emotional, like it brings you home to your family every day. In most cases, the more technical and abstract the feature, the greater the need to tie it to a tangible benefit to the consumer.

From the Outside: Benefits

Not all products have features you can promote, but all have benefits. A benefit leads to the satisfaction of a consumer's wants and needs. "Cool, crisp flavor" is a benefit (it quenches thirst and tastes good). "Firm, smooth ride" is a benefit (it pleases the senses, and gives peace of mind). "Kills 99.9% of household germs" is a benefit (you're protecting your family's health).

Anyone can write a feature ad. All you need is a spec list. As a writer, you have to translate those features into benefits that resonate within the customer. Sometimes it's as simple as listing a feature and lining up a benefit. That's the old FAB (features-advantage-benefits) approach, used for years in industrial brochures. However, we encourage you to think of more subtle and clever ways to promote the benefits. Edward de Bono, a cognitive expert, suggests that marketers pay close attention to the UBS, or unique buying state, of consumers. In the old days we called the moment consumers were most receptive *aperture*. Think camera lens. So, when you're thinking about how to leverage a benefit, consider the UBS. Another approach came from a client. He uses the formula SWWC (So what? Who cares?). If you can answer those questions, you're halfway there. Table 2.2 gives some examples of features, benefits, and how they satisfy a consumer's wants and needs.

As we'll discuss shortly, you should think in terms of an overriding benefit. Remember the adjective you need to tack onto the brand name—if that adjective is positive, it's likely an overall benefit. And don't be afraid to work with the account planners to connect your key benefit to the UBS. You might also consider the fact that many of the choices consumers make today are based on symbolic product attributes. So don't discount intangible emotions. Finally, when spinning your benefits, think back to your brand—to its promise. Can your benefit engender positive emotion leading to trust? If so, you have leveraged the feature to its maximum potential, creating great strategic advantage. Now let's get to work.

Feature	Benefit	Wants and Needs
Contains fluoride	Prevents tooth decay	Saves money, saves time
Automatic shut-off	Shuts off unit if you forget	Safety, saves money, convenience
Electronic ignition	Easier starts in cold weather	Convenience
Slow nutrients release	Greener plants, more flowers	Aesthetically pleasing, convenient

Table 2.2   Features and Benefits

Assembling the Facts

You've gathered a lot of information. Now it's time to organize it into something you can use. The following are three basic ways to organize information.

Copy Platform

The Copy Platform is also known as a Creative Strategy Statement and by several other names. It can be as simple or as detailed as you'd like. No matter what you call it and how complicated it can be, a good Copy Platform should cover the product features and benefits, competitive advantages and weaknesses, information about the target audience, the tone of the message, and a simple, overriding statement about the product. We call this the One Thing. It can also be called the Central Truth, the Big Idea, or the Positioning Statement.

The best way to start—ask this simple question:

"If you could say just One Thing about this product, it would be _____."

It's not an easy sentence to complete. When we begin working with new clients, we sometimes ask them to complete that statement. You'd be surprised how many times they struggle with an answer. The most common response is "Gee. Nobody really asked that before. It's really so many things. I can't think of just one." Then they provide a laundry list of features. No wonder they needed a new agency!

Another way to think about a Positioning Statement is to distill the essence of the consumer's identity. Then distill the essence of the brand. Then find the sweet spot that marries both of these. It's hard to do, and every agency has its own way of getting there. (Note: None of this is possible without a *lot* of research.) Here's one example using this technique: Corona. The consumers are urban professionals seeking an escape. The brand is a premium, smooth Mexican beer. The One Thing: Corona takes you away.

A Copy Platform is essential to getting you to the Positioning Statement. You'll find an example Copy Platform in the Appendix. It's a compilation of several forms used by different agencies. Each firm will have its own way to organize information, but this one will do a pretty good job most of the time.

To summarize, we use Copy Platforms for the following reasons:

- **Provide a framework for your ad:** You have all the basic facts about the target, the product, the competition, and the marketplace. If you have some blank lines, you know you need more information.

- **Identify the One Thing that's most important:** You could use a Positioning Statement. Or use a single adjective attached to the brand. Or it could be a sentence that describes what you want the consumer to believe about this product.

- **Support that One Thing with believable information:** This could be features and benefits that support product claims. In the case of a copy-free ad, only the visual supports that overriding image of the product.

- **Connect people with the product:** In your Copy Platform you should ask: What do you want the reader, viewer, or listener to do? What is the desired conviction and action step? Do you want the consumer to take a test drive? Ask for more information? Visit a website? Or do nothing?

- **Organize the client's thoughts:** A good Copy Platform is a collaborative effort between client and agency. The client can provide a lot of information, and together you can clarify and prioritize it. This should not be done by a large committee—at least not by a committee larger than one or two people per client and agency. When completed, both the agency and the client have the same road map for creative strategy.
- **Justify your creative decisions:** If the client signed off on the Copy Platform, they will be less likely to criticize your creative efforts if you can prove you're on strategy. If the client says you're off target, you can ask where and why, based on your collaboration on the Copy Platform.

Creative Brief

Creative Briefs may be prepared from a Copy Platform, or directly from the assembled information. The Creative Brief is a more linear progression from where we are to where we want to be and how we will get there. The strategy is more clearly defined than in most Copy Platforms. The Virginia Commonwealth University Brandcenter used one of the best Creative Brief formats we've seen. If these questions are answered correctly, you've got just about everything you need to start concepting an ad.

- What do we want to accomplish? (Objective)
- Who are we talking to? (Target audience)
- What do they think now? (Current position)
- What do we want them to think? (Reinforce position or reposition)
- Why should they think this? (Features/benefits)
- What is our message? (The One Thing and how you say it and show it—the tone)

The creative brief on page 35 was written by a student for Q-tips.

Consumer Profile

The Consumer Profile takes the Copy Platform and Creative Brief a step further by putting a human face on the target audience. Think of journalism's five W's in terms of the consumers: Who are they? What are their wants and needs, their buying intentions, their attitudes toward the product and competitors? What do they do for a living? What are their hobbies? Where do they live and work, and how does that affect their buying patterns? When are they planning to buy? When do they watch TV or use other types of media? Why should they consider your product or the competitor's? Based on the demographic, psychographic, lifestyles and values, and other research, a Consumer Profile puts some flesh on the bare bones of the Copy Platform. You might consider summarizing the demographics in the first paragraph and include the psychographics in the second paragraph, while you weave the lifestyles and values through the whole profile.

The list below should help you develop some basic information about the product and potential customers:

- *Who* is the prospect?
- *What* does she do, and *what* does she want?

- *Where* does she live?
- *When* does she buy?
- *Why* would she be interested?
- *How* does she buy?

The example on page 36 was written by a student to describe the ideal prospect for Excedrin Migraine. You can see how by focusing on demographics and psychographics, you can create a personal portrait of the ideal person within the target audience. From this profile, thanks to attention to her media habits, we know that an advertiser can't reach Maria very effectively through traditional media. She might notice billboards along her commute, but she's not listening to the radio. She doesn't read newspapers or magazines, and her television viewing includes a lot of noncommercial programs. Through demographics and psychographics we know our approach must be intelligent (she's smart and successful) and to the point (she doesn't have a lot of spare time). The benefit of a nonprescription remedy that could relieve her symptoms without taking time out for a doctor's visit may be the main selling point.

©Q-tips

The main objective of my campaign will be to introduce Q-tips cotton swabs to the next generation of adults, showing them the many uses as well as the quality that distinguishes Q-tips cotton swabs from the generic competition.

Who are we talking to? We are speaking to people who value a good product and want the best. More important, we are targeting the emerging Millennial crowd to sway their future buying habits.

What do they think now? The majority of our new audience is indifferent to Q-tips cotton swabs. They consider this a very menial purchase and usually pick the cheapest package on the rack. They have always depended on others to pick up this item, so this will be a brand-new purchase for them.

What do we want them to think? We want to instill a brand image into their minds, when they walk into a grocery store for personal care products; we want them to think Q-tips. We want them to pass over the generic products and choose Q-tips because Q-tips are a personal product as well as a practical one.

Why should they think this? Because Q-tips will be presented in a very edgy and fun way, we will be able to connect to our audience. This will carry over to the point of purchase and influence their buying habits. We want them to realize the importance of taking care of themselves with the highest quality of cotton swabs.

What is our message? Q-tips cotton swabs are a personal item with practical applications.

© Juan Herrera / istockphoto

Meet Maria

Maria Sanchez is a modern, 35-year-old working mom with a husband and two children, ages 10 and 3. She graduated from the University of Illinois with a degree in management, which helped her get a job in the human resources department of a large insurance company in Chicago. She has steadily advanced to become assistant department manager. She earns $65,000 and expects to continue moving up the corporate ladder. Her husband Carlos is a sales representative for a large manufacturing firm. His income varies greatly from year to year, so Maria's large and stable income is extremely important to their family. Maria and Carlos live in a four-bedroom home in Hoffman Estates, which is a 45-minute commute one way (when traffic is moving). Maria loves her job, but the stresses of caring for a family, commuting, and the usual pressures of a human resources department can sometimes trigger a migraine headache. With her busy schedule, Maria can't take time off from work and family when she has a migraine. The increased frequency of her migraines creates even more stress, but she doesn't have time to visit a doctor or make an extra trip to the pharmacy.

In her spare time, Maria likes to ride her bicycle, play tennis, and shop. She and Carlos enjoy traveling, with and without the kids. They try to set aside at least one weekend a month as "date night" to recharge their marriage. Throughout her workday she sneaks a peak at Facebook, Instagram, and Pinterest on her cell phone and spends at least an hour every night updating and responding to social media at home. She'll access the web a little at work, usually by clicking a link in her inbox. At home, Maria and Carlos will stream shows from Netflix, and when she's with her mom and sisters, they'll occasionally watch telenovelas on Univision. When her iPod isn't linked to her car stereo, she surfs SiriusXM and almost never tunes into a local radio station. She'll scan junk mail but rarely takes time to read the newspaper and has canceled most of her magazine subscriptions. Most nights she'll try to read a chapter or two on her Kindle in bed, but she usually nods off after the first couple paragraphs.

You Decide What's Important

The ad will not write itself based on a compilation of facts. Sometimes a great creative idea stems from a minor benefit and blooms into a powerful image that drives a whole campaign. David Ogilvy wrote one of the best headlines ever by focusing on a Rolls-Royce clock rather than the whole car. Our advice: Get the facts and use them, but don't be a slave to data. When you see a feature or even a rather vague benefit, be sure to ask this question:

SO WHAT?

What does that feature do for the consumer? Keep asking "So what?" until you get to the benefit that satisfies a basic want or need. Think about the questions you'd ask if you were buying something. You may not always get something you'd include in the body copy, but if you keep probing, you might get an idea for a whole campaign.

For example:

Dove soap is one-quarter cleansing cream.

So what?

It's creamier, less harsh to the skin.

So what?

Your skin looks younger, less dry.

So what?

You feel better about yourself.

Now you've got a hook. Don't tell her about your soap, talk to her about feeling young, beautiful, free, and sexy. The Dove brand was launched in 1957, and while it's changed a lot over the years, its core value is still there. Put yourself in the target customer's shoes. Luke Sullivan says, "Ask yourself what would make you want to buy the product? Find the central truth about the product . . . hair coloring isn't about looking younger. It's about self-esteem. Cameras aren't about pictures. They're about stopping time and holding life as the sands run out."[12]

"The part I love in the process is when you crack the idea and suddenly all the possibilities come flooding forward . . . like a mental orgasm mixed with a sense of relief."[13]

Ross Chowles, cofounder, executive creative director, The Jupiter Drawing Room, Cape Town, South Africa

©Apple Inc.

When Steve Jobs returned to Apple, the company had no new products. The "Think Different" campaign kept the brand relevant until the incredible wave of new products could be introduced.

Tone: Finding Your Voice

You know what you want to say: now you have to figure out how to say it. Whether you create a formal tone statement or just think about it, you really do need to define the tone of your creative effort. Another way to think about it is finding your voice: is it loud and obnoxious, soft and sexy, logical and persuasive, fun and carefree, melodramatic and sensational, or some other characteristic?

For example, if you did advertisements for a hospital, you wouldn't make jokes about kids with cancer. You'd be hopeful, respectful, empathetic, and maybe emotional. A parody ad created a huge backlash when it showed an adorable lost puppy finding his way home, only to be sold by the puppy mill owner who used GoDaddy to create her website. The twist at the end was too much for pet lovers, and the company pulled the spot. A Super Bowl ad for Nationwide Insurance featured a little boy lamenting that he'd never grow up because he died in an accident. An important topic to be sure, and one worthy of discussion—but did it set the right tone for a nacho-noshing, beer-guzzling crowd at a Super Bowl party?

The tone or voice of an ad is more than the concept. It's reflected in the selection of talent, music, editing, direction, and voice inflection. For example, Microsoft ran an ad about using technology to empower a little boy born without leg bones to live a normal life. If you just read the script, you'd miss the optimistic, heartwarming tone. As with everything else, know the target audience. Then find the right tone to communicate your message.

What Do You Want Them to Do?

Remember AIDA? The *action* component is the finish line of your advertising. If you can get the reader or viewer to contact the advertiser, most of your work is done. Although you will continue to reinforce the brand and encourage future sales to consumers who take action, your primary job is to connect buyers to sellers. It's up to them to close the deal. The main idea is to connect the reader, viewer, or listener with the advertiser. Make it easy to get more information if it's needed. If personal selling is critical to a purchase, find a way to connect the prospect with the salesperson. These connections can take the following forms:

- Easy-to-remember and meaningful URLs
- Outbound email (that doesn't look like spam)
- Mobile apps encouraging continued interactivity
- Meaningful engagement with Facebook
- Maximizing Twitter, sometimes employing hashtags
- Onsite engagement from test drives to taste tests
- Prepaid reply cards to request more information or an appointment
- QR codes leading to mobile sites
- Toll-free phone number in ads to connect to a live person

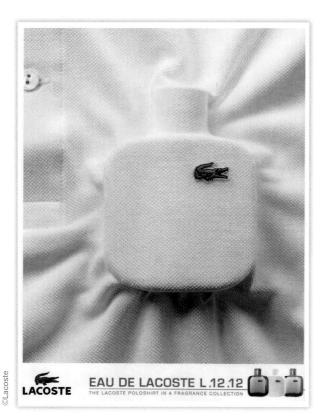

©Lacoste

Could Lacoste charge just as much for a shirt without the little alligator? Or is such blatant labeling turning off consumers? Their brand managers must think the reptile still has a lot of appeal, since they've been using it to sell their cologne as well as clothing for a number of years.

Think about the many ways customers can take action, and then make it easy to connect them with the advertiser.

Think Like a Planner, but Write Like a Creative

You've done your homework on the audience, the product, and the competition. Now you're ready to talk to a prospective customer. It's your job to give voice to that product or brand. Imagine you're talking to a neighbor over the fence. Could you tell him or her the One Thing? Do you have answers to objections or misperceptions? Could you convince that neighbor to seek more information? It's all about making that personal connection.

Here are a few samples:

Objective: Introduce new hybrid crossover utility vehicle

Type of Product: Considered purchase, high-involvement durable good

Target Audience: 20- to 30-year-old women in top 25 markets, $45,000 to $70,000 income

Possible Creative Strategy: Lots of pictures to show features, styling, captions to explain benefits (environmentally friendly, dependable, lots of space, mileage)

Tone: Convey fun, independence, adventure, and social responsibility

Objective: Encourage contributions to animal rights group

Type of Product: Emotional issue, high involvement for select few

Target Audience: 18- to 64-year-old women

Possible Creative Strategy: Show animal suffering in lab tests, long copy tells story of animal and how you can help

Tone: Tap into caretaking emotions with urgency

Objective: Introduce new style of brace for arthritic knees

Type of Product: Considered purchase, high involvement

Target Audience: 45- to 80-year-old men and women with arthritis

Possible Creative Strategy: Position as alternative to surgery and drugs, show active seniors, testimonials, and before/after stories and images

Tone: Create peace of mind, tapping into dreams of reengaging in an active lifestyle

Creative Strategy and Branding

You've gathered, organized, and prioritized the background information on the product. You've identified the target audience. You've set the tone. What's missing? How about your branding strategy? How do you put a face on that product or service that connects with consumers? Two key factors that help formulate branding strategy are **resonance** and **positioning**.

Resonance: Did You Just Feel Something?

When you achieve **resonance**, your external message connects with internal values and feelings. It connects to consumers' emotional sweet spot. Tony Schwartz comments, "Resonance takes place when the stimuli out into our communication evoke meaning in a listener or viewer . . . the meaning of our communication is what a listener or viewer gets out of his experience with the communicator's stimuli."[14]

Resonance requires a connection with feelings that are inside the consumer's mind. You don't have to put in a new emotion—just find a way to tap into what's already there. You'll see what we mean in Chapter 4. Your communication must trigger some internal experience and connect it with your message. Your brand story must be relevant. Relevance leads to resonance, which will strengthen awareness, begin building comprehension, and lead to conviction and possibly action. How's that for connecting multiple streams of psychobabble? Want a simpler explanation?

$$1 + 1 = 3$$

Resonance is connected to branding because a brand can make an emotional connection, it makes consumers feel something—something that is good, and sometimes it's bad. A harried mom with a carload of cranky kids sees those Golden Arches and rejoices, "At last—cheap food, Happy Meals, and relatively clean restrooms." The next driver turns up her nose and thinks, "Ugh—greasy food, indifferent service, and a restaurant full of cranky kids demanding Happy Meals." Both views are relevant and color the thinking about the brand.

The convergence of brand strategy and resonance theory succeeds best in brands that make consumers happy. Marketing professor Pierre Chandon states, "People align themselves with a brand that reflects what they see when they look in the mirror."[15] Meghan Casserly at Forbes.com listed the world's happiest brands.[16] Here's our take on her selections.

> **Apple**—I belong to a special group of creative nonconformists. Actually, I want to look as cool as the other people who want to look cool, and I don't even want to know if another brand is better.
>
> **Campbell's Soup**—It brings back warm feelings after coming in on a cold day. Actually, I'm too lazy to make anything from scratch and I don't care about all that extra sodium and fat.
>
> **Coca-Cola**—I remember all the good times when Coke was the ultimate refreshment. Actually, I would love to have a Coke with every meal, but other than childhood memories, there isn't one redeeming thing about sugary carbonated beverages.

Facebook—I'm in control of my own brand story. Actually I'm creeped out by people looking at my page, my mom bugs me constantly about helping her with updates, and it's turned into another advertising medium.

J. Crew—I can get classic quality for a reasonable price. Actually, I kind of like some of their styles, but when Michelle Obama endorsed the brand, it kind of lost its allure.

Johnson's Baby—My mom used it on me. I use it on my kids. Actually, if there's anything wrong with something this pure and innocent, I really don't want to hear about it.

Kraft Macaroni & Cheese—It's easy, cheesy, and sometimes the perfect food. Actually, it usually tastes like crap, but most of the time I'm too burned out to make anything else.

Assume the Position

Jack Trout and Al Ries revolutionized marketing in the late 1970s and early 1980s with their theory of positioning. Their book *Positioning: The Battle for Your Mind* introduced a new way of thinking about products and how they fit into the marketplace. This is the best definition of positioning we've found: *Simply stated, positioning is the perception consumers have of your product, not unto itself, but relative to the competition.*[17]

The key to understanding and using positioning lies in the consumer's mind. The consumer files product considerations into two broad categories: garbage ("nothing there for me") and maybe-I'm-interested. In the second category, consumers use subcategories for different products, often aligning those positions with heavily promoted brand images. For example, BMWs are fast. Volvos are safe. Jeeps are rugged. And so on. So if you asked most consumers to "position" or rank those brands in various categories, you'd probably find some resistance to the idea that a BMW is as safe as a Volvo, or that a Jeep can be as fast as a BMW, or that Volvo can be as rugged as a Jeep. All true in some cases, but not universally believed. Once a position is established, it takes a lot of effort to change it.

Before you develop the position of your client's product, you have to ask:

- What is the current position?
- What is the competitor's position?
- Where do you want to be?
- How are you going to get there? (That's strategy.)

Repositioning and Rebranding

If you don't like your product's position, you can try to change it from the top down. Here are a couple examples:

Burberry's trademark black, tan, and red check design was a favorite with minor British royalty, preppies, and stuffy country club types for well over 150 years. But when gangs started sporting Burberry plaid, something had to be done. New management overhauled the brand with a mix of modern and classic looks that included a sexier trench coat and swimwear, and snapped up high-profile celebrities like Kate Moss and Emma Watson.[18] Sales rose almost immediately, with rapid growth in Asia. Sales have remained strong across America, Europe, China and Korea.[19]

Corona beer was the light, cheap brew that fueled spring breakers in Mexico during the 1980s. As those folks grew up a little, they moved on to more sophisticated beer brands.

When Johnson's Baby rolled out the "For All You Love" campaign, they knew showing the special bond between mother and child resonates much more than showing the package.

Still a classic. This Nike ad from Mexico conveys the "Just Do It" branding without words—in any language.

Corona's sales suffered, until a new ad agency repositioned the brand as the one to relax with—the one that takes you away. Ads invoked lazy days in a hammock rather than wet T-shirt contests. The "Change Your Latitude" and "Find Your Beach" campaigns put Corona back on the map, and sales soared. After all, no matter how hard you partied in college, you can always dream about relaxing on the beach.

Judith Aquino notes, "Rebranding a company's goals, message, and culture is hard—many have tried and most fail. A successful campaign requires more than a revamped logo. It demands a vision that inspires customers, investors, and others to see the company in a new light. Through savvy marketing and better quality control, some companies discovered new ways to revive their brands and in some cases, made them stronger than ever."[20]

While Trout and Ries opened a lot of minds to the idea of positioning, we don't agree with their premise that creativity makes no difference. Sometimes it's the only difference. Another caveat is the Trout and Ries analyzed successful campaigns in the past tense and made them fit their theory. Did the 7Up creative team really think about positioning when they launched the "Uncola" campaign, or did they just want to do smart comparative advertising? Often the creative is the only thing that makes a brand memorable, and it usually takes time for it to stick.

The Power and Limits of Branding

For years we've been firmly entrenched in what marketing guru Scott Bedbury called "a new brand world." Today as social media and word-of-mouth marketing mold opinions, fewer people accept what advertisers say about their brands. In fact, more consumers, especially Millennials, have formed a significant anticorporate sentiment that has severely eroded the once powerful brands of their generation.

Before you start supporting a brand with marketing communication, you have to understand the strengths and the challenges of branding. Luke Sullivan takes the traditional view:

"A brand isn't just a name on the box. It isn't the thing in the box either. A brand is the sum total of all the emotions, thoughts, images, history, possibilities and gossip that exist in the marketplace about a certain company."[21] Companies marketing brands that have positive images experience billions of dollars in extra brand equity, worth far more than the physical assets of their firms. They protect those brands and all the symbols associated with them like a mama bear. Put an unlicensed NFL team logo on a jersey and you'll see how sharp those claws can be. Brands that are losing their luster have backed away from the most blatant identification on their products to stop their losses. As of this writing, the most uncool look for a guy is wearing a shirt with a big Abercrombie & Fitch logos, relaxed-fit Dockers, and toting a brightly colored McDonald's carry-out sack.

Brand Image

Brand image advertising and promotion sell the personality, the mystique, and the aura surrounding or emanating from the product or the company that makes it. Think of the old cliché "Sell the sizzle, not the steak." Every product has a brand image, whether weak or strong, negative or positive. Consider these two aspects of branding:

What it is: A brand is a promise. It's shorthand for all the product's attributes, both good and bad.

What it does: A brand makes its promise personal by conveying the product's personality, which reflects on the people who buy the product. It's really about relationships.

How does the brand image of BMW differ from that of Cadillac or Lexus? They all cost about the same, but have different characteristics, as do their customers. How did Apple differentiate its computers from PCs? Not as a technically superior and more expensive computer, but rather as a computer with an easy-to-use operating system favored by right-brain types. IBM told people to "Think." Apple said, "Think different." Luke Sullivan states, "Most of the time we're talking about going into a customer's brain and tacking on one adjective onto a client's brand. That's all. DeWalt tools are tough. Apple computers are easy to use . . . Volvos are safe. Porsches are fast. Jeeps are rugged. Boom. Where's the rocket science here?"[22] To support a brand's image, advertisers use simple, unique, and easily recognized visuals. Over time, the brand (and all its attributes, good and bad) comes to mind when a consumer catches even a glimpse of these visuals.

Branded Storytelling

Every brand has a story behind it. A marketer's job is to make sure it's a good story, one that can be told over and over again by satisfied customers. In the past, advertisers developed the Unique Selling Proposition. Today they're searching to create a "Unique Story Proposition." Alain Thys writes, "Great brand stories stem from the reason a brand exists. Apple wanted to free creative spirits while slaying the Microsoft dragon. Coco Chanel set out to reinvent fashion and liberate women from tradition.

Pepsi wants to be a catalyst for change for every generation. Dig into the history, people and promises of your brand to uncover its Unique Story Proposition (USP). Make this the anchor for every story you tell."[23]

Self-described marketing heretic Mark Di Somma states, "Stories are the backbones of powerful brands. Every strong brand is backed by a powerful brand story that weaves together all the brand elements into a single and compelling tale packed with truth, insights and compelling ideas."[24] Stories are driven by emotions, and consumers are expressing these emotions through their consumption choices. Think of how Nike has managed to direct all its communications toward one underlying message—the will to win. They have to do this through telling the story of individual athletic success, but always in the context of the athletic community—the Nike community. In the process consumers see themselves within these stories and thus within the Nike community. They too dream of winning, and Nike's stories represent their stories—or at least their mythological possibility. Nike's advertising provides the context for this mythology to grow. It also demonstrates how branding and the USP shape consumers' experiences.

Perhaps no brand was a greater reflection of its CEO than Apple. Steve Jobs's fanatical control over everything, including advertising, resulted in some of the greatest campaigns of all time. As a struggling upstart and later as a market leader, Apple's brand story was consistent: Create simple, easy-to-use, elegant products that make the user a better person and, as a result, the world a better place. Jobs's brand message of technology as a humanizing force was eloquently stated in the introduction of the iPad 2, his last big product launch. Even with Jobs's passing, the ethos of control remains visible in the continued dominance of the Apple brand.

> This is what we believe. Technology alone is not enough. Faster. Thinner. Lighter. Those are all good things. But when technology gets out of the way, everything becomes more delightful, even magical. That's when you leap forward. That's when you end up with something like this.[25]

Brand Agents

Consider the power of Beyoncé, Richard Branson, Ellen DeGeneres, and Phil Knight as they shape their brands. It is their personal stories that provide the mythology that shapes and sustains their brands. Thought of in this way, myths give a brand an emotional context, which provides the platform from which consumers find a sense of identity and belonging. Remember Maslow's hierarchies? Think of brands as "the narrative of mankind. It's a story told with a collective voice and a shared point of view."[26] When brands are conceived in this manner, you can see how the brand story articulates the brand promise.

Traditional branding strategy dictates that to be effective, a brand must be used consistently and must invoke meaning. Sometimes that meaning bubbles up from the bottom, as with Pabst Blue Ribbon beer. After decades of decline, PBR experienced a revival thanks to urban hipsters looking for an ironic brew to go with their flannel shirts and fixed-gear bikes. Not wishing to jinx their unexpected resurgence, the company wisely took a rather passive role in positioning, and let the market drive the brand.

Pabst limited promotion to sponsoring obscure indie bands and facial hair clubs and placed some products in a few TV shows and movies. If Pabst had taken a more aggressive approach, those nonconforming hipsters might have adopted another bland, unpopular lager.

Even with changes in how brands are perceived, marketers still need to establish recognition, differentiation, and relevance for their brands. In earlier times, the solution was to saturate every advertising medium and slap that logo on anything that won't move. However, advertising funds are limited, even for huge companies, so a more sophisticated approach was required to make that brand stick in the minds of consumers.

David Aaker, brand consultant and author of more than 14 books, suggests that the value of a brand is often rooted in the parent brand. Sub-brands are the value brands. Marriott is the parent brand, while Courtyard by Marriott is a value-based sub-brand. Aaker suggests there are three types of relationships between parent brands and sub-brands: endorser, codriver, and driver brands. Let's use Nike to walk you through. Nearly every extension of the Nike brand, from Nike Golf to NIKEiD, carries with it the cache of the parent brand. Now let's see how it plays out.

- **Endorser brand:** This brand is endorsed by the Nike parent brand—Nike+ (running gadgets).
- **Codriver brand:** This brand is equal to the parent brand in terms of its influence with consumers and sometimes appears as a competitor—Adidas.
- **Driver brand:** With this brand the parent maintains primary influence as driver and the sub-brand acts as a descriptor, telling consumers that the parent company is offering a slight variation on the product or service they have come to know and trust—Nike Women.

Next come **line extensions**. Robert Sprung, partner of a major branding services company, says, "A good line extension takes a brand with a solid core of values and applies it to an area where the brand has permission to go."[27]

Dove has done an excellent of extending its brand to reach a wider audience of women and now men. Dove's landmark "Real Beauty" campaign encouraged women who were not fashion models to love their bodies and thus embrace themselves fully. But that was only about half the population, so Dove chose to extend its brand to men's skin care products. In 2010, Dove launched Men+Care to make men "feel comfortable in their own skin." The message: real men don't lose their masculinity when they gain better looking skin. (Shhhh, don't tell them, but they also embrace themselves more fully.) Supported by a Super Bowl ad, sales promotions, mobile and web ads, and social media, the campaign appealed to men in places where they live and play, using language that resonated with them. Of course men needed to feel okay using Dove products; it's important to note that women make most personal grooming decisions for men. So having a brand women know and love for their men as well as themselves was a definite advantage.

Nike started with running shoes, and before long it was apparel, which opened the door to every other sport—for both men and women. Talk about market dominance. Marketers for strong brands naturally want to leverage that strength whenever possible.

The *Branding Strategy Insider* website lists some guidelines for successful brand extension:

- Have you identified what your brand owns in the consumer's mind? [In other words, what is your brand's position?]

- Have you identified all the areas in which the consumer gives your brand position to operate?

- Have you identified all the ways your brand and others in its category have made compromises with the consumer?

- Have you found ways to redefine your business to break those compromises?

- Have you explored ways to make your brand more relevant to the next generation of consumers?

- Do you have a way to screen all new brand extension proposals for their congruence with the brand promise and impact on brand equity? [A fancy way of asking if you've done your homework.[28]]

The End of Branding? Maybe. Maybe Not.

In 1989 Canadian Kalle Lasn founded AdBusters, an activist foundation challenging consumerism. Ten years later another Canadian, Naomi Klein, published the anticonsumption manifesto *No Logo: Taking Aim at Brand Bullies*. She railed against globalization, sweatshops, misleading advertising, American cultural dominance, and many other sins of modern marketing.

©American Express

It's not enough to be well known. People want to know if their favorite brands are good corporate citizens. American Express promotes its sponsorship of Scott Harrison's efforts to bring fresh water to impoverished areas. The QR code connects the reader to the full story.

King of the Bounce

© Adidas © Foot Locker

Adidas came out with a new sneaker technology called Bounce that was meant to compete with the Nike Shox. During the briefing session the team told us how long and hard they worked to come up with the technology to successfully compete in the market space that was currently dominated by Nike.

The technology was put through various tests until they came up with the perfect look and feel. We came up with the idea to bring the Bounce technology to life to show the quality level of the sneaker in a fun and entertaining way. What better way to do that than to have the Bounce technology compete to become a part of the shoe.

Foot Locker Inc. partnered with Adidas to create a campaign for the launch of the Adidas Bounce sneaker, which would be sold exclusively at Foot Locker stores nationwide. The mission was to promote the new technology of the Adidas sneaker created to take on the Nike Shox. The biggest challenge was to keep the urban feel, which is the heart of the Foot Locker brand, and merge it with a sport lifestyle brand of Adidas.

We created various characters, giving each a different background and personality, and the characters kept video logs of their training journeys throughout the competition.

The competition would take place in Sumo wrestling style, and each character would wear a uniform that resembled the look of the Bounce technology. We shot various videos of the characters giving the viewers insight into their process, which would be available on YouTube.

The videos were a teaser to lead up to the actual marketing event, which was held at the Chelsea boxing arena in New York City.

Clips from the training and final competition were all compiled to make the 30-second commercial for the brand. This led to Adidas doubling the estimated sells of the product. The campaign was translated into a Foot Locker in-store presence with window banners, clings, fixture toppers, tabletop designs, and out-of-home posters placed in bus shelters and wild postings.[29]

With cobranding, Adidas and Foot Locker got the bounce their brands needed.

Ellen Wagner, art director, formerly SapientNitro, New York, now freelancing

---

Together Lasn and Klein laid the foundation for what has become the antibranding movement, which one could say eventually led to the Occupy movements. While most consumers won't totally boycott big-name brands, there has been renewed interest in the corporate policies behind those brands. More people want to know what a company stands for; if it does good as it's doing well. Another outgrowth of this movement is Dara O'Rourke's Good Guide, a comprehensive resource for information about the environmental, health, and social performance of consumer products and the companies that make them. While you can use Good Guide to choose brands and products that reflect your values, we'll try to embed discussions about socially responsible branding through the book. If nothing else, in perusing Good Guide you will quickly learn that a brand is more than a logo.

A brand is everything good and bad associated with the product and its company. Our perception of a brand greatly depends on how it resonates in our lives. Brands give us an identity, and they allow us to form bonds with others like us. That's why it's no surprise to see anticapitalist protesters proudly marching in their North Face jackets, H&M tops, Uggs, and Ray-Ban aviators as they take selfies on their iPhones.

How to write
BRANDING GUIDELINES

First ask...

How will they be used?
Are they easy to follow?
Do they reflect marketing goals?
Are they scalable?

Brand personality
Professional or laid back? A personality makes your brand approachable.

Brand beliefs
Aligns with personality and marketing to build company character.

Social media tone
Use same tone across all social media platforms.

Marketing position
Knowing where you want to be gives your brand a goal.

Copywriting tone
All copy, including websites, ads, direct mail and collateral.

Source: TbA Marketing Group

What exactly is the difference between want and need?

PEPPERIDGE FARM

Milano dark chocolate

Never forget that people don't buy things. They buy satisfaction of their wants and needs. When it comes to something as delicious as Milano cookies, it's hard to tell the difference between want and need.

It's Just Like Swimming

Courtesy of Yisha Zhang

This August marks the beginning of my seventh year in the United States and the beginning of my fifth year as a strategic planner. There were many points along the way when I thought I couldn't do this anymore—when I got really homesick one month after I came to the United States for grad school and wanted to go back home; when there wasn't a permanent position open for me at the agency where I interned for a year and I didn't prepare a single thing for the job interviews I never thought I needed; and when I threw away eight not-good-enough briefs in the middle of the night and seriously questioned if I had the smarts and ability to be a good planner.

Somehow, I worked through all these and many more other challenging moments.

Today, I'm still happily getting paychecks for decoding and manipulating consumers' minds—something that I've wanted to do since high school. I'm not sure what motivated me to keep on going every time I doubted myself. Maybe it's because I really love being in advertising; or maybe because my parents already paid too much for my bachelor's and master's degrees in marketing and it's way too late to back out.

Okay, I kid.

The part that I didn't kid about is that it ain't easy to work in advertising, and it ain't easy to be a good planner. It doesn't matter whether English is my first language or second. We'll need . . . excellent work ethics to go through countless late nights, a thick skin to ignore creatives' "why should I listen to you" face when we just started, and almost blind self-confidence to believe that we can always write a better brief. Most important, we'll need the courage for learning to swim, the old-school way: just dive in and try to survive. We all know that our potential is most realized when we don't have the time to think about what if we fail.

I constantly get emails from students, mostly international students in the United States, asking whether they should stay here or go back, which agencies they should apply to, and what are the chances that they could get work visa sponsorships. I know they were earnestly seeking advice, but most of the time, I could only tell them that I didn't know. I didn't know what the right choice for them was, just like I cannot learn to swim for them. I understand that every now and then, we all have doubts. We all doubt if this is the right direction to go and how far we can go. The truth is, we will never know how far we can go if we don't go all in in the first place.

Just dive in and we will all survive. And if we train really hard on a regular basis, we might all be really good at it one day—swimming or advertising.[30]

Yisha Zhang, senior strategic planner, Team One
@teamoneusa

Christine Bronstein

Christine Bronstein used one word to launch a brand: *wives*. Her research told her that we all need wives. But, of course, only men have them. She turned the word *wives* on its head. For her, wives are your closest allies and friends. Bronstein founded A Band of Wives, now called A Band of Women, a private social community for women. It provides a safe place for women to ask for and find the support they need, to promote their businesses and talents and other cool things they do. In her day job, Bronstein is the CEO of one of the few women-run, venture-backed health and fitness companies in the nation.[31]

Marty Neumeier

Before launching and becoming president of Neutron LLC, a San Francisco–based firm specializing in brand collaboration, in 2002, Marty Neumeier was editor and publisher of *Critique*, the "magazine of graphic design thinking," which had quickly become the leading forum for improving design effectiveness. In editing *Critique*, Neumeier joined the conversation about how to bridge the gap between strategy and design, which led directly to the formation of Neutron and the ideas in his book *The Brand Gap*.

Shirley Polykoff

Shirley Polykoff was a pioneer for women in advertising and outstanding creative talent. She started out in advertising as a teenager working for *Harper's Bazaar*. After a career in retail copywriting, she took over the Clairol account at Foote, Cone & Belding, where she penned the classic "Does she . . . or doesn't she?" Polykoff reached the position of executive vice president and creative director at FCB and left to found her own successful agency.

Rebecca Van Dyck

As chief marketing officer of Levi's, Rebecca Van Dyck was challenged to make the old brand relevant to a new generation of fickle and skeptical consumers. One winning strategy was promoting the Levi's Curve ID line for women. She also expanded the iconic "Go Forth" campaign to 24 countries and debuted the "Now Is Our Time" campaign to an audience of 325 million people on Facebook, telling them they have the power to change the world. Regarding her global strategy, she said, "Initially, America was our canvas. Now, our canvas is the world." The world is buying it—resulting in significant increases in sales and profits for this venerable brand. *Adweek* named Van Dyck as a Brand Genius.[32]

The Spirit of the Time

"What makes Millennials (people born between 1980 and 2000) tick?" is probably one of the most burning questions facing the world of advertising and marketing today. This generation craves the inner, search for meaning, and authenticity and is very nonmaterialistic. In response, marketers and advertisers have introduced important perspectives such as "brand with a purpose," "experiential advertising," and "Corporate Social Responsibility." However, especially when considering the lack of trust among consumers toward advertisers, are these perspectives enough to connect with the nonmaterialistic and authentic essence of Millennials (aka consumers)?

Recent research has pointed to a new framework or a new school of thought when advertising in the 21st century—spirituality. This line of research is not suggesting a new marketing technique or another superficial way to connect with consumers; it offers a shift of consciousness of how advertising and business should be done. It brings forward a few assumptions about spirituality in advertising:

- Spiritually is not religion. It is beyond religion and a very broad concept.
- Spiritually focuses on the inner dimension of humans (by extension, consumers) and human growth.
- Spirituality is a path to achieve fulfilment and overcome obstacles in our day-to-day life.
- Spirituality focuses on meaning.

Your mission, as future advertisers and persuaders, is to figure out how the concept of spirituality could or should be implemented in advertising. Xanadu Flooring is a carpet company based in the United States. It offers very unique and authentic cultural designs. The carpets are handmade by local villagers from a small village in South Asia. The leadership of the company promotes an extremely inclusive and supportive environment for all people who work for the company or are involved with it. Purchases are conducted online through the company's website. Customers are providing rave reviews about the quality of the product and the incomparable warm and homey feelings it evokes. Xanadu hired you as a communication and advertising expert to help in building its brand recognition and brand identity. Before delving into the task and the discussion questions, please conduct the following exercise:

- Step 1: Close your eyes, sit comfortably, relax, and take a few breaths.
- Step 2: Think about associations, words that come to mind when you are thinking about the notions of the inner and spirituality. Write them down.
- Step 3: Think about Xanadu Flooring. Now, think about associations, words that come to mind when you are thinking about it. Write them down.
- Step 4: While considering all the previous steps and the above assumptions about spirituality, create a commercial storyboard, inspired by the spirituality concept, for Xanadu Flooring.

WHAT WOULD YOU DO?

1 Thinking within the spirituality framework and the upcoming Millennial crowd, how should you build your brand strategy for Xanadu Flooring? What would be the three words that define Xanadu? Would you recommend a different name?

2 As a brand manager and/or advertiser, what would you recommend Xanadu and its leadership to do in order to support the authenticity of the spiritual message you have developed earlier in the commercial storyboard (hint: think about internal policies, employees' relationships, culture, leadership, customer relations, events in a community, etc.)?

3 For Xanadu, think about a media strategy that would fit the spiritual essence and message of the brand. Where would you advertise? Which media channels would you use? Would you consider inventing a new media approach for the emerging spirituality framework in advertising?

Gilat Marmor-Lavie, lecturer, Stan Richards School of Advertising & Public Relations, University of Texas at Austin

1. What's the Big Idea, Buddy?

(Contributed by Kimberly Selber, PhD, associate professor, University of Texas–Pan American.)

This exercise is all about finding the Big Idea or the One Thing and linking it to strategy.

- Find several campaigns with at least three ads. (Try using *Archive* magazine for this assignment; the online version—http://www.luerzersarchive.net—is great, because you can easily grab all the ads together.)
- Write a Copy Platform or Creative Brief for each campaign. End with one sentence describing the overarching concept in the campaign—the One Thing.
- Compare how other students or groups interpreted your message. If the messaging is tight, the briefs should be similar. This works great as an in-class exercise or as homework in teams or solo.

2. Brand Stretching

- As a class, generate a list of five brands, from five different product categories. Now, individually generate a list of brand extensions for each product. Consider what areas the parent brand already owns and in which areas of the brand you find growth opportunities.
- Now pick one brand. Post your brand and list of potential brand extensions. Explain the rationale for each brand extension choice.
- Then, as a class, generate other possible brand extensions.

3. Tagging the Heart of a Brand

- Choose four brands. As a class, brainstorm a list of words that personify the heart of each brand.
- Break into four groups, one brand per group. Based on the words generated, write a Positioning Statement.
- Visit brandtags.net. Click on "Tag Brands" and "Explore Brands" to find brands to analyze.
- Next click on "Guess Brands" and see how many of the first 10 brands that pop up your group can guess correctly. If you guess the brand, you can be pretty sure the brand positioning is strongly articulated and maintained.
- Share your results with the class and learn which brands have strong positioning and why.

Review chapter content and study for exams. http://study.sagepub.com/altstiel4e.

- Interactive practice quizzes
- Mobile-friendly eFlashcards
- Carefully selected chapter-by-chapter video and multimedia content

Chapter 3

Ethical and Legal Issues
Doing the Right Thing

Entire books have been written about ethical and legal issues in advertising. All this book can do is candidly address a few of the challenges the industry faces, which may help you make better choices as you move through your career. Ethical issues fall into that vast gray area between black-and-white legality. Sometimes a client may provide information that may not be legally accurate. Other statements or practices that are legal might not be ethical. That's where it gets really tough. The one thing we can recommend is that you take some time to define your own individual ethical boundaries before you get into this business. Having given ethics serious consideration in advance will help you when you get mired in the vast sea of gray.

Ethical Challenges Within

The advertising industry faces a few ethical dilemmas within its own ranks. Advertising has long seen itself as a meritocracy—a place where the best and brightest compete to make it to the top. However, there are challenges within the industry. Look around and you will likely see few African Americans, Hispanics, and Asians unless you're looking within multicultural agencies. It's not a lot different for gays and lesbians, who tend to be siloed on "gay" accounts within general market agencies. The lack of minority representation in advertising was so extreme that a decade ago, the city of New York filed suit against the industry. In the end, the suit changed very little. For people from diverse communities, employment equity in advertising remains elusive. This is an ethical challenge for the industry. However, with an ever more diverse world, we suggest it's also bad for business.

A second challenge within the industry is the lack of gender diversity in creative departments. While opportunities remain vibrant for women across other departments, in creative, women make up only 20% of creative teams and only 14% of all creative directors across the world.[2] While the numbers in the United States are a bit better, it's still a problem. Women drive more than 80% of all consumption choices, yet we don't see many of them on creative teams. Wouldn't women provide relevant and salient perspectives? Some argue a good creative person should be able to climb into the skin of his or her target audience and create resonant and effective work. If that's true, that begs the question, then why are multicultural agencies thriving? Furthermore, what does the lack of women in creative suggest about the environment within creative departments and employment opportunities for women? The numbers alone suggest a masculine world within creative departments. How that influences the creative work or the environment in which the work is produced is open to debate—and undoubtedly changes from agency to agency. One thing is for sure: It certainly poses challenges for women working in creative.

Ticklish Categories, Difficult Issues

For one person, working on an alcohol brand would be a thrill. For another, it might cross an ethical line. The same might be true of working on firearms or pharmaceuticals or political campaigns or even fast foods. You'll need to find and set your ethical boundaries. And getting there may not as easy as you think. For starters we all juggle a variety of loyalties—loyalties to yourself, to your family, to your coworkers, to your client, and the list goes on. To give you an example of how difficult ethical decisions can be, we've chosen two ticklish categories to briefly consider, pharmaceuticals and politics. Candidly, this is only the tip of the iceberg.

"More exposure of actual or current women and minority creative leaders is essential to grow a new base of leaders. They cannot be what they cannot see."[1]

Diego Figueroa, senior vice president, director of strategy and participation, Lapiz

©Starbucks Corporation

Starbucks wanted baristas to discuss race issues with their customers. The much mocked campaign lasted only a week, creating a huge social media backlash and resistance from customers, both Black and White. Time will tell if this kind of "retail activism" helps or hurts the brand.

In 2012 the pharmaceutical industry invested nearly $3.5 billion in advertising drugs to consumers.[3] While pharmaceutical advertising is subject to more regulation than many other categories, keep in mind that the United States is one of only two countries (New Zealand is the other) where prescription drugs can be advertised to consumers. In the same year the fast food industry spent $4.6 billion on advertising, mostly targeting children.[4] We are talking about big money. Now consider that the vast majority of advertising dollars spent focuses on "lifestyle" drugs, anything from erectile dysfunction to social anxiety to allergy medications. Any of you who watch televised sports are aware of the Viagra and Cialis commercials that dominate the airwaves. Then in summer 2015, the Food and Drug Administration approved Addyi, the "female Viagra," which had been denied approval twice before and is "at best minimally effective and could cause side effects."[5] We are not minimizing the value of lifestyle drugs for the people who benefit from them. However, we are questioning the overall societal value of shifting money from research and development to advertising. To give you some context, the Food and Drug Administration substantially deregulated the advertising of pharmaceutics in 1996. This was driven by a substantial lobbying effort on the part of the pharmaceutical industry, and it has paid off handsomely. However, it also costs handsomely. Consider that from 1998 to 2013 the pharmaceutical industry spent nearly $2.7 billion on lobbying. That is 42% more than the second biggest lobbyer, insurance. Furthermore, lobbyists, individuals, and political action committees (PACs) connected to pharmaceutical industry have given nearly $150 million in political campaign contributions since 1990.[6] Might there be some ethical concerns involved in the myriad decisions that got us to this moment in time? We cannot understate the intersection of money, power, and ethics within the advertising landscape, which takes us to our next ticklish subject, politics.

In the current political climate we cannot help but wonder if ethical values have been tossed aside. You might be able to argue that many of the ads are partially factual. However, almost everyone can agree that they often do not represent the values of fairness and respect, which certainly calls into question whether they are responsible. Throw into the mix that corporations, labor unions, and political action committees (PACs) now have legal status as individuals when it comes to free speech. We have to wonder about the transparency and the ethical values of citizenship when it comes to ads from PACs and other special-interest groups. From the presidential race down to a local aldermanic district, it's gotten increasingly toxic. To give some perspective on spending, in 2014, super-PACs, which included unions, raised $695 billion and spent $348 billion.[7] That stockpile increased for 2016 and shows no sign of slowing down for future elections. No matter which side you're on, it's fair to say that most political advertising does not foster trust in our industry, nor does it embrace ethical values. Pharmaceutical and political advertising reflect specific categories. Yet if you drill down within any sector, brand by brand, you will likely find ethical challenges.

Women and Children First

The old notion of "women and children first," pertaining to sinking ships, seems to be long past. However, it provides a good starting point for talking about ethical issues, from gender representations to protecting vulnerable demographic groups. This does not just mean women and children.

Images of women in advertising have a long history of objectification and misrepresentation. These images have, for far too long, skewed toward portraying women as sexualized or incompetent, or making women invisible. In Chapter 4 we will talk about how to reach women, as they are still considered a niche demographic group. We know, with women making up half the population, thinking of them as a niche market is crazy. While we can't change the industry structure, we can challenge it. Why is it that GoDaddy pulled its 2015 Super Bowl ads, which humorously portrayed puppy mills? (Don't get us wrong, we are not proponents of puppy mills.) Yet in previous years GoDaddy had not batted an eyelash, so to speak, when creating ads that objectified women—competent women, no less. Remember Danica Patrick, the NASCAR driver, draped half naked across her racecar? It strikes us as ironic and troubling that there was more public outcry over the unfair treatment of puppies, while there was little to no outcry about objectifying women. Let's be clear, consumers have a role to play here. However, as long as there are agencies (72 and Sunny, to be specific) that are willing to take on clients like Carl's Jr. and create commercials that objectify women (think Charlotte McKinney walking naked through public spaces on her way to bite the big burger), the problem will remain. How can we rethink the way we, as advertisers, *choose* to speak to and about women?

The How Marketing group suggests seven wise insights about speaking to women.[8]

- First, identify unique segments based on lifestyle. Nike does this well.

- Second, "brand lite" isn't the answer. Don't make the mistake of creating a softer women's brand. Apple is a great example of a brand women love, just the way it is.

- Third, communicate product values instead of listing features. Volvo does that successfully. Women know it stands for safety and dependability.

- Fourth, understand that she's always watching. If you don't speak the truth, she will know. The NFL lost big brands, from CoverGirl to Pepsi, when it tried to soft-pedal the issue of domestic violence among its players. With a 60% increase in female viewership in the past ten years,[9] this is a mistake no brand can afford.

- Fifth, respect her. McDonald's used to have a resonant voice with women. In 2002 they introduced salads, and in 2011 they invited mommy bloggers to the press conference that introduced the addition of fresh fruit to Happy Meals. But lately they are not getting the healthy food message moms are sending; in 2014, McDonald's stock dropped by more than 4%.[10]

- Sixth, embrace high standards. Women demand quality, and reward brands that serve it up. Whole Foods has been able to charge more by promoting their strong community engagement.

- Finally, be willing to commit. If you want her to commit to you, you'd better commit to her. Dove is a brand that is committed to women, with its game-changing "Campaign for Real Beauty" followed by "Dove Sketches," and women will return the commitment. Frankly, so will men. Dove gets real people. In the end, reaching women requires that you do your homework and make no assumptions.

What about men? With apologies to Thomas Jefferson, they're not all created equal—at least when it comes to marketing. There seem to be three buckets of men: the authority figure, the unrestrained fun(ny) guy, and the village idiot.

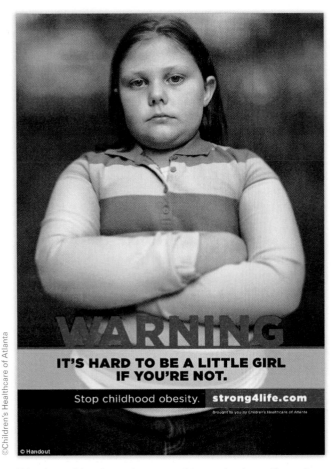

WARNING

IT'S HARD TO BE A LITTLE GIRL IF YOU'RE NOT.

Stop childhood obesity.   strong4life.com

Brought to you by Children's Healthcare of Atlanta

© Handout

Warning—this ad taps into everything we've been discussing. It's not easy to fit in when you don't meet social expectation, especially when some brands exploit those expectations. What part will you play?

Interestingly, the male authority figure is beginning to be challenged by nonwhite men and women, which surely represents a more balanced picture. The ubiquitous fun(ny) guy appears to be more and more sexualized, not unlike women have been for millennia. The village idiot is a far too common portrayal, with men being shown as unable to figure out even the slightest problem, while being mocked ad nauseam. You've seen him: the guy making selfies in the Xerox machine; the guy locked out of his hotel room wearing only his tightie whities; the guy volunteering to juggle chain saws; and the list goes on, even though most of us don't remember the brands being advertised. The 2015 Super Bowl offered a welcome reprieve from these stereotypical portrayals of men, with ads showing us real men, being real dads, in real time. To quote Coca-Cola's great slogan, that was "the pause that refreshes." Keep it coming.

When it comes to vulnerable audiences, children are not the only demographic that is at risk. In fact, in Canada, seniors (people over 60) are the most targeted demographic group and, some say, often the most vulnerable.[11] With matures, as we refer to folks over 65, you will note an increase in direct mail, and increasingly, email and telemarketing scams.[12] Matures tolerate authority, are very loyal, and appreciate a good value. At the same time the natural aging process makes some people less skeptical and more susceptible to scams.[13] We'll talk more about how to reach seniors and children in Chapter 4. However, suffice it to say, reaching out to vulnerable demographics requires deeper ethical considerations.

Targeting children is fraught with ethical dilemmas. Should advertisers even be talking to children? Maybe. Maybe not. Alex Bogusky, former partner at Crispin Porter + Bogusky, and founder of FearLess Revolution and COMMON, suggests that we consider what might happen if we stopped advertising to children. Bogusky thinks, "A lot of things would happen, and almost all seem to be for the good of society."[14] Yet it's fair to say that advertising to children is not going away. Thus, there are myriad questions that should frame decisions when it comes to children and advertising. Do advertisers bear responsibility for crafting images to children that broaden gender representation rather than continuing to narrow it? What are the consequences of advertising products that may actually harm children, be they fast food, sugary sodas, or too much screen time with video games? When and where do media placements cross a line? We know brands engage with children on Saturday mornings, in schools, online, in games, and from the moment they get their first mobile phones. It seems no place is free of branded messaging, and the consequences are not insignificant. Clearly parents and caregivers play a role here. However, placing the responsibility at their feet is an easy out for advertisers—and one that doesn't sit well with us. Advertisers have long claimed that advertising is informational, and that they simply use entertainment to engage this youthful target with useful information. However, young children do not have the cognitive facilities to discern information from entertainment.

Advertisers are the grownups and we must be responsible for our decisions.

We suggest four crucial considerations to guide you as you craft messaging aimed at children:

- First, use media and messages that are age appropriate.

- Second, consider whether the content is detrimental to children.

- Third, honestly acknowledge your role in creating and/or maintaining stereotypes.

- Fourth, honor the concerns of parents and professionals, especially when it comes to younger children.

Holding these considerations in the forefront is not only the right thing to do, but they may save you from having to engage in damage control after the fact. As we have discussed, children are not the only group that warrants serious ethical considerations. They are, however, more vulnerable than most. What will you choose to do, when it comes to advertising to children?

Let's talk about another area of gender representation. Gays, lesbians, and transgender people are affected more from invisibility, at least in advertising, than from misrepresentation. No responsible advertiser would use outrageous stereotypes for gays or lesbians. However, how many are willing to own their support of the LGBT community within their general marketing advertising? More and more every year, but overall still very few. We'll discuss effective and ethical ways to tap into that market in the next chapter.

Absolut boldly demonstrated its support of the LGBT community by running this ad, in niche print media and online. Does support for LGBT equality trump the social damage caused from promoting alcohol?

Advertising in Action

We suggest three primary ways the industry attempts to keep its moral compass balanced. First, a number of industry organizations have created codes of conduct, which have provided guidance for practitioners. Agencies often have their own set of codes of conduct as well. Second, the industry as a whole is pretty passionate about giving back to the community through either cause-related advertising or with pro bono work. Third, the advertising industry hires, retains, and promotes people with high ethical principles, who are willing to put those standards front and center *and* who are willing to push back against the status quo. Number three is still a work in progress. Diversifying the advertising workforce could also up the ethical ante.

Most industries have codes of conduct that guide professional practices. Additionally, the majority of companies also have internal codes of ethics or principles that guide employee behavior. The American Association of Advertising Agencies provides creative codes of conduct for its members. Even if you're not a 4A's member, it's good advice if followed. However, it also has limitations, as you will see.

American Association of Advertising Agencies: Creative Codes of Conduct

We the members of the American Association of Advertising Agencies (AAAA), in addition to supporting and obeying the laws and legal regulations pertaining to advertising, undertake to extend and broaden the application of high ethical standards. Specifically, we will not knowingly create advertising that contains:

a. False or misleading statements or exaggerations, visual or verbal.

b. Testimonials that do not reflect the real opinion of the individual(s) involved.

c. Price claims that are misleading.

d. Claims insufficiently supported or that distort the true meaning or practicable application of statements made by professional or scientific authority.

e. Statements, suggestions or pictures offensive to public decency or minority segments of the population.

We recognize that there are areas that are subject to honestly different interpretations and judgment. Nevertheless, we agree not to recommend to any advertiser, and to discourage the use of, advertising that is in poor or questionable taste or that is deliberately irritating through aural or visual content or presentation.[15]

The American Marketing Association also has a strong statement of ethics.[16] We've highlighted the key points because they serve as a great guide for everyone in our business:

Ethical Norms

- Do no harm.
- Foster trust in the marketing system.
- Embrace ethical values.

Ethical Values

- Honesty
- Responsibility
- Fairness
- Respect
- Transparency
- Citizenship

These codes provide a strong framework for ethical practice. Yet looking across the advertising landscape today, how many brands actually adhere to these codes? Is not exaggeration or puffery (we will talk about this in the legal section) a hallmark of much advertising? Honestly, are Reese's Puffs and Cap'n Crunch really a good way to start a child's day? And if respect is part of the equation, what was Carl's Jr. thinking when it used gratuitous nudity to sell hamburgers? Clearly the advertising industry is guided by codes of conduct;

however, sometimes you cannot help but wonder, is anyone paying attention to them? That is precisely why our third point, the hiring, retaining, and promoting of people with high ethical principles who are willing to put those standards front and center *and* who are willing to push back against the status quo, is so important. Will you be one of them?

Corporate Social Responsibility

Codes of conduct are a reflection of the direction for-profit organizations have been moving toward for some time, and reflect a trend toward Corporate Social Responsibility (CSR). When done right, CSR should be part of the corporate business model, embraced by all brands within the organization. It should be proactive and not simply reactive to negative publicity. Many forward-thinking brands that embrace CSR are supporting the "triple bottom line" —people, planet, and profits. Judges at the major awards shows are taking note. Brands that showcase CSR win big. In other words, a company can do well by doing good.

Agency practices can also reflect CSR, and many do. Aside from the millions of hours donated to great causes, which have produced memorable and impactful advertising, pro bono work leads to millions of dollars' worth of donated media annually.[17] Campaigns like "No More," to address domestic violence, with its memorable 2015 Super Bowl ad, created by Grey Advertising, have raised awareness about an issue that has long been sidelined in public discourse. Boston Strong worked to raise funds for victims of the Boston Marathon bombing. Susan G. Komen, despite recent public relations problems, has created awareness of breast cancer at an unprecedented level. International campaigns like Droga5's Tap Project, for UNICEF, have brought life-sustaining change to people around the world. Advertising truly can make a positive difference for individuals and communities, not just for the corporate bottom line.

Droga5's work for Tap Project has had a big impact across the world, raising awareness about the lack of clean drinking water while raising money to solve the problem. UNICEF could not have picked a better partner. Check it out at tap.unicefusa.org and start making a difference.

This long history of pro bono work demonstrates a dedication to raising awareness of social issues over the course of time. In 1942, in the midst of World War II, these contributions became formalized with the formation of the Ad Council. The mission of the Ad Council is to identify a select number of significant public issues and work collaboratively with members to stimulate action on those issues through communications programs. The Ad Council's goal is to make measurable differences in society. Volunteer talent from the advertising and broader communications fields work with media to facilitate messaging using the resources of the business and nonprofit communities. In the end, the Ad Council's mission is to create awareness, foster understanding, and motivate action to make positive changes in our society. Since its inception the Ad Council has done hundreds of campaigns. The inaugural campaign was "Rosie the Riveter," which helped sell war bonds during World War II. In 1944, working with Foote, Cone & Belding, the Ad Council introduced "Smokey Bear." In 1957, and for many years following, it created fund-raising campaigns for the American Red Cross. The Ad Council helped launch the 30-year Peace Corps campaign in 1961 with the tagline "The Toughest Job You'll Ever Love." The "Crying Indian" ad from 1973 won two Clio Awards while promoting an antilittering message. (However, in Chapter 4, we will expose a disappointing surprise about the Crying Indian.) The reason 99% of you wear your seat belts is due in large part to work the Ad Council began in 1985.

Some of the Ad Council's recent work that's making a positive difference in society. What will your contribution be?

In 1988, the Ad Council began its first of many AIDS awareness campaigns. Publically addressing childhood obesity began with a campaign launched by the Ad Council in 2005. In celebration of the Ad Council's 70th birthday, in 2012 it launched a campaign encouraging consumers to "Rosify Yourself" with a Facebook app.

While you might not be able to change the world through advertising, you can certainly avoid adding to the current problems. Ethics becomes even more complex when you consider the diverse and ever changing world in which we live. Much of the work you do will influence or touch consumers with sensibilities significantly different from your own. Whether these consumers hold different social values or practice a different religion or live on the other side of the globe, it is incumbent upon you to remain sensitive to the impact your work has beyond its obvious or intended audiences. The consumers you may intentionally or unintentionally touch may have very different cultural perspectives than you do, and those perspectives often pose tangled ethical challenges. Somewhere along Aristotle's golden mean we hope you can find an ethical grounding. We've provided six questions to send you off on your professional journey with your ethical compass balanced and ready to go:

1. **What is your personal moral code?** Do you know right from wrong, and, more important, do you care? And have you taken the time to think about how your personal ethical codes will translate into your professional ethical codes?

2. **Are you conforming to your company's guidelines?** Do they expect you to follow these rules, and will they hold you accountable? And what is your responsibility if they don't hold others to the company guidelines?

3. **Are you conforming to your client's guidelines?** If you're a freelancer or an agency, you need to make the effort to find out what these guidelines are. And you need to produce work that fits the client's corporate culture.

4. **Are you conforming to industry guidelines?** Many companies are part of trade associations and other organizations that have firm rules for advertising and promotion. You need to make the effort to find out what these guidelines are and adhere to them. Industry guidelines are instituted mainly to prevent unfair competition among association members, but can also be in place to promote a positive image for the entire industry. This can also mean network or station standards. For example, ads that are not accepted for prime-time broadcast may be allowed on late-night cable.

5. **Can you risk negative reaction from the media and potential customers?** Will you win a creative battle but lose in the court of public opinion? With YouTube and social media, bad news travels a lot faster than good news. The decisions you make at the front end can have significant impact all the way down the line.

6. **Are you aware of local, state, and federal regulations?** We'll get into that in much more detail, but remember: Not knowing the law is no excuse. It's your job to make the effort to find out what these regulations are and to adhere to them.

We hope we've got you thinking about some of the ethical issues involved in what you, as a creative person, actually do and what you, as a practitioner, may encounter. We also hope we've inspired you to work toward making a positive difference in the world.

Every candidate says his or her opponent stretches the truth, but few go to the extreme of disfiguring their opponents in such an insulting way. When does free speech go too far?

©Friends of Alberta Darling, Patty Reiman, Treasurer

Responsible Driving, Czech Style

Courtesy of Ondrej Gottwald

Our agency specializes mainly in societal marketing. Among other activities for international brand clients, we create social responsibility campaigns for the Czech Beer and Malt Association, which represents the most respected breweries in the Czech Republic. Recently we addressed the worrying results of research that showed an increasing drinking-and-driving problem in the Czech Republic. Our client decided to promote nonalcoholic beer for drivers as a safe alternative to their favorite drink.

Most of the usual anti-drinking-and-driving campaigns communicate the horrifying situations of car accidents and lifelong consequences. Our approach was different. We wanted to nicely thank drivers for their responsible behavior and thus strengthen awareness within wider society. This approach also allowed us to establish a successful partnership with the state police department.

Our brand ambassadors, young men and women in branded blue safety vests, were present at police checkpoints during the holiday season. At the checkpoints police randomly stopped drivers to check blood alcohol levels. If they passed, the brand ambassadors thanked the drivers and rewarded them with cans of cold nonalcoholic beer and disposable alcohol testers. The ambassadors reminded them to use the testers next time they thought about driving after drinking. To those outside the Czech Republic, this approach might sound odd. But within the Czech Republic our brand ambassadors were a huge hit. Why? Because Czech people did not expect a special thanks for simply doing the right thing. Not to mention, anyone might a bit nervous when stopped by the police.

Result? The campaign garnered huge media coverage, as well as an enormously positive reception from drivers and the general public. Without any media investment, the campaign was picked up by two of the main national TV channels and became breaking news. Not only that, coverage was also picked up by the largest daily newspapers as well as small regional papers and TV stations. The story also flooded the Internet, with drivers sharing personal stories about the experience across multiple social media platforms. I even got an ice-cold nonalcoholic beer from police while shooting footage at a driver checkpoint.

Thanks to the earned media, our anti-drinking-and-driving messages were top of mind and started discussions about responsible behavior among many Czech people. Our client had the added benefit of promoting its nonalcoholic brands. Now that's responsible driving—Czech style.[18]

Ondřej Gottwald, new business director, Garp, Prague

Just remember, it really does matter how you frame an issue, highlight a benefit, take on the competitor, select a media channel, choose a word, or create an image. Your work affects not just your client but also the consumers you touch and the world in which you live, work, and play. How you make a difference depends on you, your agency, and your client. The bottom line—it's up to you. In the end, ethics kick in where the law ends—and, as you have seen, often long before that.

Legal Issues

Legal issues are often black and white and, in most cases, backed by years of established precedents. We'll cover some basic ground in this regard. However, digital marketing has opened up new challenges that lawmakers are still trying to wrap their brains around, such as what constitutes privacy in social media and what defines intellectual property in the digital space. We will try to address some of these issues, knowing that new ones will emerge as technology continues to evolve. We will cover some of these changes here and in our online, mobile, and social chapters.

As we've said, whole books have been written on the subject of the law and advertising. However, here we will very briefly focus on two aspects that we think really matter to copywriters: claims and copyright.

Stake Your Claim

Copywriters make all kinds of claims, and most of them are perfectly legal. Yet it's worth briefly talking about what *legal* really means. All claims of fact are viewed very seriously under the law. There can be no deception. However, advertisers have a fair amount of wiggle room found in the nonfact claims they routinely use. Most of us write nonfact claims that fall into one of two categories—puffery and lifestyle—and thus we escape the scrutiny of the law.

Cigarettes are legal, but have been proved harmful. That's why they're not protected by the same freedom of speech afforded to other products. Australia has gone beyond banning cigarette advertising to forcing all brands to adopt some very graphic warnings about the dangers of smoking.

Health claims, especially for processed foods, are watched very closely. Campbell's claims its Healthy Request soups are heart healthy and provides the data to back it up.

Commercial free speech, while not as "free" as noncommercial speech, is protected under the First Amendment. For example, the government can regulate advertising products that are illegal, such as prostitution and street drugs, as well as products whose manufacture is regulated, such as prescription drugs, alcohol, tobacco, and some food products. Recently First Amendment rights have been vastly expanded, and that will affect the work you do, particularly in the realm of political advertising, where corporations, unions, and PACs are now considered "people." However, they have not been expanded enough to allow Facebook to own your "likes." A recent court decision reaffirmed that individual "likes" remain part of free speech.

Then there is **puffery**, a common tactic that involves using superlatives or obvious falsity to tout the greatness of your brand. The court assumes that consumers are bound to know that puffery is just an exaggeration. As one judge said, "The bigger the lie, the bigger the protection." The Uniform Commercial Code of 1996 states that exaggerated claims are acceptable, even if they are lies, unless someone can prove the claim was meant to be a fact. The government believes that most consumers are smart enough to see through the boasting and not take it seriously. Sometimes the puffery can be incorporated into a slogan, which blurs the intent. For example, Wal-Mart used to use the tagline "Always the low price. Always." The Better Business Bureau (instead of the Federal Trade Commission) said that this went beyond puffery to claim that the store always had the lowest prices of all retailers. Before the challenge dragged the brand into court, Wal-Mart decided to change the slogan to "Always low prices. Always Wal-Mart." The change in copy is a subtle change, but it is not as misleading.[20]

Then there are **lifestyle claims**. These indicate that a product or service will make the user's life better with such benefits as cleaner shirts, delicious food, a car that is fun to drive, social acceptance, finding the love of your life, and even a better sex life. The claims may be direct or implied. Contrast the in-your-face product demonstrations of OxiClean with the symbolic imagery found in Cialis commercials. Both of them make lifestyle claims that focus on the benefit rather than features. Since the benefit is more subjective, actually addressing the wants and needs of the consumer, the interpretation of the claim is usually given more latitude.

Now consider Skechers and Red Bull. Both brands made claims that were ultimately considered false and deceptive because their claims could not be backed up by scientific data. In short, they made unsubstantiated claims. In 2012 the Federal Trade Commission (FTC) reached a $40 million settlement with Skechers, the largest ever for the FTC.

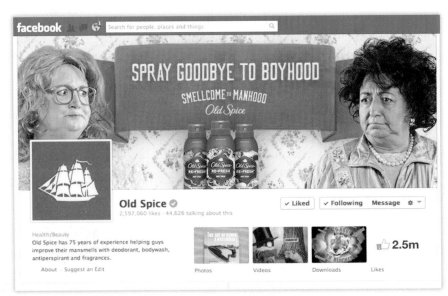

Old Spice showed clinging moms lamenting their sons' rite of passage into manhood as soon as they started using Old Spice. Print ads, TV and radio commercials, social media, and web ads were used to promote this puffery and an old stereotype.

It found that Skechers had misled consumers with deceptive advertising, for its Shape-up shoes, based on misleading and inaccurate data from its scientific studies.[21] The advertising claimed that consumers could simply walk their way to fitness. They would lose weight without ever setting foot in a gym. That's a whopper that the FTC considered far beyond puffery, and this claim was not held up by Skechers' own data. To add to the brand's misery, they had celebrity endorsements, which we will talk about later, that only multiplied the brand's distress. Red Bull also got itself into trouble by making false claims about the energy the beverage provided. In the summer of 2014 Red Bull settled a class-action lawsuit after claiming that its drink provided a bigger boost than caffeine.[22] The trouble was, there was no scientific proof that any of the ingredients in Red Bull provided any boost beyond that of caffeine. That's an unsubstantiated claim. So much for giving consumers "wings."

Substantiation means that you can, and must be able to, prove what you claim. This is especially important when you're comparing your product with the competition or when you're making an exclusive claim. Keep in mind that if the substantiation has not been obtained *before* a claim is made, the advertiser may be subject to legal action. Get the facts first, not just when you're forced to.

Some advertisers go over the line and commit fraud. The most obvious form of fraudulent advertising is to promote counterfeit goods—knockoffs of well-known high-quality brands. Promoting something that's fake is not only unethical but also illegal. Another less blatant kind of fraud is bait-and-switch advertising—when you promote a lower price for a product that's not available with the intent to sell the customer a more expensive product. If supplies of the lower priced product are very limited, the store is obligated to tell shoppers. Even so, thousands of shoppers wait in line for Black Friday specials when they know they might not get that special deal.

Muscle Milk lost a lawsuit, forcing them to state there is no milk in their product. Another lawsuit upheld that Muscle Milk is loaded with as much sugar, fat, and calories as junk food. For the sake of their careers, let's hope the well-paid athletes promoting this product are eating healthier food.

Thank you for suing us.

Here's the truth about our seasoned beef.

The claims made against Taco Bell and our seasoned beef are absolutely false.

REAL★BEEF
QUALITY GUARANTEED

Our beef is 100% USDA inspected, just like the quality beef you buy in a supermarket and prepare in your home. It is then slow-cooked and simmered in our unique recipe of seasonings, spices, water, and other ingredients to provide Taco Bell's signature taste and texture.

Plain ground beef tastes boring.
The only reason we add anything to our beef is to give the meat flavor and quality. Otherwise we'd end up with nothing more than the bland flavor of ground beef, and that doesn't make for great-tasting tacos.

So here are the REAL percentages.
88% Beef and 12% Secret Recipe.

In case you're curious, here's our not-so-secret recipe.
We start with USDA-inspected quality beef (88%). Then add water to keep it juicy and moist (3%). Mix in Mexican spices and flavors, including salt, chili pepper, onion powder, tomato powder, sugar, garlic powder, and cocoa powder (4%). Combine a little oats, caramelized sugar, yeast, citric acid, and other ingredients that contribute to the flavor, moisture, consistency, and quality of our seasoned beef (5%).

We stand behind the quality of our seasoned beef 100% and we are proud to serve it in all our restaurants. We take any claims to the contrary very seriously and plan to take legal action against those who have made false claims against our seasoned beef.

Greg Creed

Greg Creed
President, Taco Bell

TacoBell.com
Facebook.com/TacoBell

TACO BELL

©Taco Bell

Taco Bell was sued for selling "seasoned beef" that plaintiffs claimed was only about 35% real beef and 65% something else. Their "Thank you for suing us" ad set the record straight: They stated that the product is actually 88% real beef and only 12% "secret recipe." Sounds delicious.

©MuscleMilk

Only Oscar Mayer wieners prevent cancer

9 out of 10 doctors agree

Oscar Mayer is the only brand of wiener proven to prevent all kinds of cancer. And you don't even have to eat them. Just buy them. Never worry about cancer again!

Misleading claim:
If part of the ad is false, all of it is false. You should not make claims that can't be substantiated or that you know are false. Your competitors are watching.

A healthier alternative to fast food

Less fat, more protein than a Quarter Pounder

Pound for pound, an Oscar Mayer wiener has 50% less fat than a McDonald's Quarter Pounder and 80% less fat than a Burger Kind Whopper. Pick a leaner wiener.

Substantiated claim:
If it's true and you can prove it, you can claim it. You don't always have to cite your source of proof, but you should be prepared to if challenged.

Paradise on a bun

A little bit of heaven in every bite. We've been on a roll for 75 years.

Puffery:
The more outrageous the claim, the better.

Ok so it won't prevent cancer

But it sure tastes great!

Recent ads may have led you to believe that only Oscar Mayer wieners can prevent cancer. The truth is no wiener can prevent or cure cancer. But that doesn't mean you should deny yourself the pure pleasure of enjoying delicious Oscar Mayer wieners.

Corrective advertising:
Sort of admitting guilt. Regulatory agencies or the courts usually determine the magnitude of the mea culpa.

Note: Oscar Mayer advertising samples are used for educational purposes, and none of the ads shown above were ever authorized or produced by that company. As far as we know, Oscar Mayer sells high-quality products and follows the highest ethical standards for advertising and promotion.

Copyrights

A copyright is the exclusive right granted to authors, artists, and composers to protect their original work from being plagiarized, sold, or used without their permission. It's very important to understand and respect copyright law. Legal protection is extended to the work without the need to register it with the U.S. Copyright Office. A work must be registered, however, before a copyright owner may bring suit for infringement.

You can't copyright an idea. The work must be produced or published. For example, you can't reproduce Picasso's paintings and sell them without permission. But you can create new works of art that mimic his style. This could explain why there are so few original ideas in marketing, movies, and television.

Finding an Agency That's "Just Right"

Courtesy of Jon McDonald

My interest in advertising started with a desire to write jingles. I wanted to do something I loved for work—every day. Playing music progressed to a curiosity about copywriting. I wanted to work in a creative environment rather than the boring corporate world that I saw too frequently in my textbooks. I had heard good things about marketing, and I figured if the marketing department is fun, an advertising agency is where they learn all their jokes. So, I went to the source—advertising—and landed in account management.

My career started at a traditional advertising agency in Iowa. I learned a lot by working directly with clients and the creative team, but it felt a bit small. It was educational, but not too exciting. After my first year, easing into the industry with print ads and an occasional digital banner ad, I received an opportunity to work in San Francisco. I packed my bags and moved west, away from my family, not knowing anyone in the San Francisco area. It was a bold move to take as an advertising novice, but I quickly became accustomed to my new environment.

I had moved from print ads to national TV commercials and global media campaigns. The big leagues. It was interesting and it was exciting. But it wasn't the same. It wasn't right for me. The value of the work began to outweigh the value of the people I was working with. The luster of large-scale work wore off quickly, and the agency culture didn't feel right.

So I moved back to the Midwest, landing an account position in a great agency. I had found a happy medium, creating genuine work with genuine people. After a progression very similar to that of Goldilocks, I have found myself at an agency that is "just right."

My three-city adventure has taught me how varied the advertising world is. There are many agencies, serving many clients. Each agency has its own culture and style. It's important to find a place that fits you, a place where you can thrive and enjoy every day on the job.[23]

Jon McDonald, account manager, Carmichael Lynch

@jonmcdo

Or as one cynic put it, "Imitation is the sincerest form of advertising." This is something to keep in mind when you're showing your portfolio around. Until you actually have your work produced, your ideas are fair game. An unethical person could steal your potential award-winning concept, and there's not much you can do about it. Fortunately, people in our business are part of a pretty tight community, so sleazy idea stealers don't get away with it for very long.

A published work remains protected by a copyrighter holder for the lifetime of its creator plus 70 years. If the work is created anonymously or under a pseudonym or as work for hire, it's protected for 95 years from the first date of publication or 120 years from the date of its creation, whichever is less.

So if an advertisement, a tagline, ad copy, music, a photo, a commercial, a website, a video clip, or any portion of an advertisement or other marketing communication is produced or published, no one can legally use or modify it without permission for a long, long time.

As the Internet grew, it became imperative to protect copyrighted material online. The Digital Millennium Copyright Act (DMCA) extends existing copyright laws to the Internet, while limiting the liability of the providers of online services for copyright infringement by their users. As scrapbooking sites like Pinterest gain popularity, users may risk violation of the DMCA if they post copyrighted images without permission. Bottom line: When in doubt, never display copyrighted text and images on the Internet without permission.

Work for hire means that the creators of a work sign their rights to a given work away to an employer. This may happen when a freelance writer or designer creates work for an agency, when a company for a specific assignment hires a photographer, or when an agency creates work for a client. In fact, as an employee, you are de facto producing work for hire. You don't own it, the agency does.

If the copyrighted work is used without permission, it's considered copyright infringement. Even something as simple as making photocopies or scanning another person's work is an infringement.

There is an exception to copyright protection, which is called **fair use**. In general, fair use includes the work in news reporting, teaching, scholarship, and research. The publisher of this book has determined that the images used here for education fall under fair use, so we do not need specific permission from the agencies, clients, copywriters, or designers. In this book we are using these examples as teaching aids, with comments that relate to the accompanying text, although we do have to document the sources of these materials, and we do our best to give credit where it is due.

Since the advent of the computer and the massive expansion of the Internet, art directors and copywriters have been borrowing images and pasting them into layouts as a means of illustrating concepts for their clients. The fact that they are not reproducing them for profit is what allows them the wiggle room. That's where fair use ends. After that they must either buy the images or re-create them in a manner that is substantially different so as not to be construed as copying the likeness of the images.

Use of Archive Photos

The issue of copyright infringement takes many twists and turns in our business. For example, years ago we wanted to do a series of ads for tool safety using some stills from Three Stooges films. Our target audience fit the demo for Stooges fans, and the images showing Curly's head in a vise and Larry's nose being pulled by pliers certainly made the point. Only one problem—these images, even though they were over 70 years old, were still not in the public domain. They are owned by the estate of Moe Howard, which controls their use, and at the time were prohibitively expensive. We ran into the same issue when we wanted to use a photo of Albert Einstein for another client. Advertisers quickly find out that estates, publications, or photo agencies own most of the great iconic images of famous people. The more famous the image, the more it will cost.

Photography for Hire

Typically the images taken by a professional photographer for a client or agency belong to the photographer. If the images are to be used in advertising or other commercial purposes, the client or agency pays the photographer for their use. Rates vary depending on how they are used, where they are used, and how often they are used. Sometimes a photographer or videographer will agree to a flat rate called a buyout. In this case, the agency or client can use those images just about any way they see fit.

Voice Talent

Announcers for television and radio commercials can work under union rules, which cover the session fee, pension and welfare payments, and residual use of the work. Or they can accept a buyout, which may be more or less than the costs dictated by the union. We won't discuss the pluses and minuses of hiring union or nonunion talent; however, no matter which system is in place, you usually can't use that voice track forever without permission. For example, a radio spot is scheduled to run in a small market for 13 weeks, so the talent fee is negotiated for that situation. However, if the spot starts running on a national network for a whole year, the talent fee is renegotiated, unless the talent signs off on a complete buyout. Every announcer sets his or her own payment system, but suffice it to say, law protects his or her voice.

> "Only one thing is impossible for God: To find any sense in any copyright law on this planet."[24]
>
> Mark Twain,
> American author

Music

The good news is you found the perfect song for your next TV commercial. The bad news is you can't get the rights. And even if you could, your budget doesn't allow paying for it. Music licensing is the licensed use of copyrighted music. A purchaser of recorded music owns the media, not the music itself, and has limited rights to use it. Licensing could involve a flat fee or royalty payments based on time and/or units sold. Now, if you think that any old song over 70 years old is fair game, think again. The world's best known song, "Happy Birthday to You," was written in 1893. It's now owned by Time Warner and generates over $2 million a year in royalties. It's protected by copyright extensions until 2030.[25]

Digital Copyrights

Rapid development in digital technologies has prompted reinterpretation of copyright protection. Copyrights are harder to protect, and there are more challenges to the entire philosophy of intellectual property. The legal system is constantly scrambling to catch up with technology. Suffice it to say, just because you found it on the Internet doesn't mean you can use it. If the source doesn't offer free use, don't use it.

Using Celebrities

Public figures are protected from commercial use of their names or likenesses without their permission. They can't be used in ads or other materials unless they sign off. That includes dead celebrities. The cost will depend on how and where they are used. You might wonder how paparazzi shots of celebrities can be plastered all over the tabloids. In this case, public figures have less protection than the general public because they are considered newsworthy. On the flip side, if a celebrity endorses a brand, he or she had better be using it, and it had better do what the brand claims it does. Skechers used celebrity endorsements from folks like Kim Kardashian and Joe Montana for its Shape-up shoes. Problem was, they didn't shape up anyone, including Kardashian or Montana.

Libel

Competitors and sometimes government watchdogs monitor product claims closely. But what happens when a false or misleading statement is made about a person? The legal term is *libel*, and there are some very specific tests that must be passed before a lawyer will even touch a case.

You must prove:

1. A false statement was communicated to the media. The definition of what is "false" becomes tricky in a "he said/she said" scenario.

2. The libeled person must be identified or identifiable. The person's name and/or image must be involved or some reference made where there is no reasonable doubt that the person is being portrayed in an unflattering way.

3. Actual injury or financial loss must result. This injury or loss could be a hit to a person's reputation or mental suffering, which can be very difficult to prove.

4. The person accused of libel is proved to be willfully negligent or to have malicious intent. In other words, there's a motive to smear someone.

After reading the above you're probably saying, "I see this happening every day in the news, entertainment, and politics. How can people get away with saying all these nasty things about each other?" Public figures, entertainers, politicians, and government officials are treated differently. So a movie reviewer can legally lie about a leading lady's personal life, pan the actors and director, drive people away from the box office, and be negligent or malicious with no consequence. In fact, it's expected. Politics keeps getting uglier because negative advertising works, no matter how many lies and half-truths are told. When critics demand accountability and substantiation in political advertising, the First Amendment is waved in their faces. It's freedom of speech—which does not apply to phony product claims, but certainly has helped elect a lot of phonies who make the rules.

Trademarks

Most slogans and taglines are considered protected. So are brand names.
A trademark, designated by ™ or ®, means that a brand or slogan is registered

with the federal government. When you are applying for a trademark, you will have a better chance of success if your brand has a unique spelling. For example, EZ Duzzit would be easier to register than Easy Does It. Even if you pick a brand name that is already in use, you may be able to register it when it is used in a different market. For example, both Microsoft and Volunteers in Service to America used the Vista brand.

If you really want to protect a brand, you'll need to keep a few things in mind. David Weinstein, an intellectual property lawyer, states that the easiest brand or product name to protect is a "word, picture, or symbol that conveys little or no information about the nature . . . of the products."[27] Case in point: Apple. Apple Corps was the Beatles' business holding company and, as a name, had nothing directly to do with the band. For years Apple Corps disputed the use of the Apple Computer name, which by itself had nothing to do directly with computer products. Apple Computer paid Apple Corps $80,000 in 1991 to use the name, and promised never to get into the music business. Of course, with the Mac able to play music and with the introduction of iTunes and the iPod, the surviving ex-Beatles claimed that the computer company had reneged on its promise and sued again. In 2007 Apple Computer agreed to pay Apple Corps $500 million for the name.[28] How about them Apples?

Another consideration when coining a brand name and protecting it is to include a descriptor. While Kleenex has become a generic name with consumers, it is still protected because the word *tissue* always follows it. Aspirin was a brand but over time became a generic product. The world *cola* became generic when Coca-Cola originally placed the ® between the words, thus protecting *Coca* but setting *Cola* free. When you look closely, you'll that see everything related to Coca-Cola, from the bottle shape to the contour design to the word *Coke*, is trademarked and rigorously protected.

Using someone else's slogan or tagline will get you into legal trouble, and it won't do much for your career either. You need to do your homework in order to be sure that the brilliant tagline you just thought up is not already being used by another brand somewhere, somehow. When in doubt, run it by a colleague or do a word search and check online government resources such as the Trademark Electronic Search System. If you're still in doubt, contact legal counsel. In short, don't make assumptions.

In the end, if you have a concern about what you are doing, check in with yourself, then check in with legal.

> "Every product has its own truth, its own believability zone. Stray and your readers will know. Oh yes, they'll know."[26]
>
> Jim Durfee,
> copywriter and founding
> partner, Ally & Gargano

Chapter 3

Alex Bogusky

After joining Crispin and Porter Advertising in 1989 as an art director, Alex Bogusky became creative director five years later and a partner in 1997. In 2008, he became cochairman of Crispin Porter + Bogusky (CP+B), the same year he was inducted into the Art Directors Club Hall of Fame. While at CP+B, he created the "Truth" campaign and helped Al Gore debunk the notion of "clean coal." In 2010, he left CP+B to create COMMON and FearLess Revolution, a consortium of entrepreneurial creatives dedicated to educating and empowering consumers.

Nancy Hill

The first ever CEO of the American Association of Advertising Agencies, Nancy Hill began her career in 1983 at the Doner agency in Baltimore and advanced with increased responsibilities. Prior to accepting the position at 4A's, she served as CEO of Lowe Worldwide in New York. Her personal and professional interests have long focused on the high-tech sector, serving such clients as AOL, Cisco Systems, Sony, Motorola, and Verizon, among others. As CEO of 4A's she is firmly committed to the "business case for diversity . . . whether we are talking about race/ethnicity, points of view/life experience, and skill sets."[29]

Jean Kilbourne

Recognized globally for her critical work exploring images of women in advertising, Jean Kilbourne was named by the *New York Times Magazine* as one of the three most popular speakers on college campuses. She is an award-winning author and filmmaker. Her films include *Killing Us Softly*, *Spin the Bottle*, and *Slim Hopes*. Her books include *Can't Buy My Love: How Advertising Changes the Way We Think and Feel* and *So Sexy So Soon: The New Sexualized Childhood*.

Ivan Preston

Ivan Preston was professor emeritus at the University of Wisconsin–Madison and an expert on consumer ethics and fraud. In 1975, he published *The Great American Blow-Up: Puffery in Advertising and Selling*, which catapulted him into prominence. Preston frequently served as an expert witness in advertising litigation cases for both government agencies and advertisers. Although he had a brief tenure with the Federal Trade Commission's Division of Advertising Practices, he never shied away from condemning the relaxation of regulations and the commission's lack of consumer behavior expertise. Preston died in 2011.

Shelby Dunlap and Pluto's Pizza

Shelby Dunlap is an assistant account executive at Nightingale Public Relations in Portland, Oregon. She works on the Pluto's Pizza account. Pluto's is a pizzeria with four locations in Portland; the company wants to expand and add locations in Portland as well as in other markets such as Seattle and Spokane. Shelby has worked on the account for a year and reports to the account executive, Amy Gregg, and the account director, Kati Brown.

Pluto's Pizza specializes in wood-fired pizzas that are authentically Italian. The dough is handmade, ingredients are fresh and local, and the pizzas are cooked in a dome-shaped, wood-burning oven at temperatures around 1,500 degrees. This gives the pizza a charred and rustic taste with a tender crust.

Much of Shelby's time is spent managing the social media presence for Pluto's Pizza, including the brand's Facebook, Twitter, and Instagram accounts. She also monitors review sites such as Yelp and Urban Spoon to make sure that the customer experience at Pluto's Pizza is a positive one. Because occasionally customers come to Pluto's expecting the pizza to be more like that prepared by a chain like Domino's, some reviews are less than favorable. On the whole, though, most reviews are in the four-star range. Shelby prepares a weekly summary of the reviews at various sites that is shared with the client.

One Monday morning, Shelby was called into a meeting with Kati. Kati had just spoken to the owner of Pluto's, who had just heard that a competitor from Seattle, Emerald City Wood Fire Kitchen, was planning to open several locations in Portland. In addition to wood-fired pizzas, Emerald City offers steaks, salads, and sandwiches. Emerald City had a very active social media presence, with more than 3,500 followers on Facebook (compared with Pluto's 710) and consistent four- and five-star ratings.

"We need to turn up the volume on social media," Kati told Shelby and Amy. "Increase our followers, get our message out. And we really need to boost those Yelp ratings. Can you get your friends to go online and write some positive reviews for us?"

Shelby began making a list of friends who had recently eaten at Pluto's when Amy chimed in, "I have a great idea. Shelby, can you go online and write some bad reviews for Emerald City on Yelp? Maybe create one or two new accounts and post some negative stuff under different names? It would really help us compete if we all had the same number of stars."

1 Do you think Kati's direction to get friends to write reviews was appropriate? Why or why not?

2 Do you think Amy's direction to write bad reviews for Emerald City was appropriate? Why or why not?

3 What are other ideas to leverage social media in this situation?

4 If you were Shelby, what would you do?

Kim Sheehan, professor, University of Oregon

1. Supporting Your Claim

Analyze the following product claims, decide which would be legal, and explain your opinion. If you feel the claim is not supportable, how would you change it?

- Nobody makes a beer colder than Coors Light.
- With adult education classes at Bridgestone University, one night a week can change your life.
- The new Hyundai Genesis offers the luxury and performance of a BMW 5 Series for about half the sticker price.
- You can't survive in this climate without a Trane air-conditioning system.
- Mr. Coffee is the most dependable, reliable, and energy efficient coffeemaker ever made.

2. Whose Ethics?

(Contributed by Kimberly Selber, PhD, associate professor, University of Texas–Pan American.)

Find six print ads you feel are "ethically questionable."

- Write up a one-page critique of each ad. Explain why you feel it is ethically questionable—focusing on the ad and not the product itself (i.e., not that drinking is bad and shouldn't be advertised, but that ads promoting alcohol should not target minors). Focus your comments on the target, placement, the content, and so on.
- Next write a short survey. Poll 10 people from various backgrounds on the ads they found ethically questionable. Add in several neutral ads when polling your audience.
- Finally, write up the results, along with a comments section considering the following questions: Do your friends think like you do? What did you find that was surprising? End with a short reflection section. Ask yourself, what kind of socially responsible person do I want to be? What is the advertising industry's responsibility? What would I do if I was asked to work on something I felt was ethically wrong or simply bad for society at large?

3. (Dis)abled

This exercise is designed to help you think about your perceptions of people not like yourself, in this case people with disabilities.

- Your instructor will provide you with a brief and a storyboard based on that brief.
- Once you've had a chance to look it over, think about how you could insert a person with an obvious disability into the commercial. Challenge yourself to do it in a way that naturally integrates the person into the storyline. The challenge will be for the new addition to feel seamless, as if that person was part of the original spot.
- Share revised storyboards.

In Britain, legal stipulations now require advertisers to include people with disabilities in a small percentage of all advertising. Discuss how this changes people's perception of people with disabilities and how it can have a positive impact on brands.

Review chapter content and study for exams. http://study.sagepub.com/altstiel4e.

- Interactive practice quizzes
- Mobile-friendly eFlashcards
- Carefully selected chapter-by-chapter video and multimedia content

Chapter 4

Evolving Audiences
The Times They Are A-Changin'

Bob Dylan wrote the lyrics to this song over 50 years ago. He could have written them today. Look around. Does everyone look like you? Until the 1960s, advertisers must have thought the "typical" consumer was a straight, married, White suburbanite. During the past 50 years marketers have discovered a few things: Blacks purchase homes; women buy cars; gays and lesbians like vacations; Arab Americans own businesses; Latinos are tech savvy; seniors lead active lives; and singles enjoy living alone. Diversity in marketing is the number one change in advertising across the past quarter century.[1] Creating advertising that reflects our ever changing society is not only the right thing. It is the smart thing.

Our Shifting Social Landscape

Today, one in every three Americans is a person of color, and that's a trend that will only increase. In the last U.S. census, more than half of the people who identified themselves as "Black in combination with at least one other race" were under 18 years old.[2] Ways of viewing gender and sexual orientation are also changing. Equality was once only a dream for gays and lesbians. In 2015, the Supreme Court ruled in favor of marriage equality. The barriers against LGBT rights are gradually fading away, reflecting a more tolerant tone in the general population. Ironically, cohabitation, or remaining single, among straight people is on the rise.[3] In major metro markets like Atlanta, Minneapolis, San Francisco, Washington, Seattle, and Manhattan, the number of singles is climbing to over 40%.[4] Singletons, most between 35 and 64, are also fueling the consumer economy. Age-related demographics are changing too. As the generation that grew up with Bob Dylan enters retirement they are redefining what retirement means. Yes, the times they are a-changin'.

Sooner or later, your wife will drive home one of the best reasons for owning a Volkswagen.

Women are soft and gentle, but they hit things.
If your wife hits something in a Volkswagen, it doesn't hurt you very much.
VW parts are easy to replace. And cheap. A fender comes off without dismantling half the car. A new one goes on with just ten bolts. For $24.95, plus labor.

And a VW dealer always has the kind of fender you need. Because that's the one kind he has.
Most other VW parts are interchangeable too. Inside and out. Which means your wife isn't limited to fender smashing. She can jab the hood. Graze the door. Or bump off the bumper.

It may make you furious, but it won't make you poor.
So when your wife goes window-shopping in a Volkswagen, don't worry.
You can conveniently replace anything she uses to stop the car.
Even the brakes.

This ad appeared when Dylan's song was popular. Even the top creative shops ran ads that dismissed women. Yes, "the times they are a-changin'."

Once upon a time the "typical" nuclear family of mom, dad, and 2.3 kids living the suburban dream was depicted as the ideal. However, the makeup of the American family is changing the demographic landscape, and advertisers are scrambling to understand these changes and respond to them. Today 87% of Americans approve of interracial marriages.[5] And as we noted above, gay marriage is quickly becoming an accepted norm. Americans' changing attitudes are reflected in the choices of spokespersons and models, which demonstrate a fluidity of cultural definition. Some of the hottest models today have an indefinable ethnic look. Despite Tiger Woods's fall from grace, his role as a spokesperson opened the door to normalizing a broader definition of ethnic identity, and he remains one of the highest paid celebrity spokesperson. The acceptance of marriage equality has also driven some brands to reach out to openly gay or lesbian spokespeople, who often have huge appeal within the general market. Ellen DeGeneres, a married lesbian, has long been a spokesperson for big brands from American Express to Samsung, with her 2014 Academy Awards selfie promoting the brand.

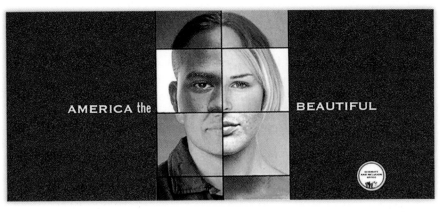

AMERICA the BEAUTIFUL

Diversity is a beautiful thing. This student-designed digital board features rapidly rotating panels reflecting our ever-changing population. Does this vision of a multicultural America ring true for you?

DeGeneres recently launched her own fashion line, E.D., and her target audience was not lesbians. The lines they are a blurrin'.

Now consider this: no matter which demographic group you look at, women are a driving force in consumer decision making. Yet advertisers still consider women a niche market—a niche market with formidable influence and spending power. Women are a growing part of the labor force, with 57% of women participating in the labor force, compared with 70% of men, and 75% of moms with school-aged children are working.[6] Even when they are not the end users, women influence over 80% of consumption decisions. If we wrap all the niche markets together, from African Americans to LGBT to retiring boomers, they would make up 84% of the total population.[7] Trust us, this chapter is worth reading.

Today, it's not a question of whether to appeal to specialty audiences. It's more a question of how to do it. How do we show people of color, LGBT individuals, or disabled people in our ads without using stereotypes? If we avoid the obvious, do we deny their identities? Can we keep it real without alienating other audiences? Advertisers need to be responsive to the social and cultural shifts suggesting that many people see themselves as having multiple, fluid identities. America is no longer a homogeneous melting pot, if it ever was. At its best, America today is more like a stew where all the ingredients, colors, flavors, and textures are equally important as they deliciously coexist. This is at the core of the current debate over whether multicultural or cross-cultural approaches work most effectively.

- **Multicultural strategy** distinguishes consumer segments by cultural factors and segmentation factors. It assumes that cultural differences affect consumer decision making and consumption behavior. Thus marketing efforts should leverage cultural insights to motivate consumer behavior.

- **Cross-cultural strategy** suggests combining cultures within a segment. It increases the diversity within segments and at the same time reduces the number of segments. This approach suggests that leveraging unique cultural insights is not as effective.[9]

One size fits all won't work any longer, if it ever did. We think multicultural strategies are the most effective. Maybe as our evolving cultural norms take root, the work of multicultural and general market agencies will also begin to merge. Maybe not. Regardless, to work in the industry today you'll need to be on the cutting edge of trends, with a sensitive understanding of the shifting lines of social and cultural identity.

"We have to first break down preconfigured stereotypes. In order to do this, we must promote workplace equality and build the awareness."[8]

Teresa Cuevas,
social media strategist, Lapiz

A Humble Disclaimer

Before we dive into the how and why of multicultural advertising and niche marketing, we offer a humble disclaimer. In preparing to write this chapter, we talked with a diverse group of advertising practitioners, conducted extensive research, and asked some trusted confidants to review our work. Along the way, we chose to focus on the three largest ethnic groups: African Americans, Hispanics, and Asian Americans. However, with the growth in LGBT advertising and generational marketing, we thought they too deserved attention. And then there are those big spenders—women. We tried to be sensitive, unbiased, and ethical regarding the various issues discussed in this chapter. Some might say we wrote too much on one group and not enough on another or that we totally missed the point or ignored other groups. Some may take issue with our content or the tone. We did our best to be sensitive and to bring complicated issues out into the open. We encourage you to think about them, because "the times they are a-changin'."

It's All There in Black and White

Advertising to the African American demographic has a long history with a handful of brands. However, it did not take off in earnest until the early 1970s. Then the trend was to make Black people look like "dark-skinned white people."[10] While some Blacks were happy to finally see themselves in mainstream advertising, others resented the lack of realistic models and situations. Add to this the fact that the language of identity changes over time. According to *Advertising Age*, many Canadians, Black Caribbean immigrants, and Europeans of African descent feel excluded by the term *African American*. They often think it doesn't accurately reflect their cultural heritage.[11] Respectfully and resonantly reaching this demographic can be tricky.

Before multicultural agencies existed, the industry lacked messages that reflected cultural experiences beyond a White world. People like Thomas Burrell, founder of Burrell Communications, now part of Publicis, and Caroline Jones, founder of Mingo, Jones, Guilmenot, now Chisholm-Mingo, were advertising pioneers. As the lines defining race and ethnicity blur, the work of reaching multicultural people becomes more challenging. Al Anderson, another early leader in multicultural advertising, suggests that the *multi* in multicultural marketing has gotten a bit blurred: "Last time I checked, all marketing is targeted at somebody."

The new Timberland PRO® TITAN™ workboot features a lightweight titanium-alloy safety toe and our exclusive PowerFit™ comfort system. Because your workload is heavy enough.

WHAT TO WEAR WHEN YOUR WORKLOAD IS MEASURED IN METRIC TONS.

©Timberland

To some people this ad might represent a stereotype of Blacks as blue-collar laborers. To others, it's just another hardworking guy who needs a good pair of work boots. What do you think?

Now how you construct this young, Black, Latino, Asian person, I don't know. I've never met one of these folks."[12] That blurring is not likely to go away anytime soon, with marketers stretching for cultural crossover, at the same time that more and more people define themselves as bi- or multicultural.

When connecting to a multicultural target, you need to leverage cultural knowledge with sensitivity and respect. For Burrell and Jones, success came by tapping into the unique cultural experiences of Blacks. They also knew the importance of media placement, and leveraged channels that resonated with their audience. But the focus on ethnic advertising agencies also highlights the fact that general market agencies seem most comfortable segregating those who create multicultural messages from those who work on the general market. As the advertising industry grapples with the dilemma of separate agencies, there is a tendency for the big multinationals to buy multicultural agencies and bring them under their corporate umbrella.

Filtering for Cultural Relevance

Brands like Coca-Cola, Ford, General Mills, McDonald's, Procter & Gamble, and State Farm have long understood the need to leverage cultural knowledge.[13] General Mills views its advertising to the Black community as steeped in respect for the community's culture, rituals, and institutions.[14] Marketing leaders at McDonald's attribute the brand's success to leading with "ethnic insights."[15] A study by Burrell Communications suggests that focusing on aspirational themes is huge.[16] We also know that stories, rooted in family and community, have a long cultural history within the Black community. Coca-Cola has leveraged this knowledge and has been reaching out to Blacks since the 1930s, focusing on families, with a huge emphasis on moms and teens. Currently, Coca-Cola's marketing group views teens as the trendsetters and moms, who play a very prominent role in family life, as the gatekeepers. Coke's recent "Pay It Forward" campaign, originally part of Black History Month, was built on a simple premise: as a community we are responsible for advancing the next generation. The campaign provides "deserving youth with an opportunity to experience a summer apprenticeship with a current celebrity or business leader and encourages others to do the same."[17] It's been a huge success.

Celebrities are often the vehicles brand managers use to tap into aspirational Black values. Originally, Black endorsements went mainly to athletes. Today we see Black entertainers topping the list of brand endorsers. Beyoncé, according to *Forbes,* is the 32nd most powerful women in the world, with earnings estimated at $40 million.[18] She appears in everything from Pepsi commercials to L'Oréal cosmetics print ads to a multiform-platform H&M campaign. Ford used comedian Kevin Hart to launch the Explorer to this demographic. The added value of using Black celebrities like Beyoncé and Hart is that they are also resonant with the general market.

Coca-Cola's early commitment to advertising to Blacks is evident in this ad from the 1950s. Its commitment has paid off handsomely, and the brand continues to "share the possibilities."

Tapping Into the African American Market

To tap into the Black market you need to know where to find them. The top three urban areas with the highest Black populations area New York, Atlanta, and Chicago. But guess what? Two thirds of African American metropolitan growth has occurred in the suburbs.[19] There is also a trend toward remigration to the South, as reflected in Atlanta's recent jump to the number two spot. We know that Black women, like women in every other demographic group, are big purchase influencers. African American affluence is also on the rise; with 10% of Blacks making over $100,000 annually, their spending power has increased by 73% since 2000.[20] Now that you know about their spending power and where they live, let's talk about what drives them. Blacks are fiercely quality conscious. They are also price conscious. They are early adopters of brands and trends. These three things combined create a conundrum for marketers. We sum it up this way: Black consumers place a high value on brands, as long as the brands offer them good value. Do that and you'll have a loyal consumer.

When it comes to copywriting, in most cases, it's best to avoid using slang. If you misuse slang it can be embarrassing at best and insulting at worst. When it comes to media, Blacks just don't see enough of themselves portrayed accurately. Beyond accurate portrayals, finding African Americans where they live, work, and play is essential. Digital plays a big role here. Blacks are more likely to watch video online and access online content via smartphones than the general market.[22] With Blacks as early adopters, it's no surprise to see music as the thread that crosses ethnic boundaries, moving easily across multiple media.

"You know why Madison Avenue advertising has never done well in Harlem? We're the only ones who know what it means to be Brand X."[21]

Dick Gregory,
civil rights activist and
cultural critic

©Ford

Kevin Hart makes driving an Explorer an unforgettable and funny adventure. The spots were popular with both dealers and consumers. Another win/win for Ford.

©General Mills

General Mills lives up to its commitment to portraying Black family values by honoring the ritual of cooking as family bonding. At the same time the Betty Crocker brand taps into moms, the family gatekeeper.

Finding a Seat at the Table

Courtesy of Keith Jamerson

I've always had an interest in people: understanding what motivates our personal preferences and behavior. Growing up I didn't see how this would relate to a career, but a childhood experience at a friend's house changed my perspective. I saw a really bad TV commercial and complained, "Man, that really sucked. I could make something much better." My friend's mom replied, "Well, why don't you?" This really struck a chord with me, and at that moment I decided I wanted to work in advertising.

Knowing what I wanted to do felt great, but as I went to college and started to prepare for the real world, the question became, "How do I fit into this world?" *Advertising* is not a job title. I needed to figure out where my skill set and interests could best be applied in a meaningful way. I stumbled upon my answer during an interview with an agency recruiter. "How do you feel about being a producer?" she asked. Not knowing how to respond, I replied, "Sounds kinda sexy, tell me more." *Producer* is a title that holds some cultural cachet because of the prominence of the TV and film business, but few know what people in that role actually do. I decided to give it a shot and accepted a production internship with Leo Burnett. I had no idea what I was getting into.

Similar to most internships, things started out slowly; lots of helping people out, shadowing and pestering other producers in the office. As I learned more about the job and began getting small assignments of my own, I fell in love with the role. Over time I learned that a producer's job is to take an idea that exists in some abstract form, perhaps a script or a series of illustrations, and turn it into something real consumers will see. This process can often be quite challenging as I work to develop schedules and budgets, collaborate with our creative teams, and work to get the most talented people involved in our projects (directors, photographers, editors, etc.) The final product could be a TV commercial, print ad, website, short film, or any other type of content that we create for our clients.

Six years later I'm still on that journey and loving it. I've worked with amazing international clients, on productions of all sizes, managed shoots on four continents, and worked with incredibly talented groups of people. Above all, the most rewarding part of my job is having a seat at the table in creating cool and engaging work. This is what makes the job worth doing.[23]

Keith Jamerson, producer, Leo Burnett

keithjamerson.com

Music is a defining part of African American cultural life and an essential ingredient in communal storytelling. But don't assume that it's all about straight-up jazz, hip-hop, or rap. The use of pop music in advertising got a big boost with Michael Jackson's 1984 "Billie Jean" Pepsi commercial. Spike Lee and Nike's early collaborations soon followed. That collaboration continues, including a video narrated by Lee about his son, soccer, and Black culture. Ultimately the advertising industry came to embrace hip-hop as a crossover sound. You will also find jazz as a common music bed for radio and television spots—across all demographics. Meanwhile, Beyoncé's voice floats above a multitude of brands and into the general market; her songs recently debuted in an H&M commercial. Music as a form of storytelling is a staple in African American culture. The key is to marry the right brand with the right sound.

¿Cómo Se Dice "Diversity" en Español?

Today over 53 million Hispanics live in the United States. That's 17% of the U.S. population.[24] They live in communities all across the nation, but the three biggest media markets are Los Angeles, New York, and Miami.[25] The Hispanic population is expected to keep growing—fast. In fact, in the next 40 years the Hispanic population is projected to double. According to Leo Olper of Expósito and Partners, if we think about Hispanics as a world economy, they would be the thirteenth largest world economy.[26]

Let's begin by taking a look at language and identity. Hispanics, like African Americans, have differing perspectives on this topic. According to Ileana Alemán-Rickenbach, chief creative officer at BVK/MEKA in Miami, 65% prefer to call themselves Hispanic.[27] However, age can be a big influence in preference. *Hispanic* is generally preferred by older people, while younger people prefer *Latino* or *Latina*, which they feel is more personal. Here's a little secret: The term *Hispanic*, as a demographic, was invented by advertisers and quietly made its way into the broader cultural lexicon.

American Hispanics come from multiple countries, representing every country in Central and South America. The top three countries of origin are Mexico, Cuba, and Puerto Rico, with 63% of Latinos being of Mexican descent.[28] What's really interesting, and what marketers need to pay particular attention to, is the trend toward people's preferring to identify themselves by their countries of origin—Chicana or Argentino or Cubana.[29] Ancestry means a lot to Hispanics, with nearly 90% learning Spanish before they learn English.[30] Today 76% of Hispanics still speak Spanish at home with their parents.[31] However, when Hispanics head to work, two thirds will speak English.[32] Among many Millennial Latinos, English is their social language, even among fellow Spanish speakers.

Now, let's consider how language works, or doesn't, as it crosses cultures. A Mexican exterminator will remove your *bichos* (bugs), while a Puerto Rican might want to protect his *bichos* (private parts). You have to do more than just find the right term, you have to understand cultural context.

Dominion Energy demonstrated its respect for Hispanic consumers with a headline that read, "For Danny Segura, Spanish is not a second language. It's a cultural heritage."

Ileana Alémán-Rickenbach of BVK/MEKA, a Hispanic advertising agency in Miami, explains that there is no single Hispanic culture but rather a "hyperreality" that blurs the difference between the symbolic and the real.

The reality is, *Hispanic* is really just a marketing term coined by the advertising industry in the United States. This hyperreal market lumps together people of Latin American and Spanish heritage under one "ethnic" classification, when in fact the 19 Latin groups under the Hispanic umbrella can be drastically different from one another.

"One of our clients, a top telecom, was launching a new international calling plan for mobile phones. Another opportunity to practice those hyperreal Hispanic Spanish skills, right?

"I started by asking Sandra, a Mexican coworker, 'How do you answer the phone?' We say, '¿*Bueno*?' (by the way, *bueno* literally means 'good'). Nereyda said Cubans answer '*Oigo*' ('I hear'). The Venezuelans told me they say, '*Aló*' (which has no meaning). Puerto Ricans say, 'Hello' (pronounced '*jel-ó*'). The Argentine said she had the only legitimate, polite, correct, and perfect phone greeting: '*Hola*.' From there on, everyone had a say; visiting clients opined . . . '*Buenas*,' '*Dígame*,' '*Sí*.' It was Babel.

"A little later, the client called to 'remind' us that we should use the proper Mexican 'dialect' for the West Coast and 'generic' Spanish for the rest. That's exactly what we did. We created a pun for the West Coast version where one character answered the phone by saying '¿*Bueno*?' ('Good') and the caller replied, '*Bueno no, buenísimo*' ('Not only good, but very good'). We sent a creative rationale explaining that literally *bueno* means good, but that in context it really means hello. That it was a play on words to introduce the retail message (great prices), etc., etc. . . . of course. She never got it. The cultural divide was insurmountable. On the other hand, we never found a Pan-Latin way of saying hello. The hyperreal had turned surreal.

"We ended up creating a funny, clever, and very effective campaign where people call their countries of origin, but no one answers the phone by saying hello. We just started the spots midway through the calls. In the world of Hispanic Hyperreality, definitely less is more."[33]

Ileana Alémán-Rickenbach, chief creative officer, BVK/ MEKA, Miami

You have to understand the cultural nuances. Here are some examples that express the delicacy of cultural nuance[34]:

- A Coca-Cola ad may use the slogan "y su comida favorita" ("and your favorite food"), but for Miami Cubans the ad shows pork loin, for South Texas Mexicans it's tacos, and for New York Puerto Ricans they use pork and rice or arroz con gandules.

- When McDonald's first developed a series of "Hispanic ads," they considered all Hispanics the same until they received complaints from Puerto Rico that the ads were "too Mexican."

- A telephone company tried to market its products to Latinos by showing a commercial in which a Latina wife tells her husband to call a friend and tell her they would be late for dinner. The commercial bombed since Latina women generally do not give orders to their husbands, and their cultural concept of time would not require a call about being late.

Millennials: Embracing Two Cultures

Many Latinos are young and prefer to consider themselves bicultural, embracing both American culture and the culture of their ethnic heritage. So what does all this mean for advertisers? For one, we know that bilingual Latinos are more influenced by advertising in Spanish than by advertising in English.[35] That means that Spanish-language media are *caliente*. It also means that marketers need to get to know Millennials, as 53% of all Latinos are below the age of 30.[36] Most Millennials were born in the United States and are big media users. In fact, Hispanic Millennials overindex when it comes to digital media. They are more likely to chat, stream video, listen to music, download apps, and play online games than non-Hispanic Millennials.[37] For Latino Millennials their identity is generational as much as ethnic. Their seamless blending of Latino and American culture makes Millennials the most "American" of all Hispanic segments.[38] In fact, "What we're seeing is that a 24-year old Hispanic may have more in common with a 24-year old African-American or Asian-American than with his 45-year old uncle."[39]

Dígame Más

Let's turn to the business of advertising for a moment. Advertising to Hispanics tends to be done through multicultural agencies, just as with advertising to African Americans. Most of the big agencies have one Hispanic shop under their umbrella, if not more: LatinWorks, Dieste, and Alma are under Omnicom, Bravo Group and Wing are part of WPP, while Conill and Lapiz find their home with Publicis. Each is connected to one general market agency. Bravo Group is Y&R's Hispanic agency, while Lapiz is linked to Leo Burnett. There are still a few stand-alone Hispanic agencies, such as Zubi in Coral Gables, Vidal in New York, and Lopez Negrete in Houston.[40]

This Ram truck ad was created with the U.S. Hispanic market in mind. The copy, "How can so many horses eat so little?" says a lot about humor, which is a cherished part of Hispanic culture.

Hispanic media spending is up. In traditional media television is king, garnering 73% of media budgets. The kinds of shows that draw Hispanics center on family, which is a huge culture identifier within Latino culture. It's not surprising that *Modern Family*, which pushes back against stereotypes while embracing family values, is a primetime TV leader among Hispanics. At the same time, telenovelas (soap operas) remain big for daytime viewing. It's all about family, family, family. And staying connected matters greatly within the Hispanic community. Social networks play a big role here, with Facebook having 82% reach among Latinos. Google sites have 95% reach, while nearly half of all Latinos are on Twitter and Pandora.[41] Hispanics follow their favorite brands and share branded web content at a higher rate than non-Hispanics. The key here is to know that Hispanics access online via mobile. Mobile is cost effective and portable. It fits their lifestyle. Mobile is economical and portable. If you want to reach Latinos, mobile is likely a great starting place.

Tapping Into the Latino Market

It's fair to say that some things are common across Hispanic cultures and tend to transcend country of origin. Family-focused activities are essential to Hispanic life. It was once common for multiple generations to share the same household. Today Millennial Latinos are eager to break away from their families, just like many young Americans have done for generations. Yet for Latinos, familial concerns trump individual needs. Additionally, everyday life within the Latino community can be a bit slower paced. There is always time for family and laughter. Humor, especially self-effacing humor, plays a big role in Hispanic life. In fact self-deprecating humor is a form of cultural expression. (You'll find this in Mexico too, as we'll discuss in the next chapter.) Sports are also a huge part of Latino culture, and enjoying sports as a family has a long tradition. A whopping 94% of male Hispanics are sports fans, with soccer and boxing at the top of the list.[43] Add to that the popularity of baseball among Cubans, Puerto Ricans, Dominicans, and Panamanians. But if there is one thing that brings Latinos together, above all else, it is music. Music is a Latin passion. (This parallels Brazilian culture. Check out Chapter 5.) The key to success is to check stereotypes against cultural understanding by learning the nuances of Latino culture. Brands that cater to the needs of Hispanic families, offering products and services that add value to their family's life, while demonstrating cultural knowledge and respect, will do well with Latinos. Within the Hispanic community brands like Procter & Gamble, AT&T, and McDonald's are hugely successful, and among the top 20 advertisers vying for Hispanic dollars are four automakers.[44] Hispanic dollars are so hot that Procter & Gamble ramped up its ad spending by 36%, and that has paid big dividends. With their income and spending on the rise, brands that take the time to understand Hispanics will be well rewarded.

"The challenge is to keep the flame burning, the flame of communicating to the Hispanic market in the language of their heart."[42]

Tere Zubizarreta,
former CEO of Zubi
Advertising Services and
Hispanic advertising pioneer

East Meets West

Like the Hispanic market, the Asian American demographic is a very diverse group. While there are some cultural similarities, you cannot use the same tactics to reach Chinese, Japanese, Korean, Indian, Pakistani, Thai, and the myriad other Asian American ethnicities represented within this niche market. At the same time, Asian Americans share some cultural similarities.

The largest group of Asian Americans are of Chinese descent, followed closely by immigrants from India and the Philippines. Vietnamese and Korean make up the fourth and fifth largest groups, with Japanese a distant sixth. Asian Americans tend to live in urban centers. Think of the coasts, the urban Midwest, and Texas, with Los Angeles and New York representing the highest density designated market areas for Asian Americans.[45] Asian Americans are the fastest growing multicultural segment, with 58% growth between 2000 and 2013, much of it spurred on by immigration.[46] They tend to cohabitate in family units, with multiple generations living together. They aspire strongly toward American values. Yet Asian Americans embrace and honor their individual cultural heritage. Interestingly, the majority of Asian Americans tend to see themselves as bicultural, which may be an indicator of their strong aspirational focus. Aspiration to embrace American norms and values combined with a passion for their individual cultural heritage and values creates an opportunity for advertisers. When it comes to purchase decisions Asian Americans focus on efficiency and convenience. Layer onto this strong aspirational desires to achieve the American dream. These values and desires shape their buying behaviors and drive purchasing decisions. Asian Americans overindex in key categories, including food, clothing, and technology. While they seek out value, Asian Americans also aspire to premium status and luxury brands. Suffice it to say, this is a complex group to reach.

A Culture of Fusion

We spoke about the importance of music among African Americans and Latinos. For Asian Americans the one thing that dominates their family and social life above all else is food. Cultural events revolve around food, with formal greetings and displays of affection often connected to edible tokens. Thus, it is not surprising to find that Asian Americans overindex on organic food, fresh produce, and dry grains. Considering Asian Americans' passion for food, it is also not surprising that the general market is obsessed by Asian fusion cuisine. No wonder Asian fusion is making a mark in gourmet dining. What is a surprise is that food and beverage marketers are not taking advantage of the ways Asian Americans influence food trends.

Family across the generations is beautifully articulated in this in-language grid layout for AARP. One does not even need to read Chinese to understand the essence of message. It is implied in the images and fits perfectly with the brand.

It might be the same message, but that 1-Hour Guarantee feels a whole lot different when it arrives in your language, spoken by someone who looks like you. The top one is in Tagalog (Philippines), the middle in Mandarin, and the bottom in Hindi.

Another place Asian American show consumer passion is in retail spending. Their aspirational values and higher incomes drive them to retail brands such as Nordstrom and Neiman Marcus at a far higher rate than the general market. The only category they have more passion for than clothing is books. Like any niche group, Asian Americans also have their aspirational celebrities. Jeremy Lin, the Harvard-educated basketball sensation, demonstrates immense potential as an Asian American spokesperson. More important, he has huge general market crossover. That fact was not lost on Nike, which signed him long before he burst onto the national media stage. Another brand, Ben & Jerry's, did not fare so well. It put its proverbial branded foot in its mouth when it released the absurdly stereotypical Linsanity ice cream made with fortune cookies. The brand quickly apologized and removed the flavor. They might have thought about limited-edition flavors celebrating the Chinese New Year. Not only would they taste better, they would likely sell better. Brands that understand this demographic, such as AT&T, HBO, State Farm, and Wells Fargo, and use Asian actors to reach them, are likely to win big.

Asian Americans may be a small market segment, making up just under 6% of the U.S. population.[47] However, they are highly educated and more affluent than any other multicultural demographic group in the United States. Indian Americans lead the way by a significant margin in terms of income and education. In fact, seven in ten Indian American adults have a college degree, while only about half of Americans of Korean, Chinese, Filipino, and Japanese descent and just a quarter of Vietnamese Americans have college degrees.[48] That's still far more Asian Americans with college degrees than in the general population. In fact, a whopping 61% of all Asian Americans have a college degree,[49] compared with 40% of all Americans.[50] To top it off, Asian immigrants claim 75% of all new visas for highly skilled workers.[51] The average Asian American household spends—not earns—$61,400. That's nearly 40% more than the average general market Millennial household.[52] Another way to think about this is that Asian Americans spend more than the average American family earns. Needless to say, they have money to spend.

Media Savvy and Digitally Passionate

The two key ways to reach Asian Americans are through in-language media and across digital platforms. This seems paradoxical, and in part it is. First, Asian Americans consume much of the same media as their non-Asian neighbors, but it's often via digital platforms. Second, despite their strong digital preference they gravitate toward in-language sources when it comes to traditional media. In Los Angeles there are 33 free Asian television broadcasters, with over 150 Asian satellite channels nationwide.[53] Asian Americans also consume a lot of in-language radio. The crucial point here is that Asian Americans seek out culturally specific programming. In fact, ads that feature culturally relevant

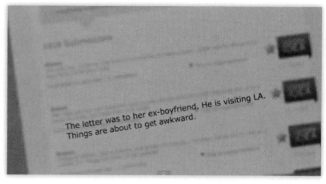

This Effie Award–winning AT&T campaign engaged Asian American Millennials to help shape the story in real time. Consumers used their mobile devices to send in suggestions, literally directing events within the unfolding story. "Away We Happened" was a viral hit, creating 13 million views and a huge fan base, not to mention serious return on investment for AT&T.

situations and characters make up 65% of the top ads among Asian Americans.[54] Cultural relevance truly does matter.

If there is one thing that stands out with Asian Americans it is their propensity toward digital adaption and innovation. A large percentage of Asian Americans are Millennials, and they are swiftly driving this demographic toward digital innovation. As a whole, Asian Americans have higher rates of smartphone use, online video consumption, and Internet connectivity.[55] In fact you could say that Asian Americans are redefining the way the general market watches, listens to, and interacts with media. As influencers Asian Americans are 15% more likely than the general market to recommend technology or electronics to others, and their smartphone penetration is an astounding 75%.[56] Now consider their digital entertainment habits. Asian Americans spend over 12 hours a month watching videos on the Internet. That is twice the rate of the general market. They are also 2.5 times more likely to download movies from a website. Plus, they spend at least 10% more time on their laptops, tablets, and mobile phones than the general market![57] This is a demographic that is truly passionate about the digital landscape and how they interact in this landscape is likely to affect all of us.

Tapping Into the Asian American Market

Now that you know a bit about where Asian Americans live, their cultural and aspirational values, their passion for digital media, and their affluence, you are probably wondering, how do you reach this dynamic and diverse demographic? Here are key takeaways[58]:

- Asian Americans are digital pioneers, adopting technology at a faster rate than any other group. Keep your eyes on them.

- In-language TV is still a dominant medium within this demographic. Learn how to speak to Asian Americans with resonance.

- Asian Americans use the Internet as a key shopping venue. Develop strategies that leverage this.

- Family and cultural heritage are key drivers shaping Asian Americans' buying behaviors. Remember this and make it work for your brand.

- Luxury brands provide aspirational value for Asian Americans. Consider how aspirational values can work for your brand, even if it is not a luxury brand.

- Asian Americans prefer information and utility in advertising messages. Leverage their high level of education for your brand.

- Culturally relevant themes are imperative within all advertising messages. Demonstrate respect for their individual cultures and Asian Americans will return the respect.

Don't Ask. Don't Tell. Just Sell.

Depending on the survey, anywhere from 6% to 10% of the American population identifies as gay, lesbian, bisexual, or transgender. Smart marketers know they can't ignore 20 million to 32 million people. Aside from the sheer numbers, the LGBT segment offers marketers other advantages. Like Asian Americans they tend to have more disposable income than the average American. Unlike Asian Americans they are not easily identifiable and often defy segmentation. However, they look fondly on brands that advertise in LGBT media or that have publicly courted them in mainstream media. Generally, LGBT households tend to be brand loyal and to seek out product upgrades at higher rates than their nongay counterparts.[59] Brands that have historically embraced this demographic include Brita, Cheerios, Chevrolet, Coca-Cola, Heineken Light, Intel, Johnson & Johnson, Revlon, Starbucks, Taco Bell, and Tide.[60] These brands are taking the lead in publically celebrating LGBTs. And it's paying off handsomely.

Just Do It

Back in the mid-1990s Nike Women ran an ad, "Canoeists," featuring two lesbians. Ironically, no one at Nike knew they were lesbians. That fact was not lost on the creative team, which consciously chose the two women because they felt they epitomized the empowerment theme and spoke to an often-ignored audience.[61] Will it take this same kind of silent protest to bring transgendered people out in the world of advertising? Some brands, such as Absolut, American Express, Cheerios, IKEA, J. C. Penney, Pepsi, and Subaru, benefit greatly from their positioning that does not exclude people based on sexual orientation. It's all about knowing your target and their tolerance threshold and being willing to step up and be inclusive. If you understand the LGBT target and show them respect, they will return the favor with brand loyalty.

Years ago, American Express began courting the gay and lesbian target when it highlighted Ellen DeGeneres as a cardholder in its "My Life. My Card" campaign. It worked well because the campaign's One Thing originally focused on celebrities. Back in the day DeGeneres fit in perfectly and slipped under the radar, but not to this community. Members of the LGBT community notice brands that reach out and include them, and they reward these brands. Just remember that backlash is always a possibility, though less and less as marriage equality takes root and tolerance of sexual orientation grows deeper among mainstream American culture.

I love wandering through Smithsonian museums, eating on H Street with friends, and going to shows at Howard Theatre.

I'm a
transgender woman
and I'm part of DC.

Please treat me the way any woman would want to be treated: with courtesy and respect.

Discrimination based on gender identity and expression is illegal in the District of Columbia.

If you think you've been the target of discrimination, visit www.ohr.dc.gov or call (202) 727-4559.

Office of Human Rights
DISTRICT OF COLUMBIA

OFFICE OF GLBT AFFAIRS

Show your support! Spread word of the #TransRespect campaign by photographing this ad and sharing on Twitter.

This public service ad by the Office of Human Rights, encouraging tolerance, respect, and employment equity for transgender people, may be a step forward.

Tapping Into the LGBT Market

If your assignment is to reinforce brand preference among LGBTs, you have several options.

One of them, however, is not stereotyping. While gays and lesbians may identify themselves by sexual preference, they also tend to strongly identify as mainstream consumers. You might run your general market campaigns in mainstream media that also have a high gay or lesbian concentration. You don't change the creative, but the media selection indicates that you're interested in their business. Running in straight and gay media at the same time also demonstrates your commitment to their community. They will notice and thank you at the checkout. Then, using visuals and copy, or both, incorporate gay themes and run those in gay publications. Reviewing gay and lesbian media, you'll notice that they tend to have the ability to laugh at themselves and the world; just be careful not to fall victim to stereotypical images. There is also the option of streaming platforms like Netflix and Hulu, which have successfully tapped into the LGBT market. Another approach is to integrate gay-themed ads across the entire campaign. IKEA, for example, has used gay themes in television commercials that also reach the general market. This demonstrates that you believe your brand is for all consumers, and you're willing to risk a possible backlash. Cheerios did this with its Cheerios Effect campaign, reaching out to gay and interracial families. It won the brand huge media praise, but also the ire of conservative groups. You can also consider keeping your mass-media advertising mainstream, or gender neutral, and focus on promotional and public relations programs that target gays and lesbians or movie trailers at movies that appeal to this demographic. Just remember that it's all about context, and respect rules the day.

Are these two brands brave or smart? Each reached out to gays and lesbians within the context of its general market campaign, and it fits perfectly. Here's where brave may come in: each openly expresses its support for gay marriage. Is this taking a brave risk or smartly appealing to the right demographic?

Generational Marketing

"You just don't understand." Every parent has heard this at one time or another, and every child has heard "When you're my age, you'll understand." Every generation sees this world differently, and advertising is definitely part of this world. This next section will offer some insight on generational marketing, including what other generations think of your generation. We'll work from the top down.

Matures and Boomers: Age is a Matter of Perception

Baby boomers are getting younger. In our last edition we reported that boomers thought of themselves as 10 years younger than they really are. This time around it's 20 years younger.[62] How do you address this demographic when many of them don't even see themselves as part of it? You begin by understanding that there are distinct groups within this market. One is the *matures*. They are over 70 and generally have a strong work ethic, are self-sacrificing, tolerant of authority, comfortable with conformity, loyal, and patriotic. They appreciate a good value and will happily spend money when they find it. Then there are the *boomers*. This group is 52 to 70, focused on self-improvement, and more than a bit hedonistic. If they could find the fountain of youth they'd be ecstatic. Boomers are nonconformist, more educated than matures, and way more tech savvy than you might imagine. They believe work should be fulfilling, feel a sense of entitlement, tend to tolerate differences, and seek adventure and new experiences. Despite their differences, matures and boomers have a fair amount in common. Both groups skew female, and together they represent about a quarter of the U.S. population.

Connecting With Boomers and Matures

When it comes to media, boomers and matures are big users, especially boomers. Today the median age of prime-time television viewers is smack dab in the boomer demographic.[63] To remain relevant, advertisers will have to rethink television messaging. However, boomers are also very savvy digital media users, and matures are earnest digital learners.[64] Consider this: boomers now spend more money on technology than any other demographic.[65] As boomers age into matures, they will take technology with them, along with social media, which is already a huge presence in boomers' lives. Today one in three social media users is either a boomer or a mature.[66] Despite their embrace of social media, both boomers and matures have a traditional streak, especially matures. Both prefer to balance social media with good old-fashioned face-to-face conversation and traditional media consumption, including tangible print, radio, and television.

No matter what the platform, for this demographic, it's the message that counts. Boomers and matures tend to respond very positively to relationships. Build them. Consider using life-stage marketing, because the mature market responds strongly to life-changing events, especially those that are personal.

Despite some backlash after running TV spots featuring a bicultural family, Cheerios brand managers did not back down. Instead they stepped it up, launching the Cheerios Effect campaign, with one spot featuring a gay couple and their adopted multiracial daughter. Just like two O's in a bowl, we all love to connect. That's the Cheerios Effect.

©General Mills

Make these events the defining moments of your campaign. Consider testimonials and endorsements to back up your claims. Give them facts. Be clear and straightforward. Let them know the benefits. Demonstrate your credibility. Education will engender loyalty. From a tonal perspective, celebrate the joys of retirement, and avoid scare tactics at all costs. Above all, don't pressure them. They will take their time to make a decision. Once they've decided your brand is the one, they will be very loyal.

Tapping Into the Boomer and Mature Market

Here are a few specific things to consider related to media. But first, here are a few tips about design that apply across most media. Make your ads visually accessible. Keep them simple, avoid clutter, and use plenty of white space. Don't forget to make type legible and a bit larger.

- **Print:** Give them information, because they tend to read more. Use bold headlines and clear subheads. Break your copy into columns to deliver information. Avoid glossy stock, because it glares.

- **Radio:** Keep background music to a minimum, and remember, they are heavy early-morning listeners.

- **Television:** Nobody watches the news like they do. However, don't forget, boomers are happy to DVR programs, so product placement and sponsorships might be good alternatives. Keep background music down, and keep titles on the screen just a bit longer.

- **Web:** Make your message meaningful and information rich. If you do, they will come, stay, and return. Give them a reason to trust you.

- **Social:** Use images when you can. Make your content meaty and relevant, and give them time to dwell. Build trust by avoiding hype and insulting jargon.

- **Mobile:** Make your message meaningful. They're on the move, with over 80% of boomers and 67% of matures packing their mobile devices wherever they go.

- **Direct:** They don't mind getting mail. In fact matures look forward to it. Boomers would also be happy to engage with you online, as long as you make it worth their while.

- **Promotion:** If something can save them money and the offer doesn't expire too soon, they will participate.

Amazon's 50+ Active and Healthy Living Store is a destination site offering a vast selection of items, from blood pressure monitors to books on traveling the world. It has a robust Resource Center filled with tips on everything from boosting brainpower to caregiving. This is a brand that understands boomers' youthful desires, spending power, and online habits.

Levi's was the brand that saw boomers through the 1960s, and they rewarded the brand by taking Dockers to work. Nobody loves a Harley-Davidson more than a boomer guy and his biker gal. Boomers are the Pepsi generation and grooved to Michael Jackson and Madonna, Ray Charles and Tina Turner. But it's not just these traditional brands that have secured a spot in the hearts of boomers. They also bought 41% of all Apple computers[67] (they actually remember seeing Apple's "1984" ad) and love to log into Facebook on their new iPhones. Treat them with respect, acknowledge their desire for an enduring youth, and if you remember their grandchildren—you'll tap into their hearts and wallets.

Gen X: Stuck in the Middle

No other generation was hit harder by the Great Recession. People in their mid-30s to late 40s face the possibility of being the first generation that will do worse than their parents and their children. They've been called the forgotten generation because so much has been said about Boomers and Millennials. But at 60 million strong, marketers can't afford to ignore them. Gen Xers are more diverse than previous generations in race, class, religion, ethnicity, and sexual orientation. They are more likely to be the children of divorced parents than previous generations. Statistically, they have the highest education levels. Gen Xers, individually, make less money in real dollars than their parents, but have higher household incomes because of more women in the workforce.[68]

Tapping Into the Gen X Market

Gen Xers have thoroughly embraced mobile technology. While not exactly digital natives, they were early adapters. They tend to like casual, friendly work environments over cubicle farms.

Feeling 20 years younger. Check. Unafraid of social media. Check. Passionate about grandkids. Check. Still cool. Check. Live, ride, drive a Jeep. Check.

Hook matures with a bit of respectful humor, then pass along the information they covet. They will reward you with loyalty.

(Seriously, what person actually likes working in a box?) They've lived through their parents' recessions and experienced the worst downturn since the Great Depression in the prime of their careers. So they are more risk averse than Boomers or Millennials and tend to be a little more careful about making major purchases.[69] Gen Xers aren't as loyal to brands and may be a little more cynical about advertising since they've been inundated by it all their lives. They're also less enthusiastic about long-term careers, being more likely to make a lateral move than moving up the corporate ladder.[70]

Here are some tips for finding and connecting with the Gen X market:

- **They value independence.** Give them a goal and let them figure out how to accomplish it.

- **Be very clear about your offer.** Don't give them reasons to be skeptical. Give lots of details, so it doesn't look like you are trying to hide anything. Offer a money-back guarantee (remember, they are risk averse).

- **Give suggestions, not rules.** Show them some things they might like and let them figure out which works best for them.

- **Consider direct mail.** Gen X seems to have a greater appreciation for direct mail than the older Baby Boomers. According to a study conducted for the U.S. Postal Service, 86% of Gen X bring in the mail the day it's delivered. Gen X rate 75% of the mail they receive as valuable.

- **Go online.** Gen X's online habits are so fractured that they're hard to pin down. However, more than any other generation, Gen X likes to research while shopping online. They read more reviews, and visit more opinion sites. This would suggest a couple of tactics: ramping up your presence on Yelp and other opinion websites, also using keyword search engine advertising.[71]

Millennials: A Marketing Dilemma

A recent Pew Research study of Millennials showed that their attitudes and opinions are markedly different from those of older generations.[72] America's Millennials are not generally attached to organized religion, but they are linked together by social media. They are also "digital natives," as 81% of them are on Facebook, with a median friend count of 250, far higher than that of older age groups. They are both skeptical and frugal, and tend to delay big purchases. Likewise, Millennials are used to sharing what they have and are in no hurry to marry. (Remember the growth of singletons?) They are, also, optimistic about the country's future. Idealism and the notion of equity tend to drive their political goals and social principles. While many Millennials call themselves political independents, they tend to support Democrats and possess liberal views on many political and social issues, ranging from a belief in an activist government to support for same-sex marriage and marijuana legalization.

Some Millennials look to celebrities for guidance on fashion, health, and beauty. For example, endorsements from pop stars like Katy Perry can influence teens to use acne medications. If that doesn't work, those with a vain streak can still Photoshop their selfies.

Millennials: BRANDS STILL MATTER

Who is a Millennial?

74.3 million population

$170 billion purchasing power

Favorite brands of Millennials:

1. Nike
2. Apple
3. SAMSUNG
4. SONY
5. Walmart
6. Target
7. Microsoft
8. Jordan
9. Coca-Cola
10. pepsi

Brands play an important role in my life...

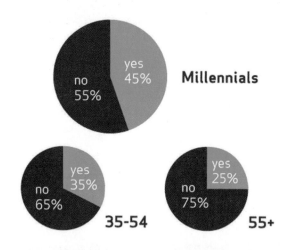

Millennials — no 55%, yes 45%

35–54 — no 65%, yes 35%

55+ — no 75%, yes 25%

Source: Moosylvania 2015 Millennial Ranking Repot, Yahoo/Digitas LBi/Razorfish /Tumblr, "Content Marketing Best Practices Among Millennials," 2014. Havasi, "Hashtag Nation," 2014.

Interestingly, Millennials are somewhat less enthusiastic than older adults about environmentalism, at least its old definition. Their idea of environmentalism may be represented in the growth of brands like Zipcar and Divvy. What they do care about is brands that act ethically. This may explain why, while Millennials may fondly remember the flavor of a Big Mac (and even long for it), they still choose not to patronize McDonald's and instead turn to brands like Freshii. In the end, Millennials represent a movement toward accumulating experiences rather than accumulating stuff.

Besides dealing with this major shift in attitudes, marketers find it increasingly hard to reach Millennials. No other generation is more distrustful of advertising or finds more creative ways to avoid it.

Tapping Into the Millennial Market

Marketing demographers sometimes disagree about how to define this generation. Are they Generation Z (born from 1994 to 2010) or Generation Y, born 10 years earlier? No matter what name you use, it's a generation defined more by values than birthdates. We shouldn't have to tell you how to talk to your peers, but when it comes to reaching the younger range of the Millennial spectrum, here are a few tips[73]:

- **Text + Mobile Video + Sharing:** It seems to be a pretty straightforward marketing equation. Invite them to opt in to a text marketing program. Create interesting mobile video content. Send them links to this mobile video. Provide an option to share this mobile video with their friends. Occasionally text them offers, invites, and discount codes that they can also share with their friends via text and social media. Teens send and receive an average of 3,330 texts per month. That's more than 6 texts each waking hour. It's also more than double any other age group. Text messaging is the number one use of a cell phone by teens.

- **Online shopping:** Nearly half of all teens have purchased something online.

- **Mobile video:** Millennials watch twice as much mobile video as other mobile viewers.

- **Sharing on social networks:** They have higher than the average number of friends on social networks, and they like to share with those networks. Ninety-three percent of Millennials have created or shared content online.
- **Don't forget traditional media:** Millennials still watch TV, listen to radio, see billboards, and pick up a newspaper or magazine. But don't think that any of those marketing communication methods will be enough to move the needle. (Return to first bullet point.)

Children: Walking a Fine Line

Reaching children requires engagement that is culturally embedded and repetitive. Characters, which have been a staple of advertising for generations, have proved to be highly effective. The Pillsbury Doughboy, Charlie the Tuna, Tony the Tiger—all of these characters have been used successfully for decades. Today Nickelodeon's

This ad from Singapore strikes just the right note, appealing to children's imagination and parents' concern about safety.

SpongeBob SquarePants has cobranding licensing agreements with a range of brands.[74] Characters offer brands a chance to emotionally engage with children with a message ensuring strong recall. This does not even address the sales power and branded cross-promotion of movies targeting children. Walk through any big-box store and you will see everything from backpacks to princess dresses splattered with icons from the latest Disney movie.

Not surprisingly, fast food, soda, and toys are product categories that have the highest recall among children. Among all these brands, McDonald's has the highest recall.[75] And remember, McDonald's is a brand that has strong loyalty among Latinos, and that community has a lot of children under 18. These two factors are not mutually exclusive. Coca-Cola is another brand that reaches out to children. In fact, Coca-Cola Classic accounted for three quarters of all branded messages targeting children in 2010, with an emphasis on the Black community.[76] With clear and compelling evidence of an obesity epidemic in America, an epidemic with particularly salient effect in Latino and Black communities, should brands like Coca-Cola and McDonald's be aggressively targeting children?

Advertising to children is fraught with ethical concerns. We invite you to remember our discussion from Chapter 3. Use media and messages that are age appropriate. Consider whether the content is detrimental to children. Honestly acknowledge your role in creating and/or maintaining stereotypes. And honor the concerns of parents and professionals, especially when it comes to younger children.

Women in Advertising: Have We Really Come a Long Way, Baby?

Advertisers have been telling women how far they've come for a long time—from Virginia Slims in 1968 to Nike in 1995 to Dove in 2004 to Always in 2014. Yet what seems missing is a holistic approach that finds the balance between objectifying women and speaking to them in a voice that lacks resonance or telling them how far they've come and how empowered and naturally beautiful they are.

The world may be changing, but advertisers are taking their time to catch up. At the same time, women remain in the driver's seat when it comes to consumer spending in both the traditional retail landscape and in the online world. If you thought women were at home with the kids, spending someone else's money, think again. Seventy-five percent of moms with school-aged children are in the labor force.[78] Women are earning and spending money. The bottom line is "women are the purchasers of this world, and understanding why she buys is the most valuable insurance policy there is."[79]

Hey, Big Spender, Spend a Little Time With Me

The idea that women are a "niche" market appears even more odd when you consider that women[80]:

- Spend close to $7 trillion annually.
- Purchase 50% of the products marketed to men.
- Represent the majority of the online market.
- Buy 68% of the new cars and influence up to 80% of all car purchases.
- Make 80% of all health care decisions.
- Influence 91% of all new home purchases.
- Buy 92% of all vacations.
- Open 89% of all bank accounts.
- Purchase 66% of all computers.
- Buy 93% of all food.
- Hold 60% of all personal wealth in the United States.

©National Organization for Women

These exceptional student ads, developed as part of a campaign, call into question how women and girls are portrayed each and every day in advertising. They are also demonstrate the power of surprinting to drive home a message. Maybe it's time to more seriously consider, what message are we sending our women and girls?

But here's the real kicker: 91% of women think advertisers do not understand them.[81] We'd say advertisers have missed the mark when it comes to women.[82] Maybe that's because advertisers still consider women a "niche" market, while White men remain the default general market.

Besides wielding an immense amount of economic power, women are also considered the leading indicators of social change. To engage women, a brand must demonstrate that it understands the meaning, significance, and direction of large social changes and how these changes affect not only women's lives, but the very fabric of society. Think of how that plays out in the work world. Women have a high preference for personal networking, and they prefer collaboration and shared authority. They thrive on conceptual thinking, consensus building, and flexible work and lifestyles. Now, think about how that plays out in women's personal lives. Women talk, whether it is one on one over coffee with friends or social word of mouth on blogs, Pinterest, or Facebook. They use brands to add convenience to their lives and joy to their family life, and they use media to gather and share information. They will sing a brand's praises or take it down with lightning speed.

Tapping Into This Influential "Niche" Market

Now that you understand a little bit about what makes women tick and what doesn't, let's talk about crafting messages they will respond to. The vast majority of women see advertising as a source of information as compared with entertainment.[83]

> "Change begins when we acknowledge how gender roles are fostered in families."
>
> Kelli Szymczak,
> associate creative resource manager, Lapiz

©Scarlet Paolicchi

Cision does an annual metrics-based review of mommy blogs, releasing its findings each Valentine's Day. Scarlet Paolicchi's fantastic "Family Focus Blog" ranked number three in 2014. With a clean and beautiful layout, smart and focused content, along with 77,700 followers, we weren't surprised to see her at the top.

These ads demonstrate humanity through storytelling. Athleta speaks of taking action to take care of yourself and offers "Power to the She," while Johnson's Baby Lotion visually connects mother and daughter as the copy provides tangible, emotive information. These are human stories that sing with resonance.

But how you give them information is based on "four emotive pathways," according to *PurseStrings* by Amanda Stevens and Tom Jordan[84]:

- **Storytelling:** Tell a story that feels real and can be told across multiple platforms. They will embrace it and share it.
- **Magical music:** Music can have a profound effect on the human body. Find out what motivates your women, and use music to tap into their emotions.
- **Embrace humanity:** Studies have documented how infants respond to faces, baby girls more than baby boys. As adults that difference remains. Add humanity to an ad, and you'll connect with women.
- **Laughter is the best medicine:** We are not talking about the typical boy humor that dominates advertising today. We are talking about merging humor with humanity and offering the ability to laugh with, not at, someone.

Women are not all the same. Young women 18 to 24 are just starting out on their own and very much reflect Gen Y. They are a lot different from 20- to 30-year-old women who work hard and play hard, and are often highly focused on their careers. Women in their upper 30s and 40s bear little resemblance to career-focused 20-somethings. They are often moms with a burgeoning family-centered focus, while trying to balance full- or part-time work with family life. Then there are women over 50. These boomers are starting a new phase of life and tend to have an adventurous streak that focuses on self-fulfillment, not to mention that they think of themselves as closer to 40. Women's age and life experiences make a huge difference in how a brand speaks to them and where the brand will find them.

The generational differences among women, as with other demographics, are huge. Do your homework. Remember, women view the world through a unique lens. Before you start talking to a woman, listen to her.

Did We Miss Anyone?

The famous "Crying Indian" ad with Espera Oscar DeCorti, an Italian American, portraying an American Indian. Did advertisers miss a moment to do the right thing?

No doubt we did. Three groups come to mind: Arab Americans, Native Americans, and people with disabilities—in large part because they are too often misrepresented or invisible. No doubt there are others too.

So, what about Arab Americans? Not all Arabs are Muslim. Not all Muslims are Arabs. How do we address them respectfully while not alienating other groups? There's a wide spectrum across Arab Americans, from conservative to secular Muslims to Christians of Arab descent to Arab Americans without any religious affiliation. While we can't begin to break down all the different segments, as a whole, American Muslims have $170 billion in purchasing power.[85] Brands such as Lowe's, Walmart, and McDonald's began courting Muslim Americans, but backed off when some groups, unfairly, accused them of supporting extremist views. Brands need to act ethically and proactively but should always be prepared for consumer responses. Brands that cave into pressure from a vocal minority often reduce their credibility with all consumers. In turn, groups with passion for their cause and the financial ability to express it need to consider the impact of their words and images. We need to find common ground in difficult times.

What about native Americans? They have been the subject of unflattering media stereotypes for generations. Historically they've been portrayed as bloodthirsty savages, humble guides, alcoholics, and of course the Lone Ranger's "faithful Indian companion." But they are rarely cast in mainstream advertising. The standout exception may be the "Crying Indian" weeping for the environment in the 1971 "Keep America Beautiful" campaign. But, here's the irony. Iron Eyes Cody, the actor who portrayed the Indian, was actually an Italian American. In hindsight, it was an epic failure, when it could have been a breakthrough. The reality is that the majority of native Americans have not lived on reservations since at least the early 1960s. For instance, Chicago, in a state without any reservations, has the third largest native American population, representing more than 100 tribal ethnic groups. Recently, broadcasters and advertisers have had to consider how to describe Washington's NFL team. Do they embrace the traditional name, which most people consider hugely offensive outside of its football context? Or do they risk alienating diehard fans by ignoring the name of their beloved team? Yes, names matter. In the end, native Americans do not see themselves as historical artifacts. They see themselves as contemporaries in diverse society. Maybe advertisers need to do the same.

What about people with disabilities? Every disability presents different challenges and may present different wants and needs. Like African Americans before the 1970s, people with disabilities are nearly invisible in today's advertising. In the United Kingdom, the VisABLE Campaign works to bring disabled people into advertising. One2OneNetwork, a mobile brand, used a man in a wheelchair as part of a slice-of-life story. In Sweden, ICA, a large grocery chain, created a long-running campaign featuring Jerry, one of its cognitively disabled employees. ICA sent home the message that we are more alike than different, and Swedes loved them for it. They also took home a Cannes Lion. Some brands do get it right, naturally. There are three reasons to use people with disabilities in advertising: It's the right thing to do. It's commercially viable. And, at least in Britain, it's a legal obligation. Maybe it's time for American advertisers to start emulating their European colleagues? And that includes people with developmental disabilities. However, for the first time, a model with Down's syndrome strutted down the catwalk during New York Fashion Week in 2015. Ever so slowly, the marketing world is beginning to realize that everyone needs to be included.

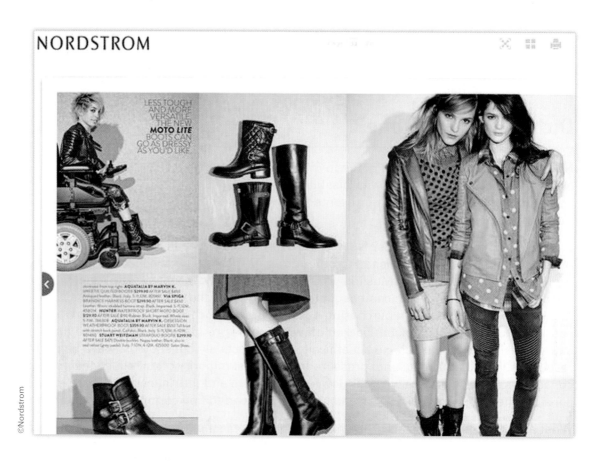

While disabled people are not as prominently featured in the United States, they are not invisible. Two status-oriented brands, Nordstrom and Guinness, take a step in the right direction. How might you use disabled people in your ads?

The Times They Are A-Changin'

There just isn't enough time or space, so the conversation about niche markets must come to a close. Despite our best efforts to avoid offending any group or individual, and our humble disclaimer at the beginning of the chapter, we have probably touched a few raw nerves. The truth is, anyone can find just about anything that's offensive if they go out of their way to look for it. It's easy to remind creative people to avoid overt racist, sexist, and homophobic language. But giving guidelines for avoiding every possible variant of subtle microaggression is far outside the scope of this book. So in the spirit of relevance and respect, we offer a few tips that apply to most niche market situations:

- Don't make assumptions or rely on personal prejudices.
- Do your homework. Talk to the people in your target audience.
- Always remember that even within a market segment, there can be huge variation.
- Get more than one opinion. What's acceptable to one person may be totally off base for a whole market segment.
- Market segments, like subcultures, are culturally bound.
- Social context matters. Be alert to subtle references that some groups may find offensive.
- Humility goes a long way.
- Act globally. Think locally.
- Above all, be respectful.

This last point—respect—needs some more discussion. John Kuraoka, a freelance copywriter, offers some great advice:

> Racism, sexism, and other us-against-them motifs are not funny. It is no more acceptable to poke fun at a middle-aged white man than it is to poke fun at a young black lesbian. It makes no difference that you, personally, are either a middle-aged white man or a young black lesbian. On reflection, it's questionable whether poking fun at anybody helps sell anything.[86]

On the other hand, don't let political correctness overrule common sense. Kuraoka has some good advice on this, too: "There is a difference between race and racism, sex and sexism. It is pointless to make a pantyhose ad gender-neutral, just as it is foolish to craft political messages about birth control without fully bringing women into the deliberation. Be aware of cases and causes in which neutering the tone of your message will degrade its effectiveness."[87] Above all remember the golden rule, and treat others as you would like to be treated.

Chapter 4

Sergio Alcocer

As president and chief creative officer (CCO) of Latin Works, Sergio Alcocer is one of the most progressive multicultural marketers in the nation. Latin Works was named Multicultural Agency of the Year three times and is consistently listed as one of the top ten ad agencies in the country. Sergio is a frequent speaker at international forums on multicultural marketing and has served twice as a judge at the Cannes Festival. He holds an MBA from the Berlin School of Creative Leadership and is currently working on his PhD at the University of Texas.[88]

Cindy Chen

Known as a fearless brand transformer, Cindy Chen pioneered real-time marketing with Oreo "Daily Twist" and Oreo Super Bowl "Blackout" tweets. During her long-standing successful career driving double-digit growth of multibillion dollar businesses in North America and Asia Pacific, she has transformed brands like Oreo from well-known ones into cultural icons. Chen has won numerous awards for reinventing brands through marketing, digital, social, and mobile innovations. Recently she was awarded seven Cannes Lions, including a Cyber Grand Prix, Effie and Clio Awards, and, among many others, a Facebook Studio Blue Award and an IAB MIXX Award as the best social media campaign of 2013. Chen is currently global head of innovation, gum category, Mondelēz International.[89]

Caroline Jones

A copywriter with a long list of firsts, Caroline Jones is often promoted as the first Black woman to have held the position. She helped many clients, including American Express, Anheuser-Busch, McDonald's, and Prudential, make their initial forays into the African American market. Jones began her career in 1963 in New York as a secretary and copywriter trainee at J. Walter Thompson. She rose to creative director in less than five years. In 1968, she helped form Zebra Associates, no small feat in an era with few Black agency principals. She cofounded the Black Creative Group and established Mingo, Jones, Guilmenot, now the Chisholm-Mingo Group. Jones died in 2011.[90]

Jimmy Smith

Jimmy Smith co-created some of the world's most iconic campaigns for brands such as Nike, Pepsi, and Snickers. Additionally, he gave birth to the rebranding of Gatorade as G and the G campaign. Soon, his talents spilled over into the world of entertainment. He has authored books (*Soul of the Game*, *The Truth* for Dark Horse Comics), co-created video games (EA Sports' *NBA Street*, Intel and Microsoft Kinect's *Discovered*), and co-created TV shows (*Nike Battlegrounds*, *Gatorade Replay*). Smith's work has been recognized by the One Show, the Emmys, Cannes, and *Time* magazine, and he was declared one of the Top 100 Most Creative People in Business by *Fast Company* magazine. In addition to his duties as chairman, CEO, and CCO of Amusement Park Entertainment, he also sits on the board of the One Club.[91]

The Faces of Diversity

Our client, Global Learning Systems (GLS), has created an educational system to help advance learning the basics—reading, writing, and arithmetic. The system focuses on early elementary learning, and thus the target is parents of children ages 6 to 10. The GLS educational system is based on an at-home educational system with an online interface. It provides support for parents and online brainteasers for children, and is framed by a systemic process, where parents can test their children's progress. GLS developed this modestly priced educational program as an at-home system specifically so that geographic constrains would not be a consideration.

To begin the process of developing insight, bring to class a photo of a child within the target age range. Have it printed on an 8½ × 11 piece of paper. Next, we will post all the faces for the class to see. Stand back and look at them. Take your time, move them around. Boys. Girls. Blondes. Redheads. Brunettes. Brown. Black. White.

Then start considering why each photo was chosen. Each picture seems to have a story. "This is my favorite picture of my little brother when he was seven." Or, "This is the kid I nanny." Eventually you may make your way around to talking about what themes you see in the faces. Then think back to the basics of the GLS educational system: it's an at-home program with online interface, including support for parents and brainteasers for children. How can you use this range of imagery to gather insights for GLS and to learn something about yourself?

1 Do the faces reflect the diversity in your community? Do the faces reflect the diversity within the potential target demographic?

2 What impact do the faces you chose have for those who may see the advertising you will eventually create for GLS?

3 How do those faces draw us into the ad—or not? How might those faces draw someone else to a GLS—or not?

4 Do the faces reflect the diversity you see in advertising? What does this say about our industry—if anything at all?

Sheri Broyles, professor, University of North Texas

The inspiration for this came from something I saw while on an accreditation site team visit. I admired it greatly. I remember talking to the faculty member about using it, but I can't recall the person or the university. If you read this and think it sounds familiar, my sincere apologies.

1. Different Voices

Choose a product. Consumer packaged goods can be good. So can home cleaning products or consumer electronics.

- Pick one brand—for example, Swiffer.

- Draw two stick people and imagine they are from two different demographic groups. As a group, create a bulleted list of demographics and psychographics that represent each group.

- Next draw a speech bubble by each stick person. Fill in the speech bubble, considering how they would greet each other.

- Now give each a thought bubble. Consider how the two stick people might think differently about each other. This is the interesting part, because it gets to an exploration of demographic, cultural, and social differences. Now fill in the think bubble. You might even begin to get at some of the deeper ethical issues, which are often hard to discuss.

2. Brands as Global Personalities

How do some brands more successfully move across the globe than other brands? Why do some take a globalized approach and others a standardized approach?

- Begin by thinking of brands as people and be prepared to trace their personalities across cultures.

- Generate a list of 10 of the most influential people on the globe.

- Discuss why each of these people is influential: What about their actions, personality, country of origin and current residence, profession and title, associations, and so on makes them influential?

- From the previously generated list consider the qualities inherent in each person. Now, link a brand to each person.

- Discuss why each of the brands exemplifies that individual.

- Now write a brand personality statement for each brand. Consider how much this statement reflects the person associated with the brand.

- Finally, discuss how these brands move across the globe based on their brand personality and cultural variations. Consider if a standardized or globalized approach is used and why.

3. Is There Really a Difference?

This exercise challenges you to consider stereotypes and how they influence advertising.

- Your instructor will connect with agency colleagues and find a campaign (ads and briefs) that involves ads for both the general market and the gay and lesbian market.

- As a class, review the brief and ad for the general market.

- Next, working in teams, brainstorm ad concepts for the gay market.

- Then select your best idea and present it to the class along with a rationale for why it's the best option to reach the gay demographic.

- Finally, your instructor will show you the ad the agency produced for the gay market.

- Open for discussion: What are the differences between the general market ad and the ad for the gay market? What were your assumptions? How did stereotypes play out?

Review chapter content and study for exams. http://study.sagepub.com/altstiel4e.

- Interactive practice quizzes
- Mobile-friendly eFlashcards
- Carefully selected chapter-by-chapter video and multimedia content

Chapter 5

International Advertising
It's a Global Marketplace

Brands seek to leverage their equity across multiple geographic regions, representing myriad cultures, while advertising agencies ramp up their knowledge of global trends. If there is one issue shaping these trends it is sustainability—a movement that grows brands through sustainable sourcing, design, and logistics, and which is transparently authentic. Sustainability, in the global marketplace, is a significant driver of return on investment (ROI). According to Keith Weed, Unilever's chief marketing and communications officer, "Our brands that most engage with our sustainability and social purpose plan are growing fastest."[1] In 2014 Unilever saw 2.9% growth worldwide and 5.7% growth in emerging markets.[2] Global branding with a focus on emerging markets is more important than ever. By 2020 the gross domestic product of emerging markets will surpass that of developed economics.[3]

Global Context

Let's consider global marketing within a geographic context. From this vantage point, here are five categories: local, national, regional, international, and global.

- **Local:** Begin in your own backyard, where you'll find local brands. These are often retail brands with small local footprints. Milwaukee's Colectivo Coffee is a good example. Colectivo is a local coffee roaster, and its advertising represents that local flavor. But the founders are also savvy business people. They began as Alterra back in 1993. Twenty years later they sold the Alterra brand name to Nestlé and pocketed the cash. The infusion of cash strengthened their bottom line and allowed them to more robustly expand their local offerings. You will also find many business-to-business (B2B) brands in the local and national category. We will talk more about them in Chapter 15.

- **National:** These brands are wedded to a single country, such America's Kroger and Nordstrom. Both brands advertise exclusively within a single national border, and the tonality tends to echo national cultural norms—albeit very different norms. In the case of Kroger and Nordstrom, they appeal to consumers at very different socioeconomic levels. Retail brands tend to dominate the national geographic category, though as we stated above, B2B has a big presence here as well. However, a new trend is emerging. As retail brands grow they tend to expand across the geographic borders of economically friendly neighbors. Nordstrom is a great example. It now has two stores in Canada, with plans to open five more by 2017. As expansion drives the 21st-century economy, some traditionally national brands may become regional brands.

- **Regional:** Here brands advertise within specific regional clusters. The French Orange telecom brand is one such brand, with a focus on Europe, North Africa, and the Middle East. Orange is Orange wherever it goes, but the offers reflect consumers' needs within the individual countries. Since cultural knowledge is key, it's worth noting that the brand had a bit of trouble in Ireland, since the color is also associated with Protestant militants. In the last edition we talked about Sonic as a national brand. Today, Sonic is a regional brand, with drive-ins across the Americas from Canada to Chile.

- **International:** These brands have broad geographic distribution. They use standardized marketing approaches, which we will discuss in more detail a bit later. In sum, standardized approaches adapt to local cultures.

> *"Ideas can come from anyone. Everyone is welcome to join in."*
>
> Ross Chowles,
> cofounder, executive creative director, The Jupiter Drawing Room, Cape Town, South Africa

Unilever and Procter & Gamble lead the way in using standardized approaches in the consumer package good arena. Tide is Tide in the United States, but Ariel from Mexico to India. The campaigns for Tide and Ariel look very different depending upon the cultural context. Another approach was taken by Iglo, which you may know as Birds Eye. Havas Worldwide, London, did a complete strategic overhaul, bringing all the brands under the Iglo umbrella, with the tagline "Better Meals Together." However, country by country, the executions reflect local culture.

- **Global:** In the global category, you'll find the behemoth multinational brands. They are hyperconsistent in their branding at a global level, with very little deviation in messaging regardless of cultural differences. Brands like McDonald's and Coke fit here. While drive-throughs throughout Europe are McDrives, the McDonald's name and the Golden Arches remain the same, no matter where they appear. The same is true for Coke. What defines happiness may have varying cultural nuances. Nonetheless, happiness itself has a universal appeal. So, the happiness you see bubbling out of shapely classic Coca-Cola bottles makes Coke's message globally ubiquitous.

fresh hai apna style on the **Coke** side of life

Coca-Cola

This Indian ad for Coke expresses its global messaging beautifully. "Hai Apna" ("My Heart") is a song made famous in Bollywood, which makes the words and the imagery spot on for the target. But you need not know much about Bollywood or India to know that Coke is spreading happiness—in perfect cultural harmony.

As the global marketplace expands and competition tightens, brands that once seemed like local jewels may find themselves sold off to new corporate parents, often far from where they were born. Take the iconic American beer Pabst Blue Ribbon. In 2000 it was acquired by a Los Angeles–based holding company. Four years later it was sold to Russia's Oasis Beverages. Why was it sold? In part because it is "the quintessential American brand—it represents individualism, egalitarianism, and freedom of expression." Was it worth its nearly $750 million price tag?[4] You bet. This speaks to the power of aspirational branding. So, next time you're in Moscow you might want to ask for a PBR.

The Power of Culture

Understanding the importance of culture will help contextualize the strategies we'll be talking about later in the chapter. We will discuss two main ways to strategically consider the impact of culture. The first is high and low cultural context. The second is the dimensions of culture.

High Context. Low Context.

The concept of high and low cultural context provides an umbrella under which you can begin to understand cultural variance. Think of high and low cultural context as primarily about interpersonal ways of communicating while socially engaging. Myriad cultural nuances define cultural context, from languages, to social interactions, to food consumption, to courtship and shopping habits.

The variations from country to country can go from subtle to extreme. It's an advertiser's job to understand them and strategically decide how important these cultural communication nuances are, thus leading to how the brand will be positioned within each country.

High-context cultures value subtlety and privacy. Within these cultures, messages are rarely explicit. In other words, you must understand the local cultural structure to understand the nuances of the cultural messages. Thus, high-context messaging is often inaccessible to an outsider. If you're not part of the culture, you may not understand the message. Asian countries are generally high-context cultures. In countries such as China and Japan messages are commonly characterized by symbolism or indirect verbal expressions. In these cultures having local people on your advertising team is essential. As an advertiser, you will quickly learn that within a high-context culture, using cultural codes, generally familiar only to insiders, is essential for success.

Beauty knows no boundaries. Dove wisely understands this. The brand asks the same questions across the world, thereby maintaining its position, while playing its role as the global advocate for real beauty.

Low-context cultures value messages that are more transparent. In low-context countries, interactions among people are generally more open. The codes embedded within messages are generally more explicit. There is also a strong emphasis on the use of words versus symbolism. The idea of "telling it like it is" is common in low-context cultures. The strategy of using words and images that can be quickly interpreted is common. In short, low-context cultures function with more direct forms of communication. In countries such as Germany and the United States, even an outsider can relatively quickly pick up on the codes within local messages. However, it's important to remember that even if these messages are understood, it does not mean that they will resonate or be accepted. That's where cultural nuances come into play.

The taglines in these Buick ads read, "Signs are there for a reason." The sympathetic appeal features victims in the locations where reckless drivers injured them. The copy, simple visual, and absence of the car work perfectly in this collectivist culture with high power distance. Its paradoxical framing implies that nothing supersedes honor.

Cultural Dimensions

Cultural dimensions are essentially six categories, which marketers use to understand nuanced cultural dimensions.[5] They were developed by Geert Hofstede and are widely used by marketers today as they shape their messages to uniquely fit an individual culture.[6] They are also very helpful for novice advertisers as they try to understand a global marketplace and how to position brands within it.

- **Power distance** refers to how much distance there is between ordinary people and powerbrokers. China has high power distance, while the United States has low power distance. Oreos are hugely popular in both countries. In China the advertising centers on children eating Oreos, reverently, and usually with family. In contrast, in the United States the brand messaging makes no reference to power differentials. Oreos are simply shown shared and enjoyed equally.

- **Individualism versus collectivism** refers to whether the individual or the family and community have stronger priority. The United States is highly individualistic, while Mexico is highly collectivist. Consider the Corona beer brand. You all know Corona as the getaway beer. It is consistently shown with the solo bottle, and the quintessential lime, on the beach. It embodies an individual experience. In Mexico drinking Corona is anything but a solo experience. It is a celebration of community. Same beer, completely different messaging.

- **Masculinity versus femininity** refers to whether social structures are dominated by masculine or feminine norms. Saudi Arabia is a highly masculine country, while Sweden is a highly feminine country. You'll find IKEA in both countries. However, in Sweden IKEA catalogues and its website show women and men sharing domestic duties. In Saudi Arabia images of women were nonexistent, which led to a huge outcry in Sweden, IKEA's home.

- **Uncertainty avoidance** refers to people's comfort or discomfort with uncertainty and their engagement in behaviors that demonstrate varying levels of avoidance. Russia has extremely high uncertainty avoidance, while India has relatively modest uncertainty avoidance. Coke recently created the "Make a Friend" campaign in India. Using touch screen technology the campaign allowed consumers in India and Pakistan, long hostile neighbors, to see each other in real time and connect—touch hands (via a screen) and send drawn messages to each other— all through a Coke dispenser. It worked fantastically because of India's modest uncertainty avoidance. It also made Coke appear as the purveyor of global goodwill by sharing happiness. It likely would not work between Russia and Ukraine.

- **Long- versus short-term orientation** refers to people's patience and their orientation to long-term gain versus cultural impatience and desire for quick results. South Korea has an extremely long-term orientation, while Brazil has a relatively short-term orientation. Korean Air is known for its focus on a luxury experience. It spends huge amounts of money to own the languid, time-bound imagery that supports this message. When was the last time you heard of a Brazilian airline? If you did it was likely a low-cost airline like Azul, whisking you quickly away, providing quick results.

- **Indulgence** refers to cultural norms around indulging children or loved ones rather than a stricter, more restrained emotional orientation. China is a low-indulgence country, while Nigeria is a very high-indulgence country. An assessment of food advertising across both countries quickly demonstrates this. Advertising imagery in Nigeria has much more focus on affectionate human interactions, while imagery in China is focused on the food itself. Indulgence versus restraint is clearly visible.

In a competitive marketplace the emphasis must be on context, but it must also be culturally relevant. Reflecting the points we have discussed above, Shankar Gupta-Harrison, vice president of 360i, suggests four ways to be sure your content has globally relevant context. First, never forget the importance of knowing whether you are engaging an individualist or a collectivist culture.

Second, consider whether your brand lives in a being or doing culture. Third, understand the importance of high and low context when it comes to choosing your communication styles. Finally, know the level of uncertainty your market can bear, and don't step beyond it.[7]

Global Growth

Looking at four main geographic regions for global branding—North America, Europe, Asia, and Latin America—we can see what brands are thriving. We can also see that technology is driving growth. In North America four of the top ten brands are in technology. Google and Apple are numbers one and two, with Microsoft, AT&T, and Amazon not far behind. Coca-Cola and McDonald's, despite some recent struggles, are also among the top ten, reflecting their global retail prowess.[8] In Europe, technology was also strong, with Spanish Movistar, Deutsche Telekom, and Vodafone leading the way. However, increasing consumer confidence in Europe also spurred luxury brands, like the French brands Louis Vuitton and Hermès, into the top ten. IKEA, though not a luxury brand, also benefited from renewed consumer confidence. Bank brands also did well, reflecting the rebounding European economy.[9] In Asia, technology and banking dominate the top ten. Tencent, a media and mobile holding company, and Baidu, the Chinese equivalent of Facebook, topped the list. South Korea's Samsung was not far behind. India's Axis Bank and the Agricultural Bank of China are key players in the top ten. Automaker Toyota also garnered a spot, reflecting growth in global distribution chains.[10] Finally, South America had slower growth than the other regions. However, Mexico and Brazil led the way in this region and remain strong. At the top are three technology brands, confirming the global technology trend. Also in the top ten South American brands were three beer brands, which reflect cultural norms as well as the growth in global distribution chains.[11] Now that you have a flavor of the landscape (as if one chapter is sufficient to discuss the entire globe) we turn our attention to emerging markets. Jump on board as we visit the emerging BRIC and MIST nations.

The BRIC nations—Brazil, Russia, India, and China—remain the focus of global growth. However, today the MIST nations—Mexico, Indonesia, South Korea, and Turkey—represent an emerging new breed of consumers. Together these eight nations represent the bulk of where advertising dollars will continue to flow. Let's follow the money and take a look at the drivers of change within these nations.

> *"The other thing is we don't believe in digital marketing. We believe in marketing in a digital world."*[12]
>
> Clive Sirkin,
> senior marketing officer,
> Kimberly-Clark, Neenah, Wisconsin

©Coca Cola; ©Base Batteries

Talk about the intersection of high and low context. This Base batteries campaign expresses the power of backup systems with high-context cultural perfection. Wife can replace husband, son can replace mother, or son can replace father—but only if you have a backup (Base batteries), and only if you understand Indian culture and politics. At the same time, the Coca-Cola backdrop expresses the simplicity of messages from low-context cultures.

BRIC Nations

Brazil

When it comes to big spending power, Brazil is a key player. It is the sixth largest economy in the world and the fastest growing of the BRIC nations, with a thriving middle class.[13] Brazilians are known for their passion for life, which is framed by music, food, and sports. But don't think that sports trump all. When it comes to media consumption soap operas trump sports.[14] From a marketing perspective three things stand out in Brazilian culture. First, Brazilians are creative and live in a culturally flexible and open society. Second, as Brazil grows into a world economic power, professionalism is imperative, and trusted relationships are the bedrock of professionalism. Third, Brazilians love social media, and marketers have quickly learned that in the social world, Brazilians blur professional and personal relationship.[15] Traditionally, Brazil has faced inward when it comes to marketing. That's rapidly changing as Brazilian brands like Natura cosmetics and Petrobras Oil are looking externally, while global brands from Adidas to Dove are seeking deeper Brazilian integration. For Adidas the 2014 FIFA World Cup provided that moment of integration for many global brands.[16] And with the 2016 Summer Olympics arriving on the heels of the World Cup, Brazil's economy will only keep booming.[17] It's been said that if "you would like to inspire rapture in Brazil, weave the 'beautiful game' (soccer) into your pitch. Incorporate the spirit of the *joga bonito* (beautiful play) in your ads."[18] Brazilians, long known for their admiration of all forms of beauty, are also huge consumers of cosmetics. With the Amazon in Brazil's backyard, an organic cosmetics brand fits perfectly, and with sustainability at the heart of global trends, Natura is poised to be a global category leader.[19] Though Brazil may be a more transparent, low-context culture, Brazilians tend toward searching out people and brands that feel "simpatico" and which they believe understand and respect them.[20] Considering the imperative nature of cultural respect and social integration, it is not a surprise that outdoor advertising has been banned in Rio de Janeiro. This duality is something advertisers must embrace if they wish to be successful in Brazil.

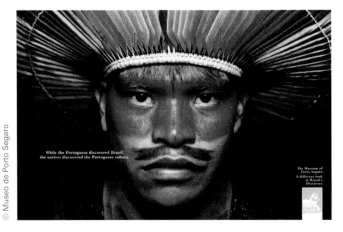

Cosmetics are big business in Brazil. Here's a different approach from the Museum of Porto Seguro.

Brazilian ads frequently reflect their joy of living often while celebrating music. Sony created a series of beautifully illustrated ads promoting car stereos that made drivers feel as if they were at a private concert.

Russia

This enormous country leads the BRIC nations in gross domestic product and has an emerging middle class. It far outstrips its fellow BRIC nations in sales growth, with a 57% average. (Its closest BRIC competitor is India at 38%.[21]) However, recent political events have begun to squeeze the Russian economy. Russian politics has been known to negatively affect foreign brands. For instance, when the Dutch led an investigation into the downing of Malaysian Airlines Flight 17 over Ukraine, Dutch flowers were burned.

Новый уровень эмоций.
BMW 5 серии в новом воплощении.

BMW 5 серии — от 40 000 евро.

Место для адреса дилера

©BMW

This upscale BMW ad appeals to the new Russian upper class, and those who aspire to join it. The headline: "A new level of emotion." Instead of the "Ultimate Driving Machine" used in North America, the Russian tagline translates as "with pleasure at the wheel."

When Russia wants to remind the United States that it has the upper hand, it bans certain California wines.[22] Adding to the pressure, the government recently banned advertising on cable and satellite stations, which will likely reduce overall foreign advertising investment, though online spending is predicted to remain strong.[23] Despite bumps in the road, the Russian economy continues to grow, driven by technology and innovation. That has brought brands like American Microsoft and Finnish Nokia into the Russian market in a big way.[24] The luxury sector is also booming as Russian wealth, particularly among those with political connections, grows. Brands like French Louis Vuitton and Italian Gucci are hot. Russian consumers tend to look to global brands over national brands. Thus, it was no surprise to see brands flock to Sochi for the 2014 Winter Olympics. At the same time, Russia brings its big and bold history with it into the present. For Russians, size matters. They appreciate brand names, big firms, and large-scale promotions.[25] The key insights on Russia are fourfold. First, focus on the growing urban middle class. Second, remember that mobile and social are key consumer entry points. Third, with over 170 ethnic groups across Russia, segmenting and cultural competency are imperative. Finally, tradition runs deep in the veins of Russians; leverage it.[26] These confounding trends strongly suggest that Russia is a mix of high and low cultural markers. The high-context markers are vestiges of the Soviet era, and the low-context markers signify Russia's growing prominence in the global marketplace.

India

With a rapidly expanding middle class, India is on the move with banking and technology leading the way. India has 22 official languages (and hundreds of nonofficial ones) and 35 distinct states. Though Hindi and English, a vestige of colonialism, are the official languages, other local languages have high emotional resonance for those who speak them. India is also a country that has historically thrived on mom-and-pop stores called "kiranas." Thus, Western-style retailing, with the rise of hypermarkets, is having a difficult time finding roots in India.[27] Combine this with the fact that digital and mobile technology are shaping India's future, and we are likely to see an entirely different way of doing retail, something marketers are calling second-wave retailing. Pop-up stores are also huge in India, with brands as divergent as Toys "R" Us to Hermès participating.[28] In India, localization will be the key to success. Reflecting this, television advertising is switching from English to Hindi, to better appeal to customers' impulses and emotions.[29] While India's entry into the global marketplace is fraught with economic and cultural dissonance, don't think for a minute that its consumers are not interested in participating in the global economy.

SHOES•CLOTHES•ACCESSORIES•MOBILE PHONES•CAMERAS•JEWELLERY•BAGS•WATCHES AND MORE!

With consumerism growing in India, Yebhi.com, an online shopping mall, uses visuals to marry traditional shopping with postmodern retailing and technology as the matchmaker. Yebhi is giving Amazon a run for its money in India.

The core message of Oreo—twist, dip, and enjoy—took a bit of explaining. Fifty years after its introduction, Oreo is a beloved brand, especially among children. The tagline reads, "Time for fun, friendship, and closeness. Only with Oreo."

Add to this the fact that India has the largest film entertainment industry on the globe—Bollywood, and it's booming. For instance, the Spanish tourism authority tapped Bollywood to create a movie featuring Indian stars Flamenco dancing across Spain. It was so successful that Indian tourism in Spain jumped 65%.[30] While Indians love their movies, they also are highly engaged with social media, and mobile drives that engagement. Surprisingly, newspapers remain a thriving media touchpoint in India.[31] So, it seems that India is a study in contrasts. Yet at its core, India is a high-context culture with a huge power distance orientation. This suggests that respect should be central to all advertising messaging. However, there will be significant challenges to interpret the nuances of respect across a country with 22 languages.

China

Let's put this very high-context culture in perspective. Five years ago China surpassed Germany, a very low-context culture, to become the third largest ad market in the world.[32] China also has the largest Internet market in the world, with the highest penetration of outdoor digital displays on the planet.[33] Certainly, many Western online media channels are closed within China. To date Google, Facebook, and Twitter are not available in China, but that hasn't slowed China's online transformation. Just check out Renren, the Chinese Facebook and you'll see how socially savvy the Chinese are. While media constraints limit advertising accessibility in China, these constraints do not appear to have dampened Chinese passion for social media. Big brands like Procter & Gamble, Coca-Cola, and General Motors are flooding into China, and tapping into social media along the way. To put this in context, Procter & Gamble spends 71% of its ad dollars outside the United States; China garnered the biggest chunk of that money.[34] In this booming marketplace, imported luxury brands from French wines to Italian Gucci bags are flying out of stores, often driven home in American Buicks. To support this booming economic growth, the banking, insurance, and telecom sectors are surging. Looking at ad revenues, China's roaring economy, and consumers' penchant for status brands,

Courtesy of Christina Semak

The first thing I ever wrote, and I mean wrote in a creative way, I didn't actually write. At three years old, I sat on the toilet in my grandparents' apartment in Moscow, Russia, in the middle of winter. And, as many people have some of their most brilliant revelations while sitting on the toilet, I too suddenly had a thought. I sat there and said out loud a poem that I had just made up on the spot.

It was something about the night being dark and the snow being cold. Deep stuff. My grandma overheard me and enjoys telling me this anecdote every once in a while. It's a funny reminder that I've loved making up stories since my baby years.

Twenty-three years later, I'm lucky enough to have a creative job as a copywriter. Every day I get to come up with new ideas about how to say something in the most compelling way possible. I'm pretty happy that I've carved out a path in life that has led to making a living doing something I've always loved doing. It makes the whole being an adult and having a job thing a lot more fun.

Don't get me wrong. It's not easy. Lots of late nights and plenty of self-doubt make this job challenging, but when I find myself in a meeting about a campaign that involves Kenny G playing smooth jazz, I smile. It's worth it.

Working in advertising has also sparked other creative outlets for me that I don't think I would have ever discovered, or even had the courage to pursue. About two years ago I started doing stand-up comedy. And again, lots of late nights and even more self-doubt often make me wonder what I'm doing at an open mic in a bar on a Tuesday night with an audience of two barely awake people. Then, when I get up on stage in a real show at a comedy club and make a connection with the audience about why Hanes are the sexiest underwear, I smile. It's worth it.

Christina Semak, copywriter, 180LA

www.christinasemak.com

it's hard to imagine that this market is anything but capitalist. There are three key drivers in China's booming economy. First, speed is everything. Second, China wants to feel like Europe. Finally, despite China's digital focus, advertisers must think locally.[35] China is the quintessential collectivist country, with significant power distance and a very long-term orientation. Any savvy advertiser knows that the key to advertising messaging in China is a subtle balancing of cultural emotions and political correctness—and we mean that literally. To understand China you "need to leave your rulebook at the door."[36]

The BRIC nations are powerful brokers in the global economy. They represent huge global populations with consumers who are eager to spend their growing disposable incomes on global brands. Over the past 25 years, advertising in the BRIC and MIST nations has steadily grown, while, relatively speaking, advertising spending in the United States has slowed. In China, and the overall Asia Pacific region, advertising spending has more than tripled.

In Latin America, where Brazil is the giant spender, advertising spending has grown nearly 10-fold. In Central Europe, with Russia as the hub, advertising spending went from almost zero to a 25-fold increase.[37] Multinational brand managers who follow the money head directly to the BRIC nations. However, more and more of them are now considering the emerging MIST nations. Consumer spending trends tell us that you had better know more than a little about the global marketplace when you enter the job market. With that in mind, let's check out the MIST marketplace.

MIST Nations

Mexico

Mexico leads the way in growth among Spanish-speaking countries in the Americas, though it has slowed a bit in recent years. Consumers in Mexico have a rich supply of global brands.
At the same time, Mexico is the production hub for the two biggest Spanish-language television stations, which broadcast across Central and North America. It is not surprising that nearly half of Mexican households have access to subscription television.[38] Add to that the fact that Mexicans use cell phones much like Hispanic Americans, leading mobile to outpace computers as the primary entry point into the digital world. That opens up enormous mobile pathways to connect with Mexican consumers. Culturally, Mexicans prefer straightforward brand promises, which help them "maintain appearances" among peers.[39] Mexicans tend to look for affordable options and rarely embrace the hunt for radical brands.[40] However, one thing advertisers can count on is a blatant lack of political correctness among Mexican consumers, who are quick to leverage stereotypes for a quick laugh. When it comes to buying habits, especially for big-ticket items, Mexicans, true to their collectivist culture, are collaborative in their decision-making process.[41] Many Mexicans still live in multigenerational homes, where brand loyalty tends to trickle down the generational line. However, if you want to build brand loyalty among young Mexican consumers, the so-called NiNis (Neither-Nors), you'd better understand their longing for heroes. In fact, "when asked for a famous person they most admired Mexican youth chose Gandhi."[42] That choice ought to give you a sense of how global the world is becoming. Mexico is a fairly low-context country with a huge passion of indulging those they love. It is also a country that is looking toward the future.

While Mexicans embrace most global brands from north of the border, they have many unique products, such as Chipiletas, a spicy and sweet candy. This commercial, featuring curious ants, reflects the irreverent sense of humor found in much of Mexican advertising.

©Chipileta

With free trade between the United States and Mexico, consumers browsing the aisles of Costco in suburban Mexico City will likely see the same brands you see at your local Costco. And aspirational brands like Nike and Gatorade have gained huge traction in Mexico.

Indonesia

When you talk about advertising potential in Indonesia, you can't help but talk about digital. Indonesia has the second biggest Facebook population in the world. It is probably also the most Twitter-obsessed nation on the planet.[43] As in Mexico, computer penetration is low in Indonesia, while mobile penetration is gigantic—six times the penetration of computers. Advertisers are following consumers' lead. Online ad spending has grown more than 200% in the past few years. Social media accessed via mobile spurred spending, grabbing a giant slice, 80%, of overall consumer spending.[45] There are four key points to consider when tapping into Indonesia. First, Indonesia is rapidly urbanizing population. Second, five cities will prove to be the central consumption hubs. Third, retail is booming at the same time that the sector remains fragmented. Finally, while Indonesians prefer local brands, the population under 30, which makes up 60% of the population, is driving a change in this preference.[46] While traditional advertising is not dead, this is a very, very digitally savvy country. Indonesia is a high-context Muslim culture, which places strong emphasis on family and the communal experiences that surround family life. So it's not surprising that broadcast channels are highly regulated in this conservative, high–power distance country. Needless to say, branded messages in Indonesia will be well vetted. Thus, advertisers tend to seek nontraditional ways of creating conversations, as a way of injecting fresh interest in brands, and circumventing regulation. This approach works well for reaching the booming under-30 demographic, who are super tech savvy, married to mobile, and a bit less conservative.

"The leadership [needs] to move the center of gravity of the company ... where babies are being born, where the new households are being formed.[44]

Bob McDonald,
chairman, CEO, Procter & Gamble,
Cincinnati, Ohio

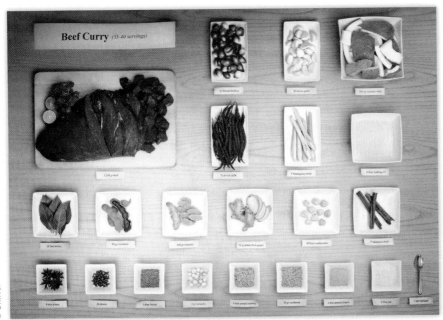

© Unilver

Unilever's Sunlight dishwashing liquid leverages cultural knowledge to send home its message. Beautifully. One tablespoon of Sunlight dishwashing liquid is enough for 40 servings. Period.

South Korea

South Korea is a high-context culture, deeply influenced by Confucian values, which stress collectivism and social harmony. South Koreans rarely show emotion in public, yet the younger generation is changing that. They tend to be more demonstrative, though still in culturally appropriate ways. Koreans are a paradoxical we/me culture. The group comes first, but individual expression is still vital to some social interactions. Thus, once a brand finds inroads into a group its popularity will rise quickly. This is particularly true for luxury brands, which have huge appeal in Asia generally. Japan and China lead the luxury category, but South Korea is close behind.[47] For South Korean consumers who cannot afford luxury brands, nonluxury retail brands have become a haven for aspirational purchases and social interaction. International brands like Zara, Uniqlo, and H&M are booming.[48] Koreans, particularity Millennials, are huge fans of entertainment television, social media, and fashion, with K-pop as the biggest cultural influence. South Koreans are avid multitaskers, with a passion for living a highly e-commerce-driven life. Brands that integrate themselves into the social world of South Koreans will fare best, reaping the biggest reward, as South Korea is one of the most digitally savvy countries on earth. Of all the Asian countries discussed, South Korea has the most long-term orientation, which means that brands that understand and leverage South Korea's link to the past will fare best in the present.

Turkey

Imagine consumer confidence ratings never going below 90%.[49] Welcome to Turkey. In this booming economy, malls are the number one hangout spot among Turkish youth.[50] Western-style shopping malls reflect cultural norms embedded in the Turkish tradition of open-air markets, but malls also represent a connection with the new Western economy. Turks, like the rest of their BRIC and MIST neighbors, are avid users of technology, with nearly half expressing the belief that staying up to date with technology is essential to life.[51] However, while technology is one of the top three most important issues for Turks, the other two might surprise you. They are religion and politics. This is, in part, because Turkey represents a mix of high and low cultural contexts. It is the high-context aspect that most likely keeps things a bit more reserved. But the spirited low-context aspect of Turkish life is driving modern consumption habits. Still, these habits are paired with Turkish cultural values that prioritize authenticity and honesty.[52]

Turkey is the bridge between East and West, as well as between modern secularism and fundamentalist Islam. This is one from a series of ads for Turkish Airlines that presents some common stereotypes of American culture as seen through Turkish eyes. They even threw in a Canadian Mountie for good measure.

If you think back across history you will recall that the Silk Road cut through Turkey, and it became a crossroads for trade. The sense of being at the hub of global movements and trade remains. Like Mexico, most of Turkey is young, with more than 50% under 30.[53] Today these young Turks use the digital landscape as their means of moshing cultures. Also like Mexico, Turkish consumers are very price sensitive. Thus, brands that are perceived as authentic, while providing good value, will be well received. Finally, the history of advertising in Turkey is not deep, so there is still a passion for more traditional media forms, such as television, newspaper, and out-of-home. But with youthful Turks driving new trends, mobile and social are paying a bigger and bigger role.[54] The bottom line: woo Turkish consumers with authenticity.

> "Culture matters. Countries similar economically are not necessarily similar in their consumption behavior, media usage, and availability patterns."[55]
>
> Marieke de Mooij, global marketing consultant, author, Amsterdam, Netherlands

Global Survival

Whether BRIC or MIST, African or Arab, American or Asian, moving brands into new markets takes a considered and culturally driven approach. Every year Millward Brown releases its *BrandZ Top 100 Most Valuable Global Brands*. This report helps global marketers understand the trends that are driving global change. *BrandZ* is one of the industry's most valued assessment tools for global branding. Here are *BrandZ's* top ten takeaways for global branding[56]:

1. **Know each customer:** Use data to truly understand each consumer and identity key events and opportunities to connect with them.

2. **Be meaningfully different:** Establish meaningful differences between your brand and your competitive set. Meaningful difference will build brand equity.

3. **Be mindfully present:** Be discreetly present, appropriate, and authentic, especially in the social media. This will help your brand stand out in the noisy media world.

4. **Be agile:** Planning is essential, and improvising in today's marketplace won't work. However, planning and flexibility must be wedded. Rigidity will doom your brand.

5. **Stay relevant:** Respect the tension between your brand's heritage and staying up to date with current trends. Make your brand's story relevant. That means fact, not fiction.

6. **Keep your eyes open:** Knowledge is power, which means you must be open to the consumer world around you, being ready to step in and invent change. Become a thought leader.

7. **Execute:** The global economy has come back. The time for putting plans on hold is over. Consumers are ready to spend. Brands must be ready to engage with them.

8. **Stand for purpose beyond profit:** Consumers, especially Millennials, are hungry for transparent, responsible brands that provide something relevant and good.

9. **Invest in brands:** There can be quantifiable ROI in brands. Since *BrandZ's* top 100 brands report was launched, eight years ago, brands in the Strong Brand Portfolios have seen an 81.1% appreciation.

10. **Employ technology for competitive advantage:** Technology can be a driver of global growth, a disrupter, or both. Don't risk your brand's competitive edge by ignoring technological opportunities.

Long before Starbucks went to China, two shoe salesmen traveled to an undeveloped part of the world looking for new business, or so the story goes. Salesman #1 returned to the U.S. headquarters with terrible news: "It's hopeless, no one over there wears shoes! We'll never sell them a thing." Later, when Salesman #2 hit town, he raced from the airport, double-parked out front, charged through the lobby, ran upstairs past the CEO's secretary, and jumped on top of the desk. "Paydirt! Every one of them needs our shoes," he shouted.

Starbucks and Salesman #2 have a lot in common. When Starbucks entered China in the late 1990s, coffee was an unknown there. Not only was there minimal awareness and virtually no demand, a competitive beverage, tea, had been entrenched for centuries with as close to 100% penetration as imaginable. But Starbucks had a plan.

Consistent with the fundamental branding mantra from Ries and Trout, "The essence of positioning is sacrifice," Starbucks carefully considered the Chinese mind-set and the food and beverage landscape before adopting a disciplined approach toward which aspects of its brand to leverage in China, when to leverage them, and what to leave out.

"We have to be thoughtful, highly disciplined and extremely respectful of local Chinese customs, food preferences and consumer behavior. In order to do that, we have to see the world through a Chinese lens," said Starbucks CEO Howard Schultz.

Starbucks arrived in China as the economy was opening and consumers were becoming more open minded and accepting of new products and experiences. China was urbanizing, and the middle class was rapidly expanding and becoming more worldly in its outlook and tastes.

As Starbucks began opening coffee shops the drink menu was a key decision point. Although even a simple cup of coffee was a novelty, Starbucks chose to launch its full selection of lattes, Frappuccinos, and so on, in China. That's partly due to the Starbucks brand being about choice and a diversity of quality coffee options. Even though it took time for much momentum to build across the drink menu, Starbucks outlets in China stocked every alternative. In addition to brand rationale, Starbucks also needed to defend against potential competitors in China who might launch products that were already on its U.S. menu.

The food menu was a different consideration entirely. Since the Chinese food palate is unique, Starbucks focused on its core coffee offerings and limited its food menu. Food options grew slowly as Starbucks became more familiar with Chinese tastes. Also missing were music CDs, the wide selection of coffee accessories and Starbucks merchandise, and Starbucks drinks and ice cream in grocery stores.

While working with Starbucks to open stores in new markets across China, media education and increasing awareness of coffee and the Starbucks brand were among the challenges. Local reporters who may have never tried coffee often didn't see any reason for it to be in their city. Since seeing and tasting are believing, we organized coffee seminars for media conducted by Chinese baristas, and Starbucks executives, including Howard Schultz, held press conferences to discuss the virtues of coffee and the company.

Today, the Starbucks brand, if not its signature coffee drinks, is on the lips of hundreds of millions of Chinese consumers. Starbucks has a footprint of more than 1,400 outlets in about 70 cities throughout China. Its food menu has expanded, bottled branded drinks are for sale off premises, and the company has broadened its corporate sustainability and employee engagement initiatives to more closely resemble programs in the United States. Throughout its expansion, Starbucks developed its brand by maintaining a disciplined approach regarding which elements of its brand to leverage.[57]

Matt Wisla, former vice president, Fleishman Hillard-Beijing; current adjunct faculty, Marquette University

Strategies for Success

Reaching consumers with resonance is at the heart of what advertisers must do as they attempt to move brands across the globe. So let's take a moment to contextualize this in terms of culture and its impact on branding across the world. In the advertising industry, we often talk about two overarching approaches: globalized and standardized.

Globalized Approaches

These tend to parallel the global geographic category, and take the view that consistent branding supersedes cultural differences. However, that is not to say that culture is not a concern. It is. For brands using a globalized approach the focus is to cultivate the brand without a huge emphasis on local culture. Brands using this approach promote a globalized Western cultural point of view. Global strategies offer brands the opportunity to maintain a highly consistent brand image throughout the world. Another appeal is that the globalized approach is much easier for brand managers when it comes to controlling all aspects of brand messaging and brand life. This approach, as common as it is, is fraught with gaps in cultural connectedness. Yet it is a favorite among Western global brand managers.[58]

©Young & Rubicam, Lima

Brand Perú wanted Americans to see it as a good trading partner, a secure place for foreign investment, and a great tourist destination. What better strategy than to come to Perú — Peru, Nebraska! Young & Rubicam, Lima, created a 15-minute television documentary merging the two cultures. Strategic, smart, and sometimes hilarious. It's just about perfect.

Standardized Approaches

On the other hand, standardized approaches suggest branding consistency, while offering flexibility. These approaches parallel the international geographic category, discussed previously. Brands in this category also have a big footprint. However, while maintaining some branding consistency, they strategically change their messaging to adapt to local cultural variance. Standardized approaches tend to create advertising messages that are more culturally resonant. When advertising a global brand, you can't afford to ignore the multitude of cultural possible pitfalls.

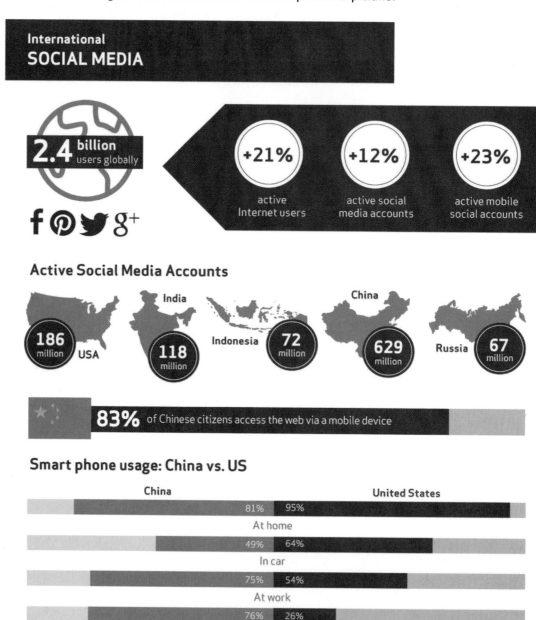

International
SOCIAL MEDIA

2.4 billion users globally

f 𝓟 🐦 g+

+21% active Internet users

+12% active social media accounts

+23% active mobile social accounts

Active Social Media Accounts

186 million USA

India
118 million

Indonesia
72 million

China
629 million

Russia
67 million

83% of Chinese citizens access the web via a mobile device

Smart phone usage: China vs. US

	China	United States
At home	81%	95%
In car	49%	64%
At work	75%	54%
While on public transportation	76%	26%

Source: We Are Social, January 2015; Tech in Asia, July 2014; GfK Media & Entertainment, August 2014

Whether you choose a globalized or a standardized approach, always be a forward-thinking global corporate citizen. What approach will help your brand sustainably return strong ROI?

While globalized and standardized approaches are the foundation, Table 5.1 will help think about how you might craft your creative strategy in a more nuanced way.

Strategy in Action

Let's end with a few examples of international advertising that has moved the needle. This time we looked for examples outside the BRIC and MIST nations. As you'll see from the four we chose, none of them feels like advertising as we once knew it.

©McDonald's

This outdoor board for McDonald's says—without a single word—that the brand understands and respects Muslims' religious practices, specifically fasting during Ramadan. With a wink and a nod the ad invites them to the restaurant when their fast is over.

Horizontal Strategies	Global	Regional
Positioning	Similar in all markets	Adapted for specific markets
Marketing environment	Similar distribution, price position, product use, legal and cultural conditions	Different types of distribution, varying legal and cultural conditions
Target audience	Similar in each market	Different segments in various markets, localized and highly segmented by income, geography, and social status
Vertical Strategies	**Global**	**Regional**
Creative development	Same slogan, look, and feel in all markets	Variations in themes, appeal, and execution of creative elements tailored to each market
Media selection	Basically the same in all markets with slight variations	Highly localized due to widely variable cultural and technological differences
Marketing communications tools	Same basic strategies and tactics in most markets	Highly variable based on legal, cultural, and technology conditions

Table 5.1   Global/Regional

Japan's Softbank created an offbeat "framily" to promote its cellular service. The popular ad series featured a talking dog as patriarch, a wife who has the *real* power, a daughter played by popular actress Aya Ueto, and a non-Japanese son played by Dante Carver. The campaign baffled most individualistic Western ad experts, but the collectivist Japanese public loved it.

Or maybe it's fair to say that none of them uses media in traditional ways.

- We begin with the work of Swiss agency Jung von Matt/ Limmat, which took the little Swiss village of Obermutten, with fewer than 80 people, and announced it to the world. The promotion set the mayor of the town at the center of the plan, by having him promise to post the photo of anyone who liked the village. With 14,000 Facebook fans from 20 countries and a huge bump in tourism, it's fair to say that this was a success. The success reflects Swiss tendencies toward indulgence and low power distance. So when the campaign took the global concept and local adaptation strategy and turned them on their head, it worked perfectly.[59]

- Argentina's Del Campo Nazca Saatchi & Saatchi helped BHG Electronics move microwaves not by developing a classic advertising campaign, but by developing a brand extension. Rather than the usual microwave that beeps at consumers when it's done, this line of microwaves plays music to announce that food is ready. They sold out immediately.[60] Considering Argentina's high uncertainty avoidance and significant tendency toward indulgence, the success is not a surprise. It is a seamless cultural fit.

- DDB Singapore created a beautiful cross-promotional campaign combining music and fashion. It teamed iTunes with StarHub Music Stores by using RFID tags attached to clothing. When shoppers entered a fitting room, the tag triggered speakers to play a musical track designed to fit the mood of the garment. This was followed by a text sent to the shopper's phone offering a free download. The campaign garnered an 84% click-through rate and boosted paid music downloads by 21%.[61] This perfectly reflects Singapore's extremely low uncertainty avoidance and delight in indulgence.

- Finally, DDB Sweden took a traditional medium, outdoor, and spun it in a very nontraditional direction. They took the global aspect of the Volkswagen brand, its 4Motion (four-wheel drive) feature, and adapted the message for the local Swedish audience. The team created a classic outdoor board featuring a car and plunked it in the middle of a frozen Swedish lake. Then they waited for the ice to melt. Progress was live streamed, and the campaign was supported by TV, print, in-store, and banner ads. By the time the outdoor board sank, sales had risen 38%.[62] Creatives from Wisconsin and Minnesota, as well as Finland and Siberia, take note. Yet this would never have worked without Sweden's orientation toward indulgence and individualism.

Lost in Translation

While the previous four campaigns illustrate home runs, you will never be able to completely avoid missteps. Life happens. However, when trying to adapt a global brand or concept to local markets, do your homework. We close with four examples to illustrate the importance of due diligence.

- The combination of General Electric and Plessey Telecommunications created the initials GPT. Not a problem in most countries, but in France, pronouncing them sounds like *j'ai pété*, which can be translated as "I passed gas."

- When Coca-Cola introduced its brand to China in the 1920s, over 200 characters could have been used to depict words that sounded like *Coca* and *Cola*. So, without a corporate standard, shop owners created their own signs. Shoppers ordering a Coke could ask to "bite the wax tadpole," sip a "wax flattened mare," or enjoy a refreshing "female horse fastened with wax." Coke finally changed the name to something that sounds like "ko-kou-ko-le," which literally means "to allow the mouth to be able to rejoice." In short, *it tastes good*—at least better than a wax tadpole.

- Coke's rival, Pepsi, also had a challenge in Taiwan. Years ago, its international slogan was "Come Alive. It's the Pepsi Generation." Somewhere in translation, the meaning was changed to "Pepsi brings your dead ancestors back to life." Now that's a pretty bold claim.

- Finally, Kraft recently named a new snack food, to be launched in Central Europe, under the new Mondelez brand. The name was a mashup of terms: *monde*, to evoke the idea of "world," and *delez*, to convey "delicious." Kraft claimed it had vetted the new name across 28 languages, including Russian. However, to Russian speakers "Mondelez" sounds like vulgar slang. The new name lasted two days. Day one, it hit the digital world via *Advertising Age*, went viral, and got trashed. Day two, it got pulled.[63] Despite the Russian adjustment, Mondelez remains the overall corporate brand name in Europe.

Goodbye, до свидания, and adiós.

Whatever your strategy, whatever your brand, as the globe grows smaller with technology bringing us closer together, culture context still matters. Perhaps more than ever. Be a wise advertiser. Do your homework. Always consider culture. And remember, your brand is a global citizen. If you do the legwork, you just might find the right strategy, hit the right tone, and discover success in the global marketplace.

WHO'S WHO?

Renata Florio

A Brazilian writer at heart, Renata Florio recently moved to New York as chief creative officer for Wing, Grey Global's Hispanic agency. Florio, from São Paulo, has worked at F/Nazca Saatchi & Saatchi, AlmapBBDO, and DM9DDB, three of Brazil's most creative shops. She has worked extensively with Procter & Gamble over the years and has won eight Cannes Lions for her work in Brazil.[64]

Dao Nguyen

Dao has worked for 18 years in technology, almost all of them at Internet businesses. She is currently BuzzFeed's new publisher. Nguyen was also director of product development for Dow Jones Ventures. She developed a deep understanding of the many aspects of online media—technical, editorial, advertising, marketing—during her tenure at Le Monde Interactif (publisher of lemonde.fr, the largest news website in France), where she was CEO for three years. Nguyen brings her business experience and programming background to excel in what she is most passionate about: developing compelling online products in all industries.[65]

Juan Tan

A native of Malaysia, Juan Tan is creative director at The Brand Union, in China. He splits his time between Beijing and Shanghai and takes the lead on a multitude of Unilever brands. Prior to joining The Brand Union, Tan was creative director at TBWA\TEQUILA\China and TBWA\Creativejuice. There his clients included Chivas, Absolut, Adidas, Häagen-Dazs, and Virgin Mobile. In the summer of 2012, he hosted the first ever Creative Counsel Asia in Shanghai.[66]

Richard Stainer

A 37-year-old triathlete, Richard Stainer grew up near Belfast. Always one to push himself, he told his mother, at age 5, that he would attend Cambridge. He did, earning a degree in modern and medieval languages. Not long ago he was the managing partner at Bartle Bogle Hegarty, heading up the global Google account, the shop's second largest after Unilever. That led to a move to BBH, in New York. Stainer is the perfect example of a truly global advertising executive.

The Happy Child Trust: Advertising in a Non-Western Society

Traditionally, South Pacific culture is very communal. Within this context standard Western advertising practices are not always appropriate. Yet sometimes they might be actually what could help solve a problem.

On the island of Fiji, Sarah Leighton, an Australian businesswoman, created a well-respected private foundation called the Happy Child Trust. The organization's goal is to protect the abused and forgotten children of Fiji. The organization houses, clothes, and feeds disabled and neglected children and also works to get child prostitutes off the street and into school. Happy Child Trust provides a 24-hour safe haven for more than 150 children. But compassion costs money. How does Ms. Leighton raise funds for the Happy Child Trust?

Ms. Leighton would prefer that people donate goods rather than money, in keeping with South Pacific culture. Additionally, she does not want to be seen as someone who exploits children to make money. However, this philosophy limits her ability to promote her organization internationally. In addition, beyond the borders of Fiji, very few people know of the Happy Child Trust.

1 Which Western advertising and integrated marketing communications principles could be used to help the trust?

2 Should Ms. Leighton allow money donations, and how can these donations be taken without sullying the reputation of the Happy Child Trust?

3 What other ways can the Happy Child Trust be advertised internationally while still maintaining the integrity of the organization?

4 What other money-generating activities and promotions could be used to support the Happy Child Trust?

Cristanna Cook, associate professor, Husson University, and visiting professor, University of South Pacific

1. Global Stretching

How far can you take one brand?

- Pick five countries, each from a different geographic area. Then select a brand that does not have a large global footprint.
- Now, generate a list of at least 10 cultural markers for each country.
- Next, find the current tagline and reshape that tagline for each individual country. Explain your rationale for the changes you made or did not make.

2. Cultural Packaging

This exercise will challenge you to think about cultural norms.

- Bring in a consumer packaged good (CPG). As a class, pick one CPG to work with.
- Select one of the BRIC or MIST nations.
- Working in teams, consider the culture of the chosen country, and develop the top three claims you would highlight on the package. Remember the need for these to be crafted in a way that makes cultural sense (language aside), and be ready to defend why you chose your three claims.
- Next, reconsider the packaging. Beside language, what would you change to make the packaging more culturally resonant?
- If you want to extend this beyond the class, jump online and see if you can find the product, or products within the same category, in the country you were working with. Then discuss how close you came to nailing the cultural nuances.

3. Messaging Across Cultures

This time we are challenging you to see how messaging changes across cultures, or doesn't.

- Using the CPGs from the last exercise, pick another one to work with.
- Make a list of countries and put them in a hat. (Each student draws one.)
- Working in teams, brainstorm thumbnails for a print ad and a social media tactic for the country you drew.
- Finally, pick your best ideas, one ad and one social media tactic, and share it with the class. Try to articulate why, from a cultural point of view, your tactics had resonance and why they worked together.
- Once the whole class has shared, look for cultural commonalities across all tactics. That will say a lot about the strength of the brand. Look for variances that will highlight cultural differences.

Review chapter content and study for exams. http://study.sagepub.com/altstiel4e.

- Interactive practice quizzes
- Mobile-friendly eFlashcards
- Carefully selected chapter-by-chapter video and multimedia content

Chapter 6

Concepts and Design
What's the Big Idea?

All creatives need to think visually. Even if the ad is all type, it's still a concept, and there has to be some kind of design that makes it work. It's hard to talk about concepts without bringing in design, so we will cover the process of developing ideas first and then talk about how you can bring them to life. Another way to say it is "ideation" and "the creative process." In this book, we'll define concepting as the development of the Big Idea. If you have a central thought, that One Thing you can say about the product, how do you say it, and how do you show it? Remember this: *concepting is the bridge between strategy and tactics*.

How to Be Creative (Concepting Strategies)

You can find many theories and recommendations on how to be creative. However, it's not a nice, neat, linear process. That killer idea may pop up in the shower. On your morning run. In yoga class. When you're playing a video game. No one can tell you when and how to think it. Concepting a single ad or a whole campaign is like making sausage. The end result can be delicious, but the outside world doesn't want to see how it's done.

While there is no single process that works for everyone, most people rely on two basic methods:

- **Adapt the strategy to the creative:** the objective of this textbook and your academic career.

- **Make the creative fit the strategy:** the approach used for winning awards, portfolio padding, and many class assignments.

Concepting by the Book

Great ideation, leading to great concepts, begins with great strategy and great research. Before you start scribbling, make sure you have the answers to the following questions:

- What is the client's real problem?

- Do I know the target audience?

- Do I know the product's features and benefits?

- What is the One Thing I can say or show about this product?

- Where is this product positioned? Where do we want to be positioned?

- Do I know the competition's strengths and weaknesses?

- What should the tone be?

Depending on the product and target audience, some of the answers to the above questions may be "not applicable." For a mature packaged good, such as deodorant, you really don't need an in-depth analysis. But you do need to understand the target audience and find the right tone to reach them.

"Too many young creative teams today . . . look at pedestrian television and print and say, 'Hey, I could do that crap.' Then they get into the business and they do that crap."[1]

Helayne Spivak,
former global chief creative director, JWT, and head of VCU Brandcenter

Guinness gives their fans credit for having a brain. When the reader connects the dots, the message is much stronger.

Concepting Approaches

As we mentioned, developing creative ideas is not a neat, orderly process. Many texts will provide formulas for concepts, which usually works great to describe a completed ad but don't help develop new ideas leading to new ads. At the risk of falling into the same trap we offer the following approaches to concepting:

Show the Product: It sounds boring, but some of the most innovative ads just show the product or logo. The benefit may be buried in the copy, implied in a tagline, or missing entirely. The main purpose is to establish a brand image or reinforce that image. For example, with most packaged goods, it's probably better to show the package or label rather than describe it in a headline. After all, it's what the consumer sees on the grocery store shelf. Sometimes you can set up a concept in a modified question-and-answer format, where the question (or problem) is stated and the product, package, or logo is the answer (solution).

Show the Benefit: In many cases this involves a straightforward declarative sentence proclaiming the main benefit. Usually the reader does not have to think too hard to get the concept. Sometimes this is the first thing you think of. From here you move on to more creative approaches. However, it may be exactly what's required, especially if you can pair your straightforward headline with a compelling, attention-getting graphic. For a soft drink, for example, you may not have any headline, but you show the can or bottle and people having fun. The benefit is implied—your product is connected with good times.

Show the Alternative: This can be a lot of fun. One extreme example is a campaign for Terminix that shows outrageous ways people keep insects out of their homes—turning the living room into an ice-covered deep freeze, for one. That's a lot more interesting than showing a clean, bug-free house. When you go back to basic wants and needs of the target audience, it becomes easier to visualize the alternative concept.

Any smart phone can take selfies. But this Samsung camera takes self-portraits that please even the most troubled artist.

Rather than stressing the benefits of its own menu, Taco Bell portrayed a routine breakfast at McDonalds as totalitarian oppression. Presumably the proletariat is expected to break free by eating Chicken Biscuit Tacos.

In most cases, you think of the opposite of basic wants and needs—hunger, thirst, embarrassment, loneliness, illness, pain, and so on. You can probably think of several extreme images for each of these that are far more interesting than their positive counterparts.

Comparison: You can compare your product with a competitor's or, by using a metaphor, compare it with just about anything. Competitive and comparison concepts: When you go head to head against the competition, keep these factors in mind:

- If you are the market leader, don't compare yourself with number two.

- When you compare product claims, make sure you are correct.

Here are some tips for comparison advertising:

- Try to make sure that your claims are as factually bulletproof as possible.

- Try to collect hard evidence in advance to support your factual assertions (your lawyer will thank you).

- Consider the risk/reward ratio—how much incremental benefit will you get from making the specific comparison, versus how much additional risk you court by doing so.

- Consider including a footnote with additional factual data, perhaps including (a) the applicable version numbers of the products in question and (b) the date of your data.[3]

Metaphors as Comparison: Since grade school, you've been instructed to use metaphors to spice up your compositions. Use what you know about metaphors and apply them visually to your ad concepts. Visual metaphors can be very direct, such as a grumpy bear morphing into a normal-looking guy after his first cup of coffee in the morning. Or they can be less obvious. Some are very obscure and require a few mental leaps to connect the visual with a product.

Sometimes you don't go head to head with a direct competitor. In this case, they're comparing what you get for 130 calories—a bite of a wrap or a whole bowl of hot hearty soup.

Sometimes readers appreciate the minor challenge of making that connection themselves. They know the advertiser gives them some credit for having a brain.

Testimonials/Case Histories: Years ago celebrities not only allowed products to attach a name to their fame; they actively pitched the products. Today, testimonials, celebrity and otherwise, are still a popular concept. To be effective, they must have credibility—sort of like an editorial feature. As you'll see in Chapter 8, longer copy works best when you tell a story—with a beginning, a middle, and an end. That's a pretty good guide for writing personal case histories.

The Concepting Process

Now comes the fun part. Time is running out. Your assignment is due tomorrow morning. You're still sitting in front of a pile of white paper, and your mind is as blank as the first sheet on the stack.

Say It Straight, Then Say It Great: If you're not blessed with a sudden bolt of creativity, how do you get started? Go back to the brief or the value proposition described in Chapter 2. At least you'll have a base to build your great idea. This is also a great way to test the strategy internally. Work up a number of straightforward concepts that look like ads. Then review them with the account team. The objective is to get the group to say, "Yeah. That's the main idea. Now how do we make it better?" This not only makes for better concepts; it helps build good relationships with your team. Take their input, and then really go to work to do something great.

You may want to start scribbling down product features or other attributes of a product and keep asking, "So what?" Those questions may lead to something that's interesting.

Brainstorming: Here's the recipe for a great concept: Combine two creative people, preferably a writer and an art director; add stacks of blank paper, Sharpies, pencils, and layout pads; mix in copies of *Communication Arts*, and hours of scanning award and portfolio websites; turn up the heat with tight deadlines and client demands; let it simmer or boil over occasionally; if cooking process takes longer, add pizza, junk food, and a long night; allow thoughts to cook until a number of rough ideas develop or one of the creative people has killed the other.

> "If a picture is worth a thousand words, a metaphor is worth a thousand pictures."[4]
>
> Daniel Pink,
> author of *A Whole New Mind*
> and other marketing books

Testimonials can be from highly paid celebrities or ordinary people. In this ad for an ear, nose, and throat clinic, the patient tells a very personal story of regaining his voice after a motorcycle accident.

From our experience, we've found that brainstorming works best with two people. Usually, the dynamic duo is the copywriter–art director team. But it may be two writers or two art directors. Or an art director–illustrator or writer–producer team. Sometimes a third or fourth party gets involved, but it's usually better to bring in those people to validate ideas rather than develop them.

Creating by committee is usually a bad idea, especially if a client is involved in the early process. Sometimes a creative team needs to really rip on the product or brand to get the silliness out of the way. That's hard to do with a client in the same room. It's always better to ask a client, "What do you think of this idea?" instead of "What do you think we should do?" The process often isn't pretty. Most times you really don't want to know how it's done as long as the finished product turns out great.

Five Tips for Better Concepts

Through years of trial and error (more of the latter) we've developed a few recommendations for developing creative ideas.

- **Just do it:** Scribble down everything. Key words. Sketches. Stick people. At this stage, there are no stupid ideas. One key word or visual could trigger an entire award-winning campaign.

- **If you're on a roll, don't stop:** Once the creative juices get flowing, keep tossing out ideas. If you're lucky, you and your partner will get on a streak and not only come up with a killer theme, but enough concepts for a whole campaign.

- **Show it, don't tell it:** One picture may be worth a thousand sales. Find an image that grabs a reader. Then develop a tagline or headline that works in synergy with that image. Just don't describe it.

- **Don't be different just to be different:** To paraphrase Bill Bernbach, don't show a man standing on his head unless the ad sells something to keep things in his pockets. Sometimes an art director will go crazy with backgrounds, weird typography, and other bells and whistles that satisfy his or her creative muse. But if they don't add anything to the concept, don't do it.

- **Keep it simple:** Don't lose sight of the main idea. You've got the concept burned in your brain, but does a casual reader get it? If not, adding subheads to explain the idea or cramming in extra inset photos won't help. Simple ideas break through the clutter and they are easier to remember.

"If an ad campaign is built around a weak idea—I don't give a damn how good the execution is, it's going to fail."[5]

Morris Hite,
account executive and
former CEO, Tracy Locke

Concept Testing—It Starts With You

You should test your concepts at three stages. First, start with yourself. You've narrowed your stack of rough ideas down to a single concept that you love. But before you start asking the creative director for a raise, make sure you do a little internal evaluation of your ideas.

Level 1: Gut check. The first level of testing begins with you. Ask yourself, does this concept feel right? If you have the luxury of time, put it aside for a few days and ask the same question.

Level 2: Two quick tests. The first is the "business card test." Can you put your idea on the back of a business card and still convey the One Thing about your product? Another quick test is the "billboard test." If you have written copy and laid out the ad, cover up the body copy so you only see the headline and main graphic. Would it make a good billboard? If so, your creative idea communicates quickly and effectively. If not, maybe you need to come up with some new ideas.

Level 3: Honest strategic evaluation. Your idea looks good and feels good. But it still has to meet some objectives. Before you fall in love with your idea, ask yourself . . .

- **Is this concept doable?** Can you pull this off within the budget constraints? Can you execute it correctly? Do you have the talent? Props? Locations? All the other things required that make this idea work?

- **Is it on target for this audience?** You love it, but will the intended buyer? You might want to try it out on a few people in the target audience . . . but don't rule it out if not all of them get it.

- **Does it have legs?** Will this idea work in an extended campaign? Is it a one-hit wonder, or can you expand this concept for use in other media?

Level 4: Consumer interplay. Okay, you're confident your idea is on strategy. You're not in love with it, but it feels right. Now the questions are: Will consumers love it—or not? And how will they interact with it? You want consumer interaction; you don't want consumer control. This is your baby.

- **Why will they love it?** Okay, you've tried it out on a few people, so now probe deeper. Why do they love it? What especially resonates with them? How can you take their reactions and extend them?

- **Once they fall in love—or not—what will they do?** This is the deal killer in today's marketing landscape. How will consumers interact with your messages? Will your ads become viral? Are they ripe for parody? Do you have a plan to address possible negative reactions across social media?

Bounce It Off the Creative Director and Account Executive

The creative director and account executive will also quickly run through the self-evaluation process listed above. They will also apply a higher standard of evaluation that includes the following questions:

- Will the client buy it, and if so, will they love it (and the people who sold it to them)?

- Does the work represent the best of this agency?

- Can we win some awards with this?

The Client Is the Final Judge

Clients are fond of telling their agencies to think outside the box. What is this "box" anyway? Typically, clients confine the box to features and benefits. Some engineering-oriented companies think of the box in terms of specifications. Marketing-driven companies think of the box in terms of solving problems for customers. Your box should be much larger. Once you start working within your bigger box, look for ways to step outside of it. It's always better to have a bunch of crazy ideas you can pull back into the box than having the client tell you to be more creative.

Do the Twist

Not to be confused with a dance from the '60s, a twist is an unexpected element of an ad or a commercial. A randy old man's last "little blue pill" falls out the window and ends up in the gas tank of a Fiat, transforming it into a larger, more muscular SUV. A techie husband berates his old-fashioned wife for using paper products for such things as drawing pictures, writing notes, printing emails, and even reading books. When he runs out of toilet paper and asks for help, you guessed it, she slides an iPad under the door with a picture of the roll.

> *"I just see so many wacky creative things that come out of young creatives.... BUT there has to be a link back to the product issue. As David Ogilvy said: We sell or else."*[7]
>
> Maureen Shirreff, senior partner, global executive creative director, Ogilvy Worldwide

Designer sunglasses cost three times more than providing access to water. This twist on a fashion ad also compares the cost of style versus survival. Talk about wants and needs.

"The client will always pick the concept that you like the least, so never present any concepts you don't like."[8]

Robert Fleege,
copywriter, art director,
graphic designer

Finding the Edge

It's starting to become a cliché, but people are still looking for an edge—some kind of creative device to separate their advertising from the rest of the pack. "Edgy" ads take risks. They may push the envelope (another overused term) to the breaking point. In summary, creatives who work on the edge:

- Risk offending the general audience to appeal to the target audience.
- Shock the reader or viewer into noticing.
- Drive a wedge between "our customers" and everyone else (us vs. them).

Never forget the risks of pushing the envelope too far. Before you cross that line, you should review Chapters 2, 3, and 4 and be sure you have the client on your side.

What to Do When You're Stuck

Everybody develops writer's block. Sometimes the slump lasts a few hours; sometimes it lasts a lot longer. Novelists have the option of waiting weeks and months for inspiration. Copywriters don't. So what happens when that blank sheet of paper becomes your worst enemy? We offer the following suggestions:

- **Back up:** Find out where you are, and you might know why you're stuck. Do you understand the product, the market, the target audience, the competition, and the tone? Did you miss something? Do you have enough information to "say it straight"? If so, you are very close to finding ways to "say it great."

- **Find inspiration:** Dive into *Communication Arts* and *CMYK*. Check out new websites that feature award winners. Look at portfolio school sites and see what your competition is doing. Keep up to date with creative blogs, *Adweek*, and *Advertising Age*.

- **Talk about it:** Find a sympathetic ear and state your problem. Don't ask for ideas. Just explain what you know about the assignment and where you're stuck. You might find that by explaining it out loud, you'll find the solution yourself. Sometimes you'll mention an idea that seems kind of lame to you and another person sees a good idea tucked within your lame idea. They might give you just enough encouragement to turn it into a great idea.

- **Take a break:** See a movie. Watch TV. Play basketball. Go for a run. Do something totally unrelated to work. This will unclog your mind and may allow some fresh ideas to sneak in. Taking a break is fine, but don't let it extend to an hour before your assignment is due.

Design: Worth a Thousand Words

Whether your talents lie with the written word or visual expression, you'd better learn how to put your concepts into visually interesting layouts. Copy doesn't exist in a vacuum. You need to marry copy with design in an engaging layout. Here's why:

- Words and visuals do not exist in isolation.

- Design visually expresses the Big Idea and sells the product.

- Good creative should engage the audience visually and verbally.

- Portfolios are important, and presentation matters.

- Multiple skills increase your value.

- Knowledge is power.

This last one deserves a little more discussion, even if you're never going to be a creative. Fine. Now, imagine yourself as an account executive who can speak the language of creative and clearly articulates design concepts to the client. Your creative team will love you and so will the client.

So You Want to Be an Art Director

Great ideas, as we've talked about, emerge from collaboration. That's why brainstorming is so important. It gets your creative juices flowing, but it also helps ideas evolve collaboratively. As an art director, you will have to find ways to visually convey the meaning in your copywriter's headline. You'll have to make body copy engaging and readable. Your layout will have to convey strategy. But above all, you must learn how to attract attention, create interest, and stimulate action. In short, art directors share the same responsibility as copywriters—create work that sells.

Of course, as an art director, you need to understand the basic principles of design and execute them with skill and sensitivity. You should also have a mastery of the latest software. Most of all, you'll need the patience to develop multiple concepts *before* you sit down at the computer. Let's repeat that another way: Ideas come first. Period.

Coming into the industry with software skills is a huge asset, but being an idea person is the key to success. At bigger agencies, art directors are often able to hand their rough concepts off to a production artist, who is adept with software and can quickly interpret the rough sketches of the art directors. Whether your career path takes you to the copy or art side of the creative business, the key is developing and communicating concepts. The key is having great ideas.

Don't Throw Away Your Pencils

We know you'd rather be playing on your computer than reading this textbook. But ideas don't live in computers. Believe it or not, the pencil is a design tool. Design starts in your head, flows onto paper or napkins or backs of folders or inside book covers via your pencil, and is executed using your computer. Remember the order: head, paper, computer. You're the genius, not the computer.

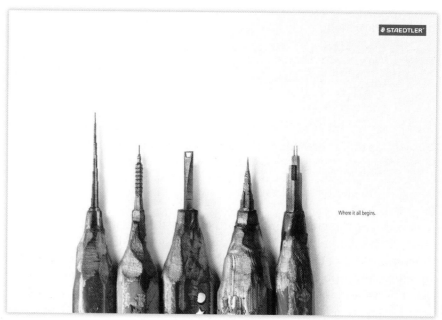

The designs for the greatest buildings in the world started with sketches, probably made with Staedtler drafting pencils. This simple combination shows where it all begins.

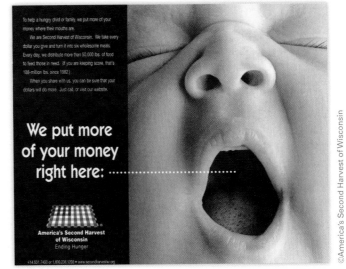

Do your planning on paper; then build it on the computer.

If you're seriously thinking about going into art direction, design, or production, you'll need to be competent with the programs that are the current industry standards. It's likely they are part of the Adobe Creative Cloud, which continually update. Finally we strongly recommend that you don't shop for visuals before you have nailed down your concept.

Basic Design Principles

Artists define design principles in their own way, and with all the blogs and books around, those opinions might seem confusing. It's just matter of perception and preference. We think Robin Williams does a great job defining design principles. Her book, *The Non-Designer's Design Book: Design and Typographic Principles for the Visual Novice*, is terrific. Taking her lead, we're focusing on the following four principles of design[11]:

- Proximity
- Alignment
- Repetition
- Contrast

Before we begin, recognize that the concept of **unity** underpins these four principles. No matter what you are trying to accomplish and no matter how you execute one, or all, of the design principles, how the layout hangs together—unity—is what matters in the final analysis. For copywriters, a good way to think about unity is to consider thematic qualities in writing. You don't change the subject midsentence, so don't change your design theme midlayout. Use each principle consistently throughout your layout. Carry your visual concept all the way through your ad—from top to bottom, left to right, page 1 to page 100, and from the landing page across every linked page.

Proximity: The principle of proximity suggests that you group related elements together based on the space between each element. You can move them physically closer so the related elements are seen as one cohesive group, or you can move them farther apart, suggesting a less important relationship. And how you align them (the next principles) will help the viewer make sense of your visual story.

All the elements have a relationship, and proximity helps viewers understand that relationship. Another way to think about it is this: Think of grouping each design elements while considering the target's needs and wants (emotions) and your strategy. See, you really can use the Creative Brief. If you tap into the target's emotion and find their sweet spot, you've hooked them.

The basic purpose of proximity is to help designers organize the elements of the layout in a way that brings the strategic concept to life. So what are the elements of a layout? They vary, but the basic ones are headline, subhead, body copy, tagline, visual(s), and logo. *Visuals* are the images that support the copy. They are almost always either photographs or illustrations. Avoid using the word *picture*. It tends to connote a photograph, which can confuse people or lock you into an unintended concept.

Alignment: Each element should have a visual connection to another element and flow from a central point. Nothing should be placed arbitrarily. Nothing should hang alone. If your alignment is cohesive, then when you (occasionally) decide to break the alignment it feels intentional. Consider alignment as the design principle that makes you a visual storyteller. Think of how a writer connects one sentence to the next, one paragraph to the next, one chapter to the next. Alignment is all about *making the verbal visual*.

Another way to think about alignment is as a system of organization. Organization is central to this principle. How elements are aligned tells the reader that no matter where an element is placed, it has a relationship to something else on that page. Alignment also guides readers from one element to the next. It allows the art director to be in charge of how readers experience the text.

The two key points to remember with the principle of alignment are visual flow and lines. *Visual flow* refers to how readers' eyes follow the layout, how they flow. The art director is in charge of the visual flow based on strategic objectives. Some novice art directors might start by centering the headline or the visual and everything that follows. That's a center-justified, top-down layout. Top-down layouts tend to be boring, but they can also be perfectly on strategy. Rather than following a formula, it's better to let the strategic message, the Big Idea, guide your alignment. A common visual flow pattern and a good standard for beginners to rely on is the *Z* or backward *S* pattern. In Western cultures, our eyes are trained to begin reading at the upper left and when work their way to the right, just like when we read a book. Then our eyes travel down, moving from upper right to lower left. This classic pattern is the reason you so often see the logo anchoring the lower right corner of a layout. Not to mention, it will be the last thing you see.

Lines are the second key element of alignment, and they are central to visual flow. Lines can be formed by the edges of visuals, the ends of lines of copy, or the lines of copy themselves. Lines can also be created by entire blocks of copy. And, sometimes, lines are just literally lines.

Robin Williams explains how lines work to hold a design together: "In any well-designed piece, you can have a wild collection of odd things with lots of energy."[13] It's the lines that hold it together.

Repetition: Repeating some design element throughout your layout is essential. It might be shape, color, lines, texture, bullets, or a particular font. It can be anything, but it needs to be visually recognizable and strategically relevant. Think of this principle as the principle of consistency. Repetition does not have to be boring. In fact, it can be downright adventurous. Every ad in your campaign should have a visually repetitious theme. Every page in your brochure should repeat similar visual elements. Every screen on your website should have visual familiarity with color, font, and type, if for no other reason than to promote ease of navigation. Repetition is what unifies your brand message.

Two main things to avoid when considering repetition are being annoying and overwhelming the viewer. Chances are if your repeated elements are annoying, they are also overwhelming.

Contrast: The two main points to consider when working with the principle of contrast are optical weight and white or negative space. Optical weight is a huge part of providing contrast. Every element in a layout has optical weight. Thin type seems light to our eyes, and we respond emotionally to that lightness. Conversely, a thick, dark line, or rule, looks and feels emotionally heavy. Optical weight can play a significant role in how viewers respond to the contrasting elements in your layout. Make it a strategic role. White space also has optical weight. It's more than just the unused portion of the layout, and it's more than just the background. In fact, white space isn't even always white. White space is the negative space surrounding elements within the layout, and it provides the backdrop for many other elements of contrast.

> *"In the best work, the visual and the verbal are so complementary that neither would be as strong on their own."*[14]
>
> Helayne Spivak, former global chief creative director, JWT, and head of VCU Brandcenter

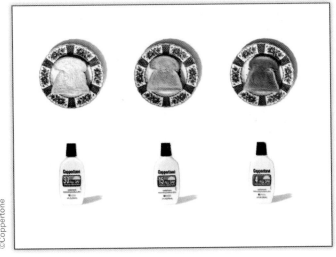

Repetition: This student-designed ad uses a visual metaphor to show the spectrum of Coppertone protection.

©Coppertone

Look closely. Do you see the letter *F* or a bus? This is one of several ads from Fiat to discourage texting and driving.

© Fiat S.p.A.

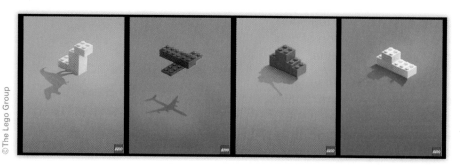

Color and continuity. The simple designs of these Lego ads not only show the power of imagination, they also hold the campaign together.

THE UGLY CARROT

IN A SOUP WHO CARES?

INGLORIOUS fruits&vegetables

by Intermarché

Alignment, contrast, and color: This is a very pretty ad for a really ugly product. The bright orange type and carrot really pop against the white background.

Why use white space? Our eyes sometimes need a rest. White space offers that. It can also frame elements or form a base on which an element can visually rest or float. Use white space to draw attention to a headline, copy block, or visual.

To test the effectiveness of your contrast, consider *mirroring*. Try to reflect the opposite weight, shape, or size in another part of your layout. Once you've mastered how to contrast visual elements and see how their weight balances the overall layout and works strategically, your design skills will improve.

Typography

Like many of the design choices you'll make, the selection of type and color goes a long way toward enhancing awareness and building strategic comprehension. Here are a few basic elements of type.

Serif or sans serif: Serif typefaces have little tails (serifs) at the ends of the strokes. Sans serif fonts do not. Probably the most important thing to remember about serif versus sans serif is that the serifs, like Goudy, tend to make the type appear more flowing and easier to read. Conversely, sans serif type, like Helvetica, tends to be more stiff or edgy and perhaps a bit more dramatic.

Weight: When we speak of the weight of type we mean optical weight, just like when we discussed contrast. One font may be much heavier than another. That is, the strokes are much more substantive, making each letter visually heavier. The weight of Arial Narrow is much lighter than the weight of Arial Black.

Size: In the graphics world, *point size* refers to the height of type. Interestingly, many styles of type vary slightly in height even if the point size is the same. The main objective is to go beyond legibility and make your copy inviting to read.

Honor your margins: We suggest half-inch margins. We also suggest that you remember white space. White space will draw your eye in. Don't run your copy edge to edge, because it pulls the reader's eye off the page instead of into the content. Also, don't cram in so much copy that it becomes intimidating to read. If you're designing a magazine ad, copy that runs to the inner edge falls in the gutter, where the magazine is bound. So honoring margins also has a practical as well as a design advantage.

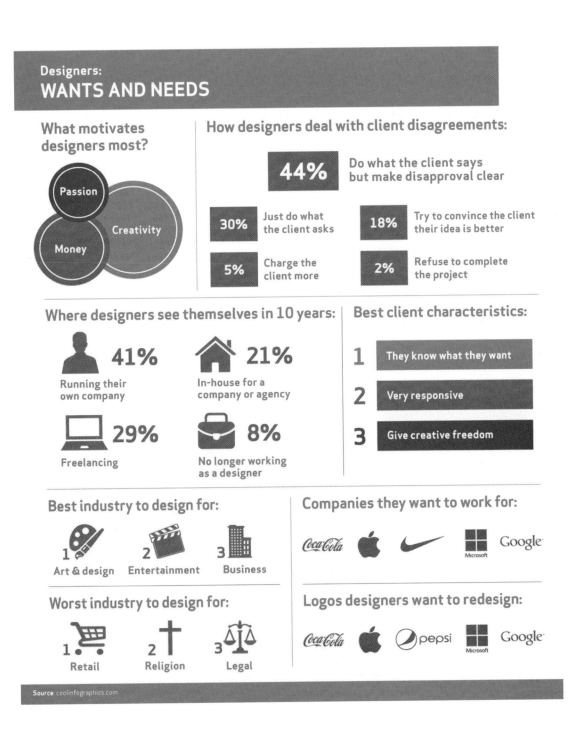

Reverse and overprinting:

Reverse is white or lighter color text over a black or dark background.

Over printing is just the opposite. It simply means the type (usually black) is printed over a lightened (ghosted) image, texture, or tone.

Other type considerations: The space between lines of text is called leading. The amount of leading depends on the size of the font, the volume of text, the desired readability, and the designer's personal preference. For example, some European designers like a lot more leading than some American designers. *Justification* describes how the type is arranged on a line. Most of the time, body copy is left justified, which means the text aligns with the left margin, with no designated alignment for the end of each sentence. See Tables 6.1 and 6.2 for examples of leading and justification.

Matching font and tone: Type plays a big role in creating resonance in the reader. For example, which of the following best matches the image of the brand?

A Diamond Is Forever

A DIAMOND IS FOREVER

A DIAMOND IS FOREVER

12/10	12/16
The lines become more compact.	The lines become farther apart.

Table 6.1   Leading

Center justified simply means the type is centered, with equal distance to each side of the page.

Right justified (as in Arabic and other languages that read right to left) means the type lines up on the right side of the page and is "ragged" on the left side of the page.

Left justified (as in Western literature) means the type lines up on the left side of the page and is "ragged" on the right side of the page.

Justified means that the type is spread evenly across the page, column, or copy block and forms smooth edges both right and left, no matter how many characters there are per line (as you would see in most daily newspaper columns).

Table 6.2   Justification

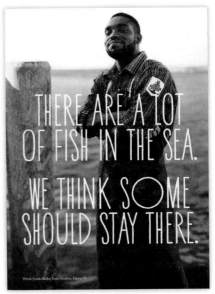

Dodge wanted to celebrate their brand's centennial by bringing back their founders. Their headlines used bold slanted caps to convey an aggressive tone that matched their cars and the attitude of the original Dodge brothers.

Reverse type can be very effective if you keep it legible. Even when overprinted, the large size and font are easy to read.

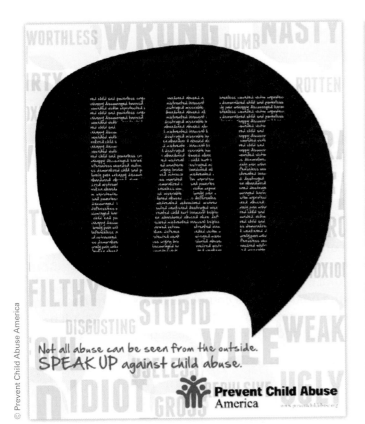

All type ads don't have to be massive blocks of black-on-white copy. This example is from a series of ads that show how words really can hurt children.

Hand-lettered type has to be a delicate balance between creativity and legibility.

The color of large corporations

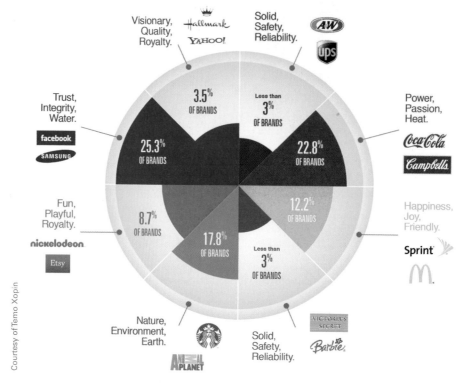

Table 6.3   The Colors of Large Corporations[15]

Color

Starting with the basics, think of colors as primary or secondary, warm or cool, and complementary or contrasting. From a designer's point of view, here are two key points:

- The human eye is most comfortable looking at warm colors.
- Complementary and contrasting colors should work to visually enhance your strategy.

Whether you're using warm or cool colors or engaging complementary or contrasting colors, you also need to keep in mind the social and cultural connotations attached to each color. Just as with words, colors can have multiple meanings. Think of the social and cultural meanings of each color. Then weigh those meanings against the brand, the colors associated with the brand, and its competitors. Also consider your audience's sensibilities when making color choices. Finally, remember that color may be applied to many elements of a layout: type, line, and backgrounds. Visual images too have an expressed color palette.

Make wise strategic choices that you can justify. Here are some questions to help you select color:

- How will color enhance the Big Idea or One Thing?
- Are the color choices in keeping with the strategy?
- Does the color support the brand?
- Will the audience relate positively to the colors?
- What are the cultural connotations of each color choice?

The "Coke side of life" campaign uses all the colors of the rainbow, including red, the color they've owned for over 100 years.

Using spot color can make a big impact, especially when it's so closely associated with the product.

Applying the Basics to Your Design

In a nutshell, design begins with your creative strategy. Work from your brief. Once you have a clear idea about what needs to be conveyed and a darned good idea about how many elements might be in your layout, start sketching or collaging. If you're more comfortable with sketching, draw thumbnails until you run out of paper. Use boxes, squiggles, and blocks to mark where various elements will be placed, as well as to indicate the general proportion of each element. Work freely and generate a lot of loose ideas. Move your boxes, squiggles, and blocks around within the confines of your layout. It you're more hands on, try collaging. The bottom line is that good design takes a lot of work. When you brainstorm a headline, you may create 50 or even 100 ideas. Most of which will be schlock. The same process holds true with layout design. In the process, you'll come to see what works best for your specific project.
One last bit of advice that bears repeating: Don't start shopping for visual images until you've nailed down your Big Idea. This process holds true whether you are designing for print, web, mobile, or an ambient structure. Only a strong design concept will lead to successful design execution.

Selecting Your Visuals

As you'll see in later chapters, certain words in headlines and copy pull in more readers. The same is true with visual elements—in print, in the digital world, or on television. As with "proven" headline words, don't use cliché visual choices just because they've generated results over the past 50 years. Try to find a new approach that gets noticed.

People, Not Things: Given a choice, people like to see other people. It's all about satisfying those wants and needs. Is that person in the ad benefiting from the product? Is that person suffering because he or she is not using the product? Will I look like that handsome or beautiful person in the ad if I use that product? The choice of showing the product or people using the product depends a lot on the product category. For example, showing a medium-long shot of a sexy sports car racing through the night could be the most effective image for that vehicle. But showing a dad with kids and a lot of stuff to carry may be the best image for a minivan.

Illustration Versus Photography: Years ago illustration was much more common. Now with Photoshop, photo manipulation creates amazing effects that were available only with illustration. However, illustration is a valid option for a lot of reasons:

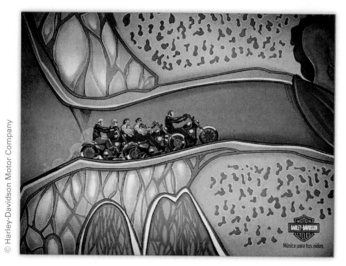

If you're a Harley rider, that distinctive rumble of American iron is music to your ears, as this illustrated ad from the Dominican Republic shows.

- **You can't show it any other way.** Cutaway drawings, blueprints, overlays, ghosted images, and many other graphic treatments are executed as artwork instead of photography and sometimes in combination.

- **You want to create mood.** Illustrations create resonance too. Sometimes you need a painting or drawing to elicit a mood or an emotion you can't get from a photo.

- **Your goal is to have dramatic effect.** Illustration can be used to exaggerate a feature, make a problem look bigger than it really is, or enhance a benefit. These visual overstatements are more accepted as artwork than when using photography.

One simple idea: FedEx delivers your package efficiently anywhere in the world.

A History Lesson With Häagen-Dazs

© Häagen-Dazs

We should always be looking forward. But sometimes you need to step back and consider some classic campaigns that got it right. With seven years of hindsight, this one still stands out.

Some of the most satisfying experiences of my career have come from the most resource-constrained situations. One example: in 2008, feeling the squeeze of big budget cuts and faced with a group of consumers who felt disconnected from the brand, Häagen-Dazs needed a turnaround plan.

It so happened that one of the hot-button issues that year was colony-collapse disorder (CCD). Scientists around the world were trying to figure out why huge numbers of honeybees were mysteriously disappearing.

So we convinced Häagen-Dazs to walk away from conventional advertising and turn their marketing lens toward the unsung workforce responsible for creating their ice cream's all-natural ingredients: the honeybee. For Häagen-Dazs, this was more than just another important environmental issue: Without bees to pollinate the plants and trees making up all-natural ingredients, 40% of the brand's flavors could go away.

For less than a million dollars all in, we launched "HD Loves HB," an integrated campaign focused on bringing the bees back. We kicked it off with a $250,000 grant to Penn State and the University of California, Davis, then created a new ice cream flavor called Vanilla Honey Bee, with all profits going to CCD research.

We launched a website, HDlovesHB.com, which educated consumers about the problem and encouraged them to help. We ran a magazine insert made of seed paper. Consumers could crumple it up, bury it in the ground and grow wildflowers that the honeybees could feed on. To dramatize the plight of the bees, we brought to life the symbiotic relationship between bees and flowers in an epic, operatic television commercial. A series of dance videos brought the problem to the attention of millions of earth-conscious YouTubers. One of the videos was awarded Favorite Website

Awards' Viral Video of the Year. If you look closely, you'll spot Casper Smart (otherwise known as Jennifer Lopez's boy toy) wearing a bee costume and break-dancing to save the bees.

Before long, our efforts paid off. Every major media channel in America picked up the story and helped champion our cause. One week after its launch, the campaign had generated 125 million PR impressions—our goal for the entire year. One Whole Foods grocery store was so inspired by the campaign that they removed every bee-dependent product from their shelves for a day.

In June 2008, Häagen-Dazs, with a coalition of national beekeepers, testified on the bees' behalf on Capitol Hill before Senator Hillary Clinton and a subcommittee of the House Committee on Agriculture.

Going from "We don't have much of a budget for this" to seeing the campaign directly affecting national policy was one of the most rewarding experiences of my life. Not too shabby either: accepting the One Show's first Green Pencil for the campaign from the rapper Ludacris (he was HUGE in 2008, I swear!).[16]

Margaret Johnson, executive creative director, partner, Goodby Silverstein & Partners, San Francisco

Design and Campaign Continuity

The four design elements, along with great copy, tie a campaign together. Lines, type, color, and layout style, in particular, provide a certain look that is carried across a campaign. Pay special attention to logo treatment and taglines. They may have to work with a wide variety of executions across multiple media. It takes discipline to maintain graphic continuity in a long-running campaign, especially when new ads are developed halfway through the campaign's run. This is when you really have to understand how the various elements interact to form a unified theme. Without that understanding, a campaign can visually fail.

Better Print Layouts

Robin Williams offers a simple yet effective approach to nurturing the creative process and developing better print layouts: "See it. Say it. Sketch it."[17]

- **See it**. Start keeping a file, scrapbook, or morgue—in other words, a collection of ads that you like. Learn to file anything that strikes you. Your scrapbook will be a great resource for ideas. Use it before you start concepting. Or when you're stuck. It's bound to trigger some fresh ideas.

- **Say it**. Write down why you like the ads you've selected. What makes them sing? Which of the four design principles are strongest? What made each one stand out? What caught your eye? If you can articulate why you like a certain ad, you are well on the way to defending your own ideas.

- **Sketch it**. Sometimes the most dreadful ads inspire great new ads. Cut schlocky ads apart and rearrange them. Or take a piece of tissue paper and draw over it. Make it better. The point is to put something on paper. You may be tempted to jump on the computer before you have a concept. Don't do it. Scribble something down first. Try some alternatives. When you're happy with your rough sketched idea, then turn on your computer. And if you're allergic to paper or you just won't turn off your computer, be sure that you treat each thumbnail document as a sketch. Don't overwork them and don't fall in love with the first one.

Layout Patterns

There are two common organizational layout systems or patterns: grids and chaotic. Each of these layout systems can be experimented with by using that wonderful design tool—the pencil. But the idea is to quickly rough out four or five thumbnails, sketching in squares or rectangle boxes for copy blocks, squiggles for display copy, and solid block shapes for visuals.

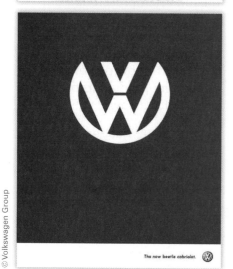

Through the years Volkswagen has produced some very clever illustrated ads.

Armed with boxes, squiggles, and blocks and using either the grid or the chaotic system as a jumping-off point, you'll be on your way.

Grids, also known as Mondrian layouts, are simply a systematic way of dividing up space using geometric patterns, beginning with the basic rectangle, which makes up your page. Grids allow us to see how elements of a layout might be organized. Consider how many elements you have in your layout. That will help you decide how many blocks you'll need to create within your grid.

Don't think of a grid layout as a stack of blocks or a boring "checkerboard" where you have to fill in all the squares. You have a lot more creative latitude. The grid simply provides a system. You use the four principles of design to arrange and rearrange your boxes, squiggles, and blocks. From a practical standpoint, grids are easier to build for print ads, web ads, and websites—which are really a collection of interconnected tables or grids.

Grid design makes it easier to create proper alignment and proportion. This one also provides a lot of opportunity to show the product in use.

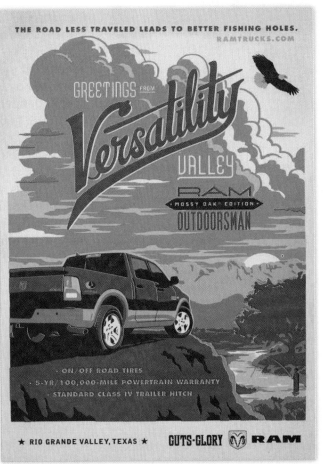

Chaotic design doesn't mean disorganized, as this beautifully illustrated truck ad demonstrates.

Courtesy of Justin Bajan

You're reading this because:

- Your phone is broken, so you can't check Instagram.
- Your annoying teacher said you had to.
- You saw my picture and thought I was hot. Maybe not.

Or maybe, just maybe like me, you're an . . . ad nerd.

It's okay. This is a safe place. I won't tell anyone.

I graduated from the University of South Carolina (Go Cocks!), where I double-majored in advertising and overachievement in advertising. That's a joke. But it's kinda true, because I was in the student advertising club and on the advertising competition team, and I founded, edited, and printed (!) an advertising newsletter. I also hung around the department head's office enough to make her think I was worthy to be entered in the American Advertising Federation's Vance J. Stickell internship program. I had to write an essay and submit some spec work that somehow earned me the gig.

Okay, check Instagram now, or Tinder, or whatever social network will be relevant by the time this is published. Done? Good.

Yeah, so at that internship I was mentored by Luke Sullivan—a superlegendary copywriter who wrote THE book on advertising: *Hey Whipple, Squeeze This*. It was like meeting the Wizard of Oz. Except Oz was GSD&M in Austin, Texas, and the Wizard was a fast-talking, mostly cursing bloke from Minnesota who told me that if I really wanted to be a copywriter, I should attend a portfolio school, like the Creative Circus in Atlanta. Thank you, Morpheus. Wrong movie, but same diff.

Anyways, long story long, I graduated from South Carolina, convinced my soon-to-be wife to get a job in Atlanta so I could siphon funds from her so I could help pay for the Creative Circus, and got my first job a month before graduating from there.

Now I've been in the biz for eight years (what?), I've lived in Boston, L.A., and now Richmond. I've done a Super Bowl spot, helped write a book for the Geico Gecko, and sired a beautiful daughter named Lydia.

Learnings:

- If you want to be a creative: watch, read, listen, play, and experience advertising all the time.
- Get an internship at an agency so you can see how the business really is.
- Go to a portfolio school so you can have a killer book in two years.
- Marry my wife, Becky, who will not only assume your debt, she'll also support you during the highest of the highs and the lowest of the lows this industry throws at you.

Capisce?

Justin Bajan, copywriter, The Martin Agency

@jbajancopymaker

Columns also function much like grids. In fact, sometimes the terms are used interchangeably.

Chaotic layouts, sometimes called circus or field-of-tension layouts, are usually not as crazy as they sound. Generally, the organizing principle that pulls chaotic layouts together is alignment. Thus, the use of lines can bring organization to a chaotic layout. Proximity is another principle that brings order. The seemingly random placement of visuals can be organized, for example, by placing captions nearby or using lines or rules to connect elements or by using repetition to create unity. Use your boxes, squiggles, and blocks to play with the layout. Some chaotic layouts, especially from novice art directors, are just that—a visual train wreck. Unless you have a well-defined design strategy and use some organization principles, we suggest you stick with something simpler.

Digital Design

Templates from Wordpress, GoDaddy, Weebly, Wix, Web.com, and hundreds more take a lot of the guesswork out of web design. But unless you have a strategy and a sense of design, these paint-by-number sites can look like Dumpster fires. After you find a template that works, keep the basic design principles in mind. However, if you are serious about learning web design, do some more homework with online tutorials.

Designing for the Web

Begin by considering a website as a collection of blocks of content, whether they click to another page or scroll down. As with any well-designed document, the four design principles—proximity, alignment, repetition, and contrast—work together to create a unified whole. Of course, you need to consider the gestural motion of touch screens, the utility of fast downloads, and the interplay of sound. But really visual consistency is what makes a website great.

Web guru Nathan Weller notes a few web design trends to watch—at least until the next wave crashes in.

> **Responsive or go home:** It's become the new standard for web design in general and WordPress in particular. With mobile coming to dominate the digital world, you can't ignore the need for responsive design.
>
> **Bigger emphasis on typography:** Most affordable template designs lock you into a handful of web-friendly fonts. But with Google Fonts and other type kits, now budget-minded designers have a lot more flexibility.
>
> **Large, beautiful background images and videos:** One of the simplest ways to make your site stand out is by having great content displayed prominently and beautifully.

With the shift to responsive design for mobile, more desktop sites are using card design and scrolling instead of clicking.

Scrolling over clicking: As the mobile web continues to grow and web design continues to skew in this direction, scrolling will continue to dominate. It's more intuitive, it's easier to do, and it cuts down on load time.

When it comes to choosing fonts, choose wisely and choose simply. Google Fonts provide a wide selection of web-friendly choices. Online, type is most easily read when it is framed within a textbox or table. In general, shorten the length of your copy within each textbox or table. Despite shorter blocks of copy, on the web you can actually provide more information than you can in print. In fact, most people go to the web to find more detailed information. So, when providing more detailed information, simply use shorter blocks of copy, but more of them.

Putting It All Together

If you really want to become an art director or a designer, it's essential that you take design classes, preferably taught by working professionals who deal with real clients every day. Learn the rules and when you can break them. Above all, there is no substitute for experience, even if most of that experience is trial and error. Practice. Practice. Practice.

- **Keep it simple.** Don't add so many elements, styles, and fonts that no one can figure out what you're trying to say. Less is more. Keeping it simple doesn't mean you can only put one element in an ad. It means you need to unify multiple elements into a cohesive design—so the reader is impressed by your idea, not your technique.

- **If you emphasize everything, you emphasize nothing.** A cluttered, confused, truly chaotic layout repels readers. No one wants to take the time to figure out your message. Again, less is more.

WHO'S WHO?

Rei Inamoto

Named in *Creativity Magazine*'s annual "Creativity 50" as well as one of the "Top 25 Most Creative People in Advertising" in *Forbes*, Inamoto is one of the most influential individuals in the marketing and creative industry today. With broad international experience in Asia, Europe, and the United States as well as an unusual combination of background in advertising, design, and technology, he brings a unique perspective to his work. As chief creative officer at AKQA, Rei is responsible for delivering solutions for Audi, Nike, Verizon, and many others. In 2009, AKQA became the first agency in history to receive five agency-of-the-year accolades from publications such as *Adweek*, *Creative Review*, and *Campaign*. It was also selected as one of *Fast Company*'s 50 Most Innovative Companies, and *Advertising Age* recognized AKQA as one of the Top Ten Agencies of the Decade. In 2012, the American Advertising Federation, honoring the top young talent of the industry, inducted Rei into "The Hall of Achievement."[20]

Helmut Krone

Helmut Krone developed a clean, uncluttered look in the 1950s that still sets the standards for modern advertising design. Working with copywriter Julian Koenig, Krone created witty, tasteful, intelligent masterpieces for Volkswagen and other Doyle Dane Bernbach clients. Krone sweated print details and advanced professionalism among creatives in his relentless pursuit of perfection. He was elected to the Art Directors Club Hall of Fame in 1976 and has been a perennial award winner as he revolutionized advertising's "look."[21]

George Lois

George Lois gained fame and major awards with bold, clean work for Doyle Dane Bernbach, Papert Koenig Lois, and Lois Holland. In 1976 he penned *The Art of Advertising*, praised as the bible of mass communication. He also became the youngest inductee into the Art Directors Club Hall of Fame. Lois's ads for Wolfschmidt Vodka, Xerox, Allerest, MTV, Maypo, Wheatena, and Edwards & Hanly, and his *Esquire* covers reflected his "loosey-goosey" style and exemplified his idiosyncratic "stun 'em and cause outrage" philosophy. Never an "establishment" model citizen, Lois is defined by his powerful early work.[22]

Charlotte Moore

Born in Chattanooga, Tennessee, and educated in Virginia, southerner Charlotte Moore found a spiritual and professional home on the West Coast when she began to work for the creative hot shop Wieden + Kennedy (W+K). Over the course of almost eight years, she worked as art director and, eventually, group creative director on accounts including Nike, Microsoft, and Coke. She left the agency in the fall of 1995 but returned as co–creative director of their European headquarters in Amsterdam. Agency ambition was interrupted by love. She followed her heart to Italy, where she currently lives with her husband and children—still doing great freelance work, some with her W+K copywriting partner Janet Champ. Her work has been recognized by *Communication Arts*, One Show, and *McCall's* Advertising Women of the Year. Moore and Champ received four nominations and two back-to-back wins in the Magazine Publishers of America's Kelly Awards for best, most effective print advertising for their Nike women's advertising work.

What's Poppin'?

For over 25 years, Bob and Betty Johansen ran their wholesale popcorn business out of their home in Sioux Falls, Iowa. Around 2010, the Johansens opened a retail store in their hometown to sell ready-to-eat popcorn as well as kernels, oil, and equipment. Their PrairiePop brand became so popular in their store that they explored ways to distribute the product through retail grocery and convenience stores.

PrairiePop is different from other ready-to-eat brands in several ways:

- It's popped in small batches, using pure coconut oil, which gives it much more flavor than air-popped brands.

- Even though it's popped in oil, it's lower in calories than the leading air-popped brands.

- It's available in large (20-ounce) clear, resealable plastic bags, in contrast to the smaller opaque bags offered by the competition. The benefits are being able to see how much popcorn is in the package and the ability to reseal the bag. The downside is that the large size discourages some consumers who don't want to buy so much popcorn, and more important, the package does not fit on a standard grocery shelf.

- The packaging on their large bags has a movie theater theme and boasts old-fashioned movie theater taste. Instead of PrairiePop being dominant, the largest graphic is "Big Bag O' Corn." There is no reference to calorie count or the other benefits (high in fiber, no trans fats, gluten free, etc.).

1 How would you change the packaging of PrairiePop to compete more successfully with Skinny Pop and other low-calorie brands? Make at least three recommendations.

2 What other types of research would you recommend? Give at least three examples and explain how it would apply to this product.

3 The Johansens need all available cash for expansion of their production facilities. Yet they need to promote their brand and its competitive advantages. How can they increase awareness and trial purchases of their product without a huge expenditure on mass media advertising? Give at least three tactics.

4 What other selling venues should the Johansens consider besides large grocery stores? Explain how the type of store or direct sales influences marketing communication strategies.

5 PrairiePop is not active in social media, although they have Facebook and Twitter accounts. Give three ideas for social medial promotions, including the themes for the promotions.

Tom Altstiel, TBA Marketing Group

Exercises

1. Failing Fast Is Fun

(Contributed by Jeff Ericksen, creative director, BVK, Milwaukee.)

Whether it's an advertising copywriter struggling to nail that one perfect headline or a software developer searching for the next killer app, there can be a method to the madness of creation. We call it Failing Fast Is Fun. Like a jazz musician or an improvisational comic, this technique allows you to build off of ideas or themes and spin them into completely new directions. One thought leads to three. Those new three each lead to another three. And so on and so on. The trick is to not stop too soon. There will be time to edit, rationalize, and flesh out later. Here's what you do:

- Write down the objective at hand.
- Grab a stack of Post-it notes.
- Limit your time. If you're doing this in a class, you might work in small groups and begin with 15 minutes.
- Unlimit your thoughts.
- Jot one idea down per Post-it.
- Review your notes and cluster them by concept. Pick your top ideas, using them as jumping-off points, and repeat.
- One you've got three or four killer ideas, see which ones have legs using the same Post-it note technique to extend each idea.
- Repeat. Repeat. Repeat.

2. Thinking Outside the Box

This exercise is designed to help you immerse yourself in a product. The specific objective is to help bring all of your senses into play. Begin with a partner and then work on your own in this three-step exercise.

Step 1

- Your instructor will stop at the dollar store and buy as many products as there are students, put them all into a covered box, and bring it to class.
- Working in pairs, one person (explorer) will explore a product with the help of his or her partner (scribe). The scribe will be in charge of taking notes based on the explorer's sensorial responses to the product. The process will then reverse.
- Without looking, the scribe will reach into the box and select a product.
- The explorer must keep his or her eyes closed through the entire process. Trust your partner!
- The scribe will place the product (still packaged) in the hands of the explorer.

- The explorer will then slowly, and with specific focus on each sense, explore the product—smell it, listen to it, touch it, taste it, and see it (last)—as the scribe writes down the explorer's words. They must trust their partner to guide them as necessary.

- Explorers should describe the product's "features" with words and phrases rooted in their sensorial experience. Be as expressive and emotional as possible. Nothing is "wrong."

- Now reverse roles. Select a new product from within the box. Do not return the first product to the box.

- Next begin to generate a list. It could be a list of all the words and images from the product's category. You could also focus on the competitor with a few "suffering points" to show the alternative is you don't use your product. Or you could do the "twist." There's also the possibility of playing with metaphors. Then again you might be so inspired that you'll think of ideas that aren't even ads and go nontraditional. The idea is to brainstorm ideas. Ultimately you will amass a benefits list.

Step 2

- Next consider who the target is and write a Consumer Profile.
- Spin the features into benefits and prioritize them into the top 10.
- Then write a Positioning Statement.

Step 3

- Next write 50 headlines, but turn in 3. No headline may be more than eight words.
- Then select the most resonant headline and execute it in a font and color that strategically speaks to the positioning of your brand (use at least 36-point type).
- Present your finished headline and discuss your rationale.

3. Five Lines

(Adapted from an exercise contributed by Mike Cissne, group leader, Bader-Rutter.)

This exercise is teacher driven and designed to help you experience how lines work as a design element.

- Take out a sheet of paper, draw five lines on it, and then sign your name and submit the sheet for review.

- Your teacher will lead a discussion, using the lines you drew, to demonstrate how many details and decisions could be involved to complete any task and that a designer should be aware of all of the choices.

- Now, generate a list of all the questions that could be asked before completing a design project that involves lines: Should the lines be thick? Should the lines be thin? Should the lines symbolize something? Should the lines touch each other? Should a ruler be used? Should the lines be short? Should the lines be long? Should the lines be parallel? How much pressure should be used when drawing the lines? Do the lines need to be seen up close or far away? What color paper should be used? What size of paper should be used? What utensil should be used? Where should the name go in relationship to the lines? And many more . . .

- Discuss how we mostly take for granted these decisions, but a good designer runs through all of these thoughts and many more before doing anything.

Review chapter content and study for exams. http://study.sagepub.com/altstiel4e.

- Interactive practice quizzes
- Mobile-friendly eFlashcards
- Carefully selected chapter-by-chapter video and multimedia content

Chapter 7

Campaigns
Synergy and Integration

Before you can create a campaign, you need to define it. From a copywriting standpoint, we prefer Maxine Paetro's simpler description:

> A campaign is a series of ads for a product (or service or company) that work individually and cumulatively to communicate the advertiser's message to the consumer.

In other words, each element of a campaign has to be effective on its own, because that may be the first and only exposure. All the elements also need to work together to build a cumulative image. With a well-executed multielement campaign, the whole is greater than the sum of its parts. Why is this important? As a complete creative person you need to know how to create comprehensive campaigns rather than a series of separate one-off ads.

What Is a Campaign?

In some cases, a campaign can include the complete MarCom arsenal, or it can be as simple as a series of three fractional-page ads, as long as they meet all of the following criteria:

Common objective: Well-defined target audience, awareness, comprehension, conviction, and action goals within a given time frame. In other words, there should be a campaign strategy.

Unified theme: Whether it's a tagline, graphic design, or copy message, a campaign needs to convey a single message so the consumer can connect that one adjective to the brand. This does not mean every ad has to look the same—but the overall message should.

Coordinated rollout: Depending on the time frame, all elements can appear at once in a blitz, or new elements can be added depending on changing marketing environments, such as seasonality and competitive response. This involves media and promotion planning, but it certainly affects creative strategy.

Overall, if you remember nothing else about campaigns, know this:

The primary purpose of a campaign is to **support the brand**.

From your clients' point of view, a campaign is a more effective, more profitable, and more stable situation for establishing their brand name.[1]

Campaigns and IMC

In Chapters 1 and 2 we outlined a few elements of integrated marketing communications (IMC). In a campaign, the operative word is *integrated*—those elements have to work together in a planned approach. Campaign strategy can involve the whole marketing communication toolbox, including public relations and media planning; however, we'll limit our thinking to creative elements.

Campaign Components

Think about any recent soda or fast food restaurant campaign. Where did you first notice it? Probably on television. But you also heard the radio commercials, saw the billboards, saw a friend mention it on Instagram, got annoyed by the brand infiltrating your mobile device, and probably glanced at a display in a store or restaurant. Each individual component conveyed the message, and collectively they pounded it into your brain. So when you see that soda on the grocer's shelf or in a vending machine, you buy it,

"One slip-up, one second-rate element, and a terrific campaign can turn into a terrific flop."[2]

Marie-Catherine Dupuy, founding partner and executive creative director, Boulet Dru Dupuy Petit

Applegate is hardly the biggest name in hot dogs, but their "Cleaner Wiener" campaign quickly established the brand as a healthier choice. Hilarious TV commercials, radio ads, digital ads, point-of-sale promotions, and a video-driven social media program worked individually and cumulatively to form a complete campaign.

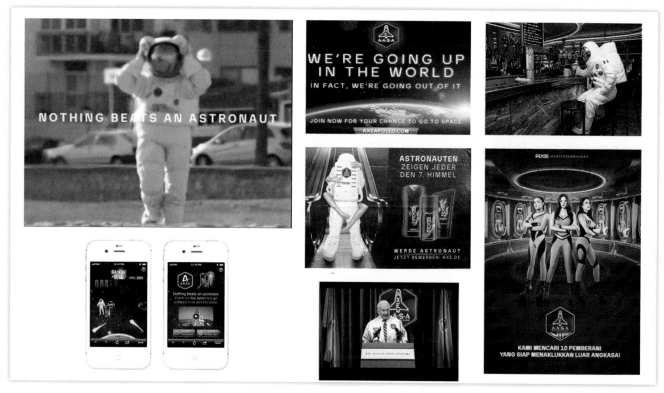

The Axe Apollo campaign was the biggest product introduction in company history. The promotion was built around a contest to award free trips on the Lynx suborbital plane. The company created the Axe Apollo Space Academy and supported the contest with a global campaign that included television, social media, point-of-purchase displays, web ads, and tons of word-of-mouth marketing.

probably without realizing how many times you've been bombarded with different messages in the various media. What made you pull into the drive-through to try that new sandwich? Maybe it was the ad on your car radio or the billboard you just passed. Again, you probably don't realize how many campaign components were working together to influence you.

Here are a few of the components that can be part of an integrated campaign:

Advertising: Consumer magazines, trade magazines and professional magazines, broadcast television, cable and satellite television, radio, local newspapers, national and trade newspapers, ambient, out-of-home, Internet banner ads.

Promotion: Short-term sales contests, special offers, discounts, rebates, incentives, sweepstakes, in-game marketing, product placement, sponsorships, events, cross-promotion with other products, publicity, and, of course, advertising of the promotion—not to mention digital promotion tools like Foursquare.

Public relations: Event planning, publicity of events, print news releases, newsletters, video news releases.

Internet marketing: Websites for computers, tablets, and smartphones; landing pages and microsites; email marketing; search engine marketing; customer relationship marketing.

Social media: Most consumer brand campaigns use social media as their hub. The focus has shifted so that advertising drives viewers to Facebook, Twitter, Instagram, Pinterest, and YouTube to continue the conversation.

Direct marketing: Database development, direct mailers (letters, cards, dimensional mailers), fulfillment (mailing information or merchandise). Direct marketing is more than direct mail: It's also telemarketing, direct selling, email marketing, and mobile apps.

If all of the above components are part of a campaign, they all have to work together, yet stand alone as individual selling tools.

How to Enhance Continuity

Continuity does not mean conformity. The biggest difference between a single-shot ad and a campaign is continuity. Continuity within a campaign means that the various components of the campaign have enough commonality that the reader, viewer, or listener should perceive a common theme and unified message.

Continuity doesn't require that the TV spot use the same dialogue as the radio commercial, or the billboards have the exact same graphics as the print ads. While it's nearly impossible to give you one set of guidelines that works for every campaign, remember this:

Don't repeat the same idea in every part of the campaign—repeat the creative strategy with different executions.[3]

Extendibility

To create an effective campaign, you need to think in two dimensions—*extending* the creative strategy across the various media and *repeating* that strategy within each medium. The first dimension—extendibility—means you use the same theme and common elements in two or more media. For example, can you carry that creative message from print to TV? Will the direct mailers look like they came from the same company as the billboards? Does the advertising support the promotion theme? Does the point-of-purchase material tie in with the campaign?

Repeatability

Repeatability is different from repetition. It does not mean rerunning the same ad or commercial until everyone is so sick of it they ignore it. That's a media decision. In a creative context, repeatability means using common elements to create a series of ads or commercials that convey the same brand message. They are not identical, but they are related. They can stand on their own, but they also work cumulatively to convey a campaign them. We can't think of a better illustration of repeatability in a campaign than the "Got Milk?" campaign. This long-running campaign has featured the celebrities of the day (and even days past), but all feature the signature milk moustache. If you want to explore the origins of this campaign, read Jon Steel's *Truth, Lies and Advertising: The Art of Account Planning*.

Another good example of repeatability is the Geico approach. They usually run three separate campaigns concurrently. One campaign ran several different commercials featuring the Gecko as the corporate spokeslizard; another series starred Max the pig to promote their mobile apps; and a third string of commercials stressed the "15 minutes saves you 15%" theme in a variety of absurd scenarios.

© Geico

Geico typically runs three campaign themes at the same time. While each campaign has its own unique look and feel, the common thread across all three is the Geico logo and money-saving message.

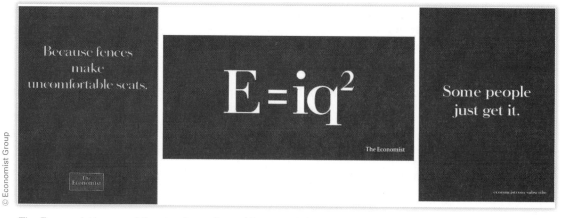

© Economist Group

The Economist has used the now legendary white-on-red design since the late 1980s. Clever headlines appeal to a smarter than average reader, or at least someone who wants to appear smarter.

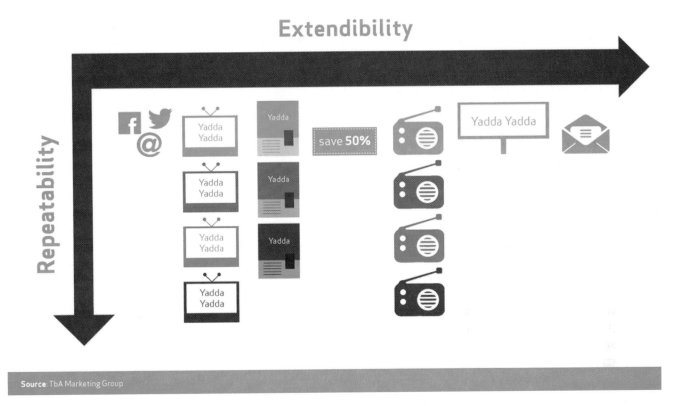

Source: TbA Marketing Group

How to Maximize Extendibility and Repeatability

We've already covered some of the creative tools you can use to provide continuity to a campaign. You can use one or all of them to help hold your campaign together.

Music

When people can't remember the words of a commercial, but can sing the jingle, you know your campaign's music is holding it together. Music is far more memorable than any other commercial element. For example, you'd have a hard time finding anyone over 45 who doesn't know the Oscar Mayer wiener song. We find it surprising how many students remember music from commercials made before they were born. There are as many ways to use music in your campaign as there are songs—probably more, with today's sampling and mixing technology. Thanks to broadcast, YouTube, and online commercials, obscure indie bands become overnight hits as millions are exposed to their music online. Sometimes the music becomes just as important as the advertising message. Philip Phillips's signature song, "Home," became a minor hit after *American Idol*, but after it was picked up as the theme music for several different companies, including American Family Insurance, Mazda, and Wal-Mart, the music never faded from pop culture.

"Creativity is just connecting things. When you ask creative people how they did something they . . . didn't really do it, they just saw something."[4]

Steve Jobs,
founder and former CEO, Apple

A Better Way

there comes
a point in
which yelling

becomes
silence

drugfree.org

Partnership
for Drug-Free Kids

The Partnership for Drug-Free Kids (previously the Partnership for a Drug-Free America) is one of the leading organizations dedicated to providing resources and information to both parents and kids regarding the dangers and problems with drug and alcohol abuse among kids in the United States.

For many years, the PDFK had been very active promoting its messages to both the general market as well as the Hispanic market. However, during the economic crisis that hit the United States in the late 2000s, the PDFK had to make some budget adjustments, and the Hispanic market was left without a tailored program.

In 2014 that all changed. The PDFK was able to secure funds to go back to the Hispanic community with a program that was tailor made and resonated with the audience. They approached us during the spring of 2014 and asked for our help to develop a comprehensive, multivehicle campaign. The overall objective was to raise awareness of the resources the Partnership for Drug-Free Kids offers by establishing them as the experts for Hispanic parents who are dealing with teen drug and alcohol abuse. This meant that, for the first time, we wouldn't be talking about prevention, but rather helping with an existing situation. This changed the focus 100%. Our creative work needed to encourage parents to take action if they suspected or knew that their teens were using drugs or alcohol.

So imagine for a second that you are one of these Hispanic parents. In a culture and group where family is at the epicenter of all we do, the prospect of facing an issue like this and

Voice

Using the same announcer throughout your TV and radio campaigns helps establish a common sound. Here are a few examples:

- **Celebrity voice-over:** A lot of very famous people provide voice-overs for commercials without identifying themselves, such as George Clooney (Budweiser), Kevin Spacey (Honda), Morgan Freeman (Visa), Tim Allen (Chevrolet), John Hamm (Mercedes), and Jeff Bridges (Hyundai), to name a few. Using famous actors may be expensive, but they often have distinctive voices that connect with viewers or listeners. Research reveals that television commercials featuring celebrity voice-overs are most influential when consumers can't identify the actors the voices belong to.[5] Research also tells us that male voices still dominate as the voice of authority. Maybe it's time to rethink that.

then openly talking or seeking help for it could be devastating. First, the feeling that you have failed as a parent. Second, you are in a "foreign" country, many times do not speak English, and you feel paralyzed, as you are not sure where to turn and how to get your son or daughter the help he or she needs. We know from research that Hispanic parents feel there is little they can do to help their teens abstain from substance abuse (61% of Hispanic callers to the PDFK help line reported not knowing what to do about their children's substance abuse, and another 25% reported not knowing where to turn for help). On top of this, there's a big element of frustration and desperation for the parents, which often results in not approaching the situation in the best way possible, resorting to yelling and screaming to make their kids understand.

Our message was about letting parents know that we understand their frustration, while telling them that there's a better way to deal with what they are going through. We wanted to arm parents with the knowledge and outlets necessary to be able to hold that conversation. The way in which we dramatized this was by showing how when we, as parents, confront our kids about these issues, they tend not to listen to us. Our pleas, and sometimes screams, become white noise. They pay no attention to us.

As an example, our TV campaign showed teens being yelled at by their parents, and while we are able to hear every single sound effect within the spot (TV, ambulance in the background, kid breathing), the parents' voices are simply muted. They scream and scream but no noise comes out. The

kid is oblivious to their pleas. At this point a super (text on the screen) appears that says, "There comes a point in which yelling become silence."

The results to date have been outstanding. As an example, the click-through rate on the banners was 3.4%, which was the highest the PDFK had seen in about eight years and well above industry average.

Thanks to this, the PDFK is planning on making communications to Hispanics once again a priority, creating more informed Hispanic parents who are ready to take action.

Leo Olper, partner, account lead, d expósito & Partners, New York

Mauricio Galvan, partner, creative lead, d expósito & Partners, New York

- **Character voices:** People are used to hearing smooth announcers. So a distinctive voice treatment can shock them into listening. Remember Gilbert Gottfried's grating Aflac commercials? The current voice of the Geico Gecko is British actor Jake Wood, although a few others have covered him, including Kelsey Grammer. Keep in mind that it's very hard to change a voice once people accept the character as a symbol for a brand.

- **Announcers:** Using the same announcer, even if he or she is not a celebrity, can provide continuity. Be careful to maintain the tone and delivery style, even though the copy changes from spot to spot. And, remember male voices do not have to be the voice of authority. It's your choice.

© Optus

Australian cable company Optus hired Ricky Gervais as an "antipitchman" who put absolutely no effort into his endorsement. In this spot he tells viewers, "You're probably watching something illegal on YouTube. You disgust me!"

Spokespersons

Back in the day, when brands were the sole sponsors of radio and television programs, the star of the show was the brand spokesperson. These days, the process is often reversed. Success in show business or sports generates instant recognition, and brands are quick to jump on the bandwagon. The key word is *success*, which transcends any considerations about race, ethnicity, or sexual orientation. Years ago, an African American woman would have limited opportunity to endorse products. In recent years, Beyoncé has stacked up endorsement deals with House of Deréon, Tommy Hilfiger, Pepsi, H&M, Armani Diamonds perfume, and L'Oréal, to name a few. And she is by no means the only African American entertainer to command top dollar for an endorsement. Nowadays, celebrity sometimes trumps prejudice.

Beyond the entertainment field, athletes are the most prominent celebrity endorsers. In his prime, Michael Jordan was one of the top commercial spokespersons, starting with Coke, then representing Nike, before branching off to McDonald's, Hanes, and many others. His celebrity transcended his fame on the court. As of this writing, Danica Patrick has not won a major NASCAR race. Regardless, she is arguably the best known professional driver in the world. Patrick became famous for her racy GoDaddy ads, which have been toned down recently. She has also pitched Peak antifreeze, Bell helmets, Coca-Cola, Can-Am Spyder, Shamrock Foods, Marquis jets, and Tissot Swiss watches, among others. One might also think Serena William's celebrity star is rising quickly. It's not. According to the Atlantic she ranks 47th among the highest paid athletic endorsers. "The only logical explanation for this gap points to long-held prejudices regarding female sports stars and how people feel they should look."[6] The commercial value of top male athlete endorsers such as LeBron James, Aaron Rodgers, and Russell Wilson is based on performance, not how they look. Tiger Woods became the symbol of Nike golf and Buick, among others. But after his various scandals his marketing value dipped, but not for long. Today, he's still one of the highest paid celebrity endorsers. Lance Armstrong has not fared as well, losing his commercial contracts along with his racing titles due to doping scandals. Besides wiping out his future income and personal reputation, he is also on the hook for some of that endorsement money. That's the high-reward/high-risk world of using celebrities. If you choose to use them, choose them wisely.

As we discussed in Chapter 6, using a celebrity works best when he or she has some reasonable connection with the product. Whether your celebrity is from the world of sports, show business, politics, or any other public venue, the main considerations should be:

- Will she or he connect with the consumers?
- Will this person enhance the brand image?
- Can we afford this person?
- Any skeletons in the closet—any future potential for embarrassing the client?

Turning Ordinary People Into Celebrities

You can create spokespersons, and if things go right, they become celebrities. One of the most successful was Jared Fogle, who lost a ton of weight eating healthy food at Subway. He was their spokesperson for over a decade, thanks to the brilliant foresight of a local Subway franchise owner who saw Jared's story "Crazy Diets That Work" in *Men's Health*. Ordinary people who become celebrities still present risks. Fogle pleaded guilty to possession of child pornography and paying for sex with minors. Meanwhile, Subway suspended his role as spokesperson as soon as the investigation began. Fogle may be gone but time will tell how the scandal will affect the Subway brand over time.

Animated Characters

For years the Leo Burnett agency was known for its "critters"—those memorable animated characters that have been the common thread of many of their long-running campaigns. Before you dismiss these mascots as throwbacks to the 1950s, consider that they've been around for a long, long time. That means the agency has created long-term brand value and, in doing so, has retained clients much longer than most of their competitors. Some characters, such as the Jolly Green Giant (1935), Tony the Tiger (1951), and the Keebler Elves (1968), are inseparable from the products.

Storylines and Situations

Storylines: Some advertisers use testimonials or case histories, all with a common theme to convey their messages. Hospitals, for example, typically feature inspirational stories of survivors who owe their lives to the advanced technology and caring doctors of their institutions. Insurance companies also use this approach, with the emphasis on caring for victims of some catastrophic event.

Situations: These are recurring themes or vignettes that involve (a) the same characters or (b) the same premise. Over the years, Budweiser has featured their iconic Clydesdales in Super Bowl commercials. Insurance companies seem to like recurring situations: besides the previously mentioned Geico campaigns, Progressive has gotten a lot of mileage from Flo's antics, Allstate has used a scruffy guy named Mayhem to represent mishaps, and Aaron Rodgers has done his "discount double check" to promote State Farm for years. A long-running series of ESPN television commercials put famous mascots, individual athletes, and whole teams in mundane 9-to-5 jobs at the ESPN offices.

Consumer-Generated Campaigns

As social media merged with marketing, advertisers used the Internet to give consumers an unprecedented opportunity to buy into their brands. Technically, anyone with a smartphone can create consumer-generated media (CGM). Encouraging consumers to create their own commercials involves them in the brand far beyond being loyal customers. Most CGM promotions include a social media component that basically says "send us an entertaining video and everyone will get to vote on it; and if they like yours the best, you get some kind of prize." Many national consumer brands have gone beyond that approach to sponsor more sophisticated consumer-generated campaigns. Perhaps the most recognizable is Doritos' ongoing "Crash the Super Bowl" promotion.

When cartoon shows dominated Saturday morning programming, cereal makers incorporated their own characters into commercials and package design. Although his look has changed a bit over the years, Kellogg's' Tony the Tiger is still a GR-R-R-EAT brand mascot.

A million bucks and international fame is a pretty good incentive to create some great concepts. Because multiple channels are involved (television, digital, point of sale, word of mouth, news media), well-publicized CGM programs are like minicampaigns. And because successful efforts are repeated every year, they can become long-term campaigns.

Despite the current trend, it's important to remember that most of these CGM campaigns are short lived, very specific in scope, and limited to a single product or brand extension. Consumer-generated work should not be used to replace long-term corporate or brand campaigns or the advertising agency. It should be used to generate high consumer engagement, but not at the expense of the brand. Pepsi learned this the hard way with the Refresh campaign. It engaged and supported community activity, in large part with CGM. In the process the brand lost market share. Why? Because its traditional brand voice went silent. In many cases, CGM could be considered a sales promotion that is supported by other media. If you're planning to use CGM as the main focus or even part of your campaign, keep these tips in mind:

- Don't separate your CGM from the main objectives for the brand or company—integrate it. Determine how your CGM will support your brand, not detract from the brand message.

- Be honest about your intentions. You want people to create ads. Don't call it something else. Too many CGM programs have crashed because they weren't transparent.

- Encourage participation—not just from entrants but also from people who can vote on the best submission. It's like Chicago politics—get them to vote early and often.

- Facilitate syndication. Use viral seeding to get the videos out to a wider audience. Empower syndication by making it simple to upload and embed in blogs.

- Consider long-term implications and opportunities. Can your CGM be leveraged into a longer running campaign? Can it be mainstreamed into your primary branding campaign?

> "There's a difference between a campaign concept and an ad concept. Are the ads different executions to illustrate the same point or are they different ways of doing the same idea? The former is a campaign"[7]
>
> Tom Monahan, author of *The Do-It-Yourself Lobotomy*

© Allstate

Allstate uses Mayhem to personify the disasters that cut-rate insurance may not cover. The long-running campaign uses humor to make its point, while another Allstate campaign uses actor Dennis Haysbert to deliver more serious messages.

Integrating Sales Promotion Into the Campaign

A lot of students tend to think of a campaign as just a collection of ads and sometimes treat sales promotion as one more action item. As we'll see in Chapter 13, sales promotion takes many forms, but in every case, it has to be promoted. That requires the integration of print, broadcast, online, social media, public relations, out-of-home, direct marketing, and point of sale to encourage consumers to participate in the promotion. By its nature, sales promotion is designed to yield short-term results rather than long-term brand building, so all that activity is usually compressed in a few months.

Integrated Digital Campaigns

As we'll see in the next chapters about online marketing and sales promotion, the web has become the hub of many advertising campaigns. While consumers may not want to read a 100-word ad, they might read 500 words on a website or blog. Sometimes the purpose of a multichannel campaign is to direct people to a single hashtag promotion. Small Business Saturday was a campaign started by American Express in 2010 to encourage people to shop at their local small businesses the day after Black Friday. It's a completely social campaign in which American Express encourages businesses to connect with their customers via Facebook, Twitter, and YouTube. It's supported by Facebook and banner ads and through the news media reports, as well as point-of-sale material provided to retailers who accept American Express.

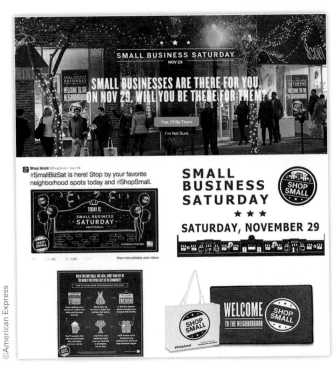

American Express launched their Small Business Saturday campaign on social media to support local independent retailers. Participating small business owners received access to marketing tools, advice, and free geo-targeted advertising.

Honda created a campaign that perfectly fit the bicultural mind-set of Latino Millennials. Featuring comic Felipe Esparza, the campaign used social media, television, and banner ads in Spanish and English.

Start at the Beginning

A complete campaign actually begins at the first links of the supply chain, with trade advertising, direct marketing, trade shows, product literature, dealer kits, co-op ad programs, point of sale, and a lot more. The dynamics of repeatability and extendibility also apply to trade campaigns, although the scope depends greatly on the time line and number of wholesale and retail outlets. We'll discuss a lot of these tactics in Chapters 13 and 15, but for now, don't forget about all the work that needs to be done before the consumer campaign launches.

Taglines: The String That Holds Campaigns Together

We call them taglines, but you could also say they're slogans, signatures, or theme lines. Usually, they are the catchphrases that appear after the logo in a print ad or at the end of the commercial, and, in most cases, they are very forgettable. In 1947 Frances Gerety crafted "A Diamond Is Forever." Her tagline cemented DeBeers' reputation for romance and quality, and many experts consider it the best of the last century. It still works, so why change it? A diamond is forever . . . and so is their slogan. When it comes to using a symbol and slogan to unite a campaign, no one has done a better job than Nike. Their long-term campaign strategy involves a lot more than the ubiquitous swoosh, created in 1971 by graphic design student named Carolyn Davidson, whom Phil Knight paid a mere $35. Couple that with the "Just Do It" slogan, developed by Wieden + Kennedy in 1988, and you've got blockbuster branding. As a "hero" brand, Nike campaigns celebrate the fighter in every athlete, from top professionals to weekend warriors. As Nike has proved, once a look is established in the consumer's mind, extending it becomes a lot easier, which made the brand's move to embrace women in the early 1990s a welcome and logically branded shift.

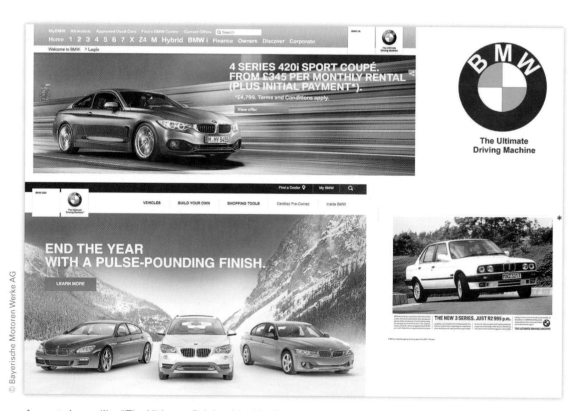

© Bayerische Motoren Werke AG

A great slogan like "The Ultimate Driving Machine" can sustain a campaign for years.

Some clients expect too much from a tagline. They don't want a little blurb to sneak under their logo. They demand a "statement" that (a) defines the company, (b) positions the product, (c) denigrates the competition, (d) reassures the stockholders, and (e) will be approved by the CEO's spouse. The more objectives a tagline tries to achieve, the more generic it becomes. When a tagline becomes too vanilla, you can put it under any logo with negligible effect. Too many taglines are written by committees and tested by management panels, many of which may not even understand branding. They're cobbled together with a few key words that mean nothing when used alone. So when a team builds a slogan, the whole mess becomes irrelevant. Before you start cranking out slogans you have to ask the client: What's the One Thing you want to say? Do you want to convey a general attitude or tone? Do you want something specific about the products? Do you want something relating to your customers? Just what the heck do you want? George Felton sums it up pretty well: "Slogans . . . had better do more than just be clever . . . they need to be smart." The smart taglines stick with you years after they first appear. They become part of the popular culture and define their places in time as well as the brand.

The primary purpose of a tagline is to establish or reinforce the brand name. To do this, the tagline should do the following:

Provide continuity for a campaign: A tagline may be the only common component of a multimedia campaign. It can also be the link between campaigns with very different looks. A good tagline transcends changes in campaign strategy. No matter what BMW is doing with their ads, the cars are always "The Ultimate Driving Machines." No matter where on earth you find a Coke or whom you drink it with, chances are you're opening a little happiness.

Crystallize the One Thing associated with the brand or product: Whether it's staking out a position or implying an abstract attitude, the slogan is an extension of the brand name. When you can mention a brand name and someone else quotes the slogan, you know you've got something. Going back to concepts discussed in earlier chapters, the tagline can help foster awareness and interest of a brand or product. A few well-chosen words can define the brand, separate it from the competition, and anchor it in the reader's or viewer's brain. Think of M&M candies that "melt in your mouth, not in your hand." It's not only a statement of a real product benefit; nobody else can say this. A good tagline increases your creative freedom. When the message ends with "Only in a Jeep," you can have a lot more fun with the content.

How to Write More Effective Taglines

The following are a few tips and techniques for writing better taglines. Of course, not every tagline is going to possess all these traits (unless you find the successor to "Just Do It"). These guidelines are offered to help you evaluate your taglines before you submit them to the client.

Keep it short and simple: VW came up with "Drivers wanted" a few years back because it stuck in the mind better than their older slogan, "It's not a car. It's a Volkswagen." After a decade of "Drivers" they came out with "Das Auto" (The Car), which may have taken German simplicity a little too far. The goal is not to keep the word count to two or fewer or to make something so obscure you need another slogan to define it. However, when you develop a slogan, think of billboards—no more than six words. Three words are even better. As Shakespeare said, "Brevity is the soul of wit." Just make sure your witticism makes sense.

Think jingle: Even if you never put your tagline to music, picture it in a TV commercial. You can use the old tricks of rhythm, rhyme, and alliteration to make it more memorable. For example, no one over 40 can forget "Winston tastes good like a cigarette should," even though cigarette advertising on TV ended in 1971. A modern example: Kay Jewelers says, "Every kiss begins with Kay."

Try to differentiate the brand: Can you come up with a simple way to separate yourself from the competition? Visa used to say they're "Everywhere you want to be," implying that American Express and MasterCard were not. They followed that with "Life takes Visa," which not only gets the product's name in the slogan, it also implies that the card is universally accepted. Celebrity spokespersons for Capital One have been asking, "What's in your wallet?" For 40 years BMW has been "The Ultimate Driving Machine." The ideal slogan can't be used by any other brand.

If you have to be generic, go global: Many brands use what could be called generic slogans. They're positive, easy to remember, and can be translated into most languages without changing their meanings. When they stand alone, these slogans could work for just about anyone. The difference is they're supported by millions of dollars of advertising and promotion. So if Joe's Burger Shack says, "I'm lovin' it," no one notices. When McDonald's does it, it becomes major marketing news. If you can remember the innocuous slogans for most mass-marketed packaged goods, it's only because they've been beaten into your brain through relentless advertising.

Play with words: A tagline can be more memorable if you take a common expression and twist it just enough to get attention. Chrysler says their cars are "Imported from Detroit," implying foreign-made quality from an American brand. Quite a change from Detroit's glory years. Years ago Panasonic promoted the ergonomics of their home electronics with "So advanced, it's simple." Sometimes you can give your slogan a double meaning. For example, a drug company targeted doctors with "Healthy concern for your practice," indicating that the drug company was successful and cared about their customers.

Don't confuse or mislead: In the effort to be creative, some writers forget that the rest of the world is not as clever as they are. An obscure one-word tagline could be misunderstood or, worse, ignored.

Justify your choices: Too many people think they are experts on taglines. So when you submit a list to the client, make sure everyone knows the parameters you were given. Too often the rules change after you've received the initial game plan.

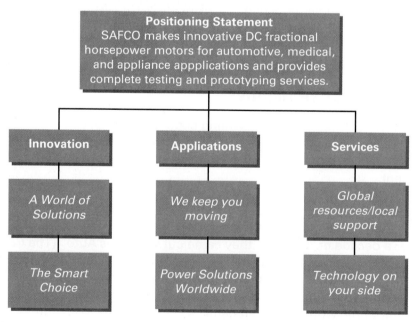

Figure 7.01   Creative Tree for Taglines

Creating Taglines From Product Information

Writing taglines is a lot like developing whole concepts. Start with the One Thing. Then say it straight. From there you can veer off in several directions, each with a list of possible slogans. Figure 7.1 illustrates a brief template for a business-to-business client, although this technique works for any product or service.

As you've probably noted, the majority of the taglines in Figure 7.1 stink. Most of the time, you'll start with a generic slogan, but as you keep working, you'll branch out. You can have as many branches as you'd like. Don't worry if some of your slogans don't fit a defined category—just keep writing. Don't start editing until you get a huge list. Then weed out the obvious stinkers. Keep refining your list until you have a group of taglines you can live with. So you might come up with something a little better, such as:

- The Power of Innovation
- Solutions in Motion
- We Power Your Ideas

Okay, they're still not "Just Do It," but don't stop trying. Keep sending out branches.

You'll find one that works as long as it stays true to the values at the base of the tree.

Taglines Need Your Support

Even "Just Do It" would not have made much sense if it had been launched in a campaign that highlighted the features and benefits of Nike shoes. It had to be paired with people dedicated to athleticism. That synergy made it magic. That's why writing taglines can be so pointless. They're usually evaluated by a committee in a vacuum, without the benefit of massive ad support or even a connection to the campaign. Once a slogan becomes established, you can vary the images and copy in the ads, but they have to be there when that tagline is introduced. Once it's established in the consumer's mind, it becomes part of the brand, transcending the creative execution that may change from year to year.

Whether it's used as a headline or tagline, the alliteration and the jingle in TV commercials makes "Every kiss begins with Kay" memorable.

Putting It All Together

Creative strategy for campaigns begins with marketing objectives. As always, you have to ask, "What do you want to accomplish?" The more specific the goals, the better your plan. When the objective is to introduce or reinforce a brand, start thinking campaigns.

No matter which celebrity delivers the Capital One message, they all close with "What's in your wallet?" A great tagline can span decades as it holds multiple campaigns together.

Thanks, Mel

Courtesy of Andre Griner

When it comes to advertising, I guess I'm what you might call a late bloomer. Flash back to 2007. I'm 27 and recently married with a young son. I had finished a year of college, but dropped out to pursue the dream of becoming a musician. Unfortunately, some dreams aren't meant to be, and it never really happened for me.

At this point, I made the decision to go back to college and get my degree. The only trouble was that I had no frickin' clue what I wanted to study. Then came what I can only describe as one of the most embarrassing inspirational moments in history. *What Women Want* came on cable (I told you), and I remember thinking how awesome Mel Gibson's character's job in advertising looked. And, just like that, I knew what I wanted to be: a copywriter.

I also knew that raising a child, working one job, sometimes two, and attending college wouldn't be easy, but it seemed like the only way for me to find a successful career. It turns out I was half right. I finished school in 2010 and discovered that I was woefully unprepared to find a job. I didn't have a portfolio or a true understanding of the advertising industry. Again, inspiration struck. A woman from Carnival Cruise Lines had spoken to my class, and told us about the great students that she had encountered from someplace called the Miami Ad School. That stuck with me, and a year later, I was accepted into the master's program there.

By the end of my time at MAS, I finally felt like I was ready to work in advertising. They helped place me with an internship in Chicago. I committed to taking full advantage of this opportunity. That meant staying late, offering assistance to others until they were actually probably a little sick of me (hopefully not), and asking as many questions as I could. For some unknown reason, they offered me a position. As I move farther into my career, I can see how frustrating advertising can be, but also how rewarding it is. I guess it's all about balance.

When I was in school, one of my professors told me that a good copywriter is not an artist, but an artisan. I think he meant that we don't make random things. They have to have a purpose and be reflective of a brand's vision. On my best days, I hope that's what I'm doing.

Andre Griner, copywriter, Lapiz

www.jondrework.co

Don't limit your thinking to repetition of the concept or even to how it will work in other media. Look at the big picture. The most famous one-shot ad of all time—Apple's "1984"—was actually part of a campaign that involved a huge amount of publicity and public relations. The commercial was shown many times—for free—after its one and only appearance, at the Super Bowl, and the buzz put the Macintosh on the map. It's interesting to note that the client was so nervous about the approach before the Super Bowl that the agency sold off their time for a scheduled second airing.

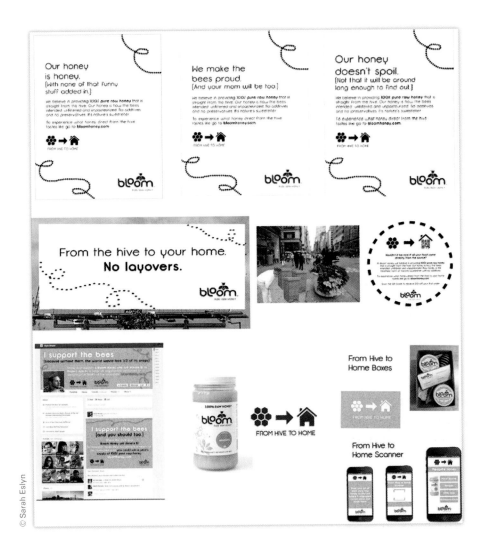

A well-crafted campaign is essential in a good student portfolio. This student kept the message and design simple throughout all print, broadcast, digital, outdoor components.

Campaign Tips

We've offered a lot of ways to improve the continuity and thus the effectiveness of campaigns. Here's some more good advice from Jim Albright:

- A campaign is a series of planned actions. Think big about a wide, multipronged attack on the marketplace.

- When assigned to write a one-time ad, check to see if the client has an ongoing look and sound and slogan. If so, make the point of the ad under the umbrella of the ongoing look, sound, and slogan.

- If the client has no continuity in its advertising, write the one-time ad so that it could be extended into a campaign, if necessary.

- When writing an advertising campaign, don't repeat the same plot in different media. Repeat the creative strategy with different executions.

> "Somehow—in the service of carmakers and brassiere manufacturers and car rental agencies— these campaigns have discovered our humanity."[8]
>
> Bob Garfield, columnist, *Advertising Age*

Client	Campaign
Budweiser	Wassup
American Legacy	Truth
Burger King	Subservient Chicken
BMW Films	The Hire
Dove	Campaign for Real Beauty
Apple	Get a Mac
UNICEF	Tap Project
Dos Equis	Most Interesting Man in the World
Nike +	Running
Proctor & Gamble	Thank You, Mom
American Express	Small Business Saturday
Old Spice	The Man Your Man Could Smell Like
Chipotle	Back to the Start
Metro Trains	Dumb Ways to Die
Red Bull	Stratos

Table 7.1   Advertising Age *Top Campaigns of the 21st Century*[10]

Advertising Age selected the top 15 ad campaigns of the 21st century. Not all of them were complete integrated marketing campaigns, but all were game changers that influenced pop culture as well as marketing.

Think extendibility from the beginning. Sometimes a strategy is so narrow that only one or two good commercials or ads can be written under that strategy. Think ahead to all the different ways you can execute advertising under your creative strategy. You may have to write a song or have T-shirts printed.[9]

Learn From the Best

We've only scratched the surface when it comes to analyzing campaigns. Some of the best minds in our business were asked to rate the best campaigns of the 21st century (at least through 2015). Their selections are listed in Table 7.1. Some choices were unanimous (Dove's Campaign for Real Beauty), but all of them were game changers. We strongly urge you to read more about these campaigns, as well as the successful campaigns from the previous century. Find the common threads, look for that One Thing, and really think about what made them stand out from the millions of other ad messages that bombard consumers every day.

"Historians and archaeologists will one day discover that the ads of our time are the richest and most faithful daily reflections any society ever made of its whole range of activities."[11]

Marshall McLuhan, historian, media expert

Chapter 7

Lauren Connolly

Lauren Connolly is an executive vice president and executive creative director at BBDO New York. She oversees the TotalWork global creative for M&M's Mars, Mountain Dew, Lowe's Home Improvement, and several pro bono accounts. She began her career as a junior copywriter at MARC Advertising in Pittsburgh before moving to BBDO in 2000. She created the iconic M&M's characters, launched AT&T's game-changing "Raising the Bar" campaign, and helped make Mountain Dew a badge brand with Millennials. Connolly is a founding member of BBDO's Diversity Council and a member of the agency's Women's Leadership Council. She was recently an honoree at the inaugural MAKERS conference, named to *Advertising Age*'s "40 Under 40," *Adweek*'s "Young Influential 20 Under 40," and one of "The 33 Most Creative Women in Advertising" by *Business Insider*.[12]

Jeff Goodby

While freelancing with partners Andy Berlin and Rich Silverstein, Jeff Goodby developed concepts for a small video game company that eventually became Electronic Arts. That client got so big that they formed their own agency, with EA as their first account. It wasn't their last. Their creative risk taking led to breakthrough campaigns for the California Milk Processor Board, Budweiser, Nike, E*TRADE, and more.

Tom Monahan

Thousands of people have improved their creative thinking thanks to Tom Monahan and his popular workshops. Through his consulting company, Before & After, he has worked with clients such as Capital One, Frito-Lay, AT&T, and Virgin Atlantic. He is also the author of one of the top business-oriented books on creative thinking—*The Do-It-Yourself Lobotomy: Open Your Mind to Greater Creative Thinking*.

Helen Lansdowne Resor

Helen Lansdowne Resor provided the creative spark in the early days of J. Walter Thompson. As the first female copywriter to write and plan national advertising, she opened the door for many women in advertising, as she was constantly creating new ways to attract readers. She brought a woman's point of view to advertising, addressing clients' conventions as she managed and supervised two thirds of the business in the JWT New York and Boston offices. She was a revolutionary inventor of a new style in advertising. Among her many achievements is one of the greatest slogans of all time, for Woodbury's soap—"The skin you love to touch."

Eat Your (Fruits and/or) Veggies!

A recent study by researchers at Oregon State University found that college students are not eating enough fruits or vegetables. Instead of the government-recommended number of servings—five fruits and vegetables per day—college students were eating five per week. Simple mistake. But people who eat more fruits and vegetables as part of an overall healthy diet are likely to have a reduced risk for some chronic diseases. Specifically, the risk for heart disease, cancer, and type 2 diabetes may be lowered. In addition, vegetables are lower in calories per cup and can be useful in lowering calorie intake. But still, five. Per week. Seriously. Yes, there are issues. It can be hard to get to a grocery store off campus. The dining halls aren't exactly inspiring confidence in their freshness. And if food is fresh, it costs more. Also, pepperoni pizza is really delicious.

So your school is putting together a crack team of students to tackle the opportunity of getting students to eat more fruits and veggies. They've tasked you with the leadership position. Yes, you.

You are expected to report back in six weeks with a plan of action that will inspire enough confidence in the administration that they'll invest the time and money you're asking for to move the needle—over time—from five per week to five per day. It's no small task. But you're up for the challenge. So let's get to work.

1 There's a lot to consider and—as with most opportunities—no right answer. So where would you start? What would your first three steps be?

2 There's a big difference between a first-semester freshman living in the dorms and a fifth-year senior living with five friends off campus. There's a big difference between men and women. And there are different strategies to trying to move the needle with people who are eating vegetables with at least some consistency already. And those are just three of the countless variables. Who would you target? How would you decide?

3 Based on your decision of who to target, what approach would take to messaging? Inspiring or fear based? Would you lead with facts or stories? Would you treat it as an awareness problem or address the potential (mis)perceptions?

4 Finally, how would you measure your progress? What behavioral measures would you use? What perceptual measures? How would you gather data? How would you define success?

Casey Flanagan, director, communication strategy, Kohler Company

1. Brand Stories

Here's a chance to learn about how personal stories influence branding.

- Pick a brand and find six people who use it.
- Next, interview each person, asking him or her to tell a story about his or her experience with the brand. Try to elicit from each person his or her emotional connection to the brand, and record your conversations.
- Review the interviews and transcribe them. Using the stories, generate a Positioning Statement that personifies the essence of the consumers' experiences with the brand.
- Next write three short branded stories, each with a headline, that embody the essence of the positioning and reflect the stories you heard. Limit your stories to 300 words each.
- As a variation, consider whom you would consider to be the perfect spokesperson for a branded campaign and write a rationale explaining why.

2. Next Ones

(Contributed by Kimberly Selber, PhD, associate professor, University of Texas–Pan American.)

This exercise works with the concepts of *extendibility* and *repeatability*.

- Find several campaigns across various categories.
- Break up into teams, with one campaign per group, and write a Creative Brief based on what your group sees in the campaign.
- Then, working with the concept of *repeatability*, concept one or two new ads that could seamlessly work with the existing campaign. You can do this with tissue roughs, the existing layouts, or full-blown creative executions.
- Next, working with *extendibility*, generate two or three new media placements or touchpoints for the campaign. Consider the executional opportunities for these new placements.
- Finally, present your group work in class.

3. Endure the Pain and Enjoy the Gain

(Contributed by Jeff Ericksen, instructor and founder, Milwaukee Portfolio School.)

All writers must suffer for their art, right? Now, I'm not talking about pursuing bad relationships, living on the streets, or abusing alcohol. Although some of those things will make for more interesting conversations at dinner parties. I'm talking about soldiering through the painful part of an ad first: writing the body copy. Here's what you do.

Exercises

- Start by writing the copy before coming up with the concept or headline. Imagine describing the client's brand, sale, or issue to your grandma in an email. Keep it clear and simple—you know how Grandma gets confused.

- When you've finished this exercise, you've accomplished a few things. You've stated your case in a manner a consumer will understand, and you're no longer staring at a blank page. Perhaps your mind is also opened up to seeing that there could be several ways to solve your problem.

- Finally, consider the subject header of your email. Maybe that's a headline?

- You might consider writing emails to the whole family. Who knows? Maybe you'll end up with an entire campaign.

Review chapter content and study for exams. http://study.sagepub.com/altstiel4e.

- Interactive practice quizzes
- Mobile-friendly eFlashcards
- Carefully selected chapter-by-chapter video and multimedia content

Chapter 8

Copy Basics
Get Their Attention and Hold It

We can show you the easy way to get an A in this class.

Got your attention, right?

That's what a headline is supposed to do. It appeals to your self-interest. It can promise a reward. It makes you want to know more. It can draw you into the ad to read more. All forms of marketing communications use headlines, even when we don't call them headlines. In television it's the start of the commercial. In radio, it's the first few words of copy. In a letter, it may be a title or the first paragraph. Once your headline grabs a reader, how do you keep the reader engaged? We'll explain that in the rest of this chapter and give you some handy tips to improve your writing skills.

Why Have a Headline?

David Ogilvy stated that the headline is the "ticket on the meat,"[1] which sounds rather simplistic for someone who wrote:

At 60 miles an hour the loudest noise in this new Rolls-Royce comes from the electric clock

He found a benefit (exceptionally quiet ride), included specifics (60 miles per hour), and twisted it with an unexpected comparison with an electric clock, probably the last thing you'd think about when buying a Rolls-Royce. At 17 words, it's very long by today's standards, but still memorable.

> *"The headline is the most important element of an ad. It must offer a promise to the reader of a believable benefit. And it must be phrased in a way to give it memory value."*[2]
>
> Morris Hite,
> account executive and
> former CEO, Tracy-Locke

David Ogilvy wrote one of the all-time great headlines using an obscure fact and a comparison anyone could understand. He didn't have to say "luxury," "quality," or even "quiet" in the headline.

Not all print ads have headlines, especially visual puzzles. However, it's important to know how to write a good headline first. Then you can decide if you need it. Some texts dissect and analyze headlines in great detail, but we'll boil their functions down to four primary points. A *good* headline does one or more of the following:

- Gain immediate attention (fishhook in the brain).
- Select the right prospect (appeal to self-interest).
- Lead readers into the text (tell me more).
- Complete the creative equation (synergy with visuals).

Types of Headlines

Categorizing headlines is usually more helpful in describing completed work than helping you develop new concepts. Phillip Ward Burton developed a list of categories that we liked.[3] We modified his list in Table 8.1.

Proven Styles of Headlines

Additional research has shown that certain styles of headlines tend to pull in more readers. Once again, it is far more important to write a headline that achieves one or more of its purposes than to have some empty bit of fluff that fits some formula.

This directive headline bluntly tells people what to do with the product.

Type of Headline	Use This When
News	. . . you want to introduce a new product, new brand, or new feature.
Direct benefit	. . . you want to promise a reward or highlight the prime benefit in the headline.
Emotional	. . . you want to sell the image and/or invoke resonance in the reader.
Directive (command)	. . . you want the reader to do something.
Comparison	. . . you want to differentiate your brand from the competitor or use a metaphor to describe your product.
Label	. . . you want to focus on the brand name, product name, or campaign tagline rather than discuss features or benefits.

Table 8.1   Types of Headlines

These three proven styles are:

- Question
- How to
- Quote

The first two are effective because they involve the reader. If you ask a question (and the reader is interested), you stimulate involvement. The same is true with a "how to" headline, but you have to finish the sentence with something that interests the reader. Quotations can be effective because they are usually connected to a person . . . and people are interested in other people, be they celebrities or ordinary Joes or Janes. A quotation hints at a story, which, if it interests the reader, fosters involvement. We offer some examples in Table 8.2.

Style	Headline	Visual	Client
Question	Ever see a grown man cry?	Broken bottle of whiskey on floor.	Crown Royal
How to	How to write an obituary for your teenager	(All-type ad)	Partnership for a Drug Free America
Quote	"I need an torque wrench as tough as my schedule."	Blue-collar worker in a maintenance application.	Enerpac

Table 8.2   Styles of Headlines

Echoing their TV and online advertising, Microsoft Surface goes head to head against Mac laptops and iPads.

A compelling question headline followed by a rather disturbing subhead. The two work together beautifully in this ad from Scotland.

Creating Headlines From Product Information

First start with a Positioning Statement, description, or that One Thing you can say about the product. This is not a headline, but it will give you some idea starters to build one or several. The image below shows how the process starts with the same type of Creative Tree we use for tagline development. You can keep adding more branches as you think of them. As with all creative writing, if you're on a roll, don't quit. Keep writing headlines even if 99% of them are awful. A real stinker may trigger a winner. You may end up with something that has no direct relationship to a specific product feature, but if it attracts readers and pulls them into the ad, you've done your job.

Writing Headlines With Style

If you work on it, you can try to add a little spice to your list of headlines. The following are a few suggestions. Try to work some of them into your long list and see if they lead to anything worth keeping.

Be specific: Let's go back to Ogilvy's classic. Do you think it would have been nearly as good with "This is one really quiet car" or "The clock is louder than the engine"? Without turning it into a laundry list of specs and features, see if you can work some details into your headline. Brooks Brothers quietly, but very specifically, states the value of its brand (reprinting a pitch for a 1942 newspaper ad): "It pays to buy at Brooks Brothers." Consider the economic parallels between 1942 and today, and you'll see how timeless simplicity can be.

Rhyme, rhythm, alliteration: As with taglines, using rhyme, rhythm, and alliteration can make a headline more memorable. Some might say a rhyming headline is clever. Others may think the same headline is cheesy. If it's memorable and sells something, who cares? Rhythm usually involves connecting a few well-chosen short words, such as "Coke is it." Alliteration, for those who can't remember English composition, combines two or more words with the same initial sound, such as "The Joint Is Jumping" or "Every Kiss Begins With Kay."

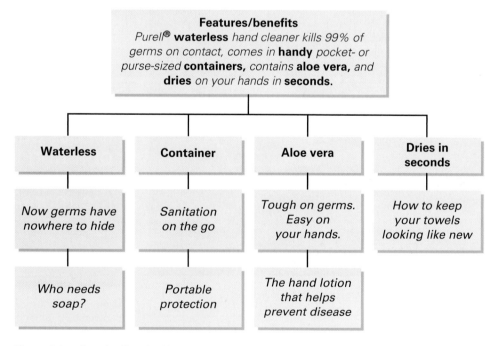

Figure 8.1   Creative Tree for Headlines

Judicious use of puns and wordplay:
Sometimes puns work. We did an ad for a luxury boat company that showed our product docked at a marina with many other fancy boats. Some of the other owners were checking out our client's product. The headline: "Pier Pressure." Cute? Stupid? You decide. This tip could also include wordplay and double meaning. As with puns, be careful.

Parallel construction: This is just a fancy way to say you're combining phrases or sentences with similar key words to make a point. A few years ago Florida tourism used the line "When you need it bad, we've got it good." Now, consider the timely rhythm of these words from Crate & Barrel: "Oven-proof. Dishwasher-proof. 401(k)-proof." A student wrote an ad for Purell waterless hand cleanser, making the point that money is full of germs and other nasty stuff. Her headline: "Dirty money. Dirty hands."

Single-word headlines are seldom more effective than this one. In an era when advertisers would not risk saying anything perceived as negative, VW gave readers credit for reading deeper to discover the real meaning of this ad.

Parallel construction: Traditionally moms were depicted as the family caregivers. In this approach, dad's the one who can't take a day off from the kids, so he takes Vicks products.

Headlines with a twist: Not all headlines have to shout the obvious truth. This simple play on words says it all.

Try it with a twist: The headline is part of the concept, so give it a twist now and then. Another example from our luxury boat client: we showed the boat at a pier in front of a very nice house in an even nicer neighborhood. The owners of our boat were hosting a very fancy outdoor dinner party. The headline: "If your neighbors aren't impressed, move to a better neighborhood."

Involve the product: Sometimes the package or logo can be an integral part of the headline. Then you really have some synergy between visuals and text, if it's done right.

Understatement/overstatement: George Felton makes a good point in *Advertising: Concept and Copy* about headline/visual synergy and tone: "If your visual is wild and crazy or obviously excessive, then back off verbally. And vice versa. In other words, don't shout twice."[5]

Ineffective Headlines

We can't tell you how to write the perfect headline. Unless it's an all-type ad, the headline usually doesn't stand alone. So the value of a headline is usually related to how well it interacts with the rest of the ad.

Be specific: Facts and figures don't always change opinions, but in this case the number of people cured of AIDS makes a strong point.

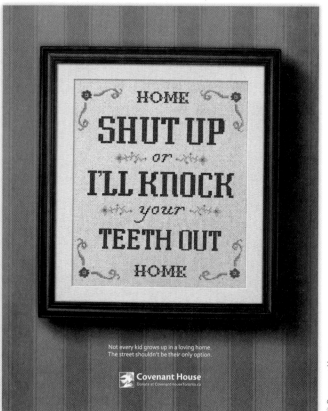

Overstatement/understatement: The headline cross-stitched in the homey sampler is so strong, you don't need pictures of domestic abuse to support it.

Crash Landing

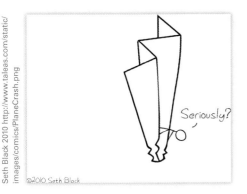

Seth Black 2010 http://www.taleas.com/static/images/comics/PlaneCrash.png

©2010 Seth Black

My grimmest battle in the trenches of advertising happened away from an agency. While freelancing directly for an airline, I watched in slow motion as my client did something so unthinkable that even writing about it here causes a feeling of posttraumatic stress disorder.

Ready? Make sure your luggage is stowed and your seatbelt is buckled, because it's about to get bumpy.

After four years of dreaming up campaign ideas for this airline—convincing travelers to pack a bag and plan a trip, no matter the season, airfares or weather—I entered some of the work my partner and I had produced into an award show that honored the best advertising targeting women. Low and behold, we won. The award organizers called to tell us the good news and to outline the announcement and PR planned for the coming weeks. They just needed a quote from the client.

The following day, the same award organizer called me back to tell me that the client had decided to do something no one had ever done before. They had decided to refuse the award. This had never before happened, and they were unsure what to do. I immediately called my client to find out what was going on. And here's what she said: "When our PR people sat down to put together their quote, they had second thoughts. They don't want to be too closely identified with marketing to women since we also market to business travelers and other segments."

At this point my memory is a little fuzzy, because I think I may have blacked out. When I came to, I reminded this client that women *are* business travelers. And that the family-friendly campaigns we had created for them that earned goodwill with parents extended into moments when these very same consumers were traveling without their children. I reminded her that one of our most valiant efforts—pulled together in 72 hours—had so successfully motivated female consumers that the client's server had crashed. I reminded her that women are not a niche or a subset group but wield the largest consumer influence in the travel category, paying the majority of her very own salary.

No dice. She kept repeating the party line that the PR people didn't want to be known as a female-friendly airline. And just like that, the award fell into the hands of the runners-up. I actually cried. Big, angry tears of frustration at the side of the road, where I had pulled over to have this crazy conversation.

I had spent eight years running an agency that specializes in marketing to women, only to find out that my biggest client had missed the point entirely. It was like running a vegetarian restaurant and discovering that your staff was secretly feasting on foie gras in the kitchen. This happened *six years* ago, and I still grimace every time I think about that client, that award, the overall business myopia. Clearly my battle scars are yet to heal.[6]

Kat Gordon, founder and CEO, The 3% Conference, San Francisco

The ultimate value of a headline depends on the expectations of the client and the results achieved. Some headlines just scream, "Think again!" Try harder when you see a headline . . .

- Asking a question that can't be answered (confusing).
- Asking a question that can be answered with a simple yes or no (no involvement).
- Used as a caption. They describe rather than interact (no synergy with visuals and limit involvement).
- Relying on stupid puns (stupid defined as having absolutely no relation to the product or market).
- Using insulting, condescending, patronizing language that annoys intelligent readers.
- Being clever for the sake of cleverness (trying to impress rather than persuade).

Evaluating Headlines

When writing headlines, you're faced with the same dilemma as with the overall concept. Do you write one that looks good in your portfolio or one that works hard at selling something? Once again, the answer is . . . that depends. Just as most people think they are experts on taglines, even more have an opinion on headlines. Some like straightforward news headlines, since there's no mistaking the message. Others like obscure references that hook a select group and leave the rest scratching their heads. Still others think silly puns are the height of creativity, while others just groan.

While there are infinite degrees of cleverness and clarity, our advice is:

If you can't be clever, be clear.

In other words, if you can't come up with at least one different, twisted, unusual, or interesting headline, then say it straight and always keep in mind that the visual is there to work with the headline, not to just sit above a caption.

Headline Checklist

Before you settle on one headline, run through the following guidelines. Your headline doesn't have to meet all these criteria, but it should cover some of them.

1. Let your headline sit for a while. Do you still love it the morning after, or do you slap your head and say, "What was I thinking?"
2. Does your headline work with the visual, or is it just a caption or, worse, completely irrelevant?

3. In your vision of the layout, does the headline look important? Is it readable? Does it have the proper proximity to the visual and body copy?

4. Can you do the "billboard test" and still have a concept that makes sense?

5. Does your headline appeal to the reader's self-interest?

6. Does your headline pull readers into the body copy?

7. Be honest. Is this the best you can do? Or can you start round two or three or four to come up with a list of great headlines?

8. Do not use a strong subhead to "explain" a weak headline. Use a strong headline, and you might not need a subhead. (Remember, less is more.)

9. Be careful with puns. There's a reason they're called the lowest form of comedy. Don't be cute just for the sake of cuteness. If a pun has a purpose, try it. Otherwise, find a more clever way to say it.

10. Think campaigns. How are you going to follow up that killer headline? Will your next five ads be just as good?

Notice the twist on a popular expression in this headline? The tagline has a twist too.

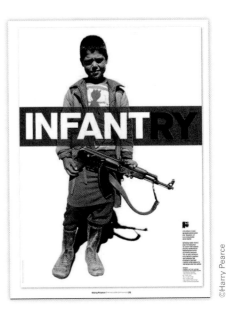

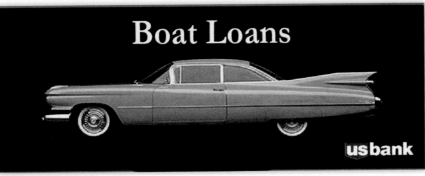

Sort of a pun. Sort of a twist. Sort of a double meaning. Sort of a waste of time, since the client rejected it.

The split headline clarifies the message in one word, while the placement and proximity to the child enhance the chilling message.

Subheads

As you would expect, the subhead is usually underneath the headline. Sometimes it immediately follows the headline, as if to say, "What we *really* meant to say is . . . ." Other times subheads are used to separate long copy blocks or introduce new thoughts in an ad. In this context they are sometimes called "breakers."

The four main purposes of a subhead are:

- Clarify the headline.
- Reinforce the main idea stated in the headline.
- Break up large copy blocks.
- Lead you into the body copy.

Subhead Traps

Too often subheads are used to "explain" the headline. You may feel the headline is too weak or that the reader won't get it. So you add a straight line so there's no mistaking the benefit. Many times this is done to convince a skeptical client that your risky ad concept really is a serious selling effort. We don't like subheads used this way for two reasons: (a) Why write a weak headline and prop it up with a subhead? Write a strong headline in the first place. (b) Use as few words as possible to convey your message. Adding a subhead can more than double the copy clutter in an ad.

Another subhead trap: Don't use the subhead to introduce a new, separate idea from the headline. Going back to our Ogilvy headline, you don't want to follow that beautiful headline with a subhead that says, "What's more, the new Rolls-Royce offers the highest horsepower of any luxury car."

Preheads

A prehead is also called an overline. Whatever you call it, it precedes the headline. You can use preheads for a number of reasons, but the four most common are:

- Set up the headline
- Define the audience
- Identify the advertiser
- Identify an ad in a series

© Mail Online

If you're looking for news about a ruthless headline grabber, the *Daily Mail* gives you two choices. This banner ad headline also reflects how newspapers now have to deliver both hard news and mindless fluff.

As with subheads, decide if the prehead is needed to explain the headline. If so, rethink the headline, and you may not need the prehead. In many cases, the prehead asks a question that the headline answers or starts a thought completed by the headline. In these cases, you could consider that prehead as an integral part of the headline.

Who Needs Body Copy?

We've said that the headline should lead a reader into the body copy. However, as you've seen in many of the examples in previous chapters, not all ads have body copy or any copy. In fact many people believe that readers won't read copy in ads and that the best we can do is get them to remember a brand name. That may be true, but a good creative person needs to know how to write body copy for print—magazines, newspapers, direct mail, and collateral. A complete copywriter also needs to know how the rules change for the Internet, mobile, and email, but we'll concentrate on traditional print media for this chapter and cover digital in other chapters.

You Never Know When You'll Need It

Versatility is one of the keys to survival in the creative field, especially in a tight job market. You might write a cool tagline now and then, but what happens when the client wants a campaign with a series of 200-word spread ads? You should know how to write all varieties of copy well. If you can't write that well, you should at least be able to recognize and respond to good writing from others.

Ads Aren't the Only Place You'll Need Copy

As we'll discuss a little later, there are many reasons to include copy in advertising. But there are so many other varieties of marketing communication where good writing skills are just as important:

> **Web Content:** An ad with one line of copy may drive a reader to a website that's chock full of copy. Writing copy for the web has its special rules, but a good portion of it is traditional advertising writing. The objectives are the same as with print ads: grab readers, hold their attention, persuade them to consider your product, and tell them how to get it.

> **Collateral:** Your ad may have only one line that says "Send for a free brochure." Who's going to write that brochure? Hundreds of millions of sell sheets, catalogs, brochures, flyers, spec sheets, magazine inserts, and other promotional items are printed every year. Somebody's got to write 'em all.

> **Direct Mail:** What makes you open a piece of junk mail? Somebody wrote something that caught your eye.

"I have always believed that writing advertisements is the second most profitable form of writing. The first, of course, is ransom notes."[9]

Phil Dusenberry, copywriter and former CEO, BBDO

Once you open it, you want to know more. Maybe it's a letter, or a brochure, or some other piece of information. Somebody wrote that too.

Reports, Plans Books, and Proposals: Who says creative writing has to be limited to promotional material? Clients appreciate a well-written, crisply edited proposal or plans book. In fact, any manager would rather read something that quickly gets to the point and doesn't waste his or her valuable time. You can take entire courses on business writing, and judging by some documents we've read, not enough people have taken these courses. Using some of the writing skills we'll discuss here will help make all your business writing better, not just ad copy.

What You Need to Know ... and Use

No matter the length or content of the body copy, you should keep a few basic concepts in mind. These apply to advertising, collateral, business documents, and basically any commercial form of writing:

- Don't write to impress—write to persuade.
- What you say is more important than how you say it.
- Remember the rules of English, but don't feel forced to use them.
- Write to the individual, not the masses.

This student-created ad tells a powerful story. It invites the reader to crumple up the sheet of paper. No matter how you try to smooth it out, the damage is done. She uses that as a powerful metaphor for childhood bullying. The government website is prominently featured to provide some help.

© Lauren Tibbs

Why Do We Need Copy in Ads?

Some ads just work better with copy. Here are a few reasons why:

Considered purchase: Whether it's an industrial flow-control valve or a power drill for a homeowner, people want to know more about the product than its brand name. Go back to the foundations of the project and find out how the product features align with the wants and needs of the intended buyer. Prioritize them and string them together with style. That's body copy.

Differentiate products: Why should a reader believe a Subaru is a better value than a BMW? Because the headline says it is, or because the copy details independent testing showing that the Subaru is faster, corners better, and performs better overall than the more expensive car? Sometimes you have to lay out the facts to make your case.

Multiple features: We hammer that One Thing into your brain. But sometimes there's more than one thing to talk about. You may lead with the main point but then bring in other key benefits to build a more persuasive case for the product. If you don't have the luxury of producing single-feature ads, you may have to find a way to weave several key points into the copy.

WITH GREAT SADNESS WE SAY FAREWELL TO:

JULIA GREENE'S
LEGS AND FEET

———————◆———————

They took her wherever she wanted to go, ever since she was a tiny toddler. From her first steps to the kindergarten gates; from music class into a class of her own at the orchestra. They gave her countless kilometers of jogging pleasure in the city park. Later, in that same park, they could barely carry her to a bench to rest. They failed her unexpectedly, shortly after her 41st birthday, on **17 August 2012**.

Regretfully,
the Williams-Greene family

WITH GREAT SADNESS WE SAY FAREWELL TO:

JULIA GREENE'S
ARMS AND HANDS

———————◆———————

They carried her little brother and later her own children. Through rolled-up sleeves, they helped with the annual, over the top Christmas Dinner preparations. They were the instruments through which her musical talent streamed; they helped her passionately produce hundreds of piano etudes and sonatas. They allowed her to strike countless chords, right up until the final, convulsive chord on **23 December 2012**.

Regretfully,
the Williams-Greene family

WITH GREAT SADNESS WE SAY FAREWELL TO:

JULIA GREENE'S
VOICE

———————◆———————

A voice she wasn't crazy about, but which her children adored. O how they loved the children's songs she sang; the bed stories she told. When they had grown into rowdy teenagers, it was the same voice that occasionally called them to order. And it was that exact voice that suddenly couldn't tell them how much she loved them, on the morning of **29 March 2013**.

Regretfully,
the Williams-Greene family

WITH GREAT SADNESS WE SAY FAREWELL TO:

JULIA GREENE'S
ABDOMINALS

———————◆———————

She adored her abdominals. Not because they gave her the perfect tummy, but because they had gifted her two sturdy sons and a darling daughter. She cursed them for hours on end when she brought them into this world. And she forlornly remembered them when they left her prematurely on **8 June 2013**.

Regretfully,
the Williams-Greene family

WITH GREAT SADNESS WE SAY FAREWELL TO:

JULIA GREENE'S
CHEWING AND SWALLOWING MUSCLES

———————◆———————

They gave her great delight in a glass of wine and simple pasta. They helped her – in all her nervousness – chew through many a pen. They allowed her to swallow the news that she was terminally ill. When she couldn't send a single bite down her throat. When she couldn't take in the sorrow anymore, on **16 August 2013**.

Regretfully,
the Williams-Greene family

WITH GREAT SADNESS WE SAY FAREWELL TO:

JULIA GREENE'S
CHEST MUSCLES

———————◆———————

She gazed at them in the mirror as a teenager. She later pressed them against the love of her life. Her children. They allowed her to heave heavy building materials during the renovation of the family home. They helped her sing heartily. And she thrust them forward, proud as a peacock, when her old son passed his final exams. They failed her for good on **29 November 2013**.

Regretfully,
the Williams-Greene family

WITH GREAT SADNESS WE SAY FAREWELL TO:

JULIA GREENE'S
RESPIRATORY MUSCLES

———————◆———————

They allowed her to regain her composure as she breathed in and out before a big performance. She used them to fog up her glasses, only to clean them afterwards. They let her sneak in a cigarette now and then, to ease the stress when she felt the need. They were instrumental in her final breath, on **6 March 2014**.

Regretfully, the Williams-Greene family

© ALS Liga België (The ALS League of Belgium)

Rather than show the damage ALS causes, this approach features a series of small obituaries for each part of the body that fails. The cumulative effect shows how devastating ALS can be.

Difficult, complicated, or controversial subjects: If you want to change someone's mind or have them do something difficult, a catchy slogan isn't enough. For example, a recent antidrug ad tells parents who smoked pot in their youth not to feel like hypocrites when they talk to their kids about drugs. That's much more effective than "Just say no."

The Case for Long Copy

Writing good long-copy ads (200 words or more) is a fast-dying art. Reason one: it's assumed no one reads ads, so why bother? Reason two: no one knows how to write long copy well enough to hold a reader's interest . . . so see reason one.

Be honest. Even in books that showcase the greatest ads ever written, do you actually read the copy? You probably don't even read the captions if they're more than five lines long. Before television shortened our attention span to 30 seconds, and the Internet cut that to 2 seconds, magazine and newspaper ads had enough copy for a beginning, a middle, and an end. We could feature many wonderful classic ads that read like well-crafted short stories, so damn persuasive that even we want to run out and buy the product. But showing these great ads from another age won't be much value if your creative solution is a three-word headline plus logo.

When we look at ads from the 1920s through the 1950s, we're amazed at the craftsmanship. The best ads had a rhythm and flow that sucked the readers in, held their attention, and, in the end, left them convinced that the right brand of baked beans or laundry soap could improve their lives. Can you imagine a 400-word ad today for any kind of commodity like detergent, cereal, coffee, cigarettes, or whiskey?

People will read a long-copy ad if they have a reason. John Caples said, "Don't be afraid of long copy. If your ad is interesting, people will be hungry for all the copy you can give them. If the ad is dull, short copy won't save it."[11]

The key to writing copy that's read, long or short, is to involve the reader. If the ad holds no reason to read on, don't expect anyone to get past a headline or visual.

Writing Structure

Types of Copy

Knowing the various types of ad copy will never be as important as knowing how to write a good sentence. However, it can be useful to recognize several copy styles and know when to use them.

On Being a Sponge

Courtesy of Alex Lahr

The path that led me to my first big-kid job in advertising wasn't illustrious or Cinderella-esque, like other creatives in the industry. I had an internship. I worked hard. And they gave me an offer. Pretty cut and dried.

But there's one piece of advice that's stuck with me ever since I heard it in a class my sophomore year of college: be a sponge. No, not a literal sponge. The path to success in advertising isn't assured by rolling around in water, despite how much fun that would be. Being a sponge means listening, collecting, and experiencing—soaking up all you can to form a better understanding of a topic. Being a sponge makes you more than an expert. It makes you an asset.

I started out doing intern stuff—pulling social media stats for reports, organizing and cleaning content on websites we'd built, writing tweets and Facebook posts, going on the occasional beer or cookie run. But there was always more I wanted to do. I craved it. Daily, I'd walk or scooter across the office and ask, "What else?" That threw my supervisors for a loop. They expected an intern who needed his hand held. Instead, they got a guy who poked and prodded for more—more work, more experiences, more liquid for his proverbial sponge.

As I was soaking up knowledge and experience at my internship, I was working my ass off with nine of my peers to develop an integrated campaign for a Milwaukee hospital system as part of our senior ad campaigns class. We spent hours speaking with and reading stories of women who had overcame breast cancer (our service line) to uncover insights that would resonate with women concerned about cancer care or considering a new health care provider.

Our campaign's messaging focused on empowerment, linking the internal resilience of our audience with the strengths and benefits of the health system. After absorbing all we could in research and strategy, then wringing it out in hours of copywriting, planning, and production, it paid off. The client selected our campaign over three others in the class, and the TV spot I wrote earned an honorable mention for student work at the Milwaukee 99 Advertising Awards.

Advertising isn't an industry where you learn everything there is to know, kick back, and watch the work roll in. Every single day you'll learn something new. Something that's exciting, baffling, boring, or maddening. And that's the beauty of it. Yes, you'll have clients that you'll find are a chore: the pesticide brand, the equipment manufacturing group, the outdoor brand with a 3% market share. But each and every one of them is an opportunity for you to learn more—about an industry, the platforms and tactics you'll be using, or, better yet, the people with whom your client wishes to connect. Every little nugget you learn makes you that much smarter, that much better at doing great things for people.

Being a sponge is what took me from intern to copywriter. I hope it does the same for you. Happy absorbing.[12]

Alex Lahr, junior copywriter, Thirsty Boy
@lonestarlahr

The story: This is also called "traditional" copy and features three main components: a beginning, a middle, and an end. Usually the beginning establishes the theme, makes a promise, plays off the headline, and in general sets up the ad. The middle is typically the sales pitch, with reasons why consumers should consider the product or service. The end is the summary and Call to Action. It wraps up the selling argument and encourages the reader to do something. A well-crafted story does not have to be a long-copy ad. But it should flow smoothly . . . as if you were telling a story that has a point.

Seth Godin has written several books about creating more effective marketing communication. In *All Marketers Are Liars*, he outlines some key points that relate to the advertising message, especially ad copy:

- Surprisingly, the less a marketer spells out, the more powerful the story becomes.[13]

- Great stories don't appeal to logic, but they often appeal to our senses.[14]

- The best stories promise to fulfill the wishes of a consumer's worldview: A shortcut. A miracle. Money. Social success. Safety. Ego. Pleasure. Belonging. Or avoiding the opposite of the above.[15]

Bullet points: Many clients will say, "No one has time to read copy. Just list the key points." In many cases, this is just fine, especially if you can't think of One Thing to say and need to list a lot of features. Usually, the points are prioritized by the importance of selling features, with the most important always going first. Too many times, the writer and client can't decide what's important, so they list everything and hope the reader will find something he or she likes.

You'll see a lot of bullet-point copy in retail newspaper ads, business-to-business magazines, and direct mail. This technique has sort of a "down and dirty" look, so it's usually not appropriate for a high-quality or brand image promotion. In addition, a long list of short bullet points takes up more real estate than a few well-written sentences in paragraph format. So if saving space is your only justification for using bullet points, measure carefully and reconsider.

One technique that can be very effective is a mix of traditional sentences and bullet points. The bullets highlight key points, and when done correctly, these draw the reader's eye to the most important selling messages.

One-liner: Sometimes the headline is the only copy in the ad. Other times the headline and visual work together to convey the main message, and a single copy line adds additional information. If you don't have to explain a lot about the product, need to direct readers to a website for more detailed information, or just want to promote a brand image, one-liners (or no copy at all) work just fine.

Writing Style

Advertising Is Not English (Even in English-Speaking Countries)

In other classes, you were told to write essays and reports with an assigned number of words, paragraphs, or pages.

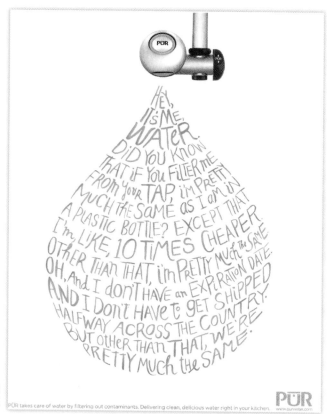

Body copy doesn't always have to be in nice neat blocks. In this ad, Pur outlines the cost savings of filtered tap water versus bottled water, all within a single drop.

These were graded for spelling, composition, vocabulary, and comprehension. Your teachers were not looking for tight, get-right-to-the-point persuasion, but rather how you could expand a one-sentence idea into a four-page paper.

In advertising classes and in the real world, your writing will be evaluated on how well you communicate. Period. Using real words. In the way real people talk. Your writing must attract a jaded reader and hook him or her in the brain. You are appealing to a consumer's wants and needs. Not to teachers who get paid to grade papers by the pound. As Shakespeare said, brevity is the soul of wit. Good advertising is both witty and brief. Now this doesn't mean you can completely ignore grammar and spelling. A copywriter can dress like a bum, but you can't write sloppy. Even though you may shatter a few rules of English grammar, the copy should be tight, easy to read, and clearly understood. Your copy style should be tailored to the target audience and the product. Remember tone? That should guide your style of writing. So an ad for a brand of chewing gum can be hip and informal, while a brochure for a million dollar yacht should be more formal and elegant.

Persuade, Don't Impress

When it comes to ad copy, you don't have to impress readers with how many words you know. Or even how much you know about the product. Instead, you have to persuade them that your product meets their wants and needs. And you don't have a lot of time or space to do it.

A common error many novice writers make is to show the client how much they know about the product, especially for new products or new clients. Or they dredge up every fancy word they can find in a thesaurus to replace the simple language most people use. You should make people believe how good the product is, not how smart you are. Some ads don't say, "Buy me," they say, "Look how I can repackage what the clients told me so I can show them I was listening." That's okay for the first draft. But on the next round, take out the meat axe and start hacking away.

When you're given a Creative Brief, or write a Copy Platform, don't forget to keep looking for the "So Whats." Find out what's really important to the consumer, and then see if the client's priorities mesh.

The "Seven Deadly Sins" of Copywriting

A lot of teachers have told you how to write. Now we're telling you how to write better—by pointing out some common mistakes and how to correct them. We call these the Seven Deadly Sins. When you see them in your writing, make a brief confession and do penance by rewriting. Even experienced writers commit these sins. As with other transgressions, you can't feel guilty until you know it's a sin.

"You have to tell a story, not give a lecture. You have to hint at facts, not announce them."[16]

Seth Godin, author of several marketing books

The Seven Deadly Sins are:

1. Advertising-ese
2. Bad taste
3. Deadwood
4. Generic benefits
5. Laundry lists
6. Poor grammar
7. Wimpy words

Let's explore each of these sins in detail and discuss ways to avoid them.

1. **Advertising-ese:** Don't confuse using proven selling words with the mindless clichés in some advertising. We've grown up with advertising jargon, so it's natural to write ads that way. Read your copy out loud. If it sounds like it should be on QVC, rewrite it.

   The best money can buy. You've seen the rest, now try the best. Isn't that amazing? Don't delay, call today. One call does it all. Nobody else offers this kind of quality at such a low price. Hurry, these deals won't last forever. Unique. New and improved. Exclusive. State of the art. Incredible. More for your money. Often imitated, but never equaled. You deserve the best. Get it now! But wait, there's more . . . and the list goes on and on.

In some cases, advertising-ese includes unsubstantiated claims or boasts of being the best without providing detail to back it up. If you can't prove it, don't say it, because you've just lost all your credibility.

Advertising-ese also includes trite punctuation, especially the dreaded exclamation point. If you have to add ! to a headline or even a line of copy, you're shouting that you can't think of anything clever or memorable. You used to see phrases like:

   It's just wonderful! The all-new 1965 Oldsmobile Vista Cruiser with the new, improved smooth-as-silk Strato-Glide transmission!

2. **Bad taste:** Sexist, racist, insensitive, offensive, and vulgar language. People can find hidden meanings in the most innocent messages. When you look at some of the ads from the 1930s and 1940s, it's amazing how African Americans were portrayed. In the 1950s and 1960s, women were shown as mindless neat freaks, more concerned with whiter shirts than careers. Today, writers who would never use stereotyped racial or sexist language think nothing of using sexual puns, vulgar language, and scatological humor. If you are appealing to a general audience, be careful what you say and how you say it. If you are going for an edgy concept that appeals to a very select group that won't be offended by your bad taste, go for it, and accept the consequences.

3. **Deadwood:** This is one of the most common sins committed by beginning writers. They say the same thing several different ways, time after time, in a very redundant fashion that wastes time and space, over and over again, ad infinitum. Say what you mean. Then tighten it up. Look for ways to eliminate unnecessary words and phrases. Don't overstate the obvious.

Original: Wamco engineers have developed several new ways to help original equipment manufacturers make products that are accepted better by their customers, which in turn makes them more profitable.

Better: Wamco makes your products more profitable.

4. **Generic benefits:** Also known as "weasel words," these benefits are so vague they could apply to almost anybody and anything. You may have attached a benefit to a feature, but have you gone far enough? Keep asking "So what?" and you'll eliminate generic benefits. Always lead with the strongest benefit. Readers may not get to it if you bury it at the end of the ad.

5. **Laundry lists:** This sin usually involves grouping features with no benefits and all have equal value. It's hard to find the "Big Idea." This is a crutch used by some writers who don't know much about the product, so they throw every feature into the copy and string them together with no relation to one another or connection to a benefit. The temptation is to cram as many copy points into an ad to let the client think you know the product. For example:

   This sleek powerboat features a powerful fuel-injected engine, two-tone gel coat finish, a tandem trailer, removable carpeting, lots of cup holders, an in-dash CD player, and a 5-year warranty. Who could ask for more in a family runabout?

6. **Poor grammar:** You should understand sentence structure, such as the need for a subject and a verb, and how to use prepositions and conjunctions and phrases. Given that, don't feel compelled to follow every rule of English composition. While you should not try to impress readers with your brilliance, you don't want them to think you are an illiterate slob.

Don't overuse the exclamation point! Also, don't overuse ellipses . . . they break up the flow and usually indicate that you haven't figured out a good transition between sentences. Use commas only when it's necessary to provide a pause or improve the readability. As long as your copy reads well, punctuation is usually a matter of personal choice.

7. **Wimpy words:** Certain words rob copy of its vitality. Writing in the passive voice also weakens copy. Beginning a sentence with a prepositional phrase or subordinate clause also dilutes the power. Some examples:

   - Usually you should never start a sentence with *there*.

Weak: There are a lot of reasons why people visit their friendly Toyota dealer. First of all there's the large selection they have.

Stronger: People visit their Toyota dealer for a lot of reasons: first, they offer the largest selection . . .

   - *That* is overused . . . try reading it out loud, with and without *that*, and see what sounds better.
   - *Be* verbs . . . "to be or not to be" is great for Shakespeare but not advertising copy. Derivatives of "to be" include *is*, *are*, *was*, *were*, and *being*.

Weak: If you have been considering purchasing a luxury sport utility, then you are in luck.

Stronger: Interested in a luxury sport utility? Lucky you.

   - **Passive voice:** Your copy should take action rather than being acted upon (even that tip reads awkwardly). The following shows one way to strengthen the message by changing from passive to active voice:

Worst: The passive voice should be avoided.

Bad: The passive voice should be avoided by writers.

Better: Writers should avoid using the passive voice.

Best: Writers should use the active voice.

The seven deadly sins of COPYWRITING

1. Advertising-ese
Write the way people talk, eliminate clichés, useless phrases, keep it conversational (read it out loud).

2. Bad taste
Watch for sexist, racist, offensive language and symbols. If it feels wrong, it probably is.

3. Deadwood
Weed out weak, redundant, unnecessary words and phrases. Keep the flow of thought moving.

4. Generic Benefit
Provide consumer benefits in terms they understand. Appeal to their lives. Lead with strongest benefit. Is one benefit so strong that it is the central truth or one thing about this product?

5. Laundry lists
Don't list features without reference to what they mean to the consumer. Weave benefits into the ad and prioritize them based on the consumer's point of view.

6. Poor grammar
Watch for errors in spelling, punctuation, and verb tense. Know the rules and when to break the rules. Use fragments if it improves readability.

7. Wimpy words
Use power words, active voice, short simple sentences. If it doesn't feel strong, it's not.

Power Writing: 15 Tips

We've discussed what not to do. Now we'll offer some recommendations that will help make any ad read easier and communicate more effectively.

- **Mix short and long sentences:** Sometimes short sentences work best, but you don't have to make every sentence three words. Mix up short and long sentences. Use the short ones for the sales message, or if you'd like, use the long sentence for the setup and the short one for the "punch line."

- **Use simple words if you can:** If you're writing a technical brochure for orthopedic surgeons, you're not going to talk about the "shin bone." But in most consumer work, simple language usually communicates best. Remember, you are writing to persuade, not to impress readers with your vocabulary. Again, we refer to the venerable John Caples: "Simple words are powerful words. Even the best-educated people don't resent simple words. But they're the words many people understand. Write to your barber or mechanic."[18] Caples found that a simple word change had an immediate impact on response rates.

Your grandparents may have told you about the KISS principle—Keep It Simple, Stupid or, more politely, Keep It Short and Sweet. While KISS is a very tired expression, it's still a good way to approach writing. You not only cut out deadwood, you can also put a little more life into your copy. For example:

Weak: You are really going to like your brighter-looking teeth.

Stronger: You'll love your new smile.

- **Write the way people talk:** Most people use contractions and speak in sentence fragments. Try to write copy as if you're talking to a friend. Read your copy out loud. Does it sound like a normal person talking or an announcer from a 1960s game show?

- **Match the copy style to the product tone:** More sophisticated products require more formal approaches (you'll never see "Yo. Check out Rolls-Royce. We got yer luxury right here!"). Copy for technical products should indicate some level of technical competence. But for the vast majority of consumer products, an informal, conversational style works best.

- **Active verbs and positive attitude:** Don't tiptoe into a benefit. Get right to the point. Use the active voice and show excitement for the product. You can't do this with every sentence, but try to make an effort to activate your writing.

- **Be specific:** "A bug-eyed Boston terrier" conveys a stronger image than "dog." Rather than using "soon," say "today." Instead of "It's been stated by many physicians," write "Doctors say."

- **Parallel construction:** As with taglines and headlines, you can use parallel construction in ad body copy. But use it judiciously and only to emphasize a point. Otherwise, it can become annoying or something even worse—poetry.

- **Alliteration, rhythm, and rhyme:** These techniques can spice up body copy. But use them carefully. You can emphasize key points, but you don't want your text to look like a string of slogans or a Dr. Seuss book. (So, you do not like rhyming text today, try it and you may, I say.)

- **Tighten it up:** The old rule is, if you want 100 words, write 200. As opposed to most good things in life, shorter is better. Find a way to say things in fewer words. Don't waste your reader's time. This is very important, so if we could say it in two words: "Write tight."

- **Use modifiers in moderation.**

Verbs are muscle. Adjectives and adverbs are fat. But you obviously don't want to write a series of two-word sentences with just a subject and verb. So use adverbs and adjectives as needed. You want your copy to be lean, not anorexic.

Weak: The appearance of your teeth is telling other people a lot about who you are.

Better: Your smile says a lot.

Too much: Whether your teeth are crooked and yellow or bright and shiny, your smile says an awful lot about the person behind it.

- Weed out overused words and phrases.

The list of overused words and phrases keeps growing *exponentially*. Wait, that's another useless term. These words and phrases pop up in daily conversation and have wormed their way into corporate speak and advertising copy. We are guilty of overusing them too. Sometimes they're still the right words. Just don't lean on them too much. It's hard to get them out of your system while you're writing. So take a pause and weed them out when editing. Find a stronger alternative. Who knows, maybe your solution will be become the next overused term *at some point in time*. Ugh. Did it again.

(Anything) on steroids

All in

At the end of the day

At this point in time

Bandwidth

Cutting edge

Focused on

Game changer

Giving 110%

Iconic

In the (whatever) space

It is what it is

Literally

Paradigm shift

Perfect storm

Push the envelope

Seriously

State of the art

Touching base

Unique

Viral

With all due respect (then insult the person)

- **Avoid being redundantly repetitive.**

Many writers feel the need to embellish a perfectly easy-to-understand word. We all do it, but the *end result* is deadwood. Here are a few examples:

End result

Final outcome

Free gift

Future plans

Going forward

Past history

Sudden crisis

True facts

- **Find inner strength.**

Some wimpy words are not necessarily incorrect, they're just a little flabby. Can you pump a little life into them? If you can't do this as you write, a thesaurus can be your best friend. But don't overdo it. Remember, the clarity of your message is more important than elegant speech. Here are a few commonly used words and some stronger alternatives.

Weak	Stronger
Cheap	Economical, affordable, thrifty, smart
Cold	Frigid, arctic, frozen, frosty, icy
Fall	Plummet, tumble, drop, dive
Find out	Discover, explore, uncover, unlock
Hot	Scorching, smoking, torrid, steamy, blazing
Large	Spacious, generous, expansive, roomy
Like	Savor, enjoy, relish
Odor	Fragrance, aroma, aura, whiff, hint of
Small	Compact, lean, efficient
Soon	Now, today, immediately

- **Write out loud:** Read your print copy out loud. If it sounds awkward, it will read awkward. If you need inspiration, read some of the great speeches of all times—fireside chats by Franklin Roosevelt, Winston Churchill's messages during World War II, John Kennedy's inaugural address, Martin Luther King's "I have a dream" speech, and Ronald Reagan's "tear down this wall" address in Berlin. They featured simple eloquence, memorable catchphrases, and vivid imagery. Most of all, they resonated in the hearts of listeners long after the speeches were delivered.

- **Edit:** And then edit your work again. Ask your roommate to edit it. Ask your brother to edit it. Ask your mother to edit it. Ask your partner to edit it. Ask your dog to edit it. In the end, our final comment on the need to edit your writing for stronger copy can be summed up in this statement. "Just do what you can to make it the best it can be." (Hint: there's a great slogan buried in there.)

For a change, we'd like to talk about *your* air bags.

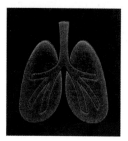

Take a deep breath. Relax. Get comfortable. You are about to read some good news.

Recently, Honda brought its advanced Low-Emission Vehicle (LEV) technology to everyone in America. All fifty states. Voluntarily.

It arrived in the form of the all-new 1998 Accord and the Civic. Both offer engines which meet California's strict Low-Emission Vehicle standard. But now you can buy one not just in California, but in Michigan. Texas. Ohio. Georgia. Wherever you live.

Both cars meet a 70-percent-lower emission standard for smog-contributing non-methane organic gases than is required by the most stringent federal standard. With no performance sacrifice or cost penalty.

Plus, in California and specific states throughout the Northeast, we're now offering our new Accord Ultra-Low Emission Vehicle (ULEV). It's the first auto certified by the California Air Resources Board as a ULEV, making it the cleanest gasoline-powered production car sold in the U.S. Ever.

That means, based on last year's sales figures, more than 60 percent of all new Accords and Civics, some 450,000 cars, will now be more environmentally friendly.

Historically, Honda has continually been a leader in fuel-efficiency and low-emission technology. Because we always think about more than the products we make. We think about the people who use them, and the world in which they live.

Which, in the end, helps us all breathe a little easier.

HONDA
Thinking.

For more about environmentally friendly Honda products call 1-888-CC-HONDA ext. 109 or visit www.honda.com. © 1997 Honda North America, Inc.

© Honda Motor Company

Even though this ad is over 15 years old, it's a great example of Power Writing. Notice the mix of long and short sentences, the use of specific information, the conversational style, and the smooth flow from beginning to end.

Checklist for Better Copy

After you've written what you think is your final draft, use this checklist. You might find that you're not done writing.

- **Strong opening line (pull-through):** Is the first line good enough to be a headline? It's got to pull the reader through. Readers take the path of least resistance—make it easy for them.

- **Appeal to consumer's point of view:** Why do I want to buy this product or service? Appeal to the reader's self-interest—what's in it for him or her? Remember the "So Whats." Is the style appropriate for the audience? Tell me about *my* yard, not *your* grass seed.

- **Clear central idea (the One Thing):** After reading your ad, will the reader be left with the one main idea you want to convey? Does your copy provide mixed messages? Go back to your Copy Platform to check.

- **Strongest sales point first:** Lead with the strongest selling point. The reader may not get to it if you bury it.

- **Strong supporting information:** Is the information persuasive and presented in a logical order? Does it support the main idea?

- **Easy reading:** Is the message clear? Does it say it in as few words as possible and as many words as necessary? Even the most intelligent people appreciate simple language. People will read long copy if they are interested in the subject.

- **Power Writing:** Can you use the active voice rather than the passive voice? Do you start any sentences with "There are"? Ruthlessly weed out unnecessary words. Get rid of the deadwood. Avoid clichés like the plague. Strip away the ad jargon and "me too" phrases.

- **Call to Action:** What do you want the reader to do? Where can he or she get more information? Where can the reader buy the product? For well-known, widely distributed consumer products this may not be necessary. But for retail it's mandatory. For technical products and other considered purchases, you need to establish a connection that may require several more contacts. The ad is merely a conduit to more meaningful communication.

Table 8.3   Checklist for Better Copy

You're Not Done Yet

You've just written a modern masterpiece of ad copy. You've avoided all Seven Deadly Sins. It's passed the checklist with flying colors. So what's next? Honest evaluation.

Give it a rest: The best advice we can give any creative person is **"Write hot. Edit cold."** In other words, if you're on a roll, keep going. Don't worry about word count, style, or even content. Write what's on your mind. Then put it away. Watch TV. Go jogging. Do anything but think about your ad. After a decent interval, look at your copy. Most people think, "Jeez, that's awful. What was I thinking?" So start the process again, this time with more focus and insight.

Mark Twain offered this advice for editing: "Kill all your darlings." In other words, get rid of words or phrases you think are cute and clever and focus on what really matters. Jim Durfee explains:

> "Advertising is a business of words, but advertising agencies are infested with men and women who cannot write."[20]
>
> David Ogilvy,
> copywriter and founding
> partner, Ogilvy & Mather

> "'Kill all your darlings.' If a single commandment could be burned into the mind of each beginning writer, it should be this one. . . . By shunning that darling of all darlings—the pun headline—I'm left with no-nonsense straight talk. . . . By avoiding cutesy-clever copy phrases I eliminate the danger of show-off writing. And when I'm writing long, flowing, beautiful, heart-pounding sentences (like this one) I know I'm in danger of spewing ego-garbage. Which endangers clear thinking. So I start over. Well, usually."[21]

Adjust your work habits: Everyone has a time when they're most creative. Unfortunately, it's usually not during the typical 9-to-5 workday. That's why it's important to write hot and edit cold. When you get an idea, jot it down no matter where you are. If you feel like writing 1,000 words at 2 AM, that's great. Email it to work and edit as long as you can stay awake.

Get help: Most good writers are excellent proofreaders—of someone else's work. They are usually criminally sloppy when it comes to their own writing. For proper editing, you need diligent, objective, and independent proofreaders. Don't rely on a computer spell checker. *You may have the write spelling butt the wrong meaning.*

Mark it up: Whether you're editing another writer's or your own work, document the problems or change them. This requires printing a hard copy and scribbling comments, just like your great-grandparents did. We've included a selection of editing marks in the Appendix. Use these when you're proofing your copy.

Don't stop: We can't think of a single project that we couldn't do better the second or third time (including this book). If you have the luxury of time, keep improving your copy. Replace weak words. Cut out the deadwood. Say it better with fewer words. Keep polishing that copy until it shines.

WHO'S WHO?

Janet Champ

Janet Champ started her career in advertising as the 15th employee, the receptionist, at Wieden + Kennedy. But Champ dreamed of being a writer and had the talent to back it up. Over her 15 years at Wieden + Kennedy, she worked on everything from Coca-Cola to Microsoft, but it was her work for Nike Women that made her famous. Champ won gold at Cannes, Best of Show at the One Show, and two consecutive Kelly Print Awards—the only writer in history to do so.

She was recognized by the National Women's Law Center, the National Women's Health Board, and the Office of the U.S. Surgeon General for the Nike TV spot "If You Let Me Play." In 1999 she was named *Adweek*'s Copywriter of the Year. Champ also has the painful distinction of having been sued by the surviving Beatles for the use of their song "Revolution" in the first TV spot she ever worked on. Since 1999, she has been a freelance copywriter "trying to do good, instead of evil."

Jim Durfee

As copywriter and cofounder of the Carl Ally agency, Jim Durfee was one of the leaders of the Creative Revolution. His philosophy was that advertising is a product, not a service. "A product," Durfee said, "is something that is molded, produced, thought out and set out before the person: 'We have made this for you, we think this will help.' A service is hat-in-hand and through the side door. It was a completely different attitude toward what an agency was and what an agency made."[23]

Jane Maas

Jane Maas began her advertising career as a copywriter in 1964. She worked her way up, eventually becoming a creative director and later a top executive at Ogilvy & Mather. Being a woman in advertising in the 1960s was not easy, and Maas, like others, endured what we now call "sexual harassment." With no place to take her complaint, at least back then, she eventually went to the top, speaking directly with David Ogilvy.

Ogilvy reassigned her, but made no changes regarding the creative director who had harassed her. She later joined Well Rick Greene. Her most famous work was the "I Love New York" campaign, which helped rescue New York City from bankruptcy and still echoes around the world. She has authored three books. Her most recent, *Mad Women: The Other Side of Life on Madison Avenue in the '60s and Beyond*, is a must-read.[22]

David Ogilvy

Founder of Ogilvy & Mather, David Ogilvy was, first and foremost, a copywriter. One of the pioneers of image advertising, Ogilvy also wrote two best sellers, *Confessions of an Advertising Man* and *Ogilvy on Advertising*. He was one of the most eloquent and influential voices in advertising and today is still one of the most quotable.

Puppy Bowl—Unlimited Creative Thinking for Out-of-Home

WHAT WOULD YOU DO?

Why is the Puppy Bowl so popular? This is the show aired by Animal Planet that spoofs the Super Bowl. Some people simply might say that puppies are naturally cute. Others might consider it a gentle alternative to football. For these and other reasons, the 2014 Puppy Bowl aggregated 13.5 million viewers over the length of the entire broadcast marathon lasting half a day.[24]

From its Facebook group to its YouTube videos, humans are watching and enjoying the antics of adoptable puppies. We know they're not playing football, but we ascribe human characteristics such as athleticism and teamwork to the puppies in a lighthearted manner.

Suppose we ascribed characteristics of consumerism? Sitting still to watch television or read a newspaper might be a bit far-fetched to imagine puppies doing, but what about catching the attention of puppies in the out-of-home (OOH) environment? According to the Outdoor Advertising Association of America, "OOH reaches consumers no matter what their media consumption habits are. It goes where most other media can't go to surround and immerse consumers out of home, where they spend 70 percent of their waking hours."[25] We can easily connect the outdoor hours of humans to outdoor time for dogs.

Consider the characteristics of out-of-home advertising. It can do more than attract our attention. It can surround us, immerse us, and refocus us. OOH can be as simple as ubiquitous billboards, but it can also appear in surprising venues and in unexpected ways.

What would a dog find attractive in an out-of-home environment? What has canine stopping power?

The challenge is not to cast the dog in the role of a human, but rather to cast the ad agency in the role of delivering messaging to dogs.

Dorothy S. Pisarski, associate professor, advertising, Drake University

1. Discuss the outdoor behaviors of dogs. Consider how they use their senses, what length of attention they may have, and their ability to focus on one or multiple things at a time.

2. As you would do with OOH human messaging, imagine and organize some ideas for placement of your out-of-home messaging for something of interest to a dog, such as a box of biscuits. Don't limit yourself to actionable ideas just yet; come up with a list of possibilities that stretch your imagination.

3. What senses would you attempt to engage with your OOH canine messaging?

4. Now, compare your experiences working on doggy OOH to your experiences with OOH for humans. Do the OOH elements that you are accustom to seeing match in creativity to those you crafted for your four-footed friends? Why or why not? Are they as attention getting? Are they as sensory?

5. What can you take from this exercise to apply to messaging in the OOH environment for humans?

1. Chocolate Coke

(Contributed by Roy Winegar, PhD, assistant professor, Grand Valley State University.)

Your team is on the Coca-Cola account at Leo Burnett. You are all gathered in the conference room for a major announcement. The client is ready to introduce a new product and wants to hear some campaign ideas to consider. Typically, this client will consider five ideas before deciding on one to move forward. The teams are given the task of coming up with five ideas each. As always, it's a very big deal to be the team that comes up with the chosen idea.

- The announcement: Coca-Cola has decided to add chocolate to its line of flavored Cokes, cherry and vanilla. They choke on the name Chocolate Coke, though, so to start with they would like a better name.
- Come up with five ideas for a name for this product and a headline for each. Knowing what you do about the Coke brand and imagining the possibilities for Chocolate Coke, find the One Thing and then use the Creative Tree to move forward. Good luck.

2. Brainstorming

(Contributed by Sheri Broyles, PhD, associate professor, University of North Texas.)

I have a cube that sits in my office, and sometimes it goes with me to class. It's my brainstorming cube. Like every cube, it has six sides. In addition, this cube has one of the following written on each side: Describe it. Associate it. Compare it. Analyze it. Apply it. Argue for/against it.

I write the topic on the board, say, hot tamales. Then I give the cube a toss into the classroom. The first person who catches it looks at whichever side is facing up, reads it out loud, then instantly responds. "Associate it. Movies." Then the cube gets tossed to another person. "Describe it. Wrapped in corn husks." Another toss. "Compare it. Hotter than Skittles." It flies all over the room, sometimes to a repeat person but eventually to everyone in the class. As the thoughts and ideas are shouted out, I write them on the board. It's very fast, and all ideas count.

When we're done we have a long list on the board that we can then go back and sort through. Sometimes you'll find new angles. Sometimes you'll find patterns. Sometimes you'll find thoughts that can be combined. You almost always get a broader range of ideas.

It's a quick technique that allows you to look at your topic from six different perspectives. That may reveal new strategic connections and the One Thing and will lead to the perfect campaign. Along the way, you just might find the right headline or tagline.

3. Consumer Packaged Goods

We've always figured that if you can write copy for a consumer packaged good, you can write for anything. After all, shampoo is shampoo is shampoo—until you read the ads.

Instructors: Pick a brand; we like Excedrin Migraine. Provide the students with a brief, so they are all working from the same strategic document.

Students: Develop three taglines each and be ready to share your favorite. (See Chapter 2 for tagline tips.)

Instructors: Make a list of the taglines on the board. Then, across the top, write the tips for effective headlines. Use this as a matrix to discuss the merits of each. Get it down to two or three and then have the class vote on the winning headline.

Students: From here, develop an ad with a headline, a visual, and 50 to 75 words of copy—using the new tagline. Present your work to the class and discuss the rationale for your copy choices.

Instructors: Have the students use the Checklist for Better Copy (Table 8.3) to guide their critique. It's very interesting to see how the creative varies and yet how each approach fits the tagline.

Review chapter content and study for exams. http://study.sagepub.com/altstiel4e.

- Interactive practice quizzes
- Mobile-friendly eFlashcards
- Carefully selected chapter-by-chapter video and multimedia content

Chapter 9

Print
Writing for Reading

The modern advertising industry was built on print. Advertising agencies were agents for companies looking for the best places to tell their stories, which at the time meant magazines and newspapers. Today, many people say print is dead, and it's true that traditional print media is in decline, but it still packs a lot of punch. We're using print to start our section on writing for each major medium. In this chapter we cover magazines, newspapers, and collateral. While the trend is toward using less traditional media and more digital, magazines and newspapers still capture a major share of the total advertising dollar. Instead of totally fading away, they are finding ways to integrate themselves with digital marketing tools. We'll begin by looking at creative opportunities with magazines.

Magazines

A magazine ad is an ideal palette for applying all the creative strategies and tactics we've discussed in previous chapters. Magazines also present a lot of creative opportunities based on the variety of sizes, shapes, and multiple-page combinations. Finally, a magazine ad is a perfect size and shape for your portfolio—small enough to fit anywhere, large enough for long copy and to make a design statement.

Why Magazines?

From a creative standpoint, magazines offer many advantages. Specifically:

Magazines are selective. Some magazines are devoted to very narrow interests, such as water gardens or old Porsches. Many general-interest publications print special editions based on region, occupation, or income.

In most cases, the printing quality is much better than in any other medium. Four-color ads really pop. And when you run inserts, the sky's the limit for the number of inks and varnishes.

> *"I approach print [advertising] as entertainment. After all, reading should be entertaining."*[1]
>
> Helayne Spivak,
> former global chief creative
> director, JWT, and head of
> VCU Brandcenter

BROCHURE FOLDS

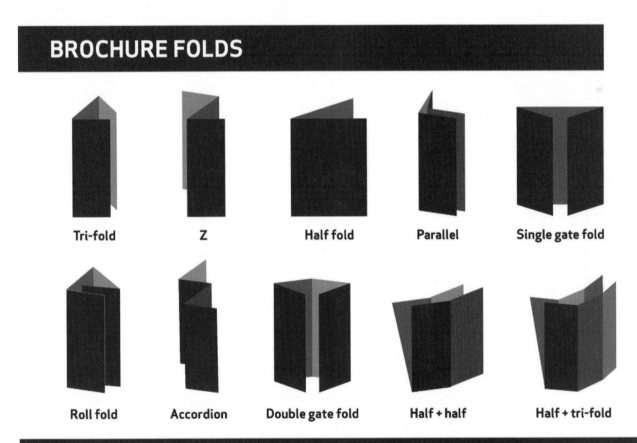

| Tri-fold | Z | Half fold | Parallel | Single gate fold |
| Roll fold | Accordion | Double gate fold | Half + half | Half + tri-fold |

Source: Alphagraphics

> *"Print copy can cover all the small differences that add up to a big reason for buying a specific brand."[2]*
>
> Hal Riney,
> copywriter and founding
> partner, Hal Riney & Partners

Full-page spreads let you create powerful concepts that resonate more effectively with well-defined target audiences.

Magazines give you a full-page palette and quality printing to stretch your creativity, as seen in this ad for a French diet dog food.

While QR codes in magazines have been around for some time, this ad takes another interactive approach. The reader can snap a picture of this ad with a smart phone to see what undetected eye cancer looks like.

Magazines usually last longer than other media. Weekly, monthly, and quarterly publications get passed around and reread. Your ads are seen longer and more often by more people.

Magazines can add prestige. Publications such as *Town & Country* reach an upscale market. So if you're selling expensive cars, jewelry, or real estate, upscale magazines are the perfect choice.

Many magazines offer value-added services to advertisers. For example, many business publications have "bingo cards" in the back where a reader can circle a number to get literature. Others offer advertisers their lists for direct mail or market research databases.

Magazines give you a lot of design flexibility. Whether you use a series of fractional pages, multipage inserts, advertorials, or a series of single-page ads, magazines give creative people and media directors a lot of options.

Magazines are integrated with the Internet. Most major magazines also have websites, which opens all kinds of promotional and cross-promotional opportunities for print and online advertisers.

Magazines and Campaigns

Magazines and campaigns seem made for each other. You can have a campaign within a single issue with multiple insertions. The periodic nature of magazines also fits many campaign strategies.

Magazines provide an opportunity for compelling messages that are even more powerful in a campaign. This series from Colombia encourages guerrilla fighters to come home for Christmas. The headline in each: "Before being a guerrilla you are my son (daughter)."

Since the readership of various magazines transcends demographics, it's natural to run ads in several magazines to maximize impact. Magazines also fit well as part of an integrated marketing campaign. Here are just a few examples:

- Use cross-promotion with a compatible brand to cosponsor a contest, sweepstakes, or special offer.
- Run a series of short-copy ads that direct readers to a website for more detailed information.
- Use tear-out mini-inserts that include coupons.

If they will fit within a magazine, include product samples in your insert.

Where to Find the Best Magazine Ads

You can find a treasure trove of great print ads in Ads of the World, Coloribus, and the major award show websites. We did. But you may also find inspiration in casual reading of ordinary magazines. We did that too. You'll also find some pretty creative uses of print media space in actual magazines that you usually don't see in concepts designed to win awards. If you are in charge of generating results in the real world, keep that in mind.

Buying a half-page spread dominates the spread so you can stretch media dollars.

Inserts give you a lot more creative options, including gatefold, barn-door designs.

This die-cut insert gives a three-dimensional effect.

Another way to dominate a spread is to combine a full-page ad with a facing fractional page. Leveraging editorial content when possible can also strengthen your exposure.

For years, the Association of Magazine Media presented the Kelly Awards for the best magazine advertising. Winning a Kelly was a major accomplishment. When asked what it took to win, Mal MacDougall, chief creative officer of Christy MacDougall Mitchell, gave the following advice, which applies to all print advertising:

> Keep it simple. Don't try to be crazy. Don't try to go to your computer and think you can do something off the wall. Do something within a very narrow strategy. The narrower the better. The strategy is a very short sentence; the soul of the brand you're trying to talk about. Simplicity is what's going to work. You cannot win a Kelly award with a complicated message. Get to know who is really reading that magazine. Decide whom you really want to talk to.

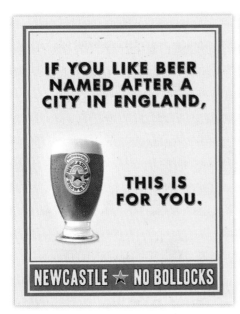

Newcastle leverages its cheeky British humor in print, as well as on TV and online. This series shows nice continuity in design and copy content.

Narrow it down to a tiny few people. Then you know exactly who is reading this golf magazine, fishing magazine, fashion magazine or gardening magazine. Make your message simple, clear and aim it right at them.[3]

Newspapers

What's black and white and read all over? Not necessarily newspapers. Today they use almost as much color as magazines. Read all over? Not anymore. Readership has dropped drastically, especially in people under 40. Even boomers who grew up reading the daily paper have shifted online, disdaining the cost and irrelevance of the *dead tree* medium. Still, in terms of advertising dollars spent, newspapers are a major force, especially when ads are packaged with both the print and online versions of the paper.

Why Newspapers?

From a creative standpoint, newspapers offer many advantages. Specifically, they are:

- **Local:** They fill in small niches, so you can pinpoint advertising in a city or suburban area.
- **Timely:** Ads can be changed within hours of appearance; they can promote short-term events.
- **Widespread in their coverage** (although readership is declining).
- **Controlled by the readers:** They can scan, skip, or plod through the paper (allowing long-copy ads).
- **Well suited for co-op opportunities:** National advertisers develop ads and help pay for them.
- **Specialized:** They include supplements and special-interest sections (sports, features, etc.).
- **Believable:** They offer news and sports first; entertainment is secondary.
- **Convenient:** Papers can be taken anywhere—trains, restaurants, bathrooms.
- **Large size:** A newspaper page offers a huge canvas for your ad. A full-page magazine ad is only a fraction of the size of a full-page newspaper ad.

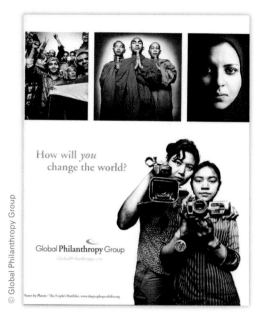

Upscale magazines are perfect for selling luxury products to the 1%, but they can also appeal to more worthy causes like global philanthropy.

Newspapers give you a larger palette to tell your story. Sometimes you need that extra space for a serious topic like wage inequality.

Retail Advertising

About $4 out of every $5 spent in newspapers goes to retail advertising. Retail is also called "local" advertising; however, with national chains running traditional-looking retail ads in national newspapers like *USA Today*, it doesn't seem proper to call them local.

Retail is different from other advertising in the following ways:

- **Urgent:** Consumers act on it quickly ("Buy me today or you miss your chance"). It works quickly or not at all.

- **Price oriented:** Most national magazines do not feature price; most retail newspaper ads do.

- **The cheaper the merchandise, the more elements in the ad:** Tiffany's does not have 24 different items with prices in their ads, like Walmart.

- **The store personality is very important:** What is the personality—bargain prices (Walmart), service (Nordstrom), "cheap chic" (Target), organic foods from sustainable growers (Whole Foods), or class (Lord & Taylor)? Remember, the merchandise could be the same at every store, so making the store image different is the key.

Online car shopping sites have basically killed the newspaper classified ad. But VW found a clever way to get their message out in a familiar format.

Tom McElligot, copywriter and funding partner of the legendary Fallon McElligot Rice, helped create some of the most iconic ads of his generation, but he had a soft spot for retail newspaper ads.

> There's no better place for a young writer than retail advertising. You learn the limits of aesthetics. You discover the world has no time for self-indulgence. You have to write ad after ad, and meet deadlines that force you to be fast. And every ad is judged on the basis of sales—period.[6]

The biggest challenge in designing retail advertising is organizing the various elements. You may have two, four, or a dozen different products featured in an ad. How do you arrange them in an attractive layout that stresses the brand, price, and store personality? When it comes to writing the copy, consider the following guidelines:

- **Tailor the copy to the customer:** Your tone should be in keeping with the prices of the products, the clientele of the store, and the types of products.

- **Be brief:** Just the facts.

- **Use direct benefits if you can:** Mention features if you must.

National Newspaper Ads

Most national newspaper ads are like magazine ads. However, if it's a daily paper, you can change the message every day if necessary. For large retailers with multiple outlets, you obviously can't list every store location, but you can convey a store's personality.

National newspapers are also ideal for corporate image, public service, and open-letter advertising. In fact, national newspapers are great vehicles for any message you want to convey quickly to a large audience.

When you want the best color reproduction or really want to make a spectacular splash, you can produce full-page (or larger) inserts. *USA Today* has included some huge inserts. One for a hotel chain in Florida folded out to 20 by 48 inches.

Sometimes advertisers insert whole sections in newspapers. Many readers pull out these inserts and keep them like brochures.

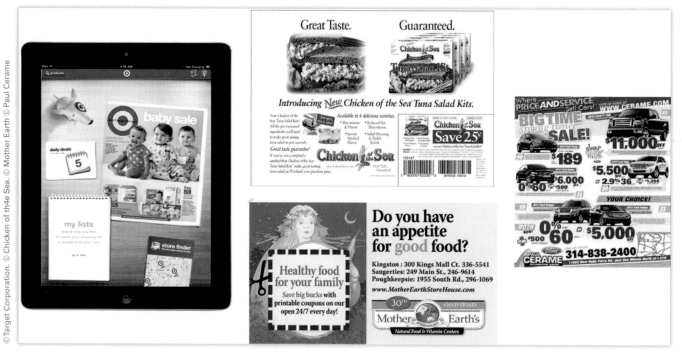

The purpose of a retail ad is to get people to come into the store. Now! There's no time to build relationships. Coupons, special deals, and limited offers generate store traffic, not brand loyalty. As far as design, they can be fairly classy, but most often resemble an explosion in a type factory.

© Georgina Flores

For more than 80 years, Allstate has built its reputation as the trusted brand that helps all people protect what matters most. Inclusive diversity has long been a core value. And since the mid-2000s, they have engaged the lesbian, gay, bisexual, and transgender community with targeted marketing campaigns.

But in 2011, the LGBT community identified insurance as one of the industries *least* supportive of them.[7] Inconsistent and complicated state laws meant that same-sex couples couldn't always get the same insurance discounts as married couples. It led to an increasing skepticism of superficial LGBT corporate "support."

There was an opportunity to use Allstate's Good Hands promise to connect with the LGBT community in a meaningful way. Our task was to win the hearts of this significant group. Not only did we need to demystify insurance but, more important, prove that Allstate was supportive during a time when acceptance of the LGBT community in the United States was split.

We started by understanding the unique set of challenges facing the LGBT community, unearthing a challenge entirely foreign to heterosexual people: *holding hands in public.*

It should be one of the best feelings in the world. It's an innocent gesture that says, "We are connected. We belong together. We are a couple." But for the LGBT community, this romantic act means publicly outing themselves. And that can sometimes be frightening.

Tackling this tension head on, we created "Out Holding Hands": a bold, integrated campaign that celebrates love, regardless of sexuality. It defends the LGBT community's right to show their affection publicly while acknowledging and commending the bravery it takes for them to do so.

To seed our message and rally support, we teamed up with our singer-songwriter Eli Lieb to create an animated short film called *Safe in My Hands*. It features an emotional song he wrote exclusively for the campaign.

The film tells the story of a man who feels ostracized and alone until he finally finds his perfect match. His unusually large hand is a visual metaphor for being different and feeling like an outsider, something that almost anyone—straight or gay—can identify with.

To further demonstrate Allstate's support of the community, we placed ads in both LGBT-targeted and general-market media, driving people to a dedicated LGBT Allstate website (allstate.com/lgbt), where they could watch the *Safe in My Hands* film, download an exclusive remix of the song, find a local Allstate agent, and get relevant insurance tips. And by using the #OutHoldingHands hashtag, photos and tweets aggregated in the #OutHoldingHands gallery on the site.

The campaign saw an outpouring of positive support on social media. And in a national survey in fall 2014, Allstate ranked seventh in unaided mentions among all brands that advertise to the LGBT community[8]—the first time Allstate has ever been on this list.

The "Out Holding Hands" campaign not only demonstrates Allstate's strong support of the LGBT community, but provides a platform for people everywhere to celebrate their love loud and proud. Because . . .

Everyone deserves to be in good hands.[9]

Christopher Warmanen, senior vice president, creative director, Leo Burnett

Newspapers and Campaigns

Newspaper advertising can fit very well into an overall campaign strategy. You can maintain continuity with other creative elements, plus you have the flexibility to make rapid adjustments. For example, you may want to use TV and magazines to establish an image for a product but use newspapers to promote its price or guide readers to local retail stores. Many tourism accounts show beautiful images of their destinations in color magazine ads and run price promotions in small black-and-white ads in the Sunday travel sections of local newspapers.

Making Your Newspaper Ad Work Better

The guidelines for writing good newspaper ads are basically the same as for other media. But note a few special rules for retail:

- Establish a store character (a store is also a brand).
- Use a simple layout (fine detail can be lost in newsprint).
- Use a dominant element if you can.
- Let white space work for you (or negative space if your ad is in color).
- State the price or range of prices (especially for retail).
- Specify branded merchandise (especially for retail).
- Urge your readers to buy now (especially for retail).

The Future of Newspaper Advertising

With continuously shrinking readership across the board, newspaper publishers are particularly alarmed about the decline among women and young adults. The Newspaper Association of America launched a rather desperate campaign to promote the values of newspapers to these two target groups.

If seniors need important information, they'll probably find it in the newspaper before they look online, as this ad explains.

Research shows that before bullies start hurting other people, they take out their aggression on helpless animals. This insight led to a campaign to promote humane treatment of dogs and cats, which may strengthen empathy for humans. Let's hope these people are reading the paper.

The "Smart Is the New Sexy" campaign used digital and social media to highlight the multiplatform experience of newspapers. It remains to be seen if the campaign just reinforced all the alternatives to the paper or actually brought young people back into the fold. In some cities, being seen with a real newspaper has become another ironic hipster trend, like skinny jeans, Pabst Blue Ribbon, and misplaced self-importance.

Collateral

Collateral is a big catchall category that includes printed material used for personal selling, handouts, and sometimes direct mail. The materials can be as elaborate as a coffee-table book featuring the illustrated history of a company or as cheesy as a black-and-white single-page flyer stuck under your windshield. Most students don't dream of writing the great American *brochure*. But somebody has to do it. And it takes some special considerations to do it right.

Collateral includes, but is not limited to, the following items:

- Product brochures
- Corporate image brochures
- Catalogs
- Sell sheets
- Capabilities brochures
- Personal selling kits
- Trade show handouts
- Annual and quarterly reports

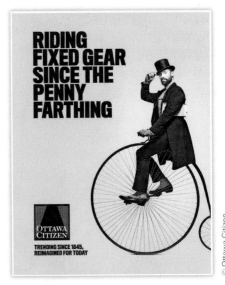

The *Ottawa Citizen* newspaper attempts to remain relevant to younger readers, claiming to be "trending since 1845" and "reimagined for today." Are you buying it?

Some form of collateral supports virtually every product, whether it's business-to-consumer or business-to-business. Collateral is included in direct mailers, personal selling kits, point-of-sale displays, meeting support material, to name a few uses. When you're writing collateral pieces, especially multipage brochures or a series of pieces, keep the following tips in mind:

- **Have a theme** and carry that theme throughout the brochure, whether it's a graphic or text theme (or both).
- **Think of the brochure as a campaign**—each major element has to work by itself and collectively with other parts of the brochure.
- **Appeal to wants and needs of the readers.** To do this you have to know and understand the intended target audience.
- **Think visually.** Even technical pieces need good, attention-getting graphics.
- **Pay attention to typography**, especially for copy-intensive pieces.
- **Stretch your thinking.** Consider gatefold pages, pockets, inserts, die cuts, windows, and other creative devices to liven up the design.
- **Consider printing limitations when doing your layout**. Don't forget that in most cases you have to *think in terms of four-page units* (unless you have one or more gatefold pages).

There are no other rules for collateral, except following good design and copywriting practices. Other than budget, there are no restrictions on paper stock, number of colors, binding technique, or paper size. Many businesses have drastically cut back on printed literature. Instead, they post PDF documents so customers can download them. This not only saves a lot of money in printing costs, but there's no inventory, and you can make changes whenever you want. If printing quality is not an issue and you don't need a salesperson to walk a prospect through the literature, it makes a lot of sense.

Collateral can range from high-end catalogs to Insty-printed flyers. No matter what size and shape they take, someone has to write the copy. A complete creative person should know how to design and write a variety of collateral pieces.

Shifting Gears: Print Versus Online Writing

As readers' tastes change, magazine and newspaper ads don't tell the whole story. Many people don't have the attention span to read a detailed print ad. Very often, print ads are not the primary media buy, but serve as mere reminders of campaign themes established in television ads and as a means to connect readers to websites or social media. A lot of creatives who want to just make nice-looking ads would be happy to eliminate most of that messy copy and kick the detailed work over to the web people. However, as a writer or creative director, you may be in charge of both functions. If you're in charge of a campaign, you know that each element has to stand alone and work with other components. So it's important to know how to connect with readers in print as well as online.

Following a Gut Feeling

Courtesy of Brenda Martinez

It was 2010. I was months away from graduation and beginning a career in finance. At least until mentors told me to interview for the Leo Burnett strategy intern position, saying it sounded "so me." I had no idea what Leo Burnett/Lapiz was or what a strategist did (strategize?). Yet, the second I started looking into the ad industry, I got the gut feeling that this was for me—I want this. Choosing an internship with no promise of a job in an unfamiliar field instead of a job in business, which I had a degree in, was very risky. But it just felt right.

And so I set foot in my first ad agency a month after graduation, and the rest is history. Four and a half years later, I still have that same sense of adventure and curiosity as I did on day one. That's actually my favorite part about the industry—it forces you to see the world through the eyes of a child. If, for example, I need to know what's going on with food trends in America, I go out and interview people on the street, check out school menus, walk the aisles of a grocery store, interview chefs, chat with my friend's mom, you name it. The key is to never assume or take your surroundings for granted.

I was hired at the end of a great summer internship and have been with my company ever since. From day one, my supervisors (now my mentors) included me in meetings with upper management, allowed me to make presentations to senior clients, sent me on business trips, and encouraged me to pursue projects of personal interest. I was truly challenged and set up to succeed, and for that I will always be beyond thankful.[10]

Brenda D. Martinez, senior strategist, Leo Burnett Group-Lapiz

lapizusa.com

WHO'S WHO?

David Aaker

Brand consultant and CEO of Prophet Consultancy, David Aaker is the author of more than 14 books, including *Managing Brand Equity*, *Building Strong Brands*, *Brand Leadership*, *Brand Portfolio Strategy*, and *Spanning Silos: The New CMO Imperative*.

Professor emeritus at the Haas School of Business, University of California, Berkeley, Aaker has been awarded four career awards including the Paul D. Converse Award for outstanding contributions to the development of marketing.

William Bernbach

Although he was the third name in Doyle Dane Bernbach, there is no doubt who was in charge of the creative process. Bill Bernbach revolutionized advertising from the late 1950s through the 1970s, insisting that advertising was more an art than a science. DDB broke from the tradition of lone writers who handed their copy to artists to render.

Instead, Bernbach worked in tandem with great art directors to create groundbreaking work for Volkswagen, Alka-Seltzer, Polaroid, Avis, Orbach's, and many others. Doyle Dane Bernbach not only changed advertising forever, the agency also spawned many the creative superstars of the 1970s, '80s, and '90s, who formed their own shops.

Helayne Spivak

Since taking the job as director in 2012, Helayne Spivak has led the VCU Brandcenter in its mission of helping the industry navigate change and fueling it with transformational leaders. Before joining the Brandcenter, she was chief creative officer of Saatchi & Saatchi Wellness. Throughout her advertising career she has held several CCO positions at such agencies as Y&R NY, JWT NY, and Ammirati

Puris Lintas. Spivak has been recognized by the *Wall Street Journal*'s Leaders Campaign, *Working Woman* magazine, the Matrix Award for Women in Communications, and as one of the Top 50 Women in Business by *Business Week* (1992). She has received many creative awards, including awards from the Clio Awards, The One Club, Cannes, the Andy Awards, and the Effie Awards.[11]

Joyce King Thomas

As a copywriter, Thomas was best known for MasterCard's "Priceless" campaign, which runs in 100 countries and has been spoofed by everyone from Ralph Nader to Bart Simpson. During her 17-year tenure, she rose to chief creative officer of marketing efforts, from advertising to digital and events. During her time at McCann, the agency won over a billion dollars in new business from brands like the U.S. Army, Verizon, Nikon, and Weight Watchers. She led the creation of iconic ideas, such as the Staples "Easy Button" campaign, which went beyond an ad campaign to become Staples' best-selling product. She is currently chair and chief creative officer at McCann XBC. *Advertising Age* named Thomas one of the 100 most influential women in advertising.[12]

Celebrations and Traditions

Matthew and Margaret met in college and had a great friendship. By their senior year they were dating each other exclusively. They went to graduate school in neighboring states, Matthew in Iowa and Margaret in Minnesota. Through some weekend visits and much communication technology, Matthew and Margaret were able to continue and deepen their relationship. After earning their graduate degrees and building their relationship long distance, they each began professional careers and started paying off their educational loans. Each felt dedicated to their relationship but also dedicated to being on a solid financial footing before taking on big bills for a wedding, honeymoon, and new home. By age 27, Matthew was ready to propose to Margaret.

After seeing a few free-standing inserts from jewelers in the Sunday newspapers, Matthew was no closer to figuring out where to buy an engagement ring. It seemed to Matthew that the glossy ads with stylized designs were too focused on young couples who could get caught up in the glamour of the diamond and not the years of commitment such as he'd made with Margaret.

It appeared to Matthew that engagement ring jewelers were not using their advertising to recognize anything more than young romance, and especially were ignoring the professional man who wanted to choose an engagement ring as a symbol of a serious commitment to a lifetime together. Matthew felt like these jewelers might not even offer high-quality gems. He knew several friends who had become engaged in college and had settled on selecting small, flawed diamonds or cubic zirconia that were big but not good investments. Neither of those options was appealing to Matthew.

Frustrated rather than enlightened, Matthew sought other ways to find a reputable jeweler who would give him personalized service and help him in picking the best quality gem in his price range.

1. Discuss how one person might view an engagement ring as an end goal, while another person might view an engagement ring as the start of a lifetime commitment.

2. How do you see advertising influencing traditions of events such as engagements, weddings, and funerals? Can you share any examples from family or friends?

3. Find some examples of ads for engagement rings in magazines and Sunday inserts. Do they appear to be targeting men or women? What makes you think so?

4. Choose one of those ads and prepare a list of changes you would make to the ad so that it addresses the opposite audience, for example,

   - a professional man
   - who wants to make a purchase decision based on logic and not emotion
   - and still wants to uphold the tradition of proposing with a diamond ring.

Dorothy S. Pisarski, associate professor, advertising, Drake University

1. Branded Shopping

Doing some ethnographic homework to understand consumers can be insightful for every creative. Let's get going.

- *Instructors:* Pick a branded product available at a local retail venue: Toyota Prius, Crest toothpaste, Apple MacBook Pro, Hoover vacuum cleaners, Lancôme cosmetics, or another brand.

- *Instructors:* Provide a Consumer Profile. Now that students know the product and the target, send them off to observe consumers in the retail environment. But first, have them do some initial secondary research on the brand.

- *Students:* Hit the streets, observing at least 10 shoppers interacting with the product and potentially its competitive set. Then generate a list of questions that will later help you access the retail environment and shoppers' experiences within that environment. What was the retail environment like? How did it feel, look, and sound? What was the sales staff like? How long did consumers spend in the retail environment? How many competing brands did they also interact with? Did they shop alone, and if not, who were they with, and how did they interact? How long did they spend with the brand? What were their physical responses?

- *Students:* Taking your ethnographic knowledge, concept three print ads with the objective of increasing traffic.

- *Students:* Share your ads in class and discuss how your ethnographic research in the retail environment influenced your creative.

2. Retail Roulette

(Adapted from an exercise shared by Sue Northey, chief strategy officer, Connecting Brands and People.)

- *Instructors:* Consider a particular retail client, the overall competitive set, and the target audience. Brainstorm a list of 50 adjectives that might apply to the category generally. Put each word on individual note cards (and save them for next semester).

- *Instructors:* In class, post the names of your retail brand along with its main competitors. Now hold up each word and let the class shout out which brand it fits. Create a stack of word cards by each brand. Where there is obvious debate, toss out the word card. For added depth you can also use images.

  - *Students:* Using each stack of adjectives, work in groups to create a profile of each brand.

  - *Students:* Now take the adjectives for each brand and use them as a seedbed for generating headlines.

  - *Students:* Pick one headline each and write copy for a newspaper ad, dropping it into a comped layout with a visual.

  - *Students:* Share your ad among the group and watch the brief come to life.

3. Going Traditional

We sometimes think of print as traditional media and digital as new media. Frankly, today it's more about what works than whether it's old or new. In truth each has a place.

- Come to class ready to share your favorite digital campaign. Your instructor will randomly select one student to present his or her campaign. Be prepared to talk about why you think yours is smart and on brand.

- Next, work in pairs to create a billboard for that brand. The trick is to make the billboard match the digital campaign. You also need to consider geographically where you would place it and why.

- At the end of class, share your concept. Everyone will be surprised what they find out.

Review chapter content and study for exams. http://study.sagepub.com/altstiel4e.

- Interactive practice quizzes
- Mobile-friendly eFlashcards
- Carefully selected chapter-by-chapter video and multimedia content

Chapter 10

Radio and Television
Interruptions That Sell

Broadcast media face new challenges from digital media that we couldn't even imagine ten years ago. Podcasting and Pandora have changed the face of traditional radio, and with it, radio advertising. Changes in television have been even more breathtaking. We see what we want, when we want, on any device we want. Netflix CEO Reed Hastings boldly predicted, "Clearly over the next 20 years, Internet TV is going to replace linear TV."[1] Still, commercial radio and television command a huge share of the total advertising dollar. As the lines between broadcast, cable, streaming, and online video blur, many of the tried-and-true principles still apply. We'll cover them here and discuss how to apply them in digital as well as traditional broadcast worlds.

Radio

So how do you get people to listen? More than anything, you break out of the audio wallpaper that radio has become. From a copywriting standpoint, radio presents a perfect opportunity for you to flex creative muscles in totally new ways. You're using words, music, and sound effects instead of pictures. When you're the writer or producer, the radio commercial is your baby, and the art director can't save your lame idea with a great layout.

Why Radio?

For advertisers and the people who write the ads, radio offers many unique advantages:

- It's everywhere, and it's free. There's nothing to buy (other than a radio) and no effort to find programming.
- You can stimulate immediate action. And, you know if your spots are successful.
- It supports local retailers and national brands. You can combine national campaign themes to support local stores.
- It features segmented markets. You can personalize your messages. Radio has become a very personal medium, so you can tailor specific messages to reach specific demographics.
- Radio personalities sell. Well-known voices have built-in credibility with key listener demographics.
- It offers creative opportunities. It's the ultimate creative challenge to create mental images with music, voice, and sound effects.
- Digital technology, such as podcasts, provides radio programming on demand

Streaming Music Services Versus Local Broadcast Radio

Commercial broadcast radio's slice of the total advertising pie has been declining for years. Music downloads, legal and illegal, have filled up iPods as younger people turn off their radios. Satellite radio, while not living up to its full potential, continues to eat into commercial radio's listener base. Led by Pandora, the Internet radio industry streams free music to its subscribers. Since the music is free, the online music providers live and die by advertising revenue or subscription fees. While the streaming music industry will continue to grow, especially with the rapid expansion of mobile, it still can't match the power of broadcast commercial radio.

> "Production is where 90 percent of all radio spots fail."[2]
>
> Luke Sullivan, author of *Hey Whipple, Squeeze This!*

Whether it's traditional broadcast or online, listeners control the content they hear, so advertisers can target audiences based on their musical, entertainment, or informational tastes. The listener determines the genre, artist or playlist, which allows advertisers to match their messages to the music. As with any advertising, the effectiveness comes from knowing the audience. Listeners of Pandora, Spotify, and MOG skew younger, so digital audio advertising needs to appeal to that skeptical, fickle, short-attention-span, tech-savvy audience. In contrast, commercials for commercial broadcast radio have to be produced to reach an older, more traditional listener who's content with blocks of 30- or 60-second commercials interrupting the programming.

Podcasting began as a novelty and has become a mainstream advertising medium. Most syndicated radio and many local radio programs are podcast for downloading to computers, MP3 players, smartphones, and tablets. Where popular programs go, advertising follows. However, with podcasting, advertising standards are not as stringent as with the typical broadcast message. For example, Durex, a condom manufacturer, ran rather risqué ads in podcast programming that probably would not have been acceptable on traditional broadcast radio.

Production Considerations

In most cases, the copywriter plays a big role in production. In smaller shops, he or she may be the sole decision maker for production—the person who selects the talent, music, sound effects (SFX), and production studio. As writer/producer, you supervise the recording and editing sessions, making sure everything matches your vision.

Where to start: When you're a beginning writer, the list of people who can and will help you is rather limited. Just for timing and testing purposes, any voice will do. But before you actually record the spot, think carefully about talent. Perhaps you can work with other beginning writers who are really into broadcast—people who work at the campus radio station or broadcast students. Check out your school's drama department. Those trained actors could be natural voice-over talents. If you're looking for the proverbial man on the street, take your recorder.

Motel 6 has used humorist, author, TV and radio personality Tom Bodett as a spokesperson since the 1980s. His signature line, "We'll leave the light on for you," was twisted a bit at the end of this spot.

CLIENT: Motel 6

TITLE: Zombies

:30

TOM BODETT: Hi, Tom Bodett. What's the big deal with zombies? Seems every day there's some new show about groaning, shuffling, half-dead people. Sounds a lot like business travelers. Well, use your brains folks, before they're eaten, and check in to Motel 6 for a clean, comfortable room at a great low rate. You'll sleep much better knowing that we'll leave the light on for you. 'Cause that'll scare the zombies away. Or maybe attract 'em. You know what, never mind about the light. Book online at Motel6.com.

It Takes Talent to Cast Talent

In the real world, when you work for a shop that's able to pay talent, your possibilities open up considerably. If you're not familiar with specific voice talent, you can get demos online from talent agencies.

Online firms such as Voice Jockey give you a wide range of talent choices and prices. Most voice talents are capable of many different styles, so listen carefully. If you're looking for multiple voices, you don't have to select them from the same agency or even have them work face to face, thanks to the beauty of digital editing. When you pick your talent, depending on the budget, you may want to hold an audition, especially if you have to sell the client. Preferably you can arrange free auditions with talent reading your copy.

Spend some time considering the voice talent. Even if you just need a straight announcer, there are many styles. Some sound "authoritative"; others are warm and friendly, with "a smile in their voice." The casting of character talent is especially critical. Be very specific about the voice tone, inflection, accent, and timing. You might need to write casting specs to help the talent agent find the perfect voice. Keep a file of voices you'd like to use for future commercials. However, don't lock yourself into the voice du jour—you know, the guy who's suddenly doing every commercial on the air. No matter how great you think your commercial is, it will start to sound like all the others.

Many folks nearing retirement would love to give this speech. Notice how many times the client's name is mentioned and that the announcer does most of the selling.

CLIENT: *Mutual Fund Store*

TITLE: *Retirement Speech*

:60

SFX: APPLAUSE IS ENDING

RETIREE: Thank you. First I'd like to thank most of the folks on 4, 6, 7, and 12. I spent a little time on each of those floors, usually moving up or down after some company acquired the company that acquired us, and I honestly don't even know what company I'm retiring from anymore. But, I do know that I'm happy to retire from it, and for that I thank the Mutual Fund Store. Without them, I would have been stuck in this godforsaken, soul-stealing, mismanaged corporate torture chamber for who knows how many more years. Instead of retiring today. Thank you. I'm out.

SFX: CROWD BEGINS MURMURING

ANNOUNCER: You work hard and the Mutual Fund Store works hard for you. We listen to you and your plans. Then we invest accordingly. Unlike many investment advisers, that's not the end. In fact, it's just the beginning. We keep watching your investments and listening to you. So let us help start building your retirement today. The Mutual Fund Store: let's put your life's work to work. Get started today by calling your local investment advisers at the Mutual Fund Store. Or find out more by visiting MutualFundStore.com.

Timing Is Everything

Beginning writers (and clients who fancy themselves as broadcast writers) sometimes have a hard time with the immutable time constraints of radio. They write beautiful 45-second spots and can't cut them down to 30s. Or they pack in a lot of useless filler to stretch them to 60s. How to make your creativity fit? One way is to count words. If you have a 60-second straight-announcer commercial, you should have between 130 and 160 words. As you approach that 160-word limit, your announcer is likely to talk faster, so the whole spot seems frantic and poorly planned. A 30-second announcer spot should be between 60 and 75 words. The announcer will thank you if your word count runs a little on the short side.

The best way to make your spot fit is to time it. Get a real stopwatch or use the app on your phone, and read the commercial the way you'd like it delivered, leaving room for music and/or sound effects that will take time. If you time out at 60 seconds, it's too long—because nine times out of ten, you'll read it faster than a professional. Try to give the announcer and producer a few precious seconds to play with.

Is This Funny? (Comedy in Commercials)

Few topics are less humorous than a dissertation of comedy. If you are naturally funny, you don't have to be told how to make people laugh. If you're not gifted with a funny bone, chances are no textbook can tell you how to use humor effectively. However, most people can appreciate humor in advertising, even if they can't deliver it. After toiling to write a funny commercial, you may find that drama or music may be a better way to go. Or you may discover that you have a gift. You'll never know until you try. So, what's funny? Comedian Carol Burnett said, "Comedy is tragedy plus time."[3] Most comedic situations are about pain or the threat of pain—physical or mental. That pain can be as obvious as dropping a piano on a person's head or as subtle as a mildly embarrassing situation.

Rejection is one of our most powerful psychological fears. So being exposed as stupid, uncaring, socially inept, weak, uncool, or just different can be very painful. And even a threat of rejection brings that pain to the forefront. But it's only funny when it happens to someone else, and then you need some distance in time or space to minimize the tragic effect.

Sometimes using pain in commercials is anything but humorous. This Ad Council spot uses kids' voices to give personal narratives about bullying.

CLIENT: Ad Council

TITLE: Learned

:60

GIRL #1: Today in school I learned a lot. In chemistry I learned that no one likes me. In English I learned that I'm disgusting. And in physics I learned that I'm a loser.

(GIRL'S VOICE CONTINUES IN BACKGROUND AS BOY'S VOICE BEGINS IN FOREGROUND.)

BOY #1: Today in school I learned that I'm ugly and useless. And in gym I learned that I'm pathetic and a joke. In history I learned that I'm trash.

(BOY'S VOICE CONTINUES IN BACKGROUND ALONG WITH THE FIRST GIRL AS SECOND GIRL'S VOICE BEGINS IN FOREGROUND.)

GIRL #2: Today in school I learned that I have no friends. In English I learned that I make people sick. And at lunch, I learned that I sit on my own because I smell. In chemistry I learned that no one likes me.

(GIRL #2 JOINS THE PREVIOUS VOICES AND CONTINUES IN BACKGROUND AS NEW VOICE BEGINS IN THE FOREGROUND.)

BOY #2: In biology I learned that I'm fat and stupid. And in math I learned that I'm trash.

GIRL #1: The only thing I didn't learn in school today . . .

GIRL #2: The only thing I didn't learn today . . .

BOY #1: The only thing I didn't learn . . .

(PAUSE.)

BOY #2: Is why no one ever helps.

ANNCR: Kids witness bullying every day. They want to help but they don't know how. Teach them how to stop bullying and be more than a bystander at stopbullying.gov. A message from the Ad Council.

When you're writing radio, first listen to a lot of commercials. Then think about what makes them funny. Or annoying. Or boring. These are some of the common threads in commercials we thought were funny:

- **Be outrageous.** While radio is theater of the mind, it can also be theater of the absurd. Stan Freberg was a master of using radio to turn the absurd into memorable commercials. To demonstrate the power of radio, one of his spots conjured up images of draining Lake Michigan and filling it with the world's largest ice cream sundae. The helicopter bringing in the giant cherry was the perfect way to top off the commercial.

- **Do something unexpected.** Remember the "twist" in Chapter 6? That's what we're talking about here. You introduce a topic, sound effect, or musical cue, and then take the listener in an unexpected direction. You can also take a seemingly straight commercial out of the ordinary with twisted copy. The deeper you get into it, the more it twists. Avoid the trap of giving away so much that the listener is ahead of the twist. Sometimes the gimmick is too obvious. It's as if you're saying, "Here's the joke . . . get ready . . . here it is . . . the joke is coming . . . and bingo, here's the punch line you already knew."

- **Use detail.** The combination of sound effects, music, and voice can provide a rich visual image. Radio can't provide detailed information about the product itself, but used the right way, details can make a commercial funnier and more memorable.

- **Combine extreme situations with realistic dialogue.** Some of the funniest commercials feature the most outrageous situations but use downplayed dialogue. Some of the most annoying commercials are just the opposite. The casting, timing, unscripted expressions, overlapping of lines, and subtle sound effects combine to make an outstandingly well-produced and funny spot. There is no way to convey this in print. You have to hear it to appreciate it.

Again, think about the commercials you find funny. Then analyze them for their structure. But keep in mind, it's not the formula that makes it funny—it's the content. A funny commercial without an idea behind it is useless. Above all, you have to be honest with yourself. If you're not funny, face it and move on. Most people aren't funny, and those who are funny might be a little screwed up in other parts of their lives. If, after all your introspection, you find that your sense of humor just doesn't come out in your commercials, try a new tactic.

The Most Interesting Man in the World still prefers Dos Equis beer. Here is a new chapter in this long-running series of verbal puffery.

CLIENT: Dos Equis

TITLE: Best Dressed Man in the World

:60

ANNOUNCER: His shadow frequently appears on best dressed lists. On multiple occasions he has vouched for himself. When he holds a woman's purse he looks intimidating. He can play Chopin on the drums. His tailgate parties have caused game delays. Eskimos have seven different words to describe his beard. Even his nod sounds like a plan. He is the most interesting man in the world.

MOST INTERESTING MAN: I don't always drink beer, but when I do, I prefer Dos Equis.

ANNOUNCER: Enjoy Dos Equis responsibly. Imported by Cervezas Mexicanas, New York, New York.

MOST INTERESTING MAN: Stay thirsty, my friends.

A Word or Two About Dialogue

Some writers forget how real people actually talk. In their effort to cram the client's name and as many features and benefits as they can into 60 seconds, they turn ordinary folks into aliens from Planet Schlock. Here are the three biggest problems with radio dialogue.

Problem: Consumers Become Salespeople

You've heard commercials where neighbors, friends, spouses, or whoever launch into spirited and highly detailed conversations about laundry detergent, motor oil, or feminine protection products. It usually starts with one person stating a problem. The other person comes up with a solution with lots of reasons why it's so great. The first person is instantly convinced and relieved that the problem is finally solved.

Solution: Use the announcer for the sales pitch. Let the characters talk like real people, and let the announcer do the heavy lifting. People expect an announcer to deliver a sales message, whether it comes at the end or separates the dialogue.

Solution: Use an "authority" figure. This can be a sales clerk, a doctor, a teacher, or anyone who is expected to know more about the product than the consumer. While the authority may be better suited to pitch the product, you still need to keep the conversation real.

Problem: Stilted Language

Even if characters don't become salespeople, many radio commercial conversations sound awfully fake. In reality, people interrupt, step on each other's lines, slur words, say "uhh" and "umm," and are generally pretty inarticulate.

Solution: Write the way people talk, and allow ad-libs. If you listen closely to some of the best dialogue commercials, you'll notice people hesitate, overlap each other's lines, use contractions and sentence fragments, and, in general, talk the way real people talk. To do this right, you need the right talent and the flexibility to let them ad-lib. Give the talent the general premise and have them improvise as they rehearse. The announcer can be as polished and articulate as you like, but keep him or her out of the conversation, especially for dialogue. Read both parts yourself or have someone else read with you. If it sounds phony, keep trying until it sounds natural.

Problem: Gaps in Conversation

Slight pauses between lines ruin many dialogue commercials. In real conversations, most people don't wait a beat before answering a question or responding in a conversation. Sometimes they take a dramatic pause, but more often they start answering while the other

"The best advertising comes out of a sense of humor ... and a realistic perspective on the importance of the product in our lives."[4]

Jeff Goodby,
copywriter and founding partner,
Goodby, Silverstein & Partners

person is finishing, so that words overlap. Dialogue should not be a tennis match where everything happens on either one side or the other.

Solution: *Compress.* Whether you do it in the actual recording or in editing, look for ways to close the gaps. That does not mean you want the spot to be one breathless run-on sentence, but go for good natural flow—in other words, the way real people talk.

Give Me a Jingle

As we discussed in Chapter 7, music can tie a whole campaign together with one catchy jingle. Most original music is not all that memorable, or if it is, it's remembered for being annoying. Maybe that's why you hear so many recycled popular songs in commercials today. Think about your target audience. Then think about the music they listened to when they were teenagers. That's when music was most important in their lives and what brings back the strongest memories. It's all about resonance.

Perhaps inspired by Axe's approach, Old Spice promises sex appeal in a spray can. In this musical-driven campaign, however, it's the moms who lament their sons' new confidence. The theme was already established with heavy TV play to give the radio a little more relevance.

CLIENT: *Old Spice*

TITLE: *Mom Song*

:30

MUSIC: IN AND UNDER

WOMAN SINGER #1: Oh, I didn't see it coming, but it came in a can.

WOMAN SINGER #2: Now my sweet son's been sprayed into a man.

WOMAN SINGER #3: Old Spice (SFX: SPRITZ SOUND) sprayed a man of my son.

WOMAN SINGER #4: Now he's kissing all the women and his chores aren't done.

WOMEN (SINGING IN TURN): Old Spice, new sprays, sprayed a man of my son. Now he smells like a man and they treat him like one.

MUSIC: WHISTLED OLD SPICE TUNE

MUSIC: OUT

Tips and Techniques

- If you forget every other tip, remember this: **Keep it simple.** Remember, one main idea per commercial—preferably one main idea per campaign.

- **Get to the point early and stick with it.**

- **Identify SFX creatively; don't label them.** For example, if you use a thunderstorm effect, don't have a character say, "Uh-oh. Looks like we're having a thunderstorm." Use something like "Looks like we're stuck inside all day."

- **Use music to evoke a place or mood.** For example, mariachi music in the background says you're in Mexico, so the announcer doesn't have to.

- **Repeat the client's name.** Some people say you should do this at least three times, more if it's retail. We don't have a magic formula, but if you do repeat the brand or store name several times, make sure it flows naturally and isn't forced.

- **Capture attention early.** The first five seconds are critical, whether it's drama, comedy, or music.

- **Use voices to create visuals.** For example, an old lady with a soft, kind voice is a loving grandma. The same voice that's harsh is a witch. Remember the importance of casting specs.

- Make sure your copy is **tailored to the market**. A hip-hop music bed is not going to work on a classic hits station.

- **Avoid using numbers**, especially long phone numbers and street addresses. Instead, feature the website where all that information is available.

- **Help your announcer.** Keep the copy a little shorter and watch for hard-to-pronounce words and awkward phrasing. Listen to the announcer if he or she has suggestions for making it sound better.

- Write the whole spot and **read it out loud** before you decide it's not going to work.

Parodies of news reports have been used since radio was invented. Students frequently rely on this approach because it's so easy to execute. This spot takes a long time to set up the situation. When the announcer finally comes in, he has to cram the client's name in six times before it's over.

CLIENT: Toro

TITLE: S'No Risk Weather Guarantee

:60

ANCHOR (TOM): Now it's time for weather, or not, with chief meteorologist Dick Hurlbrink.

WEATHERMAN (DICK): Things will cool off overnight tonight, Tom, with lows between 0 and 75 degrees, really no surprises there. Moving over to the Doppler radar, I'm seeing a mix of sun and clouds, and I'm going to go out on a limb and say we've got a possible certainty of rain, sleet, or snow.

TOM: A possible certainty, Dick?

DICK: It's certainly possible, Tom, sometime in the next fortnight.

TOM: Fortnight?

DICK: So, if you have any outdoor plans, you're going to want to make sure you pack an umbrella, some mittens, and a whole lot of sunblock, because it's going to be hot, or cold, that's my pinpoint-precision forecast, backed always by the Dick Hurlbrink spot-on guarantee. Back to you, Tom.

TOM: Oh geez.

ANNOUNCER: If you want a guarantee on the weather, don't look to the weatherman. Look to Toro. Buy a Toro snowblower by November 15th, and if your area gets less than 10% of its average snowfall this winter, you can get a full refund, thanks to the Toro S'no Risk Guarantee. Even half the average snowfall means you get 10% back. Either way, you get to keep your Toro. Visit Toro.com for details. Toro. Count on it.

Television

Mention advertising in a casual conversation and the discussion quickly turns to television commercials. They are still the most powerful form of advertising based on media spend and influence on consumer behavior. Television offers the glamour of show business plus the impact to make or break a brand virtually overnight. Creating a major TV ad campaign not only lets millions of people see your work; it may also shape pop culture for years. There is a reason some brand managers are willing to shell out nearly $9 million dollars just to buy one minute of air time on the Super Bowl. And that doesn't even take into account production costs. No other medium does a better job of delivering those three motivators— fame, fortune, and fun.

Technological innovation in digital television broadcasting continues to present new challenges and opportunities for advertisers. These advertising challenges are compounded by consumer access to video on demand through the use of smart TVs, video game consoles, and Blu-ray disc players.

> *"The advertisers who believe in the selling power of jingles never had to sell anything."*[5]
>
> David Ogilvy,
> copywriter and founding partner, Ogilvy & Mather

Serious topics, such as promoting smoking in children, require serious dialogue. The realistic dialogue here is far more effective than a typical announcer.

CLIENT: *Minnesota Department of Public Health*

TITLE: *Classified Ad*

:60

SFX: PHONE RINGS

CLERK: Good afternoon, classified ads.

EXEC: Umm. I wanted to put an ad in the paper.

CLERK: What would you like your ad to say?

EXEC: I want it to read, "Lost—tobacco executive's soul."

CLERK: (Pause) What?

EXEC: Uh. I lost my soul.

CLERK: What will the rest of the ad say? Just give me the general—

EXEC: The general gist of it is—I'm a corporate tobacco executive and responsible for promotions like giving free cigarettes away to kids during recess in other countries—stuff like that.

CLERK: Oh my goodness.

EXEC: I'm sorry—I missed what you said there.

CLERK: I just—the idea of somebody giving away free cigarettes at recess—it almost knocked me off my chair.

EXEC: Yeah, so I guess you can understand why I feel emptiness inside.

CLERK: Uh-huh. So, are you planning on staying with the company?

EXEC: Well, yeah. I mean, it pays really well.

ANNOUNCER: Corporate tobacco knows that if they don't get you hooked before age 18, they probably never will.

Technique	Variations/Applications
Straight announcer	Serious news style
	Humorous read
	Distinctive accent
	Voice modification (fast or slow)
Dialogue/interview	Two or more characters (slice of life)
	Announcer/consumer interaction
	Authority figure/consumer
Dramatization	Mini play
	Reenactment
	News/historical event
	Outrageous situation (comedy)
Testimonial/case history	First-person testimonial
	Story about person's experience
	Celebrity endorsement
Music dominant	Full jingle—original music
	Jingle with "donut" for voice segment
	Popular music
	Adapted popular music—new lyrics
Combinations	Any of the above so that one component is not dominant

Table 10.1   Creative Techniques and Their Applications

Non-real-time services allow broadcast of personalized content automatically where, when, and how the consumer wants to see it. The new challenge is to create commercial messages people choose, rather than just interrupting programming.

Changing Standards

Moving into the future, the 30-second spot may no longer be the standard. If users seek more information, they may tolerate a two-minute message. Or a series of 10-second prerolls may be all that's needed to reinforce a brand. This convergence allows advertisers to target precise types of traffic and tailor ads based on a user's watching history in a much more accurate way than the old Nielsen reports. Despite disruptions in viewing technologies, TV is still the dominant advertising medium, making up about 38% of the total U.S. spend, with digital amounting to about 28%. But this balance is expected to change in a few years when digital ad spend will surpass TV ad spend.[6] No matter how the ad is delivered, copywriters will still need to understand the basics of crafting a television commercial.

Courtesy of Christina Knight

In Sweden, there is a strong common belief that the state takes care of everything. Therefore, the general public is not aware that children's cancer research gets *no* funds whatsoever from the state, but is in fact entirely dependent on donations from individuals and corporations.

In 2012, when we won the pitch for The Swedish Children's Cancer Foundation, our assignment was to create an awareness of this fact and raise much, much more money for research.

Three hundred children in Sweden get cancer every year. Eight out of 10 survive, 2 don't, often due to the fact that research has not yet enabled new treatment methods and medicines to combat some, often more rare, forms of children's cancer.

Communication for charity organizations is always a tricky challenge. How emotional can you be or do you need to be in order to create an incentive to give, and how do you avoid crossing the fine line where it gets too emotional, so that the receiver simply cannot bear it anymore and looks the other way?

We decided to fill our concept with hope and convey the message that we've almost, but not quite, reached our goal of all children surviving cancer.

As we gradually got to know several children suffering from cancer, we also got to know them as champions, facing a gruesome and often painful fight, every minute, every day, often for years. We decided these children deserved to be celebrated as heroes, supported in the way we normally cheer on our greatest athletic heroes. The world of sport is full of superstars as well as of loyal supporters, but we decided to turn things around. The real heroes are not the sportsmen and sportswomen, but the children who fight against cancer every day. So we decided to turn a child into the hero and the traditional hero into a supporter.

In the world of Swedish sports, hardly anyone could be a bigger star than ice hockey legend Peter Forsberg, twice a Stanley Cup winner, twice a winner of the World Championships and the Olympics, and recently elected to the NHL Hall of Fame. We filmed Peter Forsberg as he met with Mattias, a 7-year-old cancer fighter, where Forsberg states that all the success and physical fights he himself has been through mean nothing in comparison to Mattias's challenge. The campaign launched on national TV and the web in March 2015, and to date has received close to half a million views on YouTube, which is a lot in a country with only 9 million people. But the most important thing is that the number of "Child Supporters" increased by 255% compared with the month prior to the launch, supporters who will bring much needed money to cancer research, enabling us to reach our goal of 100% survival.

We changed the name of regular donators from "Monthly Donators" to "Child Supporters," lending better status to those giving. Monthly donation is the optimal the form of donation, as money is withdrawn automatically every month from the donator's account, and donators tend to stay loyal for 5 to 7 years.[7]

Christina Knight, creative director, INGO – Ogilvy & Grey, Stockholm, Sweden

Why Television?

In addition to the above considerations, television offers other creative advantages:

- **Impact:** With the exception of the Internet, no other medium does a better job of combining sight and sound.

- **Universal access:** Almost everyone has a TV. Most American homes have three or more sets. TV is the great disseminator of pop culture.

- **Huge audience:** More than 110 million people watch the Super Bowl each year. But even the lowest rated late-night show attracts millions of viewers.

- **Segmentation (programming, time of day, cable and satellite):** Specialized programming makes it easier to deliver highly targeted commercials.

- **Integrated marketing:** TV is ideal to promote a promotional campaign.

- **It's perfect for cross-promotion:** With advancing technology, TV and the Internet are becoming a seamless entertainment and information medium.

- **More ways to view content:** You can watch your favorite program on DVD, or on your desktop or notebook computer, smartphone, or tablet.

Limitations of Television Advertising

- **Time limits:** Except for some cable channels and infomercials, you are limited to 10-, 15-, 30-, 60-, and 120-second messages. While it's easier to show and tell on TV than on radio, you still have to make every second count.

- **High cost:** While some websites offer TV commercial production for as low as $1,000 a spot, it has been estimated that the average cost of producing a 30-second national TV commercial is nearly $350,000.[8] Please notice that we said *average*, which falls somewhere between a Hollywood director's overproduced minimovie and a local used car dealer's camcorder spot. As with any other form of advertising, a television commercial can be as simple or as complicated as you want to make it. The best place to start is with freelancers or small production agencies. Some local television stations may offer to produce a commercial for you at a highly discounted (or even free) rate if you agree to advertise on their stations. Then there's the cost of airtime, which is subject to when the spots run, where they run, and how often they run. Availability and costs depend on the laws of supply and demand, rising and falling on economic trends. The cost of airtime is usually the media buyer's headache—unless the content of the commercial is connected to a specific program and the total package is a negotiated buy.

- **TV commercials are the most intrusive form of advertising:** Everyone says they hate commercial interruptions. It's when people go to the bathroom, get a snack, or just groan about "another stupid commercial."

- **Technology might stifle creativity:** Some people spend a lot of money on devices that let them avoid commercials. Online programs present new challenges to advertisers.

How to Solve Those Special Problems

Concepting. Really study the commercials you see. What makes them funny? Why do you remember them? Then analyze them—how do they handle transitions between scenes, camera angles, lighting, sound effects, music, and titles—everything that makes a commercial great? The rest of this chapter offers some ways you can analyze commercials and, we hope, use that information to create your own great commercials.

You may have to limit your concepts to spots you can shoot and produce. You probably can't visit or even simulate some exotic location, indoor shoots present problems without proper lighting, you're not going to have blue-screen or other computer-generated effects, and you're not going to get a movie star for your spot. Be realistic about what you can accomplish if you're planning to actually produce the spot.

Conveying your concept. Computers can help you produce professional-looking print ads. They can also help you put together a good-looking storyboard. Stock photos and scanned images work well in storyboards. If you're showing a progression of scenes using the same characters, you'll probably need to shoot your own still photography. Whether you use photos or marker renderings (hand-drawn art), make sure your storyboard captures the key frames to convey the concept of the commercial.

Postproduction. Since the advent of camcorders, shooting a commercial has not been the problem. The trick has been editing. Now with iMovie, Premiere, and other video editing software, it's easier than ever to make your own commercials. It still takes time, talent, and experience to know how to do it right. Make sure you have the patience to review every frame of your commercial for days until you get it right. The temptation is to say, "It's good enough" but it usually never is. Also keep in mind that even the slickest production can't save a weak concept.

Showing it. If you have a great TV commercial, you can import it into a PowerPoint or Flash program. You can also mix in your print and radio samples to make a multimedia portfolio. If you don't have produced spots, you can put storyboards in your book, but they have to be as good as your print work.

Consumer-generated content. Got a camcorder, digital camera, or smartphone? You can be a commercial producer. In this YouTube generation, the quality of the image takes a back seat to the content. In fact, if your commercial or video looks too slick, you may lose some credibility. Many marketers user consumer-generated content to generate buy-in from customers, drive traffic to their websites, and, if they're lucky, create a mainstream media buzz on traditional television.

> *"It is difficult to produce a television documentary that is both incisive and probing when every twelve minutes one is interrupted by twelve dancing rabbits singing about toilet paper."*[9]
>
> Rod Serling, television writer, producer, and creator of *The Twilight Zone*

Apple's iconic "1984" Super Bowl commercial consistently ranks as one of the best commercials of all time. It appeared only once but generated tremendous media and ad industry buzz years before social media.

Every year filmmakers hope to win fame and fortune ($1 million) in the Doritos "Crash the Super Bowl" competition. The formula is simple: people doing outrageous things to either get or keep their Doritos, a twist ending, and lots of product shots.

A number of major consumer brands have asked customers to come up with ideas for commercials. Is this a lazy way to avoid paying for creative ideas from their agencies or a clever approach to involve customers in the creative process? Doritos has established a tradition of hyping consumer-generated commercials on the Super Bowl. Most others have not been that successful as broadcast spots. However, through social media, consumer-generated videos have become one of the most popular components of online campaigns. Refer to Chapter 7 for more detail on consumer-generated campaigns.

How to Show Your Concept

You have several ways to convey your concept for a commercial. The one you use depends on the stage of development and conceptual ability of the person approving it.

Storyboards can be as simple as stick figures in frames. Many agencies still use marker renderings. If video and photography is already available, photo storyboards work even better. Animatic storyboards add a little motion with a soundtrack.

Script: This is the most basic and often the only method you may need to show your concept. It's written in the same way as a radio script, except there is a column on the left, "VIDEO," that lines up with the "AUDIO" column on the right. As with radio, the directions and effects are in CAPS.

Storyboard: For more detail, you can create a storyboard, with pictures of key scenes from beginning to end. The audio and video directions are under each frame. A storyboard can be sketched by hand or created with photography. Storyboards really help the producer, director of photography, and postproduction crew, as well as the client, understand the spot.

Key Frame: This should be the most memorable scene of a commercial. It may be the "punch line" or "payoff frame" in the spot. Think of the single image that a newspaper or magazine might use to describe a TV commercial, and you'll know what we mean.

Scenario: This is a brief description of the commercial concept. Typically, it starts with an introduction such as "We open on a . . . ." The scenario can describe scenes in more detail and can also work in marketing and creative strategies.

Styles of Commercials

Describing different kinds of commercials won't make you creative. However, if you start to analyze the various styles of commercials, you'll see a pattern. You may begin to understand why they are moving, or funny, or hard selling. A lot of the styles blend together, so you may have a celebrity in a problem-solution format or a vignette with a strong musical theme. We offer the following list of styles not as formulas, but rather to help you watch and then create commercials with a critical eye and ear.

Slice of Life (Problem-Solution): In the so-called Golden Age of Television, many commercials featured a slice of life (which was more often a parallel universe) in which a frustrated housewife couldn't solve some kind of cleaning problem. A helpful neighbor, an announcer, or a cartoon character told her about the advertised product and, like magic, her problems were over. Today's commercials (except for most infomercials) are not quite that cheesy, but they're still using problem-solution formats.

Demonstration: It didn't take advertisers long to figure out that TV is a natural to show a product being used. Especially one that moves. Demonstrations have also been very effective in showing what a product can do. The following are various types of demonstrations:

- Straight product in use (Apple iPhone)
- Torture test (Ford F-150 truck)
- Comparison with competitor (Microsoft Surface vs. MacBook Air)
- Before and after (Nutrisystem)
- Extreme/exaggerated demonstration (Volvo trucks)

The new steering system on Volvo trucks is so stabile, action actor Jean-Claude Van Damme can do the splits between two trucks—while they're moving at high speed—in reverse. This incredible product demonstration commercial won an award at Cannes.

© Volvo

Spokespersons: You don't have to be famous to pitch a product, although if you do it right, you might become famous. Some brands are associated with a single character, created just to promote that brand, such as the Maytag repairman, played by several different actors over three decades. Whether it's the CEO or an actor, some companies use the same person to represent them on TV. Progressive's Flo is a great example, although after a while they started running out of ridiculous situations to put her in.

When done right, a company owner or CEO becomes a brand's most believable spokesperson. Papa John's founder John Schnatter has done a great job pushing pizzas for years. Jim Koch, CEO of Samuel Adams brewery, brings a personal touch to his brand. Vacuum cleaner innovator Sir James Dyson is the perfect spokesperson to hype his products. A few years ago *Forbes* magazine stated, "The results of our analysis show that, in general, ads featuring CEOs outperform ads that do not feature CEOs. Across every metric we measure, ads featuring CEOs had slightly higher average scores vs. other ads in the same category."[10] Keep in mind that they said "in general" and "slightly higher average" scores. See Chapter 7 for more information about using celebrity spokespersons in television commercials.

Celebrities attract attention, but that's basically all they do without a strong connection to the product. Marie Osmond claims she lost 50 pounds with Nutrisystem and makes some personal statements as to why she needed to lose weight. Sometimes the same celebrity can be used to promote a product and ridicule the competition in the same commercial. Movie star Rob Lowe looked great as the spokesperson for DirecTV but also appeared as far less attractive Crazy Hairy Rob Lowe and Scrawny Arms Rob Lowe, the unattractive losers who subscribe to cable. While they were very popular, competitors challenged the actual product claims, and the whole campaign was pulled and eventually replaced with alternate versions of NFL stars such as Peyton Manning, Randy Moss, and Tony Romo.

Celebrity can be taken to ridiculous extremes. Jeff Goldblum, as famous person Terry Quattro, demonstrates how superior lighting can make an ordinary nobody more attractive (at least in his own mind).

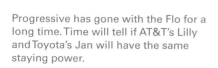

Progressive has gone with the Flo for a long time. Time will tell if AT&T's Lilly and Toyota's Jan will have the same staying power.

Courtesy of Derrick Harmon

In my early years, all I wanted to do was draw cartoons. I remember my mother trying to guide me toward more fine art, but I constantly rebelled. That rebellion meant that every piece of scrap paper, every notebook cover, every envelope left on the counter, was subject to a *toon*. Then came the popular interest in graffiti art. By the time I was a senior in high school, I knew I had to pursue some form of art education. The following September, I was enrolled in the Savannah College of Art & Design (SCAD); amongst the creative introverts, misfits, and outcasts, I felt right at home.

Four quarters into my education, financial complexities led me to take a brief five-year hiatus. But in that time, I was able to explore another creative outlet, hip-hop. Some other SCAD ex-pats and I formed a crew, Dope Sandwich, and in the coming years, we became Savannah's official hip-hop scene. I was officially labeled an MC.

During the Sandwich's rise, I decided to go back to SCAD and finish what I had started five years prior. Advertising design was a fairly new major, but seemed a bit more lucrative than cartoonist. I had recognized the similarities between rap and ads almost instantly. These two forms of communication both rely on specific messages to be packaged and delivered in a memorable way, usually by a clever character. I can do this. I'm going to do this.

After graduation, I decided to continue with my music, but after two additional years of mixtapes and tours, I felt like I needed a new challenge. I still had a flicker of a flame in my heart for advertising, so with the last of my savings and a couple packed suitcases, I hopped a plane for Chicago, challenge accepted. My portfolio was subpar, I had no industry contacts, and I was working as a bouncer in Wrigleyville wondering, "Is this what I signed up for?" But through a few well-timed emails, I found myself at Burrell Communications as a junior art director. There, I was able to dive head first into the industry, while finding ways to inject a little of my culture into my craft. Reese's Puffs became the first of my brands to fully embrace that culture, allowing me to package their key messaging in some tasty verses. With hip-hop culture becoming more prominent in mainstream advertising, I look forward to seeing more *heads* like me, finding creative opportunities in this industry.[11]

Derrick Harmon, senior art director, Burrell Communications

derrickharmon.com

Storyline: This may be a minimovie, with a beginning, a middle, and an end. Budweiser has produced a series of popular brand-reinforcing commercials featuring their iconic Clydesdales. For example, in one classic spot a Clydesdale meets a circus horse and chases across the country to find her, and the two run away, presumably to live happily ever after. Several commercials from Thailand became Internet sensations through the combination of great cinematography and a positive message of pay-it-forward kindness to strangers.

Chapter 10 *Radio and Television* 259

To commemorate the 100th anniversary of the "Christmas Truce" of World War I, Britain's Sainsbury's produced a beautiful long-format commercial that had many viewers in tears.

Vignettes: These are usually made from a series of short clips that are strung together, usually with a strong musical track to hold it all together. Vignettes can be used to show different people using the same product or a variety of products with the same brand. A good example of using vignettes was the global "I'm Lovin' It" campaign for McDonald's. The initial spots showed a wide variety of ages and races. An example of different products for the same brand would include some Honda corporate spots that showed cars, lawnmowers, motorcycles, generators, and all the other products that Honda makes. Each vignette could be a separate commercial, and short clips from two, three, or four of them could be strung together to make a longer commercial or online video. Usually you need a strong musical score to hold them together. Another campaign consideration is adapting the concept from a series of print ads into a vignette commercial.

Musical: It's hard to separate music as a category, since it's so integral to commercials today. However, we'll consider this as a unique type when music is the dominant factor of the commercial. Car manufacturers typically show a lot of quick cuts of dramatic action sequences, backed by a fast moving soundtrack. The TV jingle is still alive, but usually done for comedic effect. For example, Old Spice ran a series of commercials with distraught mothers singing about how using Old Spice made their boys into men.

©Thai Life

Some longer format commercials from Thailand became Internet sensations thanks to their beautiful production techniques and powerful, positive messages. In "The Unsung Hero," the poor but noble hero begins helping strangers in small ways. Their lives improve and his is enriched. So we all shed a tear, share the spot, and think about helping others. At least that's the theory.

Humor in TV

It's hard to be academic about humor. It's not a science; it just happens. But it touches the most basic human need to laugh at our troubles. Maybe that's why the commercials people remember most seem to be the funny ones. Probably 9 out of the top 10 Super Bowl spots each year are meant to be funny. As with radio, don't start out to create a funny television spot. You may have a good joke, but it's not a commercial unless it sells something. Luke Sullivan offers some excellent advice for writers who want to make their mark with humorous TV spots: "Don't set out to be funny. Set out to be interesting. I find it interesting that the Clios had a category called Best Use of Humor. And curiously, no Best Use of Seriousness."[13]

What Makes It Funny?

Some of the funniest commercials include at least some of the following elements:

- **The unexpected:** Throw in a surprise ending, a twist, a zinger, something they don't see coming. Many times that unexpected ending involves pain—physical or mental.

- **Pain or risk of pain:** The old formula of tragedy plus time works for TV even better than radio, because you can show it as well as tell it.

- **Exaggeration:** Making things extremely bigger, smaller, faster, or slower than expected can be humorous. So can giving animals human traits or vice versa. Extreme behavior can be funny too.

© Anheuser-Busch

Budweiser perennially wins the top honors for Super Bowl commercials with a proven formula: cute puppy, iconic Clydesdales, heartwarming storyline, and very nice production values. What's not to love?

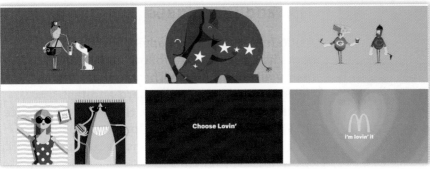

© McDonald's

Facing declining sales and negative publicity, McDonald's launched the "Lovin' beats hatin'" theme that complemented, but did not replace, the venerable "I'm lovin' it" slogan. The music-driven animated spot showed archenemies united by their love of McDonald's in a flat art style similar to 2013's "Dumb Ways to Die."

When it comes to advertising effectiveness, humor has some limitations:

- Humor may build awareness of a brand, but not much comprehension of what makes that brand better. (Snickers)

- Humor usually doesn't add much credibility to a spokesperson. In fact, an "authoritative" spokesperson is usually a parody. (Jeff Goldblum for GE lightbulbs)

- Humor works better for radio, TV, and online video, not so much for print. So if your campaign is strongly based on humor, make sure it can be extended to other media. (Chick-fil-A)

- Humor is used most often to connect with younger, upscale, male audiences. We're not saying older women don't have a sense of humor. Maybe it's because young, affluent men write most of the commercials.

What Makes It Good?

You need more than a funny situation to make a good commercial. Many humorous ideas fall flat because of poor production. The best humorous commercials need all four of the following:

- **Good direction:** The writer and director need to know when to use a wide shot, when to zoom in, how many scenes to use, and all the other intangibles that make a good spot great.

- **Attention to detail:** Do the sets look real? Are little kids dressed like real children? Are the props accurate for the time frame depicted? Little things mean a lot, and they show.

- **Talent/acting:** This is perhaps the most critical element. The same qualities that make a great comic actor different from a clown apply to commercials. Remember that with TV, you can show subtle expressions and nuances in close-ups. You don't need the broad gestures of a stand-up comic or stage actor.

- **Editing:** Well-executed postproduction makes a huge difference. The timing and transition of scenes can turn a "cute" concept into a truly funny commercial.

Tips and Techniques

Aside from the general advice for humorous spots listed above, the following tips apply to nearly all commercials. These are offered as rules of thumb and not as hard-and-fast guidelines you must follow. However, experience shows that you can have a lot better results if you heed most of them when you are critiquing commercials.

© Honda Motor Company

In a holiday campaign, Honda animated the must-have presents from the early 1990s to attract Millennials thinking about buying a new toy. Consumers could vote online for the video featuring their favorite toy to raise money for urban little league.

- **Get immediate attention.** The first 3 to 10 seconds are critical. Make the first couple of seconds visually interesting.

- **Stick with one main idea.** Keep it simple. Don't try cramming more than 2 or 3 scenes per 10 seconds or more than 10 scenes per 30. If you're using vignettes, you might need a lot more.

- **Think about brand awareness.** Show the product and involve characters with it.

- **Use titles to reinforce key points.** But not so many that viewers feel like they are reading the commercial.

- **Think visually.** Consider how you want to move within a scene, transition between scenes, and change scenes.

- **Don't forget synergy.** Don't show what you're saying or say what you're showing.

- **Audio is still important.** Use music and SFX to describe place or mood.

- **Make every word count—count every word.** The rule of thumb is about 2 words per second and about 60 words for a 30-second spot. That's less than radio.

- **Give the viewers some credit.** Let them complete the creative equation.

- **Don't overexplain.** They'll remember it better, too.

- **Keep conversation real.** Dialogue should be natural, not forced. Let the announcer be the salesperson, if you have to have one.

- **Don't save it all for the ending.** A commercial should be entertaining throughout the whole spot. Don't have a sloppy buildup to a punch line.

- **Think in campaigns.** Make your commercial compatible with, but not identical to, the other elements. It should not be a video version of the print ad. Think in terms of extending a concept without repeating the same idea in subsequent spots.

- **Study great commercials.** Look for style, camera angles, editing techniques, and so on. Understand what makes them great.

Power Writing for TV and Video

Writing isn't limited to print or the Internet. Television and video are perfect places to tell a brand's story, and using Power Writing techniques helps make that story more memorable. One of the best examples of Power Writing was used in the 1998 Apple "Think Different" launch. Actor Richard Dreyfuss delivered the 60-second "tone poem," but the sentiment is pure Steve Jobs:

Lincoln hired Matthew McConaughey to ponder his existential crisis as he drove their new cars. He spent over 5 minutes in a YouTube video watching the rain and thinking deep thoughts such as, "In a perfect world I'd be endorsing marijuana cigarettes, not cars."

Here's to the crazy ones. The misfits. The rebels. The troublemakers. The round pegs in the square holes. The ones who see things differently. They're not fond of rules. And they have no respect for the status quo. You can quote them, disagree with them, glorify them, or vilify them. About the only thing you can't do is ignore them. Because they change things. They push the human race forward. And while some may see them as the crazy ones, we see genius. Because the people who are crazy enough to think they can change the world are the ones who do.

Checklist for Your TV Commercial

When you've finished your script or storyboard, let it rest. Then come back to it and check the following:

- Does the video tell the story without audio, and how well?
- Did you specify all the necessary directions? Could a director take your script and produce the spot?
- Do the audio and video complement each other, and are they correctly timed for each other?
- Are there too many scenes (can some be omitted)? Do you need more scenes?
- Have you identified the product well?
- Does your script win attention quickly and promise an honest benefit?
- Have you provided a strong visualization of the One Thing that will linger in the viewer's memory?
- Could a competitive brand be substituted easily and fit well?
- Is it believable?
- Are you proud to say you wrote it?[15]

Presenting Your TV Commercial

Okay, your spot meets all the requirements in the checklist. Now you're ready to show it to the boss. It's not a print ad that you can just hand in. You have to sell it. The following is a pretty good procedure for presenting a TV commercial, especially to a small group.

Product demonstration is one of the oldest techniques in television advertising. Apple Watch demonstrated dozens of different functions in this simple yet sophisticated 60-second commercial.

- If it's a stand-alone concept, review the creative strategy and state the One Thing you want to convey.
- State your main creative theme for the commercial.
- Describe main elements—music, effects, actors.
- Walk through the video portion; describe what's happening.
- Hit the key visual points, with emphasis on the key frame.
- Once the visual path is established, go back and read the copy.
- Summarize the action in a brief scenario.

The Future of TV Advertising

As technology changes the way use television, commercials have to adapt to the new challenges. Personal video recorders, such as TiVo, allow viewers to fast-forward through recorded commercials. Automatic commercial elimination makes it even easier to avoid broadcast and cable commercials. So how can advertisers make sure viewers get their brand message? Digital rights management technology, used on some DVDs, could be encrypted into a program so it's either impossible to copy it or to forbid playback without the commercials. This would require disrupting the current viewing technology all the way to the TV monitor. Using such heavy-handed approaches will certainly not win many friends for the advertised brands.

A more user-friendly approach would be TV-for-pay with interactive ads to be seen at the viewer's discretion. The more ads the viewer chooses and the more questions he or she answers about the advertised product, the lower his TV bill. In essence advertisers would pay people to engage with commercials. Such an approach could drain a lot of the subtlety and drama from a commercial in favor of providing a dry list of features and benefits. New advertising solutions are developing constantly. Geico's "unskippable" preroll spot is a good example. Chipotle's "Scarecrow" animated short had 5 million views in the first week and as of May 2015, 14 million views, elevating the art and purpose of branded content through video.[16] Data-driven automation of TV advertising is on the rise. Ads will be created and sold based on demographic and interest-based targeting rather than traditional genre-based ad selling. Google has developed personalized TV ads that account for a person's viewing history and when they're done watching the show.[17] As of this writing, American execs have been cautious to adopt programmatic ads. But as traditional TV ad spend continues to decrease in favor of digital, we will probably see the programmatic marketplace grow. This kind of micro targeting would mean the creation of a number of ads, each aimed at a specific, narrowly defined audience.

This commercial followed the path of a totaled Subaru from the crash scene to the junkyard. At each stop, the simple phrase, "They lived" reinforced the safety of the vehicle. At the end, the dad says, "We lived" as the family climbs in their new Subaru.

Television Viewing:
HOW IT'S CHANGING

60 million
Americans have cancelled
cable and satellite TV

18-24 year olds spend **3 hours less per day**
watching TV than 2 years ago

500 million online videos
are watched by young people every
month, from over **75 billion**
available online.

53%
visit social media while
watching TV

34% of Millennials
watch more online video
than television

You Tube

Brand
on TV

41% of people use
a mobile device to browse
for a product after seeing
the ad on TV

Sources: New York Times 2013; Media Bistro 2013, Nielsen 2014; 20Gfk, 2013;
Comscore Video Matrix 2014; emarketer 2013

Algorithms would determine who sees each commercial and under what kind of viewing environment. Randall Rothenberg predicted, "Three things are certain: Consumers want access to great content. Brands want to deeply engage with their consumers. And television will no doubt evolve to survive."[18]

The series finale of *Mad Men* is a prime example of the relationship between television and social media. The much anticipated final episode ended with Don Draper in a yoga pose, finally at peace, as he chants "Om" on the California coast. Is his little smirk a sign of inner bliss or the satisfaction of finally getting his mojo back? The answer comes immediately as Coca-Cola's classic 1971 "Hilltop" commercial fills the screen, featuring the syrupy philosophy of Don's sensitivity training and singers who look just like his new hippie friends. *Advertising Age* reported, "As it turns out, Coke lucked into the kind of free PR all brands crave . . . the online conversation sparked a 991% increase in Coke's digital consumption after the episode aired. There were 21,204 tweets involving Coca-Cola in the three hours following the *Mad Men* finale. The free exposure is 'pretty unprecedented in the history of television,' according to Amobee Brand Intelligence, a digital marketing company. 'It's turned the singalong spot into an instant viral hit 44 years in the making; with Coke already having gotten two weeks' worth of consumption around them in less than a day.'"[19]

Beyond Television

Desktop computers and mobile devices provide a much wider audience for commercial messages. They can be 10-second prerolls before longer video content, repurposed 30- or 60-second spots, or longer versions of broadcast commercials. Advertisers also have the ability to add content such as behind-the-scenes action or include information about the stars of the commercial or the product itself. While nothing matches television for delivering viewers, most TV advertisers hedge their bets and make sure their spots also appear online.

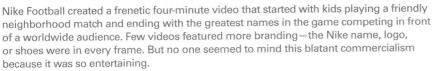

© Nike, Inc.

© Tecumseh

Online video gives brands widespread exposure when they can't afford the high cost of broadcast and cable ads. YouTube channels and other social media sites maximize the coverage and create a conversation.

Nike Football created a frenetic four-minute video that started with kids playing a friendly neighborhood match and ending with the greatest names in the game competing in front of a worldwide audience. Few videos featured more branding—the Nike name, logo, or shoes were in every frame. But no one seemed to mind this blatant commercialism because it was so entertaining.

Sometimes, the spots are previewed online, such as before a Super Bowl appearance, to build awareness and favorable opinion in the all-important polls of Super Bowl ads. More often, advertisers shift their commercials to online-only media buys due to the growing influence of digital and the high cost of broadcast.

You should also be thinking of online videos that go beyond the constraints of a 30-second ad. Video is huge for Millennials. In fact 95% of 18- to 29-year-olds watch or download online video.[20] As we'll discuss in Chapter 11, video is a critical component of nearly every effective website. Whether it's an ongoing series, a simple feature/benefit presentation, or a testimonial, video provides the impact of a TV commercial in a more controlled and welcome environment. Even obscure business-to-business brands have their own YouTube channels.

As with digital television commercials, real-time media buying (RTB) gives video advertisers an opportunity to deliver their messages to the right audience at the going market price. Currently video RTB accounts for about 25% of the online video ad spend.[21]

Chances are you won't be writing network TV commercials in an entry-level job, but you may be very busy creating online video for websites and social media platforms. Most of the principles in this chapter apply to online video.

Lee Clow

Lee Clow was the art director and creative force behind some of the most influential advertising of his generation. His work for Chiat\Day and later TBWA\Chiat\Day includes the famous Apple "1984" spot as well as the Taco Bell Chihuahua, Nike's "Air Jordan," and the Energizer Bunny.

Dan Wieden of Wieden + Kennedy, another creative giant of the modern era, described Clow this way: "Lee Clow's heart has been pumping this sorry industry full of inspiration for longer than most its practitioners have been alive. He is the real thing. He is indefatigable. I hate him."[22]

Monique L. Nelson

In a milestone transition in 2012, Monique L. Nelson became chairman and CEO and majority shareholder of UniWorld Group, the third largest African American ad agency. She joined UniWorld five years ago from the client side as senior vice president of brand integration, after nine years at Motorola, where she was the global lead for entertainment marketing.

With a solid client roster including Ford Motor Company, Home Depot, and the U.S. Marine Corps, UniWorld won the African American category at the Association of National Advertisers' annual Multicultural Excellence Awards for the agency's Ford Explorer TV campaign, and also picked up the prize for best print work, for Marines recruitment ads.[23]

Andrew Keller

Currently the CEO and a partner at CP+B, Keller began as an art director in 1998. Since that time, he has played a lead role in the U.S. launch of the Mini, the turnaround of Burger King, and the Domino's brand rally. During his time as creative director and chief creative officer, his

contributions to the creative vision of the agency have played a major role in CP+B's being named agency of the year 15 times in the trade press, Interactive Agency of the Year 3 times at the Cannes International Advertising Festival, and Agency of the Decade by *Advertising Age*.[24]

Greg Hahn

As a copywriter, Hahn was behind some of the industry's most groundbreaking and award-winning work for brands such as HBO, FedEx, AT&T, and GE, among others. He is now chief creative officer at BBDO in New York. Hahn was executive creative director for the award-winning "HBO Voyeur" which, along with winning multiple Grand Prix Lions at Cannes, was selected by the One Club as one of its "Best of the Digital Decade." He also helmed the acclaimed "HBO Imagine" project. Recently, Greg was named one of the "100 Most Creative People in Business" by *Fast Company* magazine. Prior to joining BBDO, he created the "Live Richly" campaign for Citibank, the Buddy Lee advertising for Lee Jeans, and the Cannes Lion–winning print campaign for *Sports Illustrated*. Other award-winning work includes the "Cat Herders" spot for EDS and the famed "BMW Film" series.[25]

Starting Over

Kacey had been writing commercials for a number of years when she was asked to write TV and radio spots for a well-known cement company. The TV commercials would also live on the company's website. Kasey decided to use a new approach and crafted four 30-second commercials, rather than one long spot. Each would appear during a one-hour television show, airing at 5 p.m. on network television. The radio spots would air at 1 p.m. daily.

The first commercial depicted a cement waterfall being built on a hot summer day. The second displayed a new structure being built in the fall, with leaves flying all around. The third was a cement driveway being snow-plowed and showing no signs of wear. The fourth was set in the spring and depicted a cement duck pond with baby ducks floating around. The music that accompanied each commercial matched the seasonal theme. Each commercial had a voice-over, using the owner of the cement company, whose voice was neither expressive nor memorable.

Kacey approached her new supervisor with the storyboards and scripts. Kacey was surprised by a strongly negative reaction. With minimal feedback, Kacey was told to scrap the concept and start over. With the exception of four shorter commercials, rather than one, this was the same type of work Kacey had been doing for years. What went wrong?

1 Name the protocols for creating memorable campaigns, and why are they so important? Where might Kacey's concepting have gone wrong?

2 Considering what make radio effective, what would you recommend to enhance the radio spots?

3 Considering the intended audience and the chosen platforms, what changes might you suggest to enhance the campaign's success?

Joni Koegel, assistant professor, Cazenovia College

1. Sketching in Words

(Adapted from an exercise shared by Kimberly Selber, PhD, associate professor, University of Texas–Pan American.)

This exercise will help you get outside the demographic cube and into the psychographic menagerie and get you closer to radio, TV, and video production. Create a character sketch of someone you know—as if you were describing a character in a movie or novel.

- Write a short one-paragraph introduction of who this person is, and what your relationship to this person is.
- Next describe the following in great, juicy detail:
  - Physical appearance: gender, age, body type, hair, eyes, facial features, dress, posture, movements, mannerisms, speech . . .
  - Background: education, religion, family, childhood experiences, financial situation, profession, marital status, other relationships, habits, surroundings/environment, health . . .
  - Personality: distinctive traits, self-image, yearnings/dreams, fears/apprehensions, sense of humor, code of ethics, attitude (optimistic? overly sensitive?) . . .
  - Other details: hobbies, skills, favorite foods, colors, books, music, art . . .
- Evaluate as a class, focusing on the following: Did you bring the person to life for the reader? If an actor was going to play the role of this person, would he or she have enough insight to justly portray the person?

2. Audio Hunting Expedition

Let's see how sound can inspire you.

- Think of one brand—a brand that is a big part of your everyday life.
- Go out on an audio hunting expedition to collect audio recordings of sounds connected with this brand. Then record 10 people expressing their affection for the brand—anything goes.
- Now do some secondary research on the brand. Consider if anything you found out about the brand matches the audio images you've collected.
- Inspired by your audio hunting expedition and grounded in secondary research, sketch out a quick 30-second radio spot.
- If you're really adventurous, record it using some of the footage you've collected. You could do your own voice-over or find a brave and willing friend (preferably from the drama department!).

3. Telling Your Story

This exercise is designed to help you craft a storyline that feels real—a storyline that identifies your brand.

- Craft a 60-second commercial that tells the story of your brand: "brand you."
- Here's the rub. The story has to begin with your first day of college and end with landing your advertising dream job. The point is not about the job you land but about telling the viewer who you are in a resonant way.
- Your instructor will collect your scripts at the beginning of the next class, without your name, which will be added later, and randomly hand out scripts.
- Take a few minutes to review the script you received (it could even be your own).
- Now, present the script you received. One by one, try to identify which script belongs to which person.
- The idea here is to see which scriptwriters were able to create a story that resonates with who they are—resonates enough that the class could identify "brand you."

Review chapter content and study for exams. http://study.sagepub.com/altstiel4e.

- Interactive practice quizzes
- Mobile-friendly eFlashcards
- Carefully selected chapter-by-chapter video and multimedia content

Chapter 11

Websites
Copy and Content

The first edition of this book predicted the dawning of a digital age, which was not a very bold forecast, even before the advent of Facebook or iPhones. Subsequent editions embraced the growing digital revolution and attached marketing principles to new technology. Sometime between the last edition and this one, a new buzzword emerged to describe the marketing communication landscape: *postdigital*. It's not that we've moved past digital technology. Rather, it describes an era when *everything* is digital and there's no reason to differentiate it as a thing. It just *is*. Digital will continue to integrate nearly every machine we use, whether it's a refrigerator or mobile device, and it change the ways we can deliver brand messages to consumers, who in turn are using technology to avoid receiving those messages.

A New Creative Revolution Online

As we enter this postdigital age, we can talk less about the technology of advertising and more about what it can do for us in terms of building branded relationships that connect consumers with marketing messages. Keith Reinhard, former CEO of DDB Worldwide, sums it up brilliantly: "I believe we are on the cusp of even more promising period . . . .where the lessons we learned during the creative revolution about craft and storytelling with emotion and humor will combine with the tools and data brought to us by the digital disruption."[1]

Our challenge with this chapter is not to get too bogged down in *how* things work or even where this data-driven business is headed. Instead, we will gloss over a lot of the technical jargon and try to deal with how to make all that left-brain stuff merge with right-brain creativity. So we will focus on two main areas of discussion: the medium (display advertising: banners and beyond) and the message (web content: strategy, concept, design, and copy).

Social media is woven so tightly into so many advertising programs that we find it hard to isolate it as a separate topic. However, there is so much to cover in the social space that we have pulled most of it out of this chapter and address it in more detail in Chapter 12.

"The irony is that while there have never been more ways to reach consumers, it's never been harder to connect with consumers."[2]

Brad Jakeman,
chief creative officer, Activision

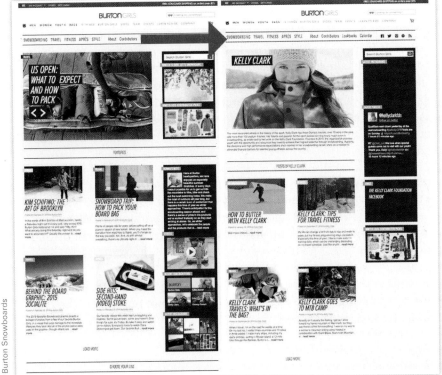

© Burton Snowboards

As one of the top manufacturers in the business, Burton realized that not only are snowboards different for men and women; so are their attitudes. Burton has a section on their site called "Burton Girls" featuring blogs as well as articles on clothing, health and beauty, and travel.

While email is certainly a digital marketing communication tool, we'll discuss it in the context of direct marketing in Chapter 14. Mobile marketing also fits in the digital realm, but we will discuss it more as a technology best suited for direct marketing in Chapter 12. At the same time, you'll see similar threads of wisdom woven across all these chapters—just like great branded campaigns are woven across the entire media landscape. Repetition is not a bad thing.

The Three Things

Despite all the changes in devices, the basics of online marketing are pretty simple. When you are creating a website, microsite, landing page, or mobile site, there are only three main things you need to do:

Get them to come.

Get them to stay.

Get them to come back.

Do all three, and you will be successful. They have to find you. They have to find something interesting when they find you . . . and you hope you can persuade them to form a favorable opinion, request more information, give up their email address, "like" you, and ultimately buy something, whether it's direct from your site or through some other channel. Finally, they have to keep coming back to extend the relationship. The following sections will discuss how all of this can happen.

Display Advertising

Advertisers are moving ad dollars from TV toward video advertising on the web, thanks in part to standardization of formats and technologies that allow advertisers to reach larger audiences across multiple sites. As social network platforms such as YouTube and Facebook grow as credible advertising vehicles, we'll see more opportunities to personalize ads. With much more refined segmentation, video ads have become more than repurposed 30-second TV commercials. At the same time, new online media firms can place ads on thousands of sites, so advertisers can not only personalize but also achieve incredible reach.

Digital technology makes it easy to test and measure display advertising and website readership. Because changes can be made in minutes with a few keystrokes, it's easy to test multiple concepts. This is called A/B testing (Version A vs. Version B). Website analytics measure traffic, page popularity, and visitor behavior to help make informed decisions about optimizing your site.

- **Text ads:** These all-type ads look pretty much like Google or any other search ads. You might catch someone's eye with a clever headline, but unless they are highlighted, they're basically ignored.

- **Image ads:** Banners have been the staple of Internet advertising. Traditionally, banners have not been all that effective for generating traffic but can still have a powerful branding effect. The trick is matching content to the brand and getting people to respond. Banners have to be creative to stand out in all the clutter of a typical webpage. Better targeting methods and more accurate analytics have made banner ads less of a hit-or-miss proposition. Display ads are targeted, based on browsing history, keywords, geolocation, past purchases, demographics, or hundreds of other variables. Online advertising networks also offer the convenience of reaching many sites with a single buy, helping you save time and make the most effective use of your budget.

- **Rich media ads:** Rich media banners go beyond the ordinary banner ad to add dropdown boxes, sound-on mouse-overs, animated bits, and even interactive games. Rich media banners and badges provide advertisers with ways to present additional content and interaction within traditional ad sizes. They can also lead to significant increases in response, brand perception, and recall.

Tips and Techniques for Creating Effective Display Ads

- **Think billboards:** Your little banner ad has to compete with the space around it, just like a billboard.

- **Keep it simple:** Just like a billboard, the fewer words, the better. You have to get their attention first. Then they can click for more detail.

- **Offer an incentive:** Everyone probably knows your brand. So convince them they'll get a special deal, a discount, free stuff, or whatever if they click on your ad.

- **Change the offer:** People check their browsers several times a day. Keep your message fresh with new looks and new incentives. This not only increases involvement, it also functions as a good test to measure which appeal pulled the most click-throughs.

- **Engage the viewer:** Use a contest or a quiz, and ask provocative questions. Make them feel like their opinions matter, and then use what you learn to keep them coming back.

- **Don't forget the brand:** Don't get so caught up in cute gimmicks that you forget what you're really selling—brand recognition.

> *"Words like 'digital' and 'traditional' will lose their meaning. They will blend into one word called 'advertising,' the art of connecting brands with people."*[3]
>
> Keith Reinhard,
> chairman emeritus of
> DDB Worldwide

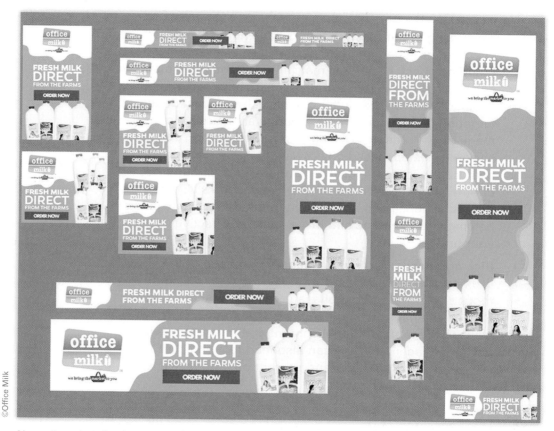

No matter what size they are, traditional web banners are usually ignored, just like cluttered print ads. Rich media display ads generate a few more clicks. Even with the most sophisticated tracking algorithm, the creative has to generate a click.

A little animated GIF banner opens the door to a very rich YouTube page that includes a series of branded videos about consumers driving Mustangs. The stories are engaging, the cars look great, and the production values are first rate.

Here's where content, native advertising, and display ads intersect. The news story is about obesity. Rather than a typical diet product ad next door, there is a display ad for Samsung phones with a cartoon relevant to the news item.

Web Copy and Content

We briefly touched on website design in Chapter 6. You can design a site from scratch, but more companies are relying on the rapidly growing selection of open-source web generators, especially those with automated conversion to mobile-friendly designs. You can't separate copy and content from web design any more than you can in print. But here we will focus on the written word and show how it's integrated into the total design.

Web Copy Mechanics

As a copywriter, you may be involved in website design in several ways, ranging from developing a total site to writing a headline for a banner ad. As an art director, you may have to develop a design for whole sites down to fourth- or fifth-level pages or landing pages that instantly capture the user's attention. No matter your role, you need to have a Big Idea for the site. What's the One Thing that people will take away from looking at your landing page or website?

- **Think campaigns.** The components of your site have to work individually and cumulatively. Make sure your design has the same look and feel throughout the website, even though many pages will have different functions. Most designers start with the most complicated page. If you can make that work, the simpler pages will be easier to lay out.

- **Design at different levels.** Your first-level and subsequent pages should have the same look and feel as the homepage, even though they have different functions. This does not mean they have to look exactly the same, but consider font size, colors, graphic style, and all the other design elements that hold together a campaign.

- **Prioritize.** To paraphrase Howard Gossage, people read what interests them, and sometimes it's a website. But there is a limit to what they are willing to read, and website visitors have short attention spans. There's just too much to see on any given site, so it's natural to jump around. It's critical to put the most important information up front and display it prominently.

- **Don't forget the navigation.** Think about how visitors find their way around your website. *Primary navigation* on a homepage directs visitors to the major sections or first-level pages. *Secondary navigation* directs visitors to content inside a specific section. *Universal navigation* is on all pages—for example, links to the homepage, "search," or "contact us."

- **Keep it simple.** Besides overdesigning a website from a graphic standpoint, you can also overdo the technology. Too much movement is annoying and pulls readers away from the text. Don't use technology for its own sake. Instead, concentrate on strategy: what you want to accomplish, not how cool you can make it.

While most of the basic writing guidelines we've presented in previous chapters apply, writing copy for websites also has its own set of rules. First of all, people do not like to read a lot of copy online—mainly because it's harder to read a screen than the printed page. Instead, they scan copy, much the same way they look at full-size newspapers. Bold headlines and pictures catch their eye and may draw them into the copy for more detail. In many cases, visitors print pages to read later rather than wade through a lot of text on screen. Yet, even in the postdigital age you need to be able to write well. Here are a few tips for writing website content that people will want to read:

- **Call out important words.** Use boldface and/or color to highlight important words. But don't overdo it. You still want to make it easy to read.

- **Use subheads to break up major copy blocks.** Since people scan rather than read, make sure your subheads have some meaning related to the body copy. Don't be so cute with your subheads that visitors miss the point of your content.

- **Keep it simple.** Stick with one main idea per copy block or paragraph. Don't introduce too many new ideas per section. In some ways a text-heavy website is like a bad PowerPoint presentation—too much copy on too few slides.

- **Convert paragraphs to bullet points.** This is especially critical if you have several key features and/or benefits. Make it easy to see the key copy points.

- **Limit your text links.** The beauty of the web is the ability to navigate within and to other sites. However, too many links interrupt your message. You don't want to hook readers and then lose them to another topic or even another website, which may take them to yet another destination.

- **Lead with the main message, then drill down.** This is the inverted pyramid style of journalistic writing. You state your main message up front and gradually add more detail to support that message. Many times, the opening paragraph will be enough to hook the readers or at least get them to download the whole message.

- **Keep it short.** The rule of thumb is to use half as many words as you would for a comparable print piece. As we mentioned, people read text on screen much more slowly than they read print.

- **Scrolling is okay.** In the past, conventional wisdom said we should avoid scrolling at all costs. So web copy was telegraphic, and we clicked from page to page. Today, scrolling is not that big a deal. In fact, with responsive design, scrolling is mandatory, and with more mobile users every day, scrolling rules.

User Experience

User experience (UX) involves all the aspects of end users' interactions with companies and products. We've moved from Web 1.0 (brochure-ware), where we simply told viewers what we wanted them to know, to UX, where we must engage and provide value to be successful. If you don't think UX is important, just look at the fallout from the botched rollout of HealthCare.gov. Good UX lets users get the information they need faster, easier, and more completely. UX deals with a user's wants and needs (remember those?). Ultimately good UX means higher conversation rates. There are many factors used to measure and improve UX, from ethnographics (watching people use sites) to eye tracking and persona creation.

User experience metrics are a bit different from the metrics used in sales, marketing, or finance, because they reflect human behavior and attitude. We paraphrase some of the key performance indicators web expert Armen Ghazarian uses to evaluate user experience:

- *Task success rate:* percentage of correctly completed tasks by users.

- *Time on task:* the amount of time it takes for the user to complete the task.

- *Use of search versus navigation:* do users make an online purchase through navigation within the site or give up and go back to search?

- *User error rate:* how many mistakes were made.

- *System usability scale:* based on user surveys and requires user participation.[4]

Airheads reaches out to adolescents with a rich digital experience offering games, tours, and contests while linking them to branded experiences on Facebook. Invitations to meet "Big Time Rush," a not-so-subtle nod to being high, or to "like us" on Facebook encourage young consumers to share information, setting up a lifelong habit of opting in.

Now that's a lot to digest for a beginning copywriter—excuse us, content provider. But if you work for a firm with a dedicated UX and/or search engine optimization (SEO) team, they will beat you up if your content doesn't measure up.

Maximizing Web Copy Impact

We've listed a few ideas on how to structure a site. Here are few more for getting the most from your web copy:

- **Multiple devices multiply opportunity:** Today's consumers are multitaskers, especially Millennials. But even older generations are seeing information delivered across multiple devices at the same time, which opens up all kinds of new potential for integration of advertising

Apple manages to stay current with a number of emerging design trends, but always keeps their trademark simplicity and elegance.

messages. Tim Cadogan comments, "Simply put, the fact that we use multiple devices in sequence and at the same time is creating opportunities to tell stories to consumers sequentially on multiple devices rather than simply presenting the same ad on every screen."[5]

- **Humanizing the message:** A landing page or microsite may try to convert a user into a customer. But copy on many multipage sites also tries to connect with audiences on a deeper and more meaningful level. So you have to develop rapport and inspire loyalty. It's embedded into all the text across a site, not just attached as content.

- **Interactive storytelling:** The text is not the only part of the site you can control. You can use all the content to tell a story about your product or brand. Fonts, images, video, widgets, and apps all work together to tell your story. It can be an elegant site like Tesla or iPhone or a site with multiple stories like Harley-Davidson or Burton snowboards. The image you portray tells your brand's story.

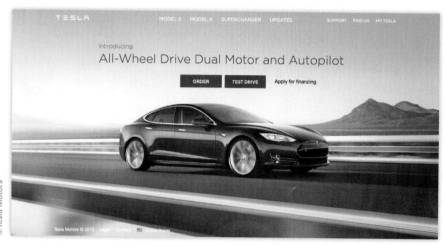

The Tesla site uses large images, long scrolling, embedded infographics, and interactive storytelling to explain their five FAQs.

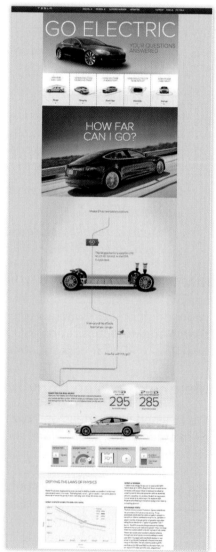

Video in Websites

Whether it's embedded in the site or linked to YouTube or Vimeo, video is a powerful tool that can increase the popularity of your webpages, generate leads and sales, show features and benefits more effectively than static art, and move you up in the SEO ranks. Video could be hook that gets them to come, stay, and come back. Video can have many purposes in a website:

- Virtual tour of your facilities

- Feature and benefits of the product or service

- Interviews with corporate spokespersons

- Testimonials from satisfied customers

- Third-party endorsements from credible experts

- How to use or apply the product

- Show the product in use

- Company procedures, such as safety guidelines
- Company policies
- Online tutorials and testing
- Promotion of a special event or sale

In addition, using video has some functional benefits. Video can drive traffic to your site. In fact, search engines love video. Tag your videos with targeted keywords, share your video on as many sites as you can to increase links to your site, and keep producing new videos to keep content fresh.

Branded Entertainment

Online video and content marketing have merged into a fast growing digital component sometimes called branded entertainment— basically telling your brand message in a format and style people will actually enjoy watching. There are many forms of branded entertainment, from consumer-generated fake commercials to repurposing TV commercials on the web and even sponsoring a series of slickly produced webisodes starring well-known celebrities.

"Building a website without video is like taking a knife to a gunfight."[6]

Kirk Strong,
founder, Smart Interactive Video

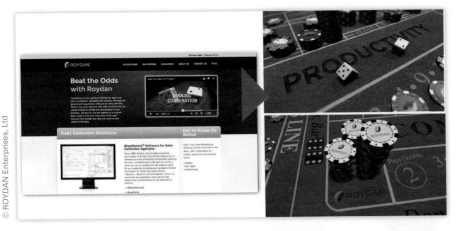

© ROYDAN Enterprises, Ltd

This corporate site provides a lot of content about software for debt collection agencies. It may seem like a rather technical, even dry, subject. But the video provides a quick, entertaining, and benefit-rich story about how using this software can improve the odds for their customers.

© Harley-Davidson Motor Company

Harley-Davidson's corporate site features "Harlistas," an authentic look into Latino motorcycling culture told through four pivotal stories of real-life characters.

Webisodes can be original programs on YouTube, such as *Funny or Die* or *Between Two Ferns*, full episodes from broadcast and cable programs, or brand stories that may feature products or may just be sponsored by a brand. Old Spice made history with their 183 individual responses to fans' questions. IKEA sponsored the *Easy to Assemble* online video series with guest stars like Jane Lynch and Jeff Goldblum. In 2014 Dove extended their "Campaign for Real Beauty," with mothers and daughters taking selfies of the features they disliked most. Reebok's "Be More Human" campaign featured profiles about real people, not professional athletes. Harley-Davidson includes "Harlistas" on their main website to share stories about the unique bond between Latino riders and the iconic brand.

Advertisers, entertainment networks, studios, and talent will continue to invest in digital platforms beyond the web. Branded entertainment will also become more interactive, more selective, and more accessible through mobile devices and tablets. Consumers will lead and brands will try to catch up, mainly because no other marketing channel generates a powerful buzz as quickly as the Internet.

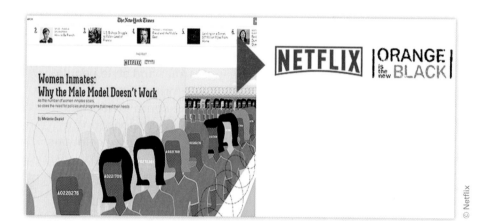

A clever bit of native synergy: Netflix advertised *Orange Is the New Black* above a *New York Times* online article about women in prison.

© Netflix

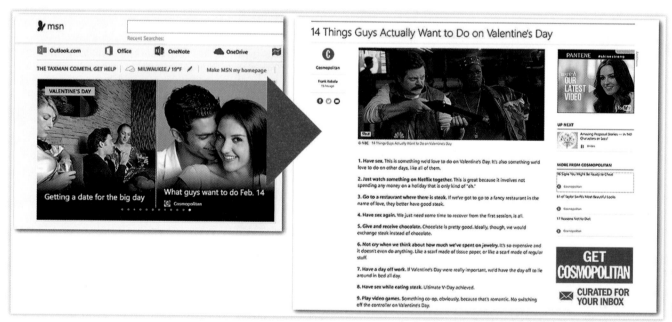

This represents the progression from native to content to display ads and more content. Click on the Cosmopolitan-sponsored news item, and you'll go to a rather silly list with links to more silly content and banner ads with links to Cosmo advertisers.

© Cosmopolitan

Search Engine Optimization

Creating content or writing web copy requires all the skills of offline writing, plus an understanding of how the web and search engines work. Even if you follow all of the tips in this chapter, your brilliant web copy or content will just lie there unread if no one visits. That's why you need to consider **search engine optimization (SEO)** to drive traffic to the site. You could fill up a whole semester learning about SEO, and many agencies either have SEO departments or outsource their web writing to SEO specialists. That's because the rules keep changing. Techniques such as packing keywords or curating information without original content used to help, but now they're punished. So it's pointless to give you the latest tricks to ensure higher rankings. However, there are a few guidelines that will most likely stand the test of time as well as the scrutiny of Google.

- Keep your copy short and to the point. It not only reads better, but there's less clutter for search engines to sift through. Break your copy up with frequent subheads, shorter paragraphs, and lists.
- Understand how to use keywords and key phrases to maximize SEO.
- Keep content fresh by updating and publishing new content often.
- Try to make your copy as original as possible. If you cut and paste too much, search engines will consider your copy duplicates.
- Don't forget a Call to Action. Tell your readers what you want them to do.
- Make sure your priorities are in order: users first, then the company, and finally the search engines. Take care of the first two, and the last one will be much more welcoming.
- Don't forget headline and subhead tags.
- Use social media to maximize search. Keep active in social media and have sharing buttons on your site.
- Search engines don't care much about graphics, but you can use key phrases as alt tags on your images.

A Word About Keywords

The concept seems simple enough. Someone types a word in a search box and a list of websites magically appears. But the ranking for the right keywords can make or break a site. As with just about everything else, knowledge is power. Keyword research allows you to respond to changing conditions that affect keyword value, such as shifts in demand and evolving market conditions. Moz.com published the very useful "Beginner's Guide to SEO." This multichapter online guide covered the basic process for assessing a keyword's value. Here's a summarized version.[7]

- **Is the keyword relevant to your website's content?** Will searchers find what they are looking for on your site when they search using these keywords? Will they be happy with what they find? Will this traffic result in financial rewards or other organizational goals? If the answer to all of these questions is a clear "Yes" then proceed.

- **Search for the term or phrase in the major engines.** Understanding which websites already rank for your keyword gives you valuable insight into the competition, and also how hard it will be to rank for the given term. Are there search advertisements running along the top and right-hand side of the organic results? Typically, many search ads mean a high-value keyword, and multiple search ads above the organic results often mean a highly lucrative and directly conversion-prone keyword.

- **Buy a sample campaign for the keyword at Google AdWords and/or Bing Ads.** If your website doesn't rank for the keyword, you can nonetheless buy test traffic to see how well it converts.

- **Using the data you've collected, determine the exact value of each keyword.** You have to factor in the number of impressions, conversions, click-through rates, and a lot of other metrics. As a writer, you probably won't be doing all the math yourself. But someone will probably evaluate your copy to make sure it's SEO friendly.

SEO & CONTENT

Social brand footprint

Provide information about your brand, answer questions and give industry insight. Produce engaging and sharable content people want to see.

Search

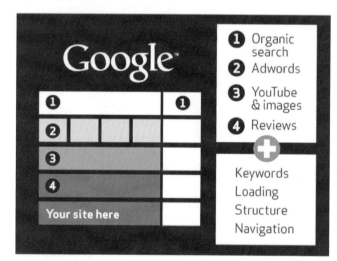

Google

1
2
3
4
Your site here

1 Organic search
2 Adwords
3 YouTube & images
4 Reviews

Keywords
Loading
Structure
Navigation

On site SEO

- Research and implement niche keywords
- Use keywords in metadata, titles & content
- Optimize site with symantic HTML structure
- Optimize site for speed
- Submit site to search engines

Sources: Gum Design + TbA Marketing Group

Web Copy Versus Content

In Chapter 14 we discuss how native advertising differs from content marketing. So we'll save that discussion for later. In this chapter we'll discuss how writing content differs from writing copy for the web. In casual conversations many marketers consider all text on the Internet content. It sounds much more trendy than the old-fashioned "copy." Recently, public relations practitioners have adopted content as they integrate it with social media. It's one more way they can distance themselves from the grubby world of advertising.

If we were to compare content with copy, we'd say that content text is meant to inform, explain, and entertain the reader. To do that content writers need to speak with authority as experts willing to share their knowledge. Selling may happen down the road after gently building good will over time, but the reader doesn't feel an urgent need to buy something. Copy, even with SEO considerations, is different. Good web copy has the same emphasis on features and benefits and encouragement to take action that we see in other advertising media.

In the end it's all writing, but not everyone can wear both copywriter and content hats. Copywriters need to get right to the point, persuade readers, and stimulate action. When you're used to doing that, it's hard to switch gears to write content designed to build an open-ended, long-term relationship. Successful content writers just don't write to bang out a couple blog posts and expect instant sales—it can take months or years to generate a critical mass of content needed to change opinions.

Web copy and web content have the same purpose—to ultimately sell something. But as Table 11.1 shows, copy and content work differently to achieve that ultimate goal.

Feeding the Content Beast

Okay. You're ready to start generating content. Typically this involves curation—collecting, archiving, organizing, and repackaging information from a variety of sources. But who has time to look for a needle of valuable information in the haystack of blogs, websites, Twitter feeds, Facebook updates, Pinterest posts, and email clutter? You could narrow your search to specific industries and markets that make data available through a variety of sources. We could give you a list of content providers, but given the number of burnouts, mergers, and acquisitions in this field, this list is bound to be obsolete as soon as it's written.

Content Distribution

We're using this chapter to discuss content development, but the distribution of that content is not limited to websites. Besides posting content on your site you can also push it out through these channels:

- Content discovery platforms
- Sharing on social networks
- Content sharing websites
- Sponsored updates
- Paid search
- Social network ads
- General and industry-specific news sites
- Influential and like-minded bloggers

As we've mentioned several times, more brands are changing their focus from technology back to building relationships online. We're moving from the "how" to the "what." *Adweek* contributor Randall Rothenberg puts it into perspective: "It has also become clear that companies need to let go of their decade-long obsession with SEO and gaming the rankings, which has content implications. Google for one has made it clear that its algorithms will reward those who produce authentic, engaging content that is also valued by others."[8]

Landing Pages

It's natural for a company to send its advertising, social media, and email traffic to a corporate homepage. Often the visitor gets lost in all the other messages, including interesting content or a blog.

Native ads for Louie CK took over New York magazine's Vulture. com site with six pieces of branded content, including articles, graphics, and videos about his show.

> *"Yet not too long down the road, tech mania will quiet down, leaving our industry to focus on what will be the ultimate competitive differentiator—superior content."[9]*
>
> Randall Rothenberg, president and CEO, Interactive Advertising Bureau

The urgency to connect about a specific product or offer fades and an opportunity is lost. The solution: create a landing page.

A landing page is a specialized website. It cuts through the clutter of a corporate website to talk about a single topic and stimulate action. A landing page quickly conveys that One Thing and then captures information—whether it's for future engagement or an immediate sale. It's all about conversion. Content marketing may build a relationship, but when trust is established, it can lead to a landing page. The lead may also come from a link in an email, social media, URLs in print ads, links in banner ads, or even a link on a corporate homepage. So, in most cases, the landing page is targeted rather than searched.

Landing pages come in handy for new product introductions, especially for diversified companies that want to launch single products. They're also great for short-term sales promotions and events.

	Copy	Content
Primary purpose	Sell	Tell
Key questions	What, where, when, (who)	How, why, (who)
Objective	Generate first-time and repeat sales	Build relationships
Information style	Facts, descriptions, emotions (reasons to buy)	News you can use—immediately useful to life or business
Engagement	One and done	Long term (if it's valuable)
Information source	Research/brief provided to the writer	Personal experience and expertise of the writer
Format	Short (just long enough to make a point)	Long (long enough to provide useful information)
Examples	Print advertisements Television and radio commercials Direct marketing Support marketing Web copy Collateral Online/mobile ads	White papers Webinars Video E-zines Teleseminars E-books Online articles Audio programs

Table 11.1   Copy Versus Content

They can also be used to discuss a single benefit of a multifeatured product. Landing pages work very well for fund-raising and charity events. Whether they provide information like prices and specs or just a list of features and benefits, the ultimate goal is to convert a visitor into a customer.

The most effective landing pages share these characteristics:

- Simple message: Don't forget that One Thing.
- Deliver value: Consider what's in it for the visitor.
- Limited navigation: Once they've landed, don't let them wander off the page.
- Make it easy to share: Provide links to social media and email.
- Focus on the lead: The reply form should be prominent and easy to use.

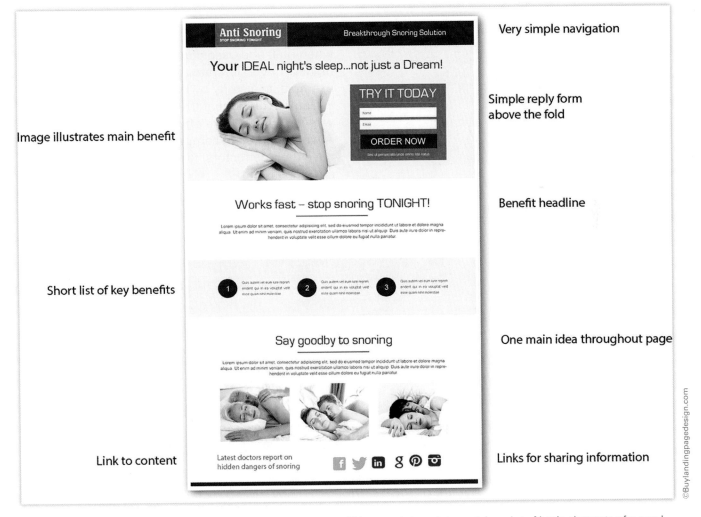

The goal of a landing page is to convert a visitor into a customer. This generic template contains a lot of basic elements of a good landing page—the greatest one being simplicity.

Microsites

Pros	Cons
Quick navigation	Pulls user away if its embedded in the main site
Better market segmentation for marketers	User may search the company and get lost in the main site
Reusable templates can save design costs	Poorly designed sites actually decrease conversions
Can be built faster than corporate parent sites	Needs to be maintained—an added cost
A/B testing is much easier	Needs to be updated to be responsive for mobile
SEO friendly, integrated with social media	May confuse users used to a known domain name for main site

Table 11.2   Microsites: Pros and Cons

Most corporate sites have become so dense, it's hard to introduce a new product, showcase a promotion, or provide specialized content on the homepage. Like a small-space ad in the newspaper, anything new gets lost in the clutter. Even worse, many corporate sites are so rigidly designed and controlled that you're handcuffed by their template, fonts, and color palette. So how do you stand out from the corporate site? Create a microsite. A microsite could be as simple as a new landing page described above. Or it could be much more content rich. They're usually one to three pages, but depending on the content, sometimes run much longer. The main things are the microsite has a separate domain name or subdomain name from the parent website, has its own navigation, a separate design, and is focused on one brand, product, or topic. For these reasons, microsites, when built and used correctly, facilitate much higher conversion rates than parent websites. For example, in a study by Forester Research, Procter & Gamble found that their BeingGirl.com microsite was four times more effective than a traditional Always marketing campaign.[11] But microsites still have their detractors. Table 11.2 lists some pros and cons.[12]

Preteen girls don't think about Procter & Gamble and its products. They're concerned with their changing bodies and all the social, emotional, and physical implications that go with it. So it makes sense for P&G to have a microsite to address those issues rather than burying content in a corporate site.

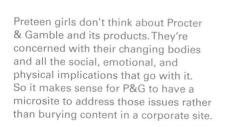

© BeingGirl

Courtesy of Rob Morrice

Trelleborg's marine systems operation designs, manufactures, and installs protective equipment for many of the world's largest ports. When a ship comes into harbor, Trelleborg produces much of the equipment it comes into contact with.

Ports are expensive to build, and the cargo that ships transport is extremely valuable and sometimes dangerous. The stakes are high, and the safe passage of vessels in and out of ports is critical. However, as a premium, industry-leading company, Trelleborg was facing a situation where low-cost competitors were claiming the same product performance. Customers didn't have the awareness of product differences needed to make educated choices. At Stein IAS, our remit was simple: turn the tide.

A key focus for the Performance People campaign was to deliver numbers on the bottom line. Traditional measures such as clicks, opens, and follows have now given way to strong business metrics, including leads, sales, and gross profit—thanks to the client's and agency's desire to prove the effectiveness of marketing. We set ourselves a personal goal too: establish the precise length of the buyer journey to gain an understanding of the type and volume of content required to most effectively nurture a lead from brand awareness to sales conversion.

The campaign was based around the most important event in the maritime calendar—the PIANC World Congress. As a platinum sponsor and PIANC partner, optimizing Trelleborg's activity before, during, and after the event was vital. A series of in-depth strategic workshops were undertaken to produce comprehensive messaging matrices and audience personas. These fueled the development of the creative, content marketing, and contact strategy. Content was critical to fueling the marketing automation system used to deploy the campaign (Oracle Eloqua). Using the messaging work, Stein IAS developed a content marketing strategy that would deliver the right messages at the right time, over the entire buyer journey.

To address each stage, a strong narrative was developed around the folly of putting price before quality, and a body of evidence built to support it (laboratory and product testing data). A series of assets was developed: an industry survey, the Barometer Report, investigated and reported back to the market on key issues, the results formed a benchmarking tool for port owners to compare performance to their peers, and a roundtable was arranged at the PIANC Congress and filmed to create a postevent asset, featuring key industry leaders discussing findings from the report.

The results surpassed previous campaigns and market expectations. The number of marketing qualified leads rose by 43% compared with the previous year, with unprecedented conversion rates (downloads) averaging over 50%. For the first time, Stein IAS was able to quantify the exact length of the customer buyer journey for Trelleborg's marine systems operation—tracking an individual's engagement from first click to sale over a 12-month period.

Most important, the tide is turning. The industry is more aware then ever of the need to put quality before price, and Trelleborg's marine systems operation is further established as a premium supplier of protective equipment for ports.

Rob Morrice, CEO, Stein IAS, Bollington, UK

Know your target audience. The top example is Corona's homepage for the United States in English. The second one is the Spanish version for the United States. Both sell Corona's laid-back lifestyle. But in the site for Mexico, it's more about the product.

Writing for a *Worldwide* Web

Except in countries where local governments crack down on Internet access, you have a global audience. So writing for global brands presents some challenges. For example, a simple literal translation into Spanish or French may mean your word count could swell by 30%. More important, people in other countries think differently, buy differently, and see things differently. Translating your text may not be enough. You have to think like your intended audience. That's why truly global brands tailor their sites to local tastes. For example, in the United States, a brand like Budweiser can show their rich heritage as an American brewer. But in other countries, Budweiser is just another American brand in a country loaded with local brews. So the website focuses on promotions and special features, rather than history.

Where Are We Headed?

A few years ago we described the evolution of the web in well-defined stages—Web 1.0, 2.0, and 3.0. Today some old-thinking companies still run Web 1.0 brochure-ware sites. Most marketers have successfully worked interactive Web 2.0 tools into the mix. Many have fully embraced the seamless integration of digital and analog worlds of Web 3.0. Others are inventing a totally new stage yet to be defined.

The German site for Samsung clearly shows the "mobile first" design mentality, which makes perfect sense when you're selling mobile phones online.

My future boss asked me why I would want to leave a dream job of working in the sports-lifestyle industry to work at an advertising agency. It's a bit of a weird question to be asked during an interview. It was as if he was persuading me to rethink my decision to jump into the advertising world.

Truth be told, I kind of fell into being interested in advertising. I went through stints as a history, teaching, and marketing major before a fateful semester when I took an advertising class because it was as close to a nonbusiness business-like elective as I could find. That class gave me my first taste of a career that would provide the mix of creative and business worlds that I could excel in. It also pushed me to get outside of the classroom. I joined the ad sales team for my college newspaper and ended up with four internships, with two in London while studying abroad. Internships matter, but my two in London really made me stand out. (I also learned a lot.)

Thinking back to that first interview at an advertising agency, my answer was simple. I genuinely wanted to work in advertising. I didn't even see the position as a job, but a rite of passage into an industry that I had been working years toward breaking into. I looked at account management as that key cog that I wanted to be a part of—and still do.

Now being four years in the industry, I've had a chance to work on amazing integrated, digital and social campaigns across brands like Verizon Wireless, Coca-Cola, and Heineken. More important, I've pushed myself further than frankly I thought was possible and in turn grown both personally and professionally. Falling into advertising maybe one of the best things that's happened to me.[14]

Freddie Chavda, senior account manager, We Are Social

@freddiechavda

In 2014, Hotels.com introduced Captain Obvious: the guy who reveals ridiculously evident observations as brilliant insights. As we write about changing technology and its impact on advertising, sometimes we feel a bit like the clueless captain. Technology evolves too quickly to announce the next bright shiny object with any expectation that it will be a big deal two years from now. Anyone who claims to be today's tech guru turns into Captain Obvious within a few weeks. When we say never stop learning, it has never been more applicable in this postdigital age.

WHO'S WHO?

Tara Lamberson

Tara Lamberson leveraged her experience with Walt Disney, Fox Television, and EarthLink to become vice president of marketing at MindComet, a digital solution agency. The range of services includes social networks, podcasting, blogs, viral seeding, email marketing, iPhone development, and brand monitoring for blue-chip clients such as General Motors, Disney, AOL, and Tyco. Lamberson leads the interactive agency strategically, developing measurable and results-focused long-term marketing strategies. She received a bachelor's degree in media arts and design from James Madison University and coauthored the book *Understanding Y: Inside the Mind of Millennials.*

Rebecca Rivera

Rebecca Rivera is chief creative officer for the 3% Conference, a digital writer and occasional creative director who recently gave up agency life to go freelance. She believes marketers get shortchanged when the people most likely to buy their products, usually women, aren't in decision-making roles at ad agencies. She should know. For more than 20 years, Rivera was a player at agencies Team One, DDB Los Angeles, McCann Erickson, Publicis & Hal Riney, Digitas Boston, and Digital Influence Group. Today she leverages her experience to bring her insights to clients, without the agency structure hemming her in.[15]

Robert Wong

Robert Wong is cofounder and executive creative director at Google Creative Lab. As a graphic designer, he is best known for his work as design chief of Starbucks. He has been honored as a Master of Design and one of the 50 Most Influential Designers in America. His work has been shown at exhibitions around the world, including the Cooper-Hewitt National Design Museum and the Museum of Modern Art (MoMA).

Simon Fleming-Wood

Simon Fleming-Wood has been the chief marketing officer of Pandora Media since October 2011. Before Pandora, he served as the founding vice president of marketing at Pure Digital Technologies, where he was responsible for the creation, development, and introduction of Flip Video. Fleming-Wood stated that Pandora's Music Genome Project is a hand-built database "of musicological DNA that allows people on the fly wherever they are to find music that they love."[16]

Drunken Pelican Water Sports Rental

Drunken Pelican Water Sports Rental is a small business located in a small city on the Florida Gulf Coast, where there are many silver-sand beaches and emerald-green waters along about 150 miles of seashore. The business has a storefront at a strip mall right next to a large public beach, renting out small water sports equipment such as paddleboards, kayaks, surfboards, and snorkeling gear. In addition, the shop also sells essential items beachgoers need, from flip-flops to beach towels to sunscreen.

Drunken Pelican has been in business for only three years. By talking to its customers, the owner of the shop, Todd, got to know that most of them are from nearby inland towns. A small portion of the customers are from other parts of the country. While Drunken Pelican gets some crowds coming during the off-season, most of its profit is generated from late May to early September, when the water is warm enough to swim in.

Todd named the store Drunken Pelican in order to give it a fun personality, mainly targeting younger visitors to the beach. The store sign has a cartoonish pelican in orange and blue attire, reinforcing its fun character.

Tourism in town has been good since the shop opened. Todd saw a steady increase in sales in the past three years. Last month, the mayor announced a strategic plan, which includes more effort to attract visitors in the next five years. Todd sees it as a great opportunity for his business to grow. At the same time, Todd feels the pressure of competition from similar stores nearby.

Todd has been looking at local newspapers and television for advertising possibilities in the past few years. However, with a limited budget, he has advertised only with a free local monthly newspaper targeting visitors and local residents. Last week, Todd saw a local attorney's banner ad while watching a YouTube video, and thought that it was a very good way to advertise the business online. In addition, he heard from a friend about Google AdWords and search engine optimization. Todd has decided that it is time to take advantage of online advertising and take his business to a new level.

1. List the advantages of online advertising over the monthly newspaper Todd has used. Is it suitable for Drunken Pelican to advertise through the Internet? If so, list at least two reasons.

2. Among all types of online advertising, Todd wants to advertise with Google AdWords first. Is it a good decision for his business? Explain.

3. Write six to ten keywords for the business. Remember, a "keyword" is actually a group of words (e.g., "beach supply" is considered one "keyword"). Think about the word combination that is most relevant to Drunken Pelican's business.

4. Todd also decides to put up some display advertising online (e.g., banner, skyscraper, and rich media). What messages should these ads deliver? What kind of visuals is ideal for those ads?

5. In what type of websites or social media should Todd place his display ads?

Ying Huang, assistant professor, University of West Florida

1. It's a Quirky World Out There

- Think of something quirky about yourself, something that sets you apart. Do you collect comic books? Are you the only unicyclist on campus? Have you been a closet juggler since middle school? Are you the only one you know who has lived through five surgeries before age 18? Do you have four toes? We guarantee there will be some quirky people in your class!

- List all the benefits of having your quirk. Have some fun with this. After all, this is advertising.

- Now write a 200- to 250-word story, along with a headline, expressing your quirkiness in vivid detail.

- Now it's time to reveal your alter ego or remain anonymous. Hop on blogger.com and create a blog that tells the world about your own unique quirk. That's right, create a blog dedicated to your very own quirkiness. You might even want to follow some of the tips in this chapter.

- Once you're done, track it for three weeks and keep blogging. Track how many posts you have each day. Are there patterns? Who is posting? What kinds of things do they have to say? At the end of the three weeks, make a list of all the branded opportunities that could be leveraged by people who share your particular quirkiness. You might be surprised by how many others share your eccentricities.

- Share your findings with the class. Yes, you have to reveal your quirkiness, at least to the class. If you like your blog, keep it and expand it. If not, game over.

2. Digital Transference

- Find a long-copy ad for a business-to-business brand.

- Dissect the copy into a series of benefits. Prioritize them based on the key message within the ad.

- Now go online and search for your brand. See if the benefits in the ad match up to the brand's web presence. If not, choose one of two options: (a) Rewrite the ad to fit the digital brand presence, or (b) rewrite the web content to fit the ad. The goal is to create seamless branded transference and make suggestions for visual consistency.

- Now that you have created a consistent print and Internet presence for the brand, suggest two other tactical opportunities that would be consistent with the revised brand voice.

3. Virtual Artifact Room

- Pick a product. Any product. It's time to find the articles that are associated with that product.

- Do enough secondary research so you are familiar with the target, and then draft a Consumer Profile.

- Now, take your ethnographic feet on the road to find objects—toys, food, music, products, photos, clothing—anything and everything that their consumer might have in his or her world. Gather it together into one place. Create an artifact room. Do this individually or as a class. We recommend doing it as a class.

- Spend time in the artifact room and get to know what objects the consumer holds near and dear. See what you can learn about the consumer's lifestyle from these objects. Compare how you "see" the consumer with how your classmates "see" the consumer.

- Now get out your pencil or pen or laptop and start writing. Begin by revising your Consumer Profile. Next write a story about your consumer, then another, and another, and another. These are the foundation for the branded story.

- Now cluster the objects in the artifact room and consider how you can make the artifact room comes to life digitally! How can you make all the objects, and what they symbolize, available to your target virtually? Is it a website, a blog, wallpaper, an app, or perhaps an alter ego? Do they arrive via a podcast, a text, or a gadget? Maybe your brand is the next to be "Simpsonized"!

- Mock up your concept and share it with the class. If you are really tech savvy, go live.

Review chapter content and study for exams. http://study.sagepub.com/altstiel4e.

- Interactive practice quizzes
- Mobile-friendly eFlashcards
- Carefully selected chapter-by-chapter video and multimedia content

Chapter 12

Socially Mobile
Reaching Communities That Buy

In our last edition we discussed the term *mocial*—the emerging integration of social media marketing and mobile marketing. Today you don't hear too many marketers talk in those terms. In this postdigital age, mobile devices have become the primary means to deliver a brand message, whether it's an app, text, a banner ad, video, branded content, a native ad, a social media post, or even a telephone call. We can't really separate digital communications into nice, neat categories. But we can explore the impact of mobile marketing, how it continues to evolve, and what the future might hold, knowing full it can't be fully separated from desktop websites and email. We'll also use this chapter to take a closer look at social media marketing, separating the use of networks as advertising platforms from branded and user-generated social marketing content.

Mobile: You *Can* Take It With You

Let's admit it. We're slaves to our smart phones. Ninety-two percent of smart phone users experience anxiety when they're not near a charger.[1] Ninety-five percent of users say their cell phone is the first thing they look at in the morning. In fact, 60% of our total media time is spent on mobile devices.[2] Sometimes we even have telephone conversations.

Mobile Web Marketing

Mobile-first web design: Most people already go to mobile first when they seek information or entertainment. Even search engines consider mobile friendliness as part of the ranking criteria. So it makes sense to consider the special user experience (UX) requirements of a small screen. One of the key factors to consider is making it easier to click on the right content. Some people, especially those who are not digital natives, have "fat fingers," which explains why almost half of digital ads are clicked by mistake.

"The concept of the front page has changed. Social and mobile are now the key distribution models."[3]

Pat Chambers,
BuzzFeed

© MensHealth

Choose a publisher   add a sponsored news story   or a sponsored photo gallery   or a sponsored video

Apps for publishers provide a lot of opportunity for native advertising. The highlighted sections show a sponsored news story, a sponsored photo gallery, and a sponsored video.

© Audi

Audi combined mobile gaming with product information. As the R8 sports car speeds past on the iPad, the user has to snap a picture. The screen shots are stored in the iPad's photo album, but only those with the car perfectly framed reveal the R8.

This also created the need for automatic spell checking for texts. Another consideration for mobile is scrolling. Most people don't mind scrolling down or across, but some sites that go both ways confuse and even irritate some mobile users. Animations take up bandwidth and sometimes complicate design aesthetics. That's why more sides are using "lazy loading" animations that are loaded in the page, but activate only when they are scrolled into view. Perhaps the biggest UX consideration is simplicity — short copy, bright colors, basic illustrations, crisp photography, and, most important, easy-to-read fonts.

Most website developers have adopted a **mobile-first** philosophy. In other words, their desktop and laptop designs are created to easily adapt to mobile phones and tablets. Designer Luke Wroblewski describes how it works: "First mock up how your website would look as a responsive layout on mobile screens. Eliminate all excess fluff and keep to only the bare essentials. From this standpoint it's much easier to scale up your design to wider screens. Navigation menus become wider, content is lengthened along with a possible sidebar. Mobile first design places a higher priority on the mobile experience, which then becomes a baseline for the entire layout."[4]

Mobile Advertising

Steve Jobs was famous for his acerbic wit as well as his creativity. One of his more memorable quotes was "Mobile ads still suck."[5] Even with the advances made since Jobs's passing, he's still right. Advertisers have not really broken through to achieve the same success in mobile as with other digital marketing. Some of the reasons are due to the nature of the device, available technology, and good old human nature. Brands can't target users on mobile devices like they can on desktop sites. Without precise targeting, advertising effects resemble the old "spray and pray" model, where success depends more on mass quantities of messages and luck. Consumers may expect that kind of marketing communication when it comes to traditional media.

© Just Eat

The rapid increase in smart phone use has driven mobile-first web design. Responsive email and website designs look fine on a desktop computer or tablet and automatically convert to a single-column design when viewed on a smart phone.

Concerns About Mobile Ads	Mobile Ad Engagement
• Crosses into personal space: 30% • Can't shut them off: 24% • Too intrusive: 18% • Too frequent: 18% • Irrelevant: 6%	• Clicked by accident: 49% • Not clicked at all: 37% • Clicked intentionally but not read: 9% • Clicked intentionally and engaged with brand: 6%
Consumers Expect Something of Value When They View These Types of Mobile Ads	**Most Important Mobile Ad Elements**
• Coupon: 27% • Banner: 25% • Video: 12% • Text message: 10% • Search: 10%	• Duration and size of ad: 57% • Relevant content: 56% • Location specificity: 51% • Freebies and rewards: 40% • Limited time offers: 23%

Table 12.1   Mobile Advertising Stats[6]

However, we have a special relationship with our mobile devices. We personalize the covers, the wallpapers, the games, the ringtones, and the apps. Our smartphones are our lives. So we don't want them invaded with unsolicited messages. It's okay to seek out information, but the biggest concerns people have about mobile advertising is the violation of personal space.

Brands are still struggling for ways to force a happy marriage between mobile and advertising. Table 12.1 shows a few reasons why it's a tough match.

Connecting Digital and Analog Worlds

Mobile technology is the gateway between the virtual and actual environments. Mobile devices are the glue that holds the Internet of things together. Marketers have been scrambling to be part of that digital/analog mix, with varying success. Here are some of the ways:

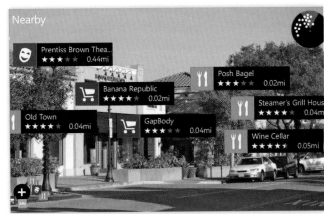

Augmented reality shows everything you're interested in within a given point of view, as indicated in the upper right corner of this screen.

Proximity marketing allows customers with mobile phones to be tracked when they enter a store, where they are at any given point of time, and for how long. The system enables special offer texts to be sent to these customers' phone. For example, a retailer could send a mobile text message to customers in their database who happen to be walking in a mall. That message could say, "Save 50% in the next 5 minutes only when you purchase from our store."

> *"Bad advertising only gets worse on a mobile phone. Bad mobile advertising is just rude."[7]*
>
> Don McNeill,
> cofounder and president,
> Digital Kitchen

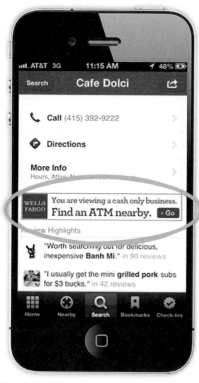

Here's another way the digital and analog worlds intersect. An ad for an ATM pops up in the middle of a review for a cash-only restaurant. Timely? Useful? Annoying?

Looking for a sweet deal? In-store beacons help you find not only the right products, but also the best price.

Mondelez International has committed to exploring proximity-based messaging, citing significant gains in point-of-purchase influence.[8]

Location-based services send advertising and other information to smart phone users based on their current locations, using a GPS chip built into the phone, or proximity to the closest cell phone towers for phones without GPS features.

In-store **beacons** are transmitters that deliver radio signals on a specified frequency from a fixed location in or around a given store. Any radio technology can be used to identify locations, but the most useful for shoppers with mobile devices are Wi-Fi, near-field communication (NFC)/RFID, and Bluetooth. Wi-Fi is readily available across smart phone operating systems and is relatively inexpensive to set up, but requires an installed app. NFC/RFID offers greater accuracy for payments and product information, but is not supported on iPhones. iBeacons are Apple's solution, which are based on Bluetooth and require the installation of apps.

Two-dimensional barcodes, such as QR codes, have connected the digital and analog worlds for a long time. Scanning that ugly little pixelated box can open the door to a beautiful website or app. QR codes have been used in billboards by Calvin Klein and Victoria's Secret, to name a few. You'll see them on virtually every for-sale sign for a residential or commercial property. QR codes on every SKU in stores like Best Buy allow shoppers to get prices and specs (making it easier to find the same product on Amazon for a lower price). Apple Passbook is a native app that uses 2D bar codes which allow users to keep coupons, tickets, boarding passes, debit cards, and credit card information via Apple Pay. **Shazam** is a 2D barcode that allows users to identify, explore, purchase, and share content by scanning audio. Most people use Shazam to identify a song on the radio, a TV show, or in a public place such as a restaurant. Shazam barcodes appear in TV commercials, print ads and out-of-home media, and, when scanned, connect the user to a brand's mobile website. Content can include coupons, discounts, a list of events, cross-promotions, and any number of sales promotion tactics. As one of the world's top ten apps, Shazam reaches more than 450 million users in 200 countries, exceeds 90 million monthly active users, and is growing by another 13 million new users each month. Shazam also makes it easy for people to share their discoveries on Facebook, Twitter, WhatsApp, Pinterest, and Google+.[9]

In-Game Mobile Marketing

Brands are now delivering promotional messages within mobile games or sponsoring entire games to drive consumer engagement. This is known as **mobile advergaming** or **ad-funded mobile gaming**. More and more game developers, especially in the social and mobile space, are offering their products for free.

So how do they monetize a free product? Brand advertising. Mobile offers a huge opportunity. As eMarketer stated, "Although mobile gamers now make up the largest and fastest-growing segment of the gaming population, mobile gaming revenues still lag behind other channels, like console games." Still, U.S. mobile gaming revenues were expected to double by 2017.[10]

There are essentially three major trends in mobile gaming right now: interactive real-time 3D games, massive multiplayer games, and social networking games. This will lead toward more complex and more sophisticated, richer game play. On the other side, there are the so-called casual games—games that are very simple and very easy to play. Most mobile games today are such casual games, and this will probably stay the case for quite a while.

Ads and Apps

For all the reasons previously stated in this chapter, people just don't like mobile advertising. Mobile devices are very personal, and they don't want that space invaded. For a marketer, responsive websites are much cheaper to develop and can offer richer content than stand-alone ads. Plus they can serve as the vehicle for ads in a native environment. Most people would be more receptive to an ad on a website they opened rather than an intrusive text message.

Shazam has long been popular to track down music sources. It's becoming more popular for TV commercials to link viewers to mobile websites.

Some brands sneak a message into a mobile game. Others are up front and sponsor the game, creating entertainment that merges the brand image with the interests of the users.

People hate mobile ads, but they love apps. The total mobile ad spend is predicted to reach $85 billion by 2018, and 86% of that will be spent on developing apps.[11] Apps deliver the highest level of engagement because people actively seek them, download them, use them and have the ability to dump them when they no longer provide value. App development is more expensive than creating mobile ads, but because people invite the messages into their lives, apps are far more engaging.

Unlike ads and responsive sites, app development depends on the platform. Apple iOS is the preferred platform for developers in North America and Europe, while Android wins everywhere else.[12] Development also varies by the core technology used to create an app. About half of all apps are developed as native apps that deliver customized content and navigation. Native apps are specific to a platform and offer strong security. As a result they are more expensive to develop than apps created in HTML5.

© American Express

American Express sponsored an app that allows the user to create a personalized panorama that syncs favorite activities and locations such as restaurants and stores with the American Express Card, Facebook, Twitter, and Foursquare.

	Pros	Cons	Examples
Native apps	Only one OS required Higher speed Integration with other features Better UX Gaming High security	Single platform programming (costly and time consuming to multiple platforms) Fragmented user base Depends on app store	Facebook Skype
HTML5 apps	Multiple OS Lower development costs (one code base) Easier to update and manage Faster to market	Not fully supported on all devices Less secure Slower Does not look or feel native	Google Docs Scribd
Hybrid apps	More flexible Easy development Integration with other features	Longer development time if used on different OS Awkward communication between web and native layer	Netflix Yelp

Table 12.2   Mobile Apps[13]

About half of all apps use HTML5 or HTML5 hybrid technology. Hybrid technology is a good compromise that has a web-based mobile app wrapped inside a native container. Hybrid apps combine the opportunity for a rich user interface developed in HTML5 with device-specific capabilities accessed through the native code. The biggest advantage is flexibility. Table 12.2 outlines the pros and cons of mobile app development tools.

While downloading apps involves a choice, address push notifications associated with those apps can become very annoying. **Push notifications** can be much cheaper compared with separate SMS (Short Message Service) marketing once they are set up. But of course, they have to be factored into the cost of the app's development. As with all mobile marketing, brands have to find that balance between providing information people want, when they want it, and bothering people. Smart marketers give the consumer the choice to opt out.

Where Is Mobile Taking Us?

All indicators point to mobile becoming the dominant force in online access. With an expected 26 billion devices in use by 2020,[14] that's an easy prediction. But it's harder to find ways to integrate mobile in a marketing communication campaign. Here are some considerations:

- Advertisers need to find ways to create adaptive messaging that flows from one device to the next. About 70% of consumers research products on smartphones, but 65% of the resulting purchases take place on other media.

- Marketers will have to balance advances in geotargeting that delivers the right message to the right person at the right time and location with privacy concerns.

- Right now, mobile's share of ad spend is pretty small, and the vast majority of marketers are not very confident in their ability to measure the return on investment (ROI) of their mobile efforts. Measuring effectiveness will have to go beyond click-through measurements to more robust metrics such as cross-channels and in-store sales attribution, postclick engagement, and brand lift.

- Mobile does not use cookies to target users. But social media platforms like Facebook and Twitter are using consumer-supplied data to follow them online. Cookieless targeting has arrived.

- Programmatic has arrived for mobile. Automating the process of mobile ad purchasing and targeting allows brands to focus on their audience and improve resonance to increase engagement.[15]

Some people look to major tech events such as South by Southwest (SXSW) to discover the next big thing in mobile and social media. Some of today's mainstream apps, such as Foursquare, Quora, and Google+, rose from SXSW. The blogosphere went gaga over live video on Meerkat and Periscope at SXSW. We'll see where that goes and what comes up next. Despite the breathless excitement about the latest hot app, we have to understand that the biggest hurdle to mobile marketing is the intimate relationship we have with our devices. Aggressive advertising on our smart phones is just as unwelcome as a pushy salesperson. For many people, their mobile device is their only digital connection that's relatively free from marketing intrusion. Mobile spam, in-game ads, location information services, and more sophisticated tracking technology threaten perceptions of privacy and receptivity to marketing messages.

Social Media Versus Social Networking

Most people use the term *social media* to cover every aspect about interactive online communication. However, to really understand it in a marketing communication context, you need to know the difference between social media and social networking. Social media is the content (media) that's distributed online. It can be a blog, a video, a newsletter, an article, a white paper, an e-zine, a review, or a personal comment. Social networking is how you distribute that content through social networking sites such as Facebook and Twitter. Social networking is all about engagement. Advertising communicates. Social networking connects—builds relationships. It should be a two-way street—where the marketer listens as much as it tells. Think of social media as the "what" and social networking as the "how" of online interpersonal communication.

Social Networking Platforms

Since we are talking about marketing communications, we'll limit this section to a brief discussion of some of the top players in social networking and how they are used to deliver advertising. Then we'll cover social media marketing and why it's different from advertising. Social media marketing does *not* include paid media on social networks. As customer experience leader and social media blogger Augie Ray states, "Go ahead and invest in advertising on Facebook and Twitter, just don't call it 'social.' The most popular forms of advertising on Facebook today are retargeting and custom audiences, neither of which are remotely social, and less than one in six dollars use social data."[16]

We can't cover all the rising stars in social media. If you're tuned into the social space, you've probably read about the next big thing in this morning's Twitter feed. Rather, we'll focus on the current leaders and how they deliver ad messages.

Facebook has rocketed from an obscure chat group to a marketing juggernaut. In fact, Don Mathis in *Advertising Age* commented, "Facebook is pushing beyond the restrictive label of 'social' and rewriting the rules of the game in digital marketing along the way. If nothing else, it highlights that social is not just a channel. Rather, social is a fundamentally different way to understand and execute digital marketing. It is far more about data than platform, and Facebook is making this vision a reality. Success in digital marketing should be about finding precise consumer audiences and identities, not abstractions like campaigns and line items. Atlas is making Facebook more people-focused than ever before, and brands and agencies would be smart to follow suit."[17] Facebook is solving one of the big problems with social media and mobile devices—inability to accurately target users. Advertisers can find appropriate audiences based on a whole new set of variables, and because targeting is based on demographics and buying behavior, it's much more efficient.

It's no coincidence that organic search on Facebook has dropped to almost nothing, forcing brands to pay for sponsored stories and advertising. Fortunately for marketers, the new advertising model is so robust that they can get better results with measurable ROI than ever before.

©Facebook.com

Facebook has become a major advertising platform that continues to change the nature of mobile and social marketing.

Experts expect these enhanced data-based campaigns to replace the old like-based Facebook advertising model. Here's an example: marketers could leverage Facebook targeting to reach consumers on the desktop ESPN.com site and then use Facebook's Audience Network to reach that same customer on the *SportsCenter* app. Besides superior tracking to aid advertisers, Facebook pages are far more detailed than Twitter accounts.

Facebook gives you the ability to promote posts that already exist on your company's page. They are best served when you are trying to reach established followers. **Boosted posts** appear higher in the newsfeed, and they will appear on a person's news feed more than once. The best time to use a boosted post is when you want to reach more of your established followers with that specific content for an extended period of time. Boosted posts don't show up in the right-hand column. That space is reserved for ads, which are being replaced with high-performing branded content and app-installed ads.

Facebook continues to evolve, with new innovations in branded entertainment. POPSUGAR Rush is a 24/7 series around trending topics. Jimmy Kimmel created a Facebook native series about hot bands appearing at SXSW. BuzzFeed put out a video featuring President Obama promoting HealthCare.gov on Facebook. The finely tuned targeting capabilities around Facebook video are grabbing the attention of marketers and challenging YouTube's primacy in branded video.[18]

Twitter is a micro blog in which 140-character messages can link to a product's website, Facebook profile, photos, or videos. Consumers can and do tweet about just about anything, including products and services. Sometimes these conversations happen organically. However, marketers soon discovered that they can't rely on having a critical mass of positive tweets at any given time. Enter **promoted tweets**. They start with a compelling piece of content, such as the announcement of an upcoming product release, a sale, or an event, and add a photo or video to drive higher engagement. Once the promoted tweet is created, Twitter's target options connect it with the right audience. Twitter lead generation cards work directly within promoted tweets to collect users' contact information in exchange for the offer. They act like embedded landing pages within the tweets, except they're much more concise and require much less work from followers. The immediacy of the information and the breadth of coverage makes Twitter a natural to take advantage of current events, as Oreo did during a Super Bowl blackout and, more recently, using the cookies to simulate a solar eclipse. When Wendy's launched their pretzel bacon cheeseburger, they encouraged customers to tweet and create Facebook posts about their new product. Each week Wendy's picked their favorite messages and turned them into love song lyrics. Popular singers such as Nick Lachey sang the tweets in elaborately produced music videos on YouTube. Wendy's claimed 7.5 million Facebook views during this campaign. More important, Wendy's stock price increased during the launch of the pretzel bacon cheeseburger.[19]

Wendy's invited people to tweet the praises of their pretzel bacon cheeseburger, which they turned into lyrics for love songs to the yummy sandwich. Singers made elaborate music videos that were shared by millions. They sold a few cheeseburgers too.

With all the Twitter marketing successes, there are also some noteworthy failures, also due to the immediacy of the information and breadth of coverage. Here are a few to serve as warnings about how quickly things can go wrong.

- Spirit Airlines poked fun at the leaked nude celebrity selfie scandal by promoting #BareFares. The airline was attacked for displaying poor taste and poor timing (as opposed to the nude celebrities). The lesson: Don't try to make a buck off other people's pain.

- DiGiorno pizza latched onto the viral hashtag #WhyIStayed, which was used by victims of domestic violence. The erroneous tweet was pulled after 20 minutes, but it spawned a barrage of angry backlash tweets. The lesson: Know what a hashtag really means before you post.

- U.S. Airways was handling a customer complaint, but instead of the usual polite "thanks for the feedback" response, the person in charge fired off a hardcore porn picture that stayed up for a full hour. The lesson: Pay attention to every tweet on behalf of your brand and know who's handling your social media.[20]

Google+ provides some features of Facebook, but is also able to intergate with the Google search engine. Other Google products are also integrated, such as Google AdWords and Google Maps. With the development of Google Personalized Search and other location-based search services, Google+ allows targeted advertising methods, navigation services, and other forms of location-based marketing and promotion. Google+ is one of the fastest growing social media networks and can benefit almost any business. We're not promoting Google, just reporting the facts.

LinkedIn is the social network for established business professionals and aspiring young professionals. Individuals and companies can create professional profiles and promote Twitter streams, blog entries, slide shows, and other content on their LinkedIn profile pages. LinkedIn provides its members the opportunity to generate sales leads and business partners.

The fine line between branded content and native advertising is even more blurry when it comes to mobile social networking sites like Twitter and LinkedIn.

Oreo has earned a reputation for using social media to quickly connect breaking news stories with their brand. They scored a major coup when they tweeted during a Super Bowl blackout. Even though they had more time to prepare for a solar eclipse, Oreo's creativity still shone brightly.

Members can use Company Pages, similar to Facebook pages, to create an area that will allow business owners to promote their products or services and be able to interact with their customers. Because of its structure and reputation, many businesspeople trust LinkedIn content more than some other online sources. When you're providing native or even sponsored content on LinkedIn, keep that in mind. It's a good idea to consider the value you offer rather than talking about yourself or your company. They want to know how you will make them more successful. Short simple copy works best, especially for busy businesspeople scrolling through their news feeds. As with all social media, photos and video get results.

Foursquare is a location-based web and mobile social networking platform where users can choose to have their check-ins integrated with other social platforms, such as Twitter and Facebook. The Foursquare Brand Platform allows companies to create pages of tips and allows users to "follow" the companies and receive special expert tips from them when they check in at certain locations. Users can unlock special badges with enough check-ins, playing into the growing trend of gamification. It can be a good marketing strategy for businesses to increase foot traffic or retain loyal customers.

Yelp consists of a comprehensive online index of business profiles. Businesses are searchable by location, similar to the Yellow Pages. The website is operational in seven different countries, including the United States and Canada. Business account holders are allowed to create, share, and edit business profiles. The may post information such as location, contact information, pictures, and service information. The website further allows individuals to write and post reviews about businesses and rate them on a five-point scale. Messaging and talk features are further made available for general members of the website, serving to guide thoughts and opinions.

Photo and Video Networking Sites

A picture is still worth a thousand words and certainly much more than 140 characters. Engagement from photo and video platforms has rapidly outpaced text-only networking sites. Here are some of the market leaders:

YouTube, owned by Google, is usually regarded as the third most popular Internet site after Facebook and Google and the second leading search engine. YouTube sells sponsorships for suites of channels, using keyword targeting rather than demo statistics. YouTube gives the advertiser a grant for video production, then splits the profits from ad sales with the advertiser after the initial investment is covered. The ads on this platform are usually in sync with the content of the video request. For example, a user who searches for a YouTube video on dog training may be presented with a sponsored video from a dog toy company.

Most brands maintain their own YouTube channels and support them with ads in social and other media. For example, Toyota ran ads using Google Preferred to promote videos starring Rhett and Link from the *Good Mythical Morning* YouTube talk show. The two-minute clip generated a modest 74,000 views on the Toyota channel, but the comedy team promoted the new Camry on six of their shows, which totaled more than 10 million views. Plugging into videos that influencers are already creating could be more effective than promoting branded videos.[21]

As demand for video, especially premium content, continues to grow, can YouTube keep up? The YouTube model is not without its detractors: producers complain about unfair revenue splits, there's little interaction between content creators and users, and the quality and relevance of content varies widely. Given those issues and the insatiable demand for video, the door is open for other players. Facebook and **Vimeo** are growing in this area. **Amazon**, **Hulu**, and **Netflix** host award-winning, must-see programs. Instagram, Twitter, and Vine are major video sources. New platforms are coming on board with a variety of improvements, including mobile-first design, interactivity with fans, sharing content offline, more favorable revenue splits, easy-to-use channel guides and more innovative revenue monetization models. Despite the emergence of these platforms, we'll bet that if there's a better way to dominate online video, YouTube will find it.

Instagram grew to over 200 million users in 2014, surpassing Twitter. But even more significant is a user engagement rate that's 15 times higher than Facebook's and 25 times higher than Twitter's.[22] When it comes to brands and businesses, Instagram helps companies reach their audiences through captivating imagery in a rich visual environment. Moreover, Instagram provides a platform where user and company can communite publicly and directly. The idea of Instagram pictures is built on the sense that event is happening right now, and that adds another layer to the personal and accurage picture of the company.

Delta Air Lines, Volvo, and a fashion eyewear company were early adopters of marketing on Instagram. Thousands more have joined, as the popularity of the site continues to grow. *Adweek* reported, "The tactic is a smart one for visually driven brands in industries like fashion and travel—especially those already dabbling in influencer marketing."[23] For example, Lululemon Athletica, with more than 350,000 Instagram followers and nearly 2 million Pinterest followers, was another early adopter of Instagram video. Its initial post, "Every Mat Tells a Story," was a series of quick cuts showing a person practicing yoga poses. The video received more than 23,000 likes and over a thousand comments.[24] Instagram's Hyperlapse video component continues to grow, with over 200 million daily users. Instagram claims the videos double the engagement rate for their photos, which is already much higher than text-based social networking messages. About half of the videos are user generated.[25] Despite increasing advertising activity on Instagram, the platform has been lagging among brands. In mid-2015, just 23% of U.S. brands are on Instagram, while 90% use Facebook, 82% are on Twitter, and 60% run videos on YouTube.[26]

If you only need 6 seconds to tell your story, use a Vine. Burberry's did when they tweeted from a fashion show; Lowe's showed quick home improvement hacks; and Dunkin' Donuts recreated the key plays from a Monday Night Football game using their products.

Vine is an app from Twitter that uses a 6-second video clip to tell a story. As of 2015, over 8,000 Vines are shared every minute with over 40 million users. The minivideos are a great way to increase the engagement with a brand message, and since the file size is tiny, they are very easy to share on mobile devices.[27]

- Burberry used Twitter to broadcast its show live during Fashion Week and created four short-form videos on Vine. The most popular featured quick images of various celebrities in attendance. The results: of the 180,000 mentions using the #LFW hashtag, 10,000 were about Burberry, more than any other brand.[28]

- Dunkin' Donuts created the first-ever TV ad from a Vine, a billboard ad unit for *Monday Night Football*. The spot quickly recreated a key play from the game (a San Diego Charger touchdown) but substituted Dunkin' Donuts menu items for the actual players.

Pinterest allows users to create and share theme-based image collections. The challenge is to connect relevant marketing messages to content created just for fun. The website has proved especially popular among women, with the popular categories being food, drink, DIY, crafts, women's apparel, home decor, and travel.[30] Pinterest does not generate its own content; rather, it draws from many resources around the web and compiles them in one convenient location for users.

Snapchat is popular with Millennials because (a) images disappear after viewing and (b) their parents haven't discovered it yet. Many experts view Snapchat as a bigger threat to Twitter than Facebook and Instagram. As more companies start using Snapchat, Twitter will feel even more pressure.[31] Snapchat Discover allows brands to interact with consumers, much like the old daily newspaper. Stories are refreshed each day, rather than hanging on to rehashed and reused content they may have already seen. *National Geographic*, VICE, and MTV got on board early to publish fresh daily content. The popular messaging app is encouraging marketers and media companies to shoot ads vertically instead of the typical wide angle landscape shots. Snapchat says shows and ads shot vertically are viewed nine times more frequently than horizontal ones. As Troy Young, president of Hearst Digital mentioned, "Mobile phones are vertical devices. Turning it sideways is a lot of work."[32] Given its rapid growth and popularity with Millennials, it's amazing that only 1% of marketers were using Snapchat in 2015.[33] That's bound to change.

> *"We should be looking at making that transition from the online experience to the offline world easier. It's all about reducing friction."*[29]
>
> Marisa D'Amelio,
> agency development
> manager, Google

Pinterest users pin what interests them—fashion, food, travel tips, decorating ideas, cat pictures, whatever. Sometimes it's branded content. Sometimes it's pure advertising.

	SEO	Brand Awareness	Customer Communication	Traffic Generation
Twitter	Tweets about a webpage generate higher search rankings.	Consistent placement of brand messaging is easy with HootSuite and TweetCaster. Sponsored tweets can be purchased to highlight brand content.	The leading platform for customers seeking customer support. Peer-to-peer communication is simple, easy to track and can be public or private.	Referral traffic growing fast. Photos and videos make Tweets more clickable. Promoted tweets reach new audiences.
LinkedIn	Not one of the top influencers in social media, but personal and company profiles contain searchable text.	Business pages, influencer posts, and publishing platform increase brand awareness. Sponsored updates provide added reach.	About half of people using social media for customer service do it through LinkedIn Company Pages and LinkedIn Groups.	Considered a second-tier source compared with other platforms.
YouTube	Plenty of text, tags, and other searchable content. With over 1 billion users, the sheer size limits the ability to find desired content.	Channels attract viewers to targeted content and subscriptions increase viewership. Videos paired with preroll ads can get lost.	Easy-to-use tools allow marketers to respond to user comments and ratings.	An important source of traffic, but ranked below LinkedIn and Google+.
Google+	Links with more +1's appear higher in search results than likes and retweets on other platforms.	Higher search placement for branded webpages as well as their authors. Higher exposure and rich platform for sharing multimedia.	Targeted messages to interest groups through Circles are available but not widely used yet.	Referral traffic lower than other platforms but rising.
Pinterest	Activity associated with a webpage is a major factor in higher search rankings.	Puts photos and animated GIFs front and center. Interests tool helps users sort through heaps of information.	Public comments and repining visual content is available, but lack of private messages limits utility.	Each photo links back to a source webpage, which helps build referral traffic.
SlideShare	Content with tags and titles but links inside PDFs with a presentation are better for SEO.	Slide presentations are easily embedded in a webpage. Linear format allows brands to build a case in controlled environment.	Links can be shared easily, but seamless interaction between brands and consumers limits effectiveness. Consider using a slide with contact information.	Not as intuitive as other platforms. Consider using embedding SlideShare presentations in a website and using links in email, newsletters to the site.
Instagram	Works better for mobile than desktop, so SEO is limited, but Facebook connection factors into searches.	Most of today's largest brands use this platform. Easy to use, with a clear interface and high visual.	Videos, ads, and private messaging enable more engaging interactions and easier one-to-one contact.	Users can't click on a link and be redirected to a brand page.

Table 12.3   The Social Media Landscape[34]

Table 12.3 is adapted from Adobe's CMO's Guide to the Social Media Landscape It provides a snapshot of the strengths and weaknesses of the major social networking sites. The color coding—green (good), yellow (okay), and red (bad)—is handy for a quick overview. Features for each platform change constantly, so check out cmo.com for the latest version.

Social Media Marketing

Social networking allows people to build (or destroy) personal relationships. The same is true of brands attempting to interact with consumers. In social media marketing, **engagement** means that customers and stakeholders are participants rather than viewers. Social media in business allows anyone and everyone to express and share an opinion or an idea somewhere along the business's path to market. Each participating customer becomes part of the marketing department, as other customers read their comments or reviews.[35]

Engagement in social media marketing can be divided into two parts:

1. Proactive posting of new content and conversations, as well as the sharing of content and information from others.

2. Reactive conversations with social media users responding to those who reach out to your social media profiles through commenting or messaging.

Traditional media is limited to one-way interaction with customers, or "push and tell," where only specific information is given to the customer, without any mechanism to obtain customer feedback. On the other hand, social media marketing is supposed to be participative, where customers are able to share their views on brands, products, and services. Traditional media gives the control of the message to the marketer where social media marketing shifts the balance to the consumer.[36]

Before companies discovered there was potential for managing this virtually uncontrolled word of mouth (WOM), most of the brand conversations were organic—they sprang up at the grassroots level and took on a life of their own, sometimes to the disadvantage of the brand. Market models developed where brands could integrate their messages on social media platforms. They sponsored stories, found bloggers who could say something nice about them, and snuck product information into content people valued. Increased sophistication of semantic technology let companies detect the right time and place to touch consumers with micro targeted campaigns. The results were impressive. Companies basked in the glow of likes, shares, followers, and all the other measures of social acceptance. However, many brands discovered that earned praise didn't translate to sales.

To create realistic expectations of what social media marketing is supposed to accomplish, you need to define it. Of all the definitions out there, this one seems to be the best: brands' use of social networks as the platform to tell their messages with sponsored stories or through influencers who share brand-friendly messages to encourage conversations about the brand. Paid advertising on these sites is not really social media marketing, because it's a top-down strategy. In these cases, Facebook or Twitter essentially has the same function as a magazine or television program, except that if people are engaged, they can share, click to visit a site, or buy direct.

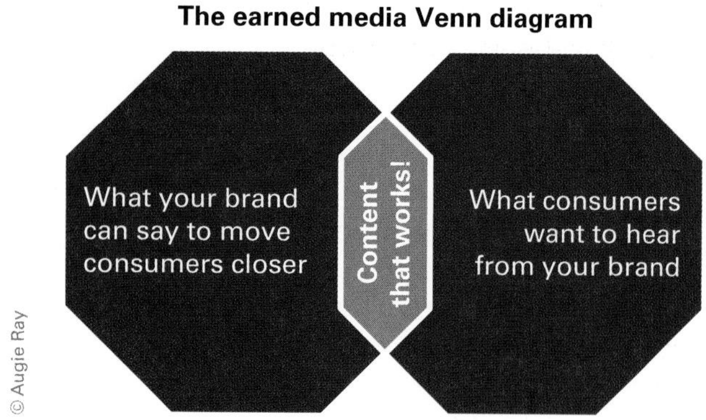

The earned media Venn diagram

© Augie Ray

Figure 12.1 Earned Media Venn Diagram[37]

The Venn diagram in Figure 12.1 shows the narrow range of effectiveness where messages from the brand intersect with receptivity from the consumer. Social media marketing outside of this intersection may generate online activity, but it may not result in meaningful marketing results.

When Social Media Marketing Works

The nature of marketing is trying to sell something. Some brands hit the sweet spot in Figure 12.1. Social media marketing works best when you can provide information about a brand that people want to hear about so that you can increase engagement. In other words, hit people at the right time, with the right information, so they buy something.

Brand Category	Examples
Narrow, select vertical markets	Sports teams TV programs Movies Style brands
Brands with a purpose (related to a cause that resonates)	USAA Chipotle
Brands with better products and service	Apple

Social media marketing can be used for good causes that resonate with consumers. Specific topics like concern over genetically modified food mesh with Chipotle's social media campaign. The cause can be even more generic, such as self-esteem and bullying. Dove and Coca-Cola took their recent happiness-oriented campaigns to Twitter using targeted campaigns to turn online hate into something positive. With branded hashtags #SpeakBeautiful (Dove) and #MakeItHappy (Coke), the brands attempted to use marketing to make the Internet a happier, friendlier place. With #SpeakBeautiful Dove hopes to foster positive self-esteem for women and girls. "Twitter allows us to send one-on-one responses to women and girls to inspire them to help change the way we talk about beauty on social media," said Jennifer Bremner, director of marketing for Dove. "It only takes one tweet to ignite a positive trend online."[38]

For Coke, #MakeItHappy uses ASCII art—which generates images out of lines of text—to target different hateful tweets and turn those words into cheery imagery. According to Coke, its campaign received 95% positive and neutral responses. Writers from Gawker pranked the brand to inadvertently tweet lines from Adolf Hitler's *Mein Kampf*, the very type of hate speech the campaign was hoping to stamp out.

Brands with strong reputations for quality have an easier time with social media marketing. Apple has no official company profile on Facebook or Twitter, yet it beats Samsung for creating buzz. Both companies introduced new products in the fall of 2014. Within a few days of the launch, Samsung generated 2,350%

more fans, followers, and subscribers on Facebook, Twitter, and YouTube, but Apple still delivered far more Word of Mouth.[39] And as we we've heard for decades, Word of Mouth is the best advertising.

When Social Media Marketing Doesn't Work

To really understand social media marketing, we have to separate the marketing from social media. Social media by itself is great for building relationships, increasing awareness, and enhancing a brand's reputation. That's why public relations and social media are so intertwined. However, as social media and customer experience thought leader Augie Ray points out, "Social media is poorly equipped to deliver trust, traffic, acquisition and purchase—the primary objectives of marketing a brand."[40] Marketers need to take an honest look at what they want to accomplish. Earning friendship is a good thing but it doesn't always lead to a sale.

Whether they use social media platforms or desktop sites, marketers who continue to pump out content that has no value to their target audience will continue to waste money and time and will eventually lose ground to the brands that have figured out how to boost engagement. Nevertheless, marketers continue to soldier on with social media marketing programs in the face of rapidly declining effectiveness. In a 2014 survey of U.S. marketers, fewer than one in six chief marketing officers (CMOs) knew if there was any positive impact from social media marketing for their brands, yet they still intended to double that investment.[41] With falling organic reach, very low engagement levels, and inability to measure quantitative success, that increase will not be sustainable. No wonder the tenure of CMOs is so short.

Social Sponsorship

Social networking sites facilitate WOM marketing by encouraging followers to retweet and repost content to spread the word. But making this happen organically gets more difficult every year. WOM traffic is hard to predict and even harder to control. So brands are improving the odds through social sponsorship. In the most simplistic terms, they are buying followers. This is how it works:

- Brands find bloggers and other influencers who already have a substantial following.
- Influencers are compensated to post content favorable to the brand (videos, photos, blog posts) and share material from other sources.
- Sponsored content is placed by the site owner or social media account holder.
- Sites and accounts are independent of brand accounts.
- Promoted tweets and boosted posts are not considered as social sponsorship.

The level of compensation varies depending on the scope of the project. It can be as economical as linking more users to the influencer's blog, or it can be a substantial cash payment to a well-known blogger to play ball with a brand. For example, Lowe's built a series of Vine "life hack" demonstrations, working with their agency BBDO and photographer Meagan Cignolis (who already had a large Twitter following). She shot the entire campaign on an iPhone, which was distributed on Twitter, Facebook, and Tumblr. Other compensation can be payment in kind, such as products, travel, loyalty points, or all of the above.

Social sponsorship can take several directions. Sponsored conversations direct to bloggers, podcasts, and social media platforms like Twitter and Facebook work great for long-format reviews, discussions, essays, and photo collections. Digital brand ambassador programs recruit content providers to comment on brand sites after sampling the product. These can range from a top-down influencer compensation program, mentioned earlier, to a more bottom-up grassroots effort.

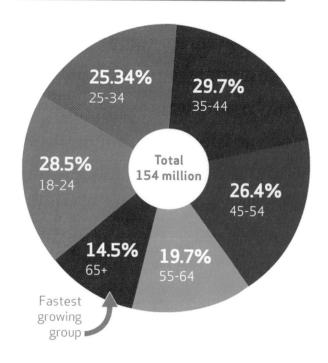

SOCIAL MEDIA USE
By Age Group

29.7% 35-44
26.4% 45-54
19.7% 55-64
14.5% 65+
28.5% 18-24
25.34% 25-34

Total 154 million

Fastest growing group

	Users (millions)	Largest demo	Trends
f	160.9	25-35	Major fall off in 18-24 Major increase in 65+
Instagram	65.3	25-34	Major increase in 18-24 Almost no activity in 65+
Twitter	57.3	18-24	Half of all users are 18-34
Pinterest	47.6	25-34	Older Millennials and Gen X'ers still active
Tumblr	21.1	25-34	Market share decreases for all demos except children 17 and younger

Source: Adweek, January 12, 2015

Social and Word-of-Mouth Marketing

Social media has altered the landscape of WOM, helping spread buzz faster and more efficiently than face-to-face communications. It's done more than simply turbocharge WOM. It has also brought this "alternative" form of marketing to the mainstream. WOM is based on the simple premise that a recommendation from a friend carries more weight than an ad message. But social media has blurred what that means. Social networking has given WOM marketers a clearer way to measure the impact of their campaigns. Marketers can see how far an influencer's opinion spreads by analyzing retweets or shares. It also becomes easier to see if an influencer's discussions are relevant and in line with positioning. Plus it all occurs in real time. When combined, WOM and social become a dynamic duo. Conversations begun online continue in person, and recommendations spread more quickly, allowing communities built around brands to gain traction. "You start conversations in one channel, continue them in a second and finish them in a third," says Karin Kane, vice president of client services for evolve24, a Maritz Research company that uses business analytics and research to measure brand perceptions, reputation, and risk. "When communication is happening in so many channels, it becomes almost impossible to separate online and offline."[42] Social media marketing is also closely tied with search engine optimization. In fact, 7 of the top 10 factors that correlate with strong Google organic search are social media dependent.[43]

Using social media to turbocharge word-of-mouth marketing can be a smart strategy. Integrated with traditional media, social media can even generate a pop culture phenomenon. Samsung Galaxy's epic Oscar selfie in 2014 is a great example. Within 45 minutes, the celebrity-packed picture was retweeted 1.3 million times. Maurice Levy, CEO of Publicis, said the tweet was worth $800 million to $1 billion in marketing value.[44] More than 37 million people saw this "spontaneous" selfie, and only 8% of the comments were negative.[45]

Then there are the epic failures. Skittles wanted to demonstrate their social media expertise. Their homepage featured tweets with the #skittles hashtag. A chatter tab had live Flickr and YouTube feeds. The Facebook fan page was displayed under a "Friends" tab. Everything started out as planned, but it didn't take long to go terribly wrong. Without a filter or moderator, profane tweets began cropping up on the homepage, which of course went viral. So much for being social media savvy.

Writing Company Blogs

Access to the blogosphere means that anyone can become a journalist. Unfortunately not everyone is a good one. The cost of traditional publishing prevents most hacks from inflicting their drivel on the public. Unfortunately there are no such restraints online. As a result, fact checking, grammar, and basic civility sometimes take a back seat to self-expression. Because blogging is such a personal activity, we'll focus on using blogs to sell something. Keep in mind, writing for style and meaning is just as critical for blogs as with print. Maybe even more important, because once it's on the Internet, it's never going away. More people can see it, share it, comment on it, and love it or hate it. Before you post your first commercial blog, you should review the body copy checklist in Chapter 8. Then set it aside and look at it a couple of days later. Remember "write hot, edit cold"? Also remember, once it's posted, it will last forever.

Here are some other purposes of blogs for business or pleasure:

- **Informational blogs:** Pick any topic, but make sure you do your research. Make sure the facts can stand up if you're making a claim. Cite your sources, and be clear when you're stating your personal opinion.

- **Company blogs:** These should reflect a more human side to a company or brand beyond a recitation of features and benefits. Perhaps personal stories, unusual facts, or other information that makes the reader want to like the company as well as buy its products.

- **Cultural insights:** Maybe you have some expertise with certain ethnicities, age groups, neighborhoods, or hobbies that you'd like to share. Marketers may be able to use your information, or it may just be entertaining to a general audience.

- **Technology updates:** Geeks read what other geeks write. Maybe you want to share what you saw at the Consumer Electronics Show. Or you tried the next killer app. A lot of people want to know what's the next big thing.

- **Industry specific blogs:** You may have some information to share about what's new in any given industry, including advertising. You can discuss what's in and what's out and look like an expert in your field. It's amazing how many blogs start with "The 10 hottest trends for _____." It works!

- **Creative rants:** It's okay to vent, just make it clever and entertaining. Give solid reasons for your criticism beyond "That really sucked."

- **Travel blogs:** Reveal hidden details the ordinary tourist never sees. Talk about the people you've encountered and share their stories. You may encourage someone to explore the world or just entertain the armchair adventurer.

- **Writing blogs:** These can be random musings about anything and everything, or they can be very focused about specific topics. More than any of the above, they must be well written. Double- and triple-check everything before hitting that send button.

Here are a few tips to make your blogs more interesting, relevant, and searchable.

- **Ask, don't tell:** Perhaps you lead with a provocative question to draw readers in (refer to Chapter 8's discussion of headlines). Or you close with a thoughtful question that encourages comments.

- **Think visually:** Visuals attract readers. Review Chapter 6 for basic design and web design trends, and find something that's compelling and relevant to your message.

- **Promote yourself:** Your blog may have its own Google+ or Facebook page. That's a perfect place to promote your latest post. It will generate more comments and help your search rankings. Tweets can also encourage visits to your blog.

- **Support other bloggers:** Use social networks to comment on other blogs and retweet other blog posts occasionally. Your support will be reciprocated.

- **Study blogs you admire:** Find some blogs you really like and follow them for several weeks or months. Discover what makes them consistently interesting, well written, and meaningful. Then interact. Let them know you value their effort. A lot of the motivation behind blogging is ego. We all seek validation.

SmartBear's blog features compelling titles, attention-getting images, and relevant content. They've taken a rather dry topic and made it fun and interesting. Plus they've connected it to social media, made it easy to comment, and highlighted other blog posts.

© AT&T

When AT&T lost an exclusivity deal with a key smart phone manufacturer, the communications giant was faced with the dual challenges of keeping users from leaving and creating loyalty among those who stayed. To reach the young Asian American demographic, a key and tech-savvy group of influencers, the interTrend advertising agency teamed up with Wong Fu Productions.

Wong Fu is a team of Asian American filmmakers that specializes in artfully portraying young Asians who rarely see accurate depictions of themselves in mainstream media. With a massive following among YouTube viewers, Wong Fu was a perfect partner to show off AT&T's powerful new devices and robust 4G network in a dramatic, cinematic web series featuring online celebrities Jen FrmHeadToToe and Victor Kim.

To maximize buzz and appeal, "Away We Happened" was shot, produced, and released in real time with a crowd-sourced plot. Having masses of viewers come together to both discuss and determine the story's developments was unique, intense, and newsworthy, but it was also a calculated way to reach young Asian Americans. interTrend's research had shown that the group is more comfortable and participatory in group settings. Young Asian Americans were also found to be more passionate about content when identifying socially and culturally with the subjects.

In addition, the campaign had a wildly popular Facebook page, allowing fans to debate each installment's developments and share observations, opinions, and excitement with friends. Feeding off the loyal fan bases of Wong Fu, Jen FrmHeadToToe, and Victor Kim, the viewership, participation, and reach of the campaign snowballed.

Everything lined up perfectly, and "Away We Happened" far exceeded the client's expectations, made headlines in entertainment and marketing circles, and earned multiple awards in the advertising industry. The message was communicated loud and clear: AT&T was proved not only to be a fun brand but a leader in technology and innovator in communication.[46]

Jon Yokogawa, vice president, interTrend Communications, Long Beach

We encourage students to write personal blogs. They are great outlets for creative writing, showcasing your work, and expressing your personality. But if a blog displays poor writing skills or an inability to make a point, you're taking several steps backward in your career. If it's not perfect, don't post it, and reread Chapter 8.

Tumblr: Dozens of great open-source sites are available to help you build a good-looking blog. But not many have the built-in marketing advantage of Tumblr. Rather than relying in simple banner ads,

Tumblr requires advertisers to create Tumblr blogs that can feature brand messages throughout the site. Tumblr ad formats include:

- **Sponsored mobile posts**—advertising blog posts that show up on users' dashboards, allowing them to like, reblog, and share the sponsored posts.

- **Sponsored web post**—the largest instream ad unit available catches users' attention when looking at their dashboards. It also allows the viewers to like, reblog, and share.

- **Sponsored radar**—picks up exceptional posts from the whole Tumblr community based on originality and creativity and allows advertisers to place their posts to earn new followers, reblogs, and likes.

- **Sponsored spotlight**—a directory of popular blogs through the community and a place where users can find new blogs to follow. Advertisers can choose several categories for placement.

The Limits of Social Media Influence

Whether you call it word-of-mouth marketing or buzz or whatever, one of its real powers is to create and sustain a brand. Where would Harley-Davidson be without a small, but rabid, gang of brand evangelists in black leather jackets? Ben & Jerry's would be just another ice cream if people didn't talk about their support for worthy causes. Macintosh might just have been another futile experiment in operating system development if dedicated art directors, designers, and other right-brainers didn't spread the word within and between agencies and studios. Without a strong brand story, digital content and viral seeding campaigns have had mixed success to create a buzz. Sometimes the most modest effort becomes an overnight viral sensation. Most times when major funds are invested in a ham-fisted push to go viral, the results are dismal. The risks are magnified. Mistakes happen faster, and they travel around the world at the speed of light. Trolls can turn a well-intended marketing effort into a global PR disaster within hours. What's more, the Federal Trade Commission has firm guidelines about disclosing compensation, and all parties should know the rules before starting a social sponsorship campaign. As with native advertising, the government wants the gullible consumer to be told that someone is paying for the content. Finally, all the warm and fuzzy good will built up with even the best word-of-mouth marketing may not convert to sales or counteract a bad customer experience after the sale.

"Social marketing eliminates the middlemen, providing brands the unique opportunity to have a direct relationship with their customers."[48]

Bryan Wiener,
CEO, 360i

Keeping Up With Social Trends

We won't take a snapshot and use it to predict a trend. The best we can do is report the facts as they stand when we write this and what some of the experts are predicting for the next few years. Katy Lynch, the portfolio director for Manifest Digital, one of the nation's leading media marketing firms, provided this view of the social media landscape[49]:

- We'll see an increase in private message platforms such as WhatsApp, Snapchat, Kik, and WeChat. With only 1% of marketers using Snapchat in 2015, there's a lot of room for growth.

- Video is everything, especially short-form video. By 2017, 74% of web traffic will come from video. Mobile users are 300% more likely to view video than laptop and desktop users. Short-form is important because 45% of viewers stop watching after 1 minute; 60% after 2 minutes. So we'll see more commercial use of Vine and Hyperlapse.

- Social commerce will continue to grow. Brands will sell more products through social media, especially now that sites such as Tumblr and Pinterest have a buy button. Half of all social media purchases happen within one week of sharing, tweeting, liking, or favoriting the product.

We're sure to see better metrics for accurate evaluation of advertising messages. We can also expect to see more blending of content and advertising. What's more, we expect to see trends toward more consolidation by the major platforms, but also more startups taking hold. But if you really want to stay ahead of the game—guess what? You can't. Even the experts have missed the mark, so we won't make too many bold predictions. However, we can say with some confidence, when platforms do a better job of engaging their users, they will be able to attract more advertising revenue than their rivals. As marketers look for better metrics and more accountability, engagement will be the most important component of ROI—far more important than a cute name, cool graphics, and racking up hundreds of Facebook likes. If people spend more time on a site, share it more often, and respond to the content, advertisers will find a way there, whether it's native advertising, sponsored content, or some new form of brand messaging. Site developers who want to become the next dot-com billionaire understand that, even though many say advertising is an evil capitalist plot.

"Social media is about sociology and psychology more than technology."[50]

Brian Solis,
principal and digital analyst,
Altimeter Group

Courtesy of Tim Kirberg

For the first 10 years of my life, there were never enough answers to all of my questions. If I couldn't learn something in an encyclopedia or at the library, it would remain a mystery. The Internet changed that. I finally had a place to exercise a mind that never rested. Where does the color go when textiles fade? What's the fewest number of pitches ever thrown in a baseball game? I had answers at my fingertips—it was like search engines were built just for me.

Everyone has a different motive when defining their career path, but I chose advertising for two primary reasons.

First, my brain doesn't have a dominant hemisphere, which really seems to throw people off. The conventional notion of "art versus science" never applied. In school I enjoyed photography and physics, graphic design and statistics. I quickly found that success in advertising often comes with an ability to understand and balance both ways of thinking. I've never encountered a target audience that was exclusively right-brained, or a totally left-brained account team. Resist being lopsided—you'll end up fighting people who tip the other way.

Second, there's a core advertising principle that always appealed to me—discovering how people think and what drives their decisions. I had the good fortune of landing an internship in brand planning (think advertising psychology) while in school. I'd sit in front of focus group tapes and take notes for days at a time. I felt like the protector of insights—the ones that would drive the strategy, that would inspire the creative, that would help a brand relate better to its customers. It was like having an exclusive news story, or a killer chili recipe. That feeling convinced me I was moving in the right direction.

Now I find myself working at Google. How did I get here? Well, search is all about understanding what people are looking for and giving them the information they need. The foundation of our business is consumer insights, not in the form of surveys or focus groups, but in the form of search behavior. Without a doubt, the kid who needed to know what bears do when they're hibernating has found a home here.[47]

Tim Kirberg, account manager, Google

thinkwithgoogle.com

Chapter 12

Sarah Hofstetter

As top marketers wrestle with the task of figuring out how to best position their brands in the fast changing digital age, many *Fortune* 500 companies have turned to Hofstetter, as president of 360i. She helped set up one of the first social media practices at any agency, which these days serves as a hub for social community management at 360i. The shop estimates that it helps top brands connect with upwards of 150 million consumers daily, and the social practice shepherded the firm as one of the fastest growing—up 75% year over year.[51]

Augie Ray

For more than 20 years Augie Ray has focused on spotting digital, mobile, and social trends and interpreting their meaning for customer experience, marketing communications, products, and services. He's been on the cutting edge of digital, as a community manager, launching websites, developing web and email programs, leading mobile application programs, and executing corporate social media programs. As a self-described customer experience leader with emphasis in social media, digital innovation, collaborative economy, and customer feedback, Augie Ray's frequent and provocative blogs provide fresh insight about digital marketing.

Jessica Rodriquez

As Univision's chief marketing officer, Rodriquez represents the new generation of Latina executives who are blurring the lines between Spanish-language programming and new media. She was former executive vice president of programming and scheduling at Univision. She believes using social media is the core of everything the network does. She comments, "What's interesting and speaks to the duality of our audience is that they'll engage with our programming in Spanish, but when they go on Twitter, they comment in English. On Facebook, it's more of a mix."[52]

Clara Shih

Clara Shih, as cofounder and CEO of Hearsay Social, has been called the most influential thought leader in social marketing on the vendor side. After being named to the Starbucks board last December, the Stanford grad—whose résumé also includes stints at Google, Microsoft, and Salesforce—stands to play a major role in the coffee chain's future. Expect Shih, author of the best-seller *The Facebook Era*, to keep the company tuned into all the latest trends—and what its customers want.[53]

Locally Owned. Locally Loved.

McHenry's is a locally owned department store offering name-brand women's, men's, and children's clothing, cosmetics, skin care and perfume, shoes and accessories, and home goods such as china, glassware, cookware, linens and towels, and other home décor. It has a long history in town and is loved by its customers.

Traditional retailing today is one of the most difficult categories in which to prosper. Factors such as the rise of e-commerce, rent, personnel, cost of goods, fickle consumer tastes, and unpredictable economic factors are constant challenges. While there is enthusiasm and nostalgia for "locally owned" or "independent" businesses, traditional retailing and even inspired, new boutiques on Main Street USA face daunting business challenges at every turn. Consumers continue to gravitate to stores such as Wal-Mart for "everyday low prices," Target for "cheap chic," or Amazon for convenience and price advantages and many other competitors. *How can a local department store such as McHenry's drive store traffic and customer loyalty?*

Here are some key factors that affect McHenry's. Currently they spend about $500,000 annually on messaging, typically in local print and newspaper. Ads primarily are sale focused. McHenry's has not used TV advertising or video. While McHenry's does have a Facebook page, this is all that it has in social media. McHenry's has a website, but it does not offer e-commerce. As a traditional, locally owned department store, McHenry's has a flagship store on a centrally located downtown street. The store is known for its quality products, name brands, and wide variety of merchandise and employs sales staff in every department. It has a loyal (but aging) customer base. Other than being a "locally owned department store," McHenry's lacks a compelling brand image to appeal to one

of its key target markets: women, ages 17 to 24, and 25 to 44. Its current messaging tagline is "Quality merchandise for all ages."

Despite some challenges, McHenry's has a number of strengths. McHenry's carries a wide range of merchandise. It features name-brand apparel, such as Ralph Lauren, along with name-brand upscale denim, such as Citizens, 7ForAllMankind, Paige, and J Brand. It also carries name-brand cosmetics and perfume. McHenry's also features special occasion apparel: formal wear, prom dresses, dress suits, and career wear. To top it off, the store carries gourmet cookware and name-brand home goods. McHenry's has very knowledgeable salespeople and a great gift registry.

1 How can a locally owned retailer compete with retail chains like Target, Kohl's, T.J. Maxx, and Macy's or specialty retailers like Banana Republic, J. Crew, Chico's, Williams-Sonoma, Sur La Table, Bed, Bath & Beyond, Pier 1, and Crate & Barrel?

2 How should the McHenry's brand evolve to become more distinct and competitive? What could McHenry's brand and creative messaging platform be?

3 What type of social media should a store like McHenry's have? How can McHenry's develop and maintain a unique voice in social media?

4 What type of promotions should McHenry's offer (special "events," sales, seasonal, and/or others) to retain a McHenry's brand identity?

Janet Rose, professor of the practice, University of Kansas

CHAPTER 12

1. Social Media Monitoring

(Contributed by Daradirek Ekachai, PhD, associate professor, Marquette University.)

Social media only works if it is well monitored. Here's one way to approach that process.

- Pick a company or brand. Generate a specific set of keywords, which might include the company name, an acronym for the company or brand, topics, issues, the tagline, and leadership (CEO names).

- Review and select a monitoring tool. Tools could include Addictomatic, IceRocket, Technorati, Google Blog Search, Social Mention, Google Alerts, and Google Insights.

- Now, identify what elements you wish to monitor.

- Having chosen a monitoring tool and elements you wish to monitor, record what you find from the online conversations and/or videos about the chosen organization or brand over the course of two weeks.

- Write a one-page report including a purpose, methodology, results, and a conclusion, and share your findings with the class.

2. Twitter School Ambassador

(Contributed by Daradirek Ekachai, PhD, associate professor, Marquette University.)

This assignment has two objectives. First, to familiarize yourself with Twitter, its writing style, its lingo, and how to tweet professionally. Second, to get you to move above and beyond tweeting what you had for breakfast or sharing what you think is cool.

- For this exercise, you will act as both strategist and writer—and you'll be a brand ambassador for your university.

- The goal is to tout the best your college has to offer via Twitter.

- Pick a topic or focus related to your school and promote it. You must begin early in the semester and tweet regularly for 10 weeks.

- Your tweets can be in the form of an original text tweet, a retweet, a reply to other Twitter users, or pictures (use photo services such as Twitpic or Instagram, or yfrog). You could also pose questions you'd like others to answer. (Tip: Use hashtags so nonfollowers can find your tweets.) Remember that your tweets are your public "digital footprints," so be sure to mix professionalism with your own personality.

- Your instructor will create a hashtag for the class and share it with the students. You are encouraged to use the class hashtag so that tweets can be easily followed. (If you like, you can have your tweets automatically update your Facebook status by placing #fb at the end of your tweet.)

CHAPTER 12

- Additionally, you must follow at least five people or accounts from within the university or related advertising or public relations media. You can also refer to Chapter 16 for ideas on whom to follow.

- After 10 weeks, turn in a summary of your tweets, including an analysis of how well you were engaged with this assignment. In other words, you will be asked to assess how successful your Twitter-based promotion was.

3. Conversations With Mom

- This exercise is crafted to help you explore and analyze the power of social media through the eyes of mom bloggers, one of the most influential groups of bloggers. This assignment could be easily reshaped to target other groups as well.

- Do a quick search of the most influential mom bloggers. We like this resource: http://www.babble.com/mom/work-family/top-mom-bloggers/

- Pick a blog and track conversations on the blog over the course of a two-week period. Be sure to note topics, images, responses, and branded sponsors.

- At the end of the two weeks, write a short summary noting topical trends as well as how copy, images, and outside links were used to support stories. Finally, note the kinds of branded sponsors the blog hosted and how the content dovetailed (or did not) with those sponsors.

- Share the finds in class and, again, look for trends.

Review chapter content and study for exams. http://study.sagepub.com/altstiel4e.

- Interactive practice quizzes
- Mobile-friendly eFlashcards
- Carefully selected chapter-by-chapter video and multimedia content

Chapter 13

Support Media
Everyone Out of the Box

So far just about everything described in this book has been pretty easy to define. Now we come to that great kitchen sink of marketing called support media. Some of it, such as outdoor advertising, is the most traditional advertising ever—older than magazines. Other support media is called *alternative media. Below-the-line media. Nonmeasured media.* And *nontraditional media.* The truth is, a lot of it is not even media in the conventional sense. Although we can't cover all of the various MarCom tools, especially the ones that will be invented as soon as this book is printed, we've split this chapter into several main categories: out-of-home advertising, guerilla marketing, native advertising, content marketing, sales promotion, event marketing, and sponsorships.

Out-of-Home Advertising

We used to call this outdoor advertising. But what do you call signs inside an airport terminal, posters in a subway station, or three-dimensional displays in a shopping mall? Some people call this *ambient advertising*, which we'll describe in much more detail later in the chapter. So we're using the term *out-of-home* to cover all advertising that's seen outside the home, but is not in the point-of-sale category. That's not a nice, neat definition, but bear with us. We think this will make sense by the end of the chapter.

Why Out-of-Home?

From a creative standpoint, out-of-home offers many advantages. Specifically, out-of-home is:

- Flexible: The location, timing, structure, and dimension of the concept give you a lot of options.

- A high-impact medium: Nothing gives you a bigger canvas.

- Exclusive: You can select a specific location.

- Economical: Low cost per impression.

- Building awareness: Ideal for establishing brand image and building rapid awareness.

- Perfect promotion: It offers ideal options for promoting packaged goods.

- Reinforcing brand image: Reinforces existing brands in the context of broader campaigns.

- Entertainment value: This is a medium that combines selling with entertainment.

Out-of-home is a great medium for copywriters and designers because it quickly conveys a concept. You have to make the point in 9 words or fewer, and often without any words. If you can create a great billboard or transit shelter, you demonstrate solid skills that carry over to other forms of print advertising. Although out-of-home marketing has been around since the first cave paining, it continues to evolve in remarkably creative and effective ways.

Posters and Bulletins (aka Billboards)

People in the outdoor advertising business don't talk about "billboards." The two main types of outdoor displays are the *painted bulletin* and the *outdoor poster*. For simplicity's sake, we'll use the layperson's term, *billboards*.

For layout purposes, all you have to know is that billboards are very wide and not very tall. So if you're using an 8.5 × 11 inch sheet of paper and your design is 10 inches wide, it should be about 4.5 inches high to have a 2.5-to-1 ratio. The reason we mention this here is that too many students treat billboards like magazine ads. When you start thinking about how they are different, it opens up a lot more creative opportunities. Which means they are much better suited to show a hot dog than a wedding cake.

Beyond the dimensions, billboards are available in several different formats or combinations of formats:

- **Standard static boards:** Your basic poster or bulletin that fits within the limits of the sign's borders.
- **Extensions:** Part of your image violates the boundaries of the board.
- **Motion boards:** These can be motorized images on a static board with sliding panels that reveal a totally different message, usually from another advertiser.
- **Illuminated boards:** The board can be lighted for night viewing or, more dramatically, to include neon, moving lights, and selective spot lighting.
- **Digital boards:** These high-definition boards project a very bright, crisp image. However, these are tremendously more expensive than traditional boards, so time on the board is usually sold by the second. Some cities regulate the time of the display, requiring longer display times so there is less distraction to drivers.
- **Three-dimensional boards:** You can add dimensional objects to and around the board, such as a car crashing through the middle, people sitting on the top edge, or parts of the poster removed to reveal the backing framework.

Digital and Interactive Out-of-Home Media

As technology evolves, out-of-home is increasingly integrated with mobile devices. *MediaLife* magazine predicted, "The future of all media is arguably mobile, which is fast becoming our preferred method of going online. Moving forward virtually every [out-of-home] campaign will have a mobile element. For instance, walking through the mall you may see a poster with a QR code that invites you to scan for a coupon for a store a little down the way in the mall."[1]

The Colorado Crisis Center used three-dimensional boards to show how stress affects people. The campaign won the Gold OBIE award for the best in outdoor advertising.

Motion-activated displays, such as those patented by MonsterVision, can be displayed in store windows, in airport and train terminals, at trade shows—basically anywhere people congregate. These displays can be quite expensive, so many advertisers use them to promote special events, launch new brands, or introduce new ad campaigns.

Tips and Techniques

The following recommendations are based on the collective wisdom of outdoor advertising professionals and our personal experience. They're not hard-and-fast rules, but factors you should consider when you're creating out-of-home advertising:

- **Be telegraphic.** The rule of thumb for billboards is nine words or fewer, with the emphasis on fewer. Some say six words is the limit. Keep in mind that someone driving by has about five seconds to get it.

- **Think big.** You've got an ad that can be seen from 600 feet away. The images and the type should be huge. Text should be at least 1 foot high to be legible—3 to 4 feet high is preferable.

- **Use bold, sans serif fonts.** Stay away from thin lines, and remember that heavy fonts blur together.

- **Go for a strong visual-verbal connection.** Think metaphors and visual puzzles. Many times you don't even need copy.

- **Stick with one main idea.** Above all, keep it simple!

- **Take advantage of location.** A sign on the side or back of a bus can be different from a static billboard because it's constantly in motion. The message on a billboard can be very local. Be aware of the season—in winter avoid whites and grays that blend in with the snow and overcast skies. In summer avoid greens that blend with foliage.

- **Use all caps for short headlines and uppercase/lowercase for longer heads.** Using all caps makes long copy harder to read.

- **Use short words when possible.** They're easier to read and you can get more on a billboard.

- **Use bold colors, not pastels.** You're trying to attract attention. That's why you see so many yellows and reds in billboards. Even white space draws attention, as long as it surrounds a bold color. High contrast is the key. Avoid colors that vibrate, like red type on a blue background.

- **Use few elements.** Remember, keep it simple!

- **Use product packaging instead of words.** Show the Coke bottle or can, not the word *Coca-Cola*. Some outdoor media companies suggest making the logo take up half the board.

> *"Any copy that runs on a billboard should fit on the back of a business card."*[2]
>
> John Pavao,
> creative director,
> Clearchannel Outdoor

OUTDOOR DESIGN

Effective font choices:

Poor font choices:

Source: Clear Channel Outdoor

Transit

Transit advertising also has its own special terminology. To make it simple, think of transit as advertising that goes on the outside or inside of things that move and at the places where you wait for things that move. Examples of transit advertising include:

- Inside- and outside-bus cards
- Outside-bus murals
- Bus shelters and benches
- Kiosks
- Train, bus, and subway stations
- Airports
- Mobile billboards: car, truck, and trailer ads

Posters

Posters can be a creative person's best bet to pad a portfolio and win awards. Technically, all you have to do is print one, post it somewhere, and, *voilà*, you've produced a real-world advertisement, seen by someone other than your roommate.

Atheists used outdoor advertising for their annual anti-Christmas greeting.

In Vienna, an advocacy group created a unique way to raise awareness and money for the homeless. Deposit 1 euro for the homeless, and a heat lamp keeps the bus shelter warm. Everybody wins. Would this kind of direct aid work in America?

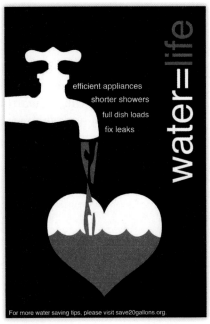

Posters give you the creative freedom to show just about anything and the flexibility to put it just about anywhere.

Guerrilla Marketing

In the 1980s, the term *guerrilla marketing* came to represent a number of nontraditional marketing communications tactics used to gain awareness without spending a lot of money (at least not as much as for traditional TV advertising). Some ambient advertising has been called a guerrilla tactic—because it's relatively low cost, but it gets people talking and the media to cover it to get even more people talking. In this postdigital age, encouraging interaction with a product or brand in the real word is a novelty. Here are three examples:

SunSmart Australia: Mixing both a sample marketing strategy and out-of-home, SunSmart Australia put together a memorable campaign for its sunscreen products. The bus poster emphasized the selling point of safety for its product, and did so in a way that was striking enough for people to take notice of. Despite the visual intrigue of the ad, however, SunSmart increased its effectiveness by adding a dispenser, where people could sample the company's sunscreen. Mixing together gratuity and shock factor, this effective campaign surely left an impression on its viewers.

BOS Sampling Robot: The BOS Sampling Robot was a campaign that impressively made the most of sampling as well as social media as a way of spreading the message of the campaign. The company set up public vending machines that operated by having consumers tweet a designated hashtag in exchange for a free sample of the beverage.

"A billboard's size only magnifies how 'OKAY' your idea is. Be outrageous."[4]

Luke Sullivan,
author, *Hey Whipple, Squeeze This!*

Automating the sampling process while making an impression on social media is a powerful combination when it comes to out-of-home marketing, and should be considered when coming up with a plan.

IBM Smart Ideas for Smarter Cities: This campaign highlighted a whole other aspect of out-of-home marketing that can be overlooked: providing value to the consumer in a way that doesn't include sampling. This truly forward-thinking campaign involved the installation of structures, branded with IBM logos that actually improved people's lives, whether it was shelter from the rain that wouldn't otherwise be there or ramps to help people get around.[5]

The Milwaukee Health Department used discarded mattresses in a guerilla marketing campaign to stress the dangers of co-sleeping with babies.

Denver has used creative ambient advertising to convince people to use less water.

When it comes to out-of-home, using guerrilla tactics can be very effective. Keep in mind that by its nature, guerrilla marketing is meant to provide big results for less money than traditional media. The goal is to generate a buzz—word of mouth (either in person or through viral channels) and earned media coverage that generates far more coverage than you can afford with traditional advertising.

Once again, the point of using these tactics is not to saturate a mass market. It's to get people talking about your brand. So it's important to make sure the creativity does not overshadow the brand message. You don't want people to remember the gimmick but not the advertiser.

Ambient Advertising

The standard billboard is fairly easy to buy from a media standpoint—you figure out how many people drive by in a given time frame and figure out a payment for a number of showings. But what if you want to make an impact where people walk, shop, recreate, commute to work, travel, or go to school? In other words, how do you make your message part of their ambient world? For the sake of this discussion, we'll consider ambient advertising as a freestanding display that attracts the attention of passers-by. The ultimate goal is not only to catch people's eye, but also to get them to talk about it to their friends, post it on Instagram, or shoot a video for YouTube. As with so many other forms of marketing communication, the impact of ambient is enhanced by word of mouth and social media.

Experiential Advertising

Where ambient advertising catches your eye, experiential advertising gets you involved. Whether it's a kinetic sculpture that invites your participation, a giant 3D puzzle you complete, or an interactive kiosk in a mall, experiential advertising helps cement a bond between the consumer and the advertiser. Experiential advertising can be as frivolous as a silly photo booth or as serious as signing a petition to help free political prisoners in oppressive regimes. The key is getting attention and them encouraging action, which when video-recorded, has viral potential.

Out-of-Home and Campaigns

Out-of-home advertising is usually used as a secondary medium. Billboards and posters are great reminders of a slogan, logo, package, or other aspect of a total campaign. Keep the two key aspects of campaign continuity in mind when using out-of-home. Can you *extend* the message by using out-of-home, and can you repeat the theme created for out-of-home?

When you are developing concepts for a campaign, you might want to go with out-of-home first. Nothing crystallizes a concept like a billboard. If you can communicate that One Thing with one billboard, you've got something you can build on.

> *"[Guerrilla marketing] requires that everyone who deals with your customers remembers the Golden Rule for Guerrillas: ALWAYS TRY TO THINK LIKE YOUR CUSTOMER."*[6]
>
> Jay Conrad Levinson, author, *Guerrilla Marketing Attack*

Tropicana spread some sunshine in airports, subway stations, taxis, and even building murals.

Native Advertising

Native advertising, also called *sponsored content*, advertorials, or infomercials, isn't really new. We just talk about it more. And not always with admiration. Newspaper advertorials, which are actually fake stories made to look like editorial content, have been around for years, and still they fool some readers into believing they're third-party endorsements. Besides the old print model, native advertising can now take the form of sponsored stories on Facebook, sponsored tweets on Twitter, sponsored emails, or sponsored articles on websites for magazines or news sites like Huffington Post or Fox News.

While many people have a hard time defining modern native advertising, don't confuse it with content marketing, which also can be difficult to define. Lucia Moses in *Adweek* commented, "It also doesn't help there's no agreement on what native advertising is or on how to measure its effectiveness. And that's before the content itself is even created, a process that by its nature is fraught because the ad has to serve the advertiser without annoying the reader."[7]

It's bad enough that hardly anyone agrees about the definition of native advertising, but it's also under fire from government agencies. The Federal Trade Commission issued a consumer warning, and the Australian government threatened legal action against deceptive native ads. The FTC warns marketers that sponsored content should be clearly identified as advertising or promotion.

This slick fashion article in the *Daily Mail* newspapers doesn't look like a L'Oréal ad, until you realize that all the products shown are from that company. Do native ads like this promote unrealistic self-image issues for women?

BuzzFeed is one of the most popular online news sources. Does it provide valuable content (or at least what some people feel is important to them), or is it a thinly disguised platform for native advertising?

Product Placement

Some companies specialize in placing their clients' products on game shows as prizes. Others concentrate on getting their clients into movies and TV shows. The classic example was in *E.T. the Extra-Terrestrial*, where the hero was lured with Reese's Pieces because M&M's would not pay for product placement. Short-term sales of Reese's Pieces skyrocketed. So when you see a character reach for a box of Cheerios, drink a Coors, or drive a new Honda, it's no coincidence. Interestingly, Apple, the most frequently placed brand, claims its spends nothing on product placement other than providing products.[8] Also called *embedded marketing*, product placement is negotiated with producers and can run into tens of millions of dollars for a single film or television program. There are agencies, mostly on the west coast, that specialize in only product placement.

Some could argue that *advertainment* is another form of product placement. The classic example is the pioneering series from BMW Films called "The Hire," featuring Clive Owen. These sponsored video programs weave the brand into the story, so it could be a form of product placement. On the other hand, since these videos are meant to be entertaining, they could be a form of branded content. See why all of this is hard to define?

Even though product placement enhances brand awareness, it still can't match traditional ads for effectiveness. According to a study a few years ago by MediaPost, more than half of viewers would buy a product after watching a commercial for it, versus about half that percentage after product placement. The conclusion was that consumers are more likely to recall brands in traditional ads than through product placement.[9] However, that doesn't seem to be slowing the growth of product placement.

Hybrid Marketing

Hybrid marketing is a term coined a few years ago to describe integration of sponsorship, product placement, commercial messages, sales promotion, and social engagement into a single broadcast or online entertainment program. In a sense, everything in this chapter taken together is a hybrid, but in a stricter definition, it applies to doing it all in one show or series. For example, Cover Girl ran a customized 40-second hybrid ad on *America's Next Top Model* to announce the Meet the Model Sweepstakes, and T-Mobile sponsored a 35-second custom ad on the American Music Awards telecast to encourage viewers to text message their votes with T-Mobile phones or to tweet their votes. For ten years, *American Idol* judges drank out of red Coke cups. Contestants sat on the red Coke couch. Of course, there were Coke commercials and sponsorship messages. You might say Coke owned *American Idol*, but with viewership at a fraction of its glory days, Coke pulled the plug on their primary sponsorship.

Each new James Bond movie usually breaks the record for product placement. Brands featured in the newest installment, *Spectre*, include Belvedere, Heineken, Samsung, Sony, Audi, Cadillac, Range Rover and, of course, Aston Martin.

Advertising images can be an active part of the game, or in the background environment, or they can change and adapt depending on the dynamics of the game, and the location and skill of the player.

In-Game Advertising

In-game advertising has come a long way from just programming a logo into a sports game. Marketers must always be monitoring current trends and how those trends may be able to positively increase brand equity. The mass adoption of social and mobile media has created users who are constantly exposed to messaging, most of which is not engaging, especially if the message comes across as advertising. Seamless integration into the media mix is essential, in order to catch the attention of prospective consumers, while they are using mediums that have high levels of frequency, such as social, console and mobile games.[10]

First, you have to know your gamers. Are they casual gamers? The kind who made Flappy Bird a short-term hit and then moved on to the next diversion. Or are they core enthusiasts, who obsess about every pixel in the latest iteration of Grand Theft Auto? Casual gamers tend to play on mobile devices and social media. Core enthusiasts tend to be console based. Ultimately, the level of branding content depends on knowing your target audience's tolerance for blatant marketing messages.

In-game advertising can be split into three main categories:

- **Advergaming:** These are usually wrapped around a product or service, for example, Mountain Dew's Dew Tour, and usually appeal more to casual gamers.
- **Static in-game ads:** These are hard-coded into the program, such as a billboard on the side of the road, signs in an urban landscape, or banners in a stadium.

Cisco offers several content marketing platforms, including Focus, their monthly online magazine. With a tightly defined target audience, content marketers can provide information their customers want to read without heavy-handed promotional messages.

- **Dynamic in-game ads:** These change the messages depending on who is playing the game, where it's played, and when, since ad messages do not have to be hard-coded into the game.

In many ways in-game advertising is just another form of product placement. However with the variety of game categories and types of games, the choice in devices, and great diversity among gamers, advertising messages can be much more focused than having James Bond drinking a Heineken.

Content Marketing

Content marketing, also called *branded journalism* or *branded content*, covers a wide spectrum of marketing communications. The one common thread is providing information a consumer actually wants *and* making sure the consumer knows where it's coming from. Compare this with the old model of interrupting entertainment with commercials or disguising commercial messages to look like editorial content (native advertising). Done right, content marketing attracts potential customers, and, more important, retains them through consistent creation and consolidation of relevant content. If you can capture and maintain their attention, and build good will toward your company or brand, you have a better chance of selling something.

Content marketing has been around for years in the form of white papers and company magazines sent to customers and other stakeholders. The Internet provided much wider opportunities for distribution of content-based information. Content marketing is especially relevant because so many people are turning away from traditional advertising. It's much easier to watch your favorite TV shows commercial free. Newspaper and magazine readership is down. Banner ads are universally ignored. However, people are still hungry for entertainment and information they can use. If it's done correctly, a company can take credit for providing that and consumers will thank them with loyalty to their brand.

Technology and financial services companies such as General Electric, Cisco, American Express, and HSBC, to name a few, have taken the lead in consistently providing content customers can use. Consumer brands have also added branded content microsites. In-depth articles, helpful hints, forecasts, trends, and profiles about interesting people are welcome news. Usually there's very little information about the company or its products. But over time, these sites position the sponsoring company as the thought leader in its field.

Content marketing extends across the whole digital spectrum, as well as print, video and broadcast executions. It's difficult to put content into nice neat silos, but for the purposes of this book, we've explored the *writing and distribution* of content—and how it differs from promotional copy—in Chapter 11.

Types of Content Marketing

Blogs	Podcasts
Events	Social media
Magazines	Videos
Microsites	Webcasts
Mobile apps	Webinars
Newsletters	Websites
Online communities	White papers

Native Advertising Versus Content Marketing

Sometimes it's hard to draw a line between native advertising and content marketing when we talk about everything in the abstract. The main distinction is that native advertising is usually designed to sell something before the consumer gets the content he or she seeks (think of a sponsored email), while content marketing gives away that content, and over time, the consumer builds a relationship with the brand (think of a monthly online magazine). The downside of native advertising is that some consumers perceive it as a sleazy gimmick and hate it even more than straightforward advertising. The downside of content marketing is that warm and fuzzy relationships don't always turn into sales, especially if your competition is warmer and fuzzier.

	NATIVE ADVERTISING	CONTENT MARKETING
PURPOSE	• Useful content is secondary to selling a product or service. • Buying the brand's product of service solves the problem.	• Build trust by providing relevant, useful information. • Generate sales or sales leads over the long run. • Sales are not expected solely as a result of one content marketing piece. • Engage with the reader and build rapport.
VALUE TO READER	• Content generally does not have inherent value without the reader buying a product or service.	• Provides value to reader that's independent of buying a product or service. The content is valuable in itself.
TONE	• Sometimes pushy and salesy. • Or a faux friendly to emulate the writing style of the publication.	• Knowledgeable, yet authentic tone that doesn't try to pressure the reader. • Acknowledges the reader's challenges or pain points and offers actionable tips or solutions. Even if those solutions don't involve the brand.
BENEFITS	• Fairly limited since readers can smell a sales pitch a mile away.	• Builds trust with readers, helps create shareable content for blogs, social media feeds, email lists, and avoids some of the potential legal issues associated with native advertising because it doesn't try to mislead.

Table 13.1   Native Advertising Versus Content Marketing[12]

Sales Promotion

Promotion is one of the four P's of marketing. In its strictest definition, all marketing communication is a form of promotion. However, in this book we'll call it *sales promotion* and define it as an activity that stimulates purchases by adding a *short-term additional value* to a product or service. In other words, the advertiser is bribing you to buy something quickly. That bribe may be as basic as a discount or as lofty as a donation to a worthy charity. Too many students think of promotion as nothing more than a boring discount coupon, two-for-one sales, and free merchandise when you buy something. But when you explore all the facets of promotion, you'll understand why it's one of the hottest fields in marketing, and when marketers cut traditional advertising in tough times, their dollars often shift to sales promotions.

East Meets West

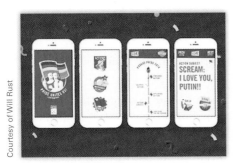

Courtesy of Will Rust

Despite huge advances in global human rights, the earth is not a safe place to be gay.

In 76 countries worldwide, a simple show of affection can lead to imprisonment, incarceration, torture, or even execution. Not always at the hands of the authorities.

When we were asked by Prague Pride to produce a promotional campaign for their 2014 pride week (which culminated in a march for gay rights) we were inspired by their concept for the whole week's program of events. "East Meets West" was meant to highlight the unusual situation in which the Czech Republic finds itself concerning gay rights. Despite being a part of what was the Eastern Bloc, the country, and Prague in particular, has become an oasis of tolerance. Many neighboring countries, especially those farther east, have appalling gay rights records by comparison. We were asked to produce a series of classic poster and TV ads to promote the parade, but we wanted to do something far more powerful. What if we could share pride with those less fortunate across our borders? What if they could attend our parade, through another human being?

LGBT Avatars was a completely new social network and mobile app developed to allow people from LGBT-unfriendly countries to take part in Prague Pride through a human avatar. A unique one-on-one connection enabling tasks and messages to be sent to Prague and live video and photo to be sent back, creating dialogue and allowing secure participation from distance. They could ask their avatars what to shout for, or request any action to perform.

The initiative was a huge success, despite limited funding. Over a thousand LGBT Avatars marched at Prague Pride, carrying the words of their brothers and sisters from afar on handmade banners. Large screens broadcast their messages anonymously at the parade, and people from 26 countries worldwide experienced pride for the first time. Since the parade, support from many high-profile human rights activists, including Sir Ian McKellen, has enforced our ultimate goal of turning this small project into a global initiative in 2016. Pride should be a right, not a privilege.[11]

Will Rust, executive creative director, Ogilvy, Prague

Most (but not all) sales promotions have specific short-term goals. They are designed to produce results quickly. Once the promotion is over, sales can slip, sometimes prompting an unending chain of new sales promotions.

The use of sales promotion is increasing, even in the service sector. Many marketers have seen diminishing returns from their traditional advertising efforts. Sales promotions, for both trade and consumer, give their sales that extra boost. This is especially common in the cutthroat world of packaged goods, where the only perceived differences between products are in their promotions. Traditionally, three fourths of the total marketing communication budget for packaged goods goes to trade and consumer promotion, while the rest goes to traditional advertising.[13]

Sales promotion is actually more of a product than an advertising medium. To be successful, promotions must be promoted. Mobile technology and social media are making sales promotion a much more powerful marketing tool for boosting short-term sales.

Why Sales Promotion?

For a copywriter, sales promotion offers many advantages, especially when it's integrated into a total campaign. Some of these advantages are as follows:

It's fast. Sales promotion accelerates the selling process and maximizes sales volume.

It can cover the whole distribution channel. Targeted promotions reach wholesalers, retailers, and consumers.

It can help retain customer loyalty. Promotions provide a way to stay in touch with current customers and to give them incentives for continuing their relationship with a brand or business.

It can increase early adoption. You provide an incentive for a customer to try a product for the first time. With the proliferation of new brands, incentives shorten the path from awareness to action.

It's measurable. In most cases sales promotion is designed for short-term sales increases, not long-term brand image. You get results (or lack of results) almost immediately.

It supports retailers. The growth of account-specific marketing, or comarketing, requires customized sales promotion programs for retail chains. For example, Sony might offer a promotional program just for Best Buy stores.

It fits the consumer's expectations. On the plus side, consumers are receptive to promotions. On the minus side . . . well, that's coming later.

It fits into an integrated marketing campaign. To be successful, most promotion needs to be promoted by traditional media.

Why Not?

For each of the major advantages, there is a flip side:

It's short acting. Because of their short-term, price-oriented nature, most sales promotions do not help build long-term brand equity.

Lack of loyalty. Although incentives can help retain customer loyalty, they can also encourage brand switching. If a brand has no perceived advantage, the consumer will base the purchase on price (or added value).

Retailers are demanding. Retailers want more, and they are getting it. So in addition to slotting allowances, retailers are demanding more generous account-specific marketing programs that often include expensive sales promotion programs.

Consumer expectations. Customers not only respond to promotions, they expect them. Automakers would love to get out of the endless chain of rebates, discounts, and other incentives. But when one offers them, the others follow suit until the whole industry suffers.

They can't stand alone. The advertiser has to weigh the short-term increase in sales against the cost of the incentive and the cost to advertise it. Sometimes an advertiser will settle for breaking even, or even a small loss if it means retaining a retail account or gaining market share.

Oscar Mayer took sales promotion to a new level. Consumers could register to win a device that turned an iPhone into a bacon-scented alarm clock.

Types of Sales Promotions

Consumer sales promotions: With the exception of long-term PR tactics such as sponsorships, most consumer sales promotion is considered to be non-franchise-building. Promotions are intended to jump-start sales and do almost nothing to build brand image. Another purpose is to gather information (give us the data, and we'll give you a prize). Either way, the ultimate goal is to stimulate action.

Contests and games: The consumer actively participates in some way by writing an essay, taking a quiz, or engaging in some other mental activity that would not challenge a first grader's intellect. In return for providing some marketing data, you have a one-in-a-gazillion chance to win something.

Sweepstakes: These involve chance more than contests do. Just enter, and you may already be a winner. Sometimes you don't have to do anything except wait for your prize. The laws governing contests and sweepstakes vary from state to state.

Product giveaways: Buy the product, and you might get the next one free. Fast food restaurants and soft drinks use this quite a bit. You have to buy something first, but you have a better chance of winning.

Samples: You can get them in the mail, in magazine inserts, or from little old ladies in the supermarket. You can give away more than pills, perfumes, and fabric softener sheets.

Roll Up Your Sleeves

Courtesy of Amanda Eggert

My parents couldn't stop me from yammering when I was younger, so yeah, communications as a career was my destiny. Motivated by a scholarship that required a high grade point average all four years of college, I busted my butt in college to make the grade, to get involved in extracurricular activities, and to network, network, network!

People in advertising often cite their unusual start in the business, and I'm no exception. An advertising professional spoke in one of my classes on a Thursday. The following Sunday, I saw him at my church. I approached him nervously, scored his business card, and got an informational interview. (Yes, he had business cards at church!)

The rest is history. I landed the internship, which lead to a full-time job offer the day after graduation. This came at a time when the economy had just tanked, and most of my graduating class was struggling to find a job. To this day I'm humbled and so very thankful. (I grew up working summers at my family's lawn and landscape company, so an old-fashioned work ethic was instilled at a young age. Looking back, I credit this for turning my internship into a full-time job.)

Starting my career at a full-service, digital advertising agency I was afforded a lot of opportunities. I started working in online media planning, placing and optimizing banner advertisements on websites. I eventually switched to social media, where that old-fashioned work ethic allowed me to start in the trenches and work my way up to a senior position, where I helped manage a department of 12+. Working in an agency setting, I learned how to manage difficult personalities, to brainstorm with diverse groups, to handle demanding clients, to juggle multiple projects, and to generally survive at a runner's pace.

After a healthy run in agency life, I landed a job at a consultation firm. This allowed me to see the business side of the equation—an invaluable perspective of how businesses run and stay profitable. At the end of the day, however, I missed the creativity of agency life. In a stroke of something I'd like to call fate, a job opportunity presented itself to move in-house at the Kohler Company. I start in two weeks. By the time this book is published, I'll be a year in (give or take).

I've spoken several times on where I went to school and am often asked how I got to where I am today. It really does come back to work ethic. Roll up your sleeves and work hard. People (employers) notice.[14]

Amanda Eggert, communications leader for digital content, Kohler Company
us.kohler.com

Paper coupons: Essentially these are little slips of paper that ensure a discount. They are distributed in a number of ways: traditionally, in magazine and newspaper ads; in freestanding inserts in newspapers; in direct mail packs (such as Valpak); and online, in a form that consumers print at home.

Discounts: These are temporary price reductions. Temporary is the key word, because a permanent price reduction creates no urgency to buy.

Digital coupons: Anyone who's bought anything online probably knows about discount codes that can significantly reduce the price. Downloadable online coupons have been around for a while too, and act basically the same way as traditional paper coupons. Location-based technology allows delivery of coupons to mobile phones when a shopper enters a specific section of a store or when the user scans a QR code.

Bonus packs: The consumer gets more of a product at the regular price. For example, detergent boxes may be bundled in a buy-one-get-one-free promotion. Bonus packs provide more value to the consumer. However, if the consumer is already a loyal customer, there is no incremental value to the manufacturer.

Rebates: Consumers are offered money back if they mail receipts and packaging to the producer. This requires more effort, and the seller bets that a large percentage of people will not bother. If they do, they have to provide information for the seller's database. Many times, prices listed contain "after rebate" in the fine print.

Premiums (merchandise): Instead of money back, the consumer gets stuff. It can be as simple as the toy in a Happy Meal (marginally harder to digest than the food) or as elaborate as thousands of dollars in water toys with the purchase of a new boat. Premiums can also be intangible items, such as frequent-flier points.

Loyalty programs: These reward customers for continuing to purchase the same brand of a product or service. Airline frequent-flier plans are the most obvious form of loyalty programs. But retailers such as grocers, discount stores, and electronics stores, where customers shop frequently, also use loyalty programs. Many consumer packaged goods companies have frequency programs that award points for purchases. The points can be redeemed for gifts, such as merchandise, or for discounts.

Cross-promotion: Some products just seem to complement each other. If so, they can work together to multiply their promotional dollars. For example, a cookie company may offer coupons for milk. Other times the lead brand in a promotional campaign will bring in partners.

Trade Sales Promotions

If you're a manufacturer, how do you motivate your sales staff, move product through distributors, and encourage retailers to stock your brands? Trade sales promotion is used for business-to-business products and for wholesale transactions for consumer goods. Some trade sales promotions include the following:

- **Financial incentives:** Lower interest rates, reduced freight costs, price discounts, and extended payments can encourage retailers to stock up on products. Some of these include *slotting allowances* to provide shelf space, *buying allowances* to reduce the introductory price, and *promotional allowances* for short-term promotions. These allowances are usually meant to be passed on to the consumer, but some retailers pocket the savings and charge full retail prices, which does not help move the product. To counter this, some packaged goods companies have dropped their everyday prices and cut back on trade allowances. *Push money*—also known as "spiffs"—can be an extra commission paid to the sales force, wholesaler, or retailer.

- **Trade contests:** Salespeople, wholesalers, and retailers receive rewards for increasing their sales. The more you sell, the more you get. These often involve travel incentives, such as a trip for two to Hawaii or tickets to a major sporting event.

- **Sales support:** The manufacturer provides displays, posters, counter cards, signage, and other point-of-sale items. Products sell better with attractive displays, which are often accompanied by price deals. The manufacturer may also provide special promotional literature for the dealer to hand out.

- **Training programs:** The manufacturer trains the distributor or dealer employees in selling the product.

- **Trade shows:** Manufacturers display their products, salespeople meet and greet potential customers, distributors and wholesalers check out new lines, and everybody sees what the competition is up to. Trade shows can be small regional events with nothing more than a few 10 by 10 foot booths or major extravaganzas such as the Consumer Electronics Show, which generates worldwide coverage. Some manufacturers spend millions every year on trade shows—for elaborate booths, celebrity talent, high-profile events, extravagant banquets, contests, and handouts. Trade shows provide a lot of opportunity for creative people. Dozens of details require creative planning: the booth design itself; displays, posters, and handout literature; event planning, preshow promotion, and premium selection; audio and video displays; and more. In a way, a trade show booth is a campaign in itself, with components that work individually and cumulatively to convey a single message.

- **Cooperative advertising:** Basically, the manufacturer helps the retailer pay for advertising its products. Sometimes the ads are provided, and all the retailer has to do is slap a logo and an address on the bottom. In many cases, the co-op ad is similar to the national brand advertising done by the manufacturer. Other times, the manufacturer provides images and copy that the retailers use to build their own ads. If you ever have to produce co-op ads, always keep the intended media in mind. For example, don't try to convert an elaborate four-color magazine ad into a black-and-white co-op ad for a local newspaper. Like consumer sales promotions, trade promotions usually have to be supported with some form of marketing communications, usually print advertising, direct mail, and the Internet.

Promotional Strategy and Tactics

Promotional strategy stems from marketing objectives. For example:

- Get 20% of Brand X users to try Brand Y within three months.

- Get 40% of current Brand Z users to increase purchases from 5 to 10 packages per month within six months.

- Expand distribution for Brand A from 40% to 80% in all X-Mart chain stores within one year.

Components of the Promotion

Assuming you know the client's objectives, you need to follow these steps:

- **Think campaigns.** If the promotion is part of a total campaign, make sure your sales promotion will fit the way the product is positioned in the market, the brand image, the target audience, and how it is sold.

- **Develop a promotional theme.** It's like a tagline. Use some of the guidelines for taglines in Chapter 7.

- **Consider the incentive.** What will you offer that adds value to the product or service and encourages quick sales? As with the theme, you have to consider the target audience and brand image. For example, a free trunk full of frozen pizzas may get a prospect into a Hyundai dealer, but it probably won't motivate a potential Audi customer.

- **Promote the promotion.** Once you have determined the theme and the incentive, how do you let people know? Your marketing of the promotion also depends on the target audience and brand image. Using multiple media, such as the Internet and print, provides for more interaction and greater involvement with the product.

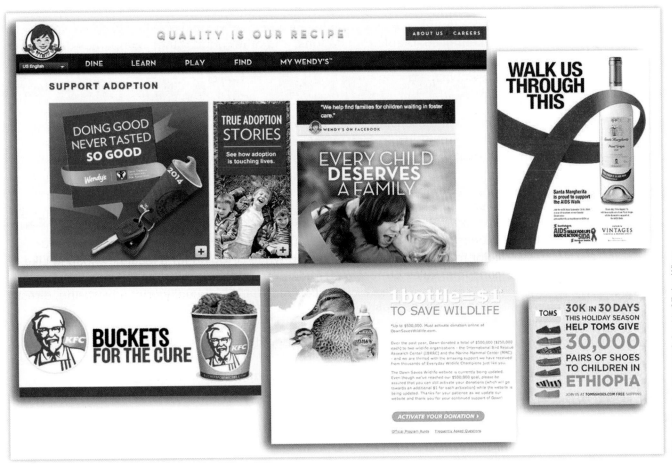

Attaching your brand to a worthy cause may buy some good will, but there has to be a reasonable connection. Wendy's has a long-term relationship with adoption. Tom's donating shoes for barefoot kids is a natural. Fried chicken and breast cancer? Not so much.

When developing a promotional campaign there are four things to keep in mind.

- First, use a memorable theme.
- Follow that up with content that relates to the product attributes (brand image).
- Then keep it simple.
- Finally, make the benefit (reward) clear.

Public Relations and Cause Marketing

In very general terms, public relations, covers any nonpaid information from a third party that mentions an identified product or service. It's also called *earned media*, since the placement of a story depends on convincing an editor to run it rather than just sending an insertion order. Content marketing is a key component of most public relations programs. The sponsor's name is there, but the sales message is usually so benign that editors are more likely to pick up the information for their own stories. There are many kinds of PR, and we're not going to address them here. Instead, we'll focus on the publicity aspect of PR and how it applies to promotion and integrated marketing communications. Examples include event sponsorship, advocacy and cause marketing, charitable foundations, and other good things companies do that deserve positive mention. Public relations can also be used to announce a sales promotion activity.

A dedicated public relations practitioner would probably cringe to see PR relegated to a subhead in a discussion of support media. We do not mean to dismiss the value of public relations. In fact, we believe PR should be the foundation of most marketing communications plans. In this context, however, we will discuss public relations in terms of creative strategy, with special emphasis on how PR can fit into a promotional campaign

Corporate advertising, as we'll see in Chapter 15, usually puts a company's best face forward. Typically the goal is get people to like the company so much they want to do business with it and/or buy its stock. *Public relations* or corporate *advertising* goes beyond the usual corporate story to promote a company's good deeds. For example, a company may run TV ads stating that they'll donate a percentage of the purchase price to a charity. Or, as was the case with a pharmaceutical manufacturer, they may announce available support plans if patients can't afford the drugs. While the quality of the food and dining experience at McDonald's can be debated, no one can doubt the good will they've created with their Ronald McDonald House charity. Even before they could shut down their leaking oil well in the Gulf of Mexico, British Petroleum used the whole MarCom tool kit for damage control. They spent millions of dollars on television and print advertising, online marketing, public events, and content marketing to tell the world how they solved the problem they created. Although litigation will continue for years, BP is probably no longer top of mind when it comes to corporate villains.

Volunteers discovered that Dawn detergent was also great for cleaning up animals affected by oil spills. Their Dawn Saves Wildlife campaign features stories, videos, and information about how people can help . . . and also a little bit how you can get softer hands and sparkling dishes.

South by Southwest has grown from a grassroots music festival to a major cultural movement that has attracted big-name "super sponsors."

Companies pay as much as $20 million to be primary sponsors of these racing billboards. As with naming rights for a stadium or a one-shot Super Bowl ad, NASCAR sponsorship can sometimes be more about stroking brand ego and pandering to its uber-patriotic fan base than building brand equity.

Organizations and government agencies create marketing communication messages to directly promote their causes—for example, public service announcements to encourage people to stop polluting, sign up for health care, adopt animals, house the homeless, end drunk driving, support cancer research, and so on. The list of worthy causes is endless. While they are not pushing products or specific brands, they are trying to increase awareness, build comprehension, and ultimately get people to take action—get more information, change their opinions or behavior, or donate money.

Other efforts attach a brand to a cause, sometimes tying in a sales promotion to sweeten the deal. For example, your promotion could be about donating money to research against breast cancer, supporting national parks, building local playgrounds, and cleaning up river walks. In addition to doing the good deed, you need to promote it through publicity releases and editorial contacts as well as traditional and nontraditional media. Marketers can't always be assured that they will earn space in a publication or TV news story. So they produce ads and commercials touting their good deeds. However, cause marketing requires more than just associating with a social issue. It takes time and effort. Companies have gotten into trouble by misleading consumers about their relationships, and others have wasted money by supporting a cause that offered little synergism.

One survey showed that more than 300 companies associated themselves with breast cancer concerns, but most became lost in the sponsorship clutter.[15] A word of warning: before you paint your product pink, make sure it's going to do your brand and the cause some good.

Event Marketing and Sponsorships

Event marketing and sponsorships are specialized forms of promotion that link a company or brand to a specific event or themed activity. Event marketing and sponsorship are sort of like public relations because they often end up building long-term good will that can enhance brand image. Marketers often participate in event marketing by attaching their brands to sporting events, concerts, fairs, or festivals. In event sponsorship, a brand or company name usually precedes the name of the particular event. Consider these: Corona Light presents Kenny Chesney in concert. The Sprint Cup NASCAR series. The Rose Bowl presented by Northwestern Mutual.

The live event is only one part of the promotion. Websites, email, text messages, and social media all work before, during, and after an event to keep the engagement going strong. For example, South by Southwest has grown into a major organizer of conferences, trade shows, and festivals, with events that include music, film, interactive, and education activities. In the past few years, social media has accelerated that growth, supported by a host of major sponsors. The 10-day extravaganza in Austin started small but now ranks as one of the top music festivals in the country, as well as a showcase for emerging technology. No matter the vehicle, positive association with a cause or performer can create the feeling of being there in person.

Box? What Box?

Thinking out of the box is finally dead. There is no box. All the nice neat categories have been overlapped, redefined, fuzzed up, and morphed into new ways to infect a consumer with an increasingly stronger immunity to advertising. Your job as a creative practitioner is to find new ways to integrate all the various marcom tools to make that connection.

WHO'S WHO?

Wendy Clark

As senior vice president of Integrated Marketing Communications, Wendy Clark was a key player in the company's drive to double revenue by 2020. She directed global design, marketing communications, media, sponsorships, interactive marketing, and marketing of the company's Live Positively sustainability platform. Her team's achievements included the successful global launch of the Coca-Cola "Open Happiness" campaign and Coca-Cola's first ever global mobile marketing campaign. A respected brand management strategist, Clark also worked at AT&T. In 2015, she took a leave of absence to help craft the brand message for Hillary Clinton's presidential campaign.[16]

Jaime Robinson

Throughout her career, Jaime Robinson has helped redesign storytelling for the social age. As executive creative director at Pereira & O'Dell, she steered major campaigns such as Intel/Toshiba's social film experiences "Inside" and "The Beauty Inside," viral hits that represent a new paradigm in branding and entertainment. Beyond that, she's made toys even more fun with Hasbro's Scrabble campaign, starring personified tiles; and in clever turns for Lego, including the "Click" community site and the accompanying short films "Click!" and "Brick Thief." Prior to her current post, she honed her chops at other creatively inclined shops, such as EVB, TBWA\Chiat\Day, and Mad Dogs & Englishmen, and translated stories for brands such as Adidas and Ray-Ban.[17]

Jay Conrad Levinson

Jay Conrad Levinson is the author of a wildly successful series of books about guerrilla marketing tactics. He cites many examples of unconventional marketing and communications programs that generated spectacular results. Typically, these guerrilla tactics use existing marketing communication tools, such as direct mail or outdoor, but in highly targeted, very creative ways.

Dave Droga

Founded in 2006, Droga5 has been named Agency of the Year three times, has appeared on *Advertising Age*'s A List four times, and was named one of *Fast Company*'s World's Most Innovative. Prior to founding Droga5, David Droga was the first worldwide chief creative officer of the Publicis Network, executive creative director of Saatchi & Saatchi London, regional creative director of Saatchi & Saatchi Asia, and partner and executive creative director of OMON Sydney. To date, he is the most awarded creative at the Cannes International Festival of Creativity and the youngest person ever inducted into the New York Art Directors Hall of Fame. He is also a laureate of the Asian Media and Marketing Hall of Fame, the AdNews Hall of Fame, the AWARD Hall of Fame, and the American Advertising Federation Hall of Achievement. Droga sits on several boards, including the New Museum, William Morris Endeavor, and the Facebook Creative Council.[18]

Zak and Zoe Sell Out

Zak Schmidley is an extreme outdoor enthusiast—mountain biking, rock climbing, hang gliding, white-water rafting, and wilderness hiking. His active lifestyle encouraged him to seek a high-energy snack for his outdoor adventures. He and his girlfriend Zoe tried many combinations of nuts, whole grains, dried fruits, and organic honey until they finally developed a winning recipe. Their bars became so popular with friends that they were encouraged to sell as many as they could make at local farmer's markets. An executive from Sunshine Farms Natural Foods was impressed and offered to manufacture and distribute their bars.

Zak and Zoe were leery of another company taking over, but having sunk every penny into their homegrown operation, they decided to work with Sunshine Farms. They became cult media stars almost overnight. With marketing support behind it, the "Zak and Zoe" brand grew from local specialty shops to major grocery chains. As the money rolled in, Zak and Zoe insisted that a portion of the profits be used to support worthy causes, such as protecting the environment and health care for Native Americans. They developed a strong following from consumers who rejected big agribusiness and food processing giants.

Due to the incredible success of Zak and Zoe bars, Genetically Modified Agribusiness Inc. (GMAI), a global power in genetically modified food and preservatives, purchased Sunshine Natural Foods. Zak and Zoe were appalled, but they also felt an obligation to keep the money flowing to their charities. Furthermore, they are locked into a 10-year agreement, with substantial penalties for breach of contract as brand spokespersons.

Tom Altstiel, TBA Marketing Group, LLC

1 As the advertising agency for GMAI, how would you position the purchase of the Zak and Zoe brand to their loyal consumers? Give three different strategies.

2 Should the company keep the recipe for the bars and change the name? If yes, explain your reason and some ideas about renaming the product. If they keep the Zak and Zoe brand, what if any changes should they make to the product or packaging? Explain your ideas.

3 How can a universally despised company such as GMAI generate good will by leveraging the Zak and Zoe brand? Give three examples.

4 Zak and Zoe had been highly respected as honest, caring individuals who raised hundreds of thousands of dollars for worthy causes. Now they are seen as corporate sellouts. How should the marketing team (company and agency) use them most effectively to preserve the integrity of the brand? Give three examples.

5 Zak and Zoe bars are now available in just one flavor. With the manufacturing and distribution muscle of GMAI, does it make sense for brand extensions into other flavors, other food categories, energy drinks, energy gum, and so on, under the Zak and Zoe brand? If yes, give some examples of other products where this has been successful. If not, give some examples where similar brand extensions have failed.

1. Brand Sensing

Using your senses may be one of your most underrated skills. Try this to ramp up your sensory tool kit.

- Make a grid. In the first column make a list of brands such as Aflac, Apple, Birkenstock, BMW, Chevrolet, Coke, Dell, ESPN, FedEx, *GQ,* Kashi, Marlboro, Motorola, NBC, Nicorette, Nokia, Starbucks, State Farm, UPS, Wii, and so on.

- Make six more columns. In each of the next five columns, note how you might experience each brand based on the five senses. How does Brand X look, feel, taste, sound, and smell? Leave the final column blank.

- Now, in class, discuss each brand and list how consumers might experience the brand with each of their senses.

- After completing the entire brand list, return to the first brand, review the sensory aspects, and in the last column list nontraditional options inspired by the sensory list.

- Continue down the list and see how the senses can lead you to see options you might never have thought of before.

2. Unusual Matches

Brainstorming as a group will very quickly expand your options when it comes to thinking outside the box (there's that cliché again!). Try it.

- As a class, generate a long list of highly unexpected touchpoints—places you might never have thought of finding advertising messages. *Unexpected* is the key word. You are encouraged to push the envelope.

- Your instructor will come to class with a predetermined list of brands, the same number of brands as students, and toss the brand names into a hat.

- Select a brand. Quickly, and relying only on your personal knowledge and/or experience with the brand, write a Positioning Statement.

- Now, present the positioning for your brand. Follow this with a discussion of who the target audience is.

- As a class, decide which touchpoint would best fit with the brand. Keep a running list of brands next to each touchpoint.

- Switch it up to the next student.

- At the end see which touchpoints have the most brands associated with them and discuss why that might be.

CHAPTER 13

3. Talking Products

(Contributed by Dorothy Pisarski, PhD, assistant professor, Drake University.)

Think of times when someone might select a Hershey's chocolate bar from all the other snacks available at a point-of-purchase display. Begin the list as a class and then continue on your own, writing five more.

- Examples: (a) on a long road trip when paying for gas inside the convenience store; (b) before a camping trip, in anticipation of making s'mores; and (c) when someone needs a not-too-serious Valentine's gift.

- Then take on the role of the chocolate bar. For each purchase occasion, complete the sentence "You won't regret buying me because _____."

- Examples: (a) I'll sweeten up your trip and make the miles go by more happily; (b) authentic Hershey's quality is needed for the best-tasting s'mores; and (c) no Valentine can resist the aroma and flavor of a Hershey's chocolate bar.

One product may have several benefits that are the result of different target groups and different behavioral situations.

Review chapter content and study for exams. http://study.sagepub.com/altstiel4e.

- Interactive practice quizzes
- Mobile-friendly eFlashcards
- Carefully selected chapter-by-chapter video and multimedia content

Chapter 14

Direct Marketing
Hitting the Bull's-Eye

Even seasoned marketing professionals sometimes confuse all the terms relating to direct marketing. Some call it *direct response*. Some only think of direct mail. Others think door-to-door selling is its main component. Obnoxious telemarketing is a direct response method. But so is an opt-in email campaign that people really want to read. For this text we'll use a definition created by Bob Stone and Ron Jacobs that covers all direct transactions:

> Direct marketing is the interactive use of advertising media, to stimulate an (immediate) behavior modification in such a way that this behavior can be tracked, recorded, analyzed, and stored on a database for future retrieval and use.[1]

In short, direct marketing is *interactive*, stimulates an *immediate response*, and is *measurable*.

Direct Marketing Defined

The five purposes of direct marketing are:

- Solicit a direct order.
- Generate a lead.
- Drive store traffic.
- Generate a measurable response.
- Grow the long-term value of a relationship between the marketer and the customer.

Why Use Direct Marketing?

From a creative standpoint, direct marketing gives you a lot of tools to reach a customer—direct mail, email, mobile advertising, telemarketing, and personal selling. No matter which one or combination you use, compared with mass advertising, direct marketing offers these benefits:

- **It's specific.** With good data, an advertiser can zero in on specific demographics and lifestyles to create a more powerful message.
- **It talks to the individual.** It's as close as you can get to one-on-one marketing.
- **It can be high impact.** If you correctly tap those wants and needs, you provide something of real value to the recipient.
- **It can be localized.** A mailer for a nationally advertised brand can include the names and addresses of local retailers.
- **It can generate sales where there are no stores.** In other words, it generates a direct response, whether it's mail order or online.
- **It can help gather information.** Given the right incentives, many people send back snail-mail or online surveys.
- **It can be used to encourage trials of new products.** Samples and discount coupons help launch many new products.
- **It delivers instant results.** You know almost immediately if your mailing is successful, based on direct sales, phone orders, visits to a location, return-of-reply cards, or other measurement methods.
- **It can be used as part of an integrated marketing program.** For example, sending direct mail fulfills requests for information in a magazine ad; you can direct people to a website for more detailed and interactive messages.

As we've discussed in other chapters, digital technology has changed the face of marketing communications, and that certainly includes direct marketing. Traditionally we thought of direct marketing as direct mail. However, there are many more methods of direct response marketing communication. So in this chapter we will explore email and mobile communication as well as direct mail.

Components of Direct Marketing

No matter if you're developing mail, email, mobile, telemarketing, interactive TV, or door-to-door, every direct marketing effort contains these three elements:

1. **The List (or Media):** Simply put, this is who you are talking to. As we'll say repeatedly, the value of the direct response marketing effort is only as good as the list.

2. **The Offer:** The offer is a promise of a reward. Is it a limited-time discount? A bonus product? Something they can't buy in a store? A new product with an incredible competitive advantage? Why should the recipient be interested?

3. **The Creative:** How do you show it, and how do you tell the story? What will get their attention, generate their interest, flame their desire, and, most of all, get them to act?

Database Marketing: Using the List

We can't stress this enough: The most creative concept ever devised is no good if it goes to the wrong person. The better the list, the more on-target your creative message will be. The more you know, the more personal the message. Some of the information you might need to develop your message is listed below. The importance of these categories will vary depending on the type of product, the marketing situation, price points, the buying cycle, and other variables.

Customer Relationship Management

Customer relationship management (CRM) tracks and organizes the interaction between the advertiser and current and potential customers. CRM usually refers to the software used to manage customer relationships, but it's just as important for the marketer to really understand the customer's wants and needs,

This student-designed 3D mailer was sent to members of Congress, urging them to vote for anti–land mine legislation. The box contained a single small shoe, the other one was no longer needed.

Everything in a letter package should encourage a response, from the outside envelope to every item within. Multiple contents give the reader more opportunities to respond.

as well as knowing who they are and when they buy. CRM is a key component of campaign management. It coordinates operational and analytical functions to target groups from a database, send emails or snail mail, and tracks the results, as well as storing and analyzing the data. Successful CRM is a convergence of traditional direct response marketing, database marketing, and online marketing. So what does all this have to do with the creative component? The key is to know the wants and needs of the target audience, because without that, there's not much of a relationship to measure.

Where to Get Information to Build Your Database

You may wonder when you pick up a stack of junk mail or when your inbox fills up with urgent requests about foreign bank accounts, "How did they get *my* name?" If you're a direct marketer, you will *never* have an accurate, up-to-date mailing list. Ever. But you can try to make it as accurate as possible so the names on your list better match the profile of the people you want to reach. Rather than going through the intricacies of database management, we will assume you will use the tips and techniques we offer below *after* you have secured information about your intended direct response marketing recipients.

Direct Mail

Direct mail (often derisively referred to as junk mail) may not have the speed and immediacy of email, but it can often be the best way to put an advertising message in the hands of a potential customer, unlike other forms of print media.

Direct response marketing not only invites; it also provides recipients with the means to take real, measurable, physical action. Carol Krol, in *Direct Marketing News*, comments, "The workhorse benefits of mail remain: it is highly customizable, it enables marketers to communicate more information in a single package; it's trackable; and it can be particularly effective when integrated with other media channels."[2] She continues, "I'd also argue the mystique of the so-called 'mail moment' has tough to replicate in another marketing channel to date."[3] Several categories of direct mail formats are available. The choice depends on the budget (production and postage), content, type of product, purchase cycle, and response mechanism.

Envelope Mailers (Letter Package)

Anything you put into an envelope applies. It may be as simple as a letter or as elaborate as a 10-piece multicomponent mailer. Keep in mind that every component has a purpose, even the envelope itself. The basic components can include a letter, a brochure, and a reply device, such as a postage-free reply card and/or prominent mention of a website or hashtag throughout the mailer. You want the outer envelope to say "open me." You can do this several ways.

> **Teaser copy:** It could be a special offer or some twist on the message. For example, one envelope for a Florida resort said, "Open carefully: contains white sand, dolphins, seashells and coconut palms."
>
> **Blind envelopes:** These are usually standard-sized envelopes that suggest normal business or personal correspondence rather than direct mail advertising. Sometimes a stamp is used rather than a meter stamp to make it look more like personal mail.

Official envelopes: These look like government correspondence, a check, or a telegram. While you might get some immediate attention with these, you're more likely to annoy people by deceiving them.

Personalized copy: Sometimes this is effective; other times it may cross the creepiness line when people wonder, "How do they know so much about me?"

Self-Mailers

A self-mailer contains the mailing address on some of the pieces itself, rather than on an envelope. Some traditionalists don't like self-mailers. They claim a letter package will have a higher response rate, perhaps because of the curiosity factor involved with opening it. A letter is more personal, while a self-mailer shouts, "I am an ad!" However, a well-designed self-mailer can be both cost effective and creative. Consider these self-mailers:

Postcards: Up to 4¼ × 6 inches is the U.S. Postal Service (USPS) postcard rate. Postcards up to 6⅛ × 11½ inches can be mailed but at a higher rate.

Folder mailers: One fold, two folds and multifolds, and three sides must be sealed.

Brochures, pamphlets, and catalogs: As with folded mailers, all outside edges must be sealed to prevent the piece from opening before it's delivered.

Newsletters: These are usually sent folded to make self-mailing easier. These must also have sealed edges.

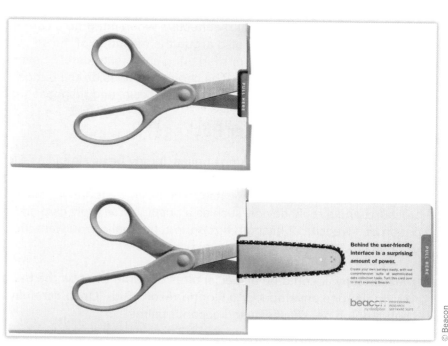

© Beacon

Self-mailers don't have to be flat or folded. A lot of options are available to cut through the clutter.

© Emery and Scuro, DMD PC

Jumbo postcards allow a little space for the mailing address and a lot of room on both sides to tell your story. They can have the impact of a billboard with the copy space of a magazine ad.

Mailers can be shipped flat and then pop up into dramatic three-dimensional pieces, as with this Ikea mailer. Levi's enlarged the idea with a life-size pop-up closet that was shipped to European fashion magazines to promote their new product lines.

© IKEA; ©Levi's

Dimensional Mailers

Some of the most innovative (and expensive) direct mailers are three-dimensional. Basically they can be anything that can be mailed or shipped. Many times the box or tube or bag will include a separate item, sometimes called a gadget. This may be a sample, a premium that might have some use, or something totally off the wall. Three-dimensional mailers are governed only by your imagination and budget.

The Fine Art of Writing a Cover Letter

When is the last time you wrote a letter? We mean a real letter. Not a long email, a Facebook post, or a hand-scribbled thank-you note to your grandma. Chances are, other than for admission to college, you have not written too many letters that were intended to persuade someone to buy something or to change his or her opinion.

© Pattex

How do you demonstrate the need for super glue? How about sending a puzzle made of broken pieces of a vase. With enough glue and several hours of patient reconstruction, you'll have something that's still totally worthless.

So we will attempt to explain that well-written letters can still be effective marketing tools, even in this age of texts and tweets. Writing still matters.

A *cover letter* lives up to its name. It covers the introduction, a sales message, and a proposal for further action. Cover letters are typically a single page, and in most cases have a beginning, a middle, and an end. These three components often amount to three or four paragraphs, but there are no ironclad rules about how to break up the information. Philip Ward-Burton offers some good advice. We've paraphrased a few of his suggestions.[5]

Cover Letter Outline

Here are seven easy steps to organize your cover letter. Each one can be a sentence or a whole paragraph.

- Promise a benefit in the headline or first paragraph—lead with your strongest sales point.

- Enlarge on your most important benefit.

- Tell the reader what he or she is going to get.

- Back your statements with proof and endorsements (testimonials).

- Tell the reader what's lost if he or she doesn't act.

- Rephrase the benefits in your closing offer.

- Incite action—set a time limit ("Buy now").

Cover Letter Style

Now that you've got some structure, you need to give it some pizzazz. Here are some ways to make your cover letter more readable.

- Start with a short opening paragraph—four lines or shorter.

- No paragraph should be longer than eight lines.

- Vary the lengths of paragraphs.

- Use deep indents and center bullet points.

- Close with a two- to three-line summary.

- Don't forget the envelope (teaser).

- Don't forget a follow-up letter—reinforce the message and refine your data mining.

Dear Jack:	Personalize with name and other information.
Here's how you can keep your Sea Ray 220SD looking showroom fresh—above and below the waterline.	Promise a benefit up front.
But when you haul it out in the fall, you know you're facing many long hours of scrubbing that green slime off the bottom. It won't come off with a pressure washer. And don't think about using harsh acid cleaners on your fiberglass hull.	Enlarge on that benefit.
Here's a better way.	Vary the lengths of sentences and paragraphs.
New BoteBrite hull cleaner cuts through that grungy bottom grime. Without hard scrubbing. Without abrasives. Without dangerous acids.	Tell the reader what's lost if he or she doesn't act.
Just spray BoteBrite on the bottom of the boat—wait 15 minutes— and rinse with a garden hose.	
That's all there is to it!	
• BoteBrite is a unique detergent that dissolves organic stains from algae and dirty water.	Use deep indents and bullet points to call out key features and benefits.
• BoteBrite will not damage fiberglass, plastic, metal, or your driveway when used as directed.	
• BoteBrite is easy to apply and even easier to clean up.	
For limited time, we're offering a Buy 2 - Get 1 Free deal. Just go to BoteBrite.com for an discount coupon. Bring the coupon to any BoteBrite retailer before September 30.	Tell the reader what he or she is going to get. Incite action.
When it's time to clean your boat his fall, do it the easy way. Use new BoteBrite for fast, safe and effective boat cleaning.	Close with a benefit summary.

Figure 14.1   Cover Letter Example

The letter in Figure 14.1 contains a persuasive sales message in a format that's easy to digest. Keep in mind, no matter how well it's written, it has to reach the right target audience.

We've been saying that you must know the wants and needs of the consumer, and technology today allows you to know more and more every year. Sophisticated database software not only provides spot-on identification but also matches it to very specific information for that recipient. The message can be personalized using variable printing techniques to deliver unique messages. The trick is not allowing big data to become Big Brother. Just because you can personalize a mailer doesn't mean you should. Grant Johnson of Johnson Direct offers this advice: "Let the target audience define how it wants to be marketed to and via what channels, then test various offers and messaging platforms based on that date to gauge results."[7]

He offers examples of marketers who excel and are exploiting the personal relevance of their brands and why they are successful:

- Starbucks: How I want *my* coffee is different from the way *you* want yours.
- Harley-Davidson: How I customize *my* bike is different from the way *you* do it.
- Apple: The music on *my* iPod defines who I am.

Is personalization a bad thing? No. But we need to let your customers and prospects tell us how to proceed.[8]

PURL: Your Personal Web Page

A PURL (personalized URL) is a landing page created for one person. Actually it could be one of hundreds of webpage templates that allow the placement of an individual's name and information derived from a database that is relevant to that person. An example of a PURL would be JohnR.Smith.TravelAdventures.com. When John Smith clicks on the link, he goes to a customized TravelAdventures landing page that may have a headline reading, "Hey, John Smith. Looking for a new adventure?" Copy on the page would use his name and weave in some information such as hiking, photography, and whitewater rafting, based on data compiled for him. John is given the opportunity to request a brochure, chat with a travel consultant, look at a blog of like-minded adventurers, and, of course, book travel online. All the time, he is providing information to TravelAdventures, which is recording the information, analyzing it, and preparing future contact with John, including more mailers, email blasts, and possibly telemarketing.

Before you consider a campaign using PURLs, consider the effect on the recipient. Has the novelty of having a personal website worn thin? Are you stepping into the creepiness zone by revealing too much too soon? Are there more effective and cheaper ways to engage a customer?

The Future of Direct Mail

Advertising mail volume has dropped off dramatically thanks to email and social media. Around 85 billion pieces are sent through the USPS, versus 167 billion emails sent daily.[10] But for direct marketers willing to embrace the future, that's not a bad thing. Lower volume means less clutter in the mailbox and the potential for better targeting. As one of the oldest forms of marketing, direct mail is still a key component in

©Cheshire Academy

Once you capture a person's name and address, you can personalize the mailer. The more you know, the more personal you can make it. In some cases, letting recipients know how much you know can creep them out. The trick is to build trust so they want to give you more information on their terms.

an integrated marketing campaign. Combining traditional direct mail with digital maximizes potential for quicker and stronger response rates. PURLs, QR codes, cross-platform integration of content to mobile, and synergy with social networks all strengthen the case for direct mail. As with web and print media, we should see more content marketing working through direct mail. With big data making targeting more of a science, direct marketers can develop mailers people actually want to open. For example, highly personalized newsletters and white papers can be sent by mail along with a small gift, coupon, or some other incentive to take action. Even postcards will benefit from tighter analytics. We'll see them tested, modified, and tweaked just like online ads and content. Regardless of how direct mail evolves, the basics still apply. The list is still the most important component. Better segmentation makes a cleaner, more finely tuned list possible. You may be able to get more activity from fewer people. The better you know the target, the easier it is to make the *offer* more relevant to encourage faster response. Finally, the creative is key to telling your story. You can quickly test *creative* concepts online before you commit to printing and fulfilling direct mailers. Creative can be tailored to accommodate new variables we've never been able to define.

Email

Email represents the best and worst of direct marketing. On the plus side, email is great for customer retention and relationship management, especially if the recipient has opted in to the campaign. Email also has been effective to gain attention and interest among new customers. Most of all, it can generate a quick response, whether it's a direct sale or clicking on a link to a more detailed website. The downside: spam. Spamming and its evil cousin, phishing (using legitimate-looking emails to scam people) have poisoned the perception of email. As a result, sophisticated mail filters screen out many legitimate emails and even quite a few that people might actually want to read. Because spam has the potential to harm your computer and potentially suck money out of a bank account, many people fear it more than ordinary junk snail mail. Besides that, email seems kind of old school, at least for personal communication. Stuart Feil in *Adweek* explains why: "Consumers will want to interact via social media. Messaging apps will take over. It's all so Y2K." But he contends, "Reports of email's death have been greatly exaggerated."[11] He cites data that shows consumers prefer receiving information about brands through email versus other media.

DIRECT MAIL INSIGHTS

Direct mail triggers an online response

The top three actions people take after receiving direct mail from a brand they're interested in:

44% visit the brand's website

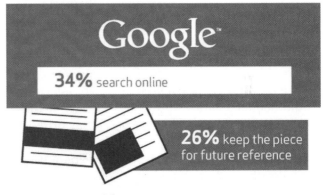

34% search online

26% keep the piece for future reference

Direct mail has a long shelf life

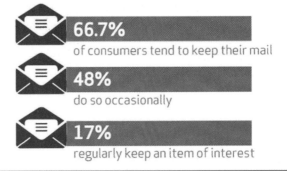

66.7% of consumers tend to keep their mail

48% do so occasionally

17% regularly keep an item of interest

Source: boingnet.com

Spark Some Fun

© Sea Doo

#SPARKSOMEFUN

SEA-DOO

SPARK SOME FUN **MIAMI** 3/23 2014 8 FEATURING deadmau5

FONTAINEBLEAU OCEAN LAWN 4441 COLLINS AVE MIAMI BEACH FL 33140

Big bulky sizes. Increasing prices. Relatively few differentiators. These were just a few factors pushing people out of the personal watercraft (PWC) market. In 2014, Sea-Doo set out to change all that with a new product called Spark.

The Sea-Doo Spark was an affordable, fun, and exciting new PWC that we knew we could use as a catalyst for riders to take to the water again. As the most accessible PWC on the market, priced right and designed to impress, we also knew we needed a communications plan for Spark that would strike a chord with an audience that overindexed with digital brand experiences and a higher Internet usage rate than other Sea-Doo buyers.

The marketing challenge was now all about grabbing the attention of our target and ultimately inspiring him to *spark some fun* of his own. In addition to TV, print, and digital ads, we layered compelling social elements that would ignite online conversation and engagement around the product to pay off this fun, vibrant attitude. We kicked off with a huge social experience that revolved around another key audience attribute—their passion for music. So, we launched with a Spark Some Fun Miami live concert that featured Grammy-nominated artist deadmau5 on the grounds of the legendary Fontainebleau Miami Beach hotel. This private concert, open only to Sea-Doo #SparkSomeFun contest winners and VIPs, was broadcast across our social channels, and the Spark experience began resonating with our audience by earning over 10,000 social mentions in the first month of activations.

From the beaches of Miami to the social networks where our audience was engaging, we continued to #SparkSomeFun by partnering with celebrities (deadmau5, Brody Jenner, and Vanilla Ice), adventure sports influencers (Aaron Colton and Gear Junkie), fellow "dad-oriented" social influencers (Bat Dad, Single Dad Laughing, and Mocha Dad), and social media sensations (Devin Supertramp, Jessica Zollman, and Dirk Dallas) that would ultimately help sway our target. Each "Spark Some Fun" influencer used his or her own special talent to create Spark-centric content and share it with their audiences.

The social influencer portion of our campaign generated over 46 million social media impressions, and the Spark ultimately became one of the hottest selling PWCs on the market.

In the end, we did much more than simply place the product in the social feeds of our target; we helped them envision it as a part of their lifestyle—something they believed could help them spark some fun.

Dave Racine, vice president,
Cramer-Krasselt, Milwaukee

Furthermore, consumers would rather use email to communicate with businesses than direct mail or text messages. What's more, the 29 minutes consumers spend each day with email is second only to the 37 minutes they spend on social media. Email open rates have actually risen in the past couple of years, largely due to mobile devices.[12] So it seems email is not extinct; it's just evolving.

Since the early days of email marketing, getting the consumer's email address was the golden ticket. After all, the list is the most important component. With big data driving email now, we keep finding new ways to fine-tune that list. Messages have the potential to be more personalized and one to one, as brands leverage both their first-party CRM data and third-party sources to target their email messages more effectively.[13]

Email has also evolved into a credible news source, especially for business-to-business marketers. Rather than accessing a random scattering of posts in social media, websites, and mobile apps, busy businesspeople increasingly rely on email newsletters to consolidate the news they need. Today, just about every established media property is delivering headlines via email. Email newsletters are on par with general and industry news sites as the top way executives keep up with news in their industry.[14]

Email newsletters should be graphically interesting and easy to read, not unlike a blog or microsite. A number of free templates are available to organize the newsletter, but someone has to write the content.

Effective email marketing doesn't end once a clean, up-to-date, and qualified list is developed. You've got to get them to open the emails and keep opening them. Permission marketing allows email recipients to opt in, so messages are sent only to people willing to receive them. Permission marketing programs are offered on websites and by telephone, direct mail, and email. Results are improved even more when permission marketing programs segment customers by demographics or buying history. Over time, recipients may get bored with a constant stream of messages, so enhancements can be introduced to renew interest. These can include sweepstakes, free information, quizzes, or other methods to keep the recipient engaged. The following list describes the steps in a permission marketing program:

- Provide the means to allow customers to easily opt in. Empower them by giving them the choice.

- Promise the kind of information the customer wants and deliver it each time.

- Reinforce this information with incentives when necessary to strengthen the relationship.

- Try to ramp up the level of participation by offering more incentives to gather more information about the customer. Make their higher level of participation worth their time.

- Continue to stay in contact and encourage feedback through social media.

Writing More Effective Emails

Like a snail-mail letter, an email has several components that are intended to spur the recipient into action. The first is the subject line, which is so important we'll discuss it in much more detail later. The next most important element is the opening line. Like the opening line of a print ad, it should hook the reader and offer a promise—why it would be worth the reader's time to keep reading. The rest of the copy should concentrate on three principles:

- Stay on topic—provide just one message.
- Provide value—tell the readers how they will benefit from taking action.
- Ask for action—what do you want the person to do?

Subject Line

The subject line is even more powerful than the headline of a print ad. It has to do all the heavy lifting without the benefit of slick graphics to attract a reader. So here are a few tips for crafting a better subject line.

Not too long, not too short: Try to stay in range of 50 to 90 characters (if you're tweeting, this should be easy).

Keep it real: People would rather get a message from a person than a company. Try to make it as personable as possible but not unrealistically cheesy. No one likes phony friends.

Provide a benefit: Don't make unrealistic claims or use advertising jargon. Try to be specific with a benefit rather than saying something generic like "Free advice on how to save big money."

Get their attention: Sometimes you have to shock a reader into reading. We recently got an email from a stock photo house that said, "Fake people stink." Made us look, if for no other reason than to see if they were talking about us.

Ask, don't shout: As with print, sometimes asking a question hooks a reader.

Your first paragraph or two should contain a miniversion of your whole email. So instead of carefully spreading out your AIDA (attention, interest, desire, and action), you should try to get all these elements in early. Online users have little patience in general, and they need to understand your whole offer fast. Avoid using hard-sell techniques. These tend to produce poor results. Readers on the Internet expect to see information on the benefits and how to order, but the tone must remain helpful. If it's too slick, your email will be trashed. Shorter is better. If some of your prospects require more information before they make purchasing decisions, include a click-through to an expanded version of your email. Consider viral marketing techniques. Prospects can pass your messages on to others they think would be interested. Always include an opt-out statement. The only thing more powerful than good will toward your company is ill will.

Years ago direct response marketing pioneer John Caples developed a list of words that were proven to increase readership and response in direct mail pieces. Today, some of those same words have just the opposite effect. When skeptical and spam-weary readers spot these words, they hit the delete button. More than likely, their email programs have already routed them to the junk folder. We suggest not using the following words if you want anyone to open your email:

Buy

Money

Discount

New

Free

Profit

Help

Sale

Hey (recipient's name)

Save

Investment

Special

And don't use ALL CAPS or exclamation points! Really good copy invites the reader in. Desperate screaming usually has the opposite effect.

Email Design

Rich mail allows graphics, video, and audio to be included in the email message. When you open up a rich email, your email client automatically calls up your Internet connection and launches an HTML page in your browser. Email clients that are offline will invite you to click on the link when you have your Internet connection open again. If your email client does not support graphics, you will receive the email as text only. Most HTML pages instantly appear, complete with the visuals, and don't require the added, and often annoying, step of downloading the graphics. As with the most successful email marketers, give recipients the opportunity to opt out by having a "please remove me from your list" link.

Today, the biggest challenge to email design is making it look good on a mobile device. As with websites, the answer is responsive design. Build an email once, and it will stay functional across all screens. Agata Celmerowski, head of marketing for Campaign Monitor, comments, "Opening email on mobile devices is now more common than opening on desktop or webmail clients. Responsive design is no longer an option for email marketers—it's a must for every campaign to ensure you get the best results."[15] Programs such as Canvas make responsive email messages a lot easier to design. Instead of requiring users to choose a template and then fit the email content into that form, Canvas has users choose a flexible style of email that matches the brand. Users can then customize how they lay out the content as they add it.[16]

Test. Test. Test.

One of chief advantages of direct marketing is measurability, and one of the key benefits of email (and other digital marketing) is the ability to test concepts, headlines, and graphics quickly and efficiently. You don't have to wait for sales figures to trickle in. With today's analytics, you know almost immediately which subject line had a higher open rate. You know that more mail was opened at 1:00 in the afternoon than at 8:30 in the morning. You know which of the three offers you tested resonates best with your target market. The response to each of the three key components—list, offer, and creative—is easy to measure. So before you send a mass emailing, with all the cross-channel connections, you'll have a much better idea what's going to work best.

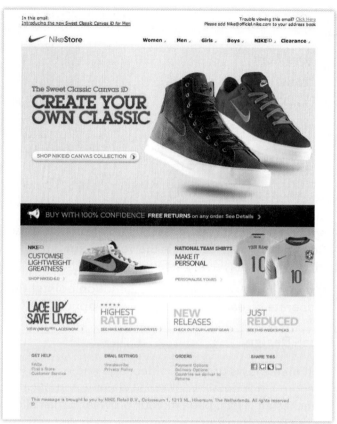

Two different email approaches. One is a direct sales pitch for Nike products; the other promotes a promotion as part of a loyalty rewards program.

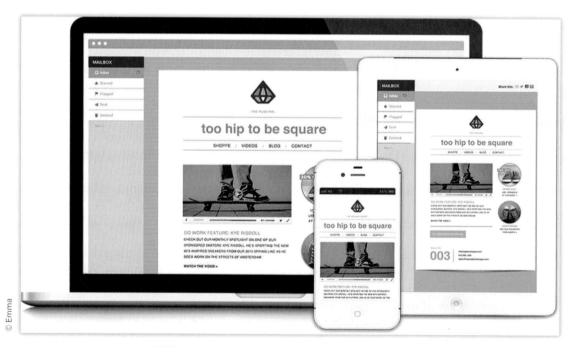

As with desktop websites, HTML emails need responsive design to be seen and read optimally on tablets and smart phones. This example shows a generic treatment for all email platforms.

Email and Cross-Channel Marketing

Email by itself can be a powerful tool, but if massive email blasts are the only means of communication, success is merely a numbers game, which is a lot like buying lottery tickets. Most people recognize spam, and response rates are appallingly low. Response rates increase significantly when email messages are coordinated with the look and feel of a company's website and other marketing communication materials. While other forms of marketing communication are learning to use digital in cross-channel marketing, email is already there. A recent study from Forrester Consulting notes, "Email is the veteran among digital channels having established presence and experienced growing pains long before its peers. Sophisticated marketers have above average integration between email and other digital channels."[17] For example, email that's integrated with direct mail, social media, telemarketing, and online tools, such as a webinar, has a much better chance of being read and generating a response. In addition, diligent use of web analytics can trigger an email response that helps close a sale. Let's say an online shopper bails out at the shopping cart. Sending an email to that shopper might get him or her to conclude the transaction. Targeted emails have a conversion rate 5 to 10 times higher than the rate for mass emails, and revenues from these follow-up emails are 3 to 9 times higher.[18]

While direct mail and email both deliver the written word to a recipient, each method has special characteristics, as seen in Table 14.1.

The Future of Email

Despite its many advantages, email can be a terrible way to communicate. Nuance, satire, humor, and sincerity are hard to express in print. Unintentional gaffes are impossible to unsend. When it comes to internal communications, many companies are phasing out email in favor of social networks and text-based programs, such as Yammer, Google Talk, and Google Voice, among others. However, as noted earlier, email is key player in digital cross-channel marketing, and it's not going away.

	Direct Mail	Email
Delivers positive brand image	X	
Higher open rate	X	
Attention grabbing	X	
Provides more information	X	
Makes recipient feel valued	X	
Believable and reliable	X	
More effective for noncustomers	X	
More effective for existing customers	X	X
Better for sending reminders	X	X
Quick and informal		X
Easier to file for future use		X
Easier to respond		X
Better for brief messages		X
Environmentally friendly		X

Table 14.1   Direct Mail Versus Email[19]

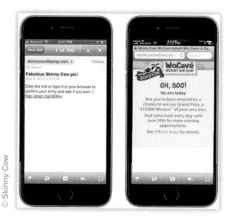

Mobile direct response marketing provides an increasingly important platform to deliver sales promotion messages.

In fact, Nancy Shaver, principal consultant, cross-channel marketing at Experian Marketing Services, says, "If you're asking where to have an authentic dialog at the lowest cost and highest impact, you'll go to email."[20]

Mobile Direct Response Marketing

As we saw in Chapter 12, mobile devices play an increasingly important role in an integrated direct marketing campaign. **SMS (short message service)** has become an increasingly important advertising channel. Unlike traditional email, mobile marketers have established guidelines in an effort to reduce mobile spam. Plus federal regulations in the United States make spamming more difficult for cell phones. A double-opt-in requirement and easy opt-out "STOP" command gives the recipient more control. Mobile marketing service expands the marketing capability of mobile direct marketing by including images, text, videos, slide shows, and audio content. **Push notifications** allow marketers to communicate directly with smart phone users. There are pros and cons, including cheaper costs over time than SMS but higher costs of initial development. The most important cost/benefit calculation to consider is the risk of alienating the recipient and losing any good will generated by pushing out unwanted or untimely information.

But Wait. There's More!

We've focused mostly on snail mail and email so far, primarily because good copywriting is so critical to their success. However, television offers direct marketers tremendous opportunities to prove P.T Barnum was right: a sucker is born every minute.

Infomercials

Most infomercials have three things in common: a product no one knew they needed, an exaggerated problem/solution format, and a hyperbolic announcer encouraging viewers to act now. You can also include cheesy production values, a prominently listed price (usually $9.99), and toll-free numbers plastered all over the screen. You won't see too many of these masterpieces at the Clios, but infomercials are still a powerful factor in direct marketing. They contain the three direct marketing elements—the list (in this case, people watching low-rated late-night cable shows), the offer (usually two-for-one deals plus a bonus item you didn't know you needed), and the creative (or what passes for it).

Some direct marketers produce longer format programs, sometimes 30 minutes or more, which attempt to have entertainment or educational value. They are a blend of native advertising, content marketing, and blatant, in-your-face sales pitches. Perhaps it's a personal fitness program hosted by a semifamous spokesperson (or couple). They address the problem (flabby, tired people), show the solution (lots of attractive people working out), and feature plenty of before-and-after testimonials. That's the soft sell. Then it's frequently interrupted with urgent pleas to order exercise equipment for just a few low monthly payments.

You might end up writing and producing infomercials, slavishly following the tried-and-true formulas to pry money out of gullible consumers' pockets. Direct marketing includes many other channels that don't require copywriting skills. If you're headed for a career in telemarketing or direct selling, you probably won't find much value in this book.

Starving for Work

Courtesy of Sarah Whalen

When I graduated, I was desperate for a job and totally clueless. For a while, I was emailing the CEO of a small but quickly rising agency in Chicago. Every Tuesday at 11:00 a.m., I would attempt to make his mouth water with descriptions of filet mignon wrapped in bacon served with garlic mashed potatoes. I would let it sink in for a minute with long-winded explanations of aromas and savory flavors and at the right moment swoop in to remind him that while he was salivating over the idea of a gourmet lunch, I wasn't hungry in the traditional sense. I didn't want a steak. I wanted a job.

My emails progressed from hungry, to starving, to famished—getting increasingly dramatic as I became increasingly desperate for a job.

And still, nothing.

After a few other failed attempts to get noticed through online portfolios, professionally printed books, and internship applications, I took the closest thing I could get to a job in advertising—working as a receptionist at DesignKitchen, a small digital agency in Chicago's meatpacking district. And in the seven years I've been there, we've changed names and gone global, and I've worked my way to senior copywriter.

My best advice would be to take whatever job you can get, as long as it gets you close to the work. Getting in is by far the hardest part. Once you're there, surround yourself with the most creative people. Ask them questions. Ask them to look at your stuff. Let your interests and strengths steer your career. And when in doubt, ask more questions.[21]

Sarah Whalen, senior copywriter, Blast Radius

Instagram @skell

The Changing Face of Direct Response Marketing

As long as the postal service pretends to deliver mail efficiently, direct mail will be a powerful marketing tool. Some people still need to hold and feel a real letter or brochure, if just for the satisfaction of throwing it away. The trick has always been to produce something that people want to open. While direct mail has always been integrated with other marketing communication channels, the potential for email, social media, and mobile marketing opens up new possibilities direct mail marketers couldn't even imagine years ago. Two reasons direct response integration works so well: connection with an individual consumer and measurability. New technology not only makes direct response marketing tools such as email and mobile more accountable; it also links traditional media such as television and out-of-home into a customized and highly measurable effort that enhances the connection between a consumer and a brand. So in addition to having our list, offer, and creative, we'll also have a lot more engagement.

WHO'S WHO?

Chapter 14

Drayton Bird

As worldwide creative director of Ogilvy & Mather Direct, Drayton Bird was a key to the success of the world's largest direct marketing agency. He went on to found what became the United Kingdom's largest direct marketing agency. With more than 40 years of experience in direct marketing and advertising, Bird wrote and published *Commonsense Direct Marketing*, *How to Write Sales Letters That Sell*, and *Marketing Insights and Outrages*—all best sellers. He also writes regular columns for marketing and advertising publications in the United Kingdom, the United States, Malaysia, India, and Europe. David Ogilvy said of him, "Drayton Bird knows more about direct marketing than anyone else in the world."[22]

John Caples

Often called the father of direct response advertising, John Caples was one of the most influential copywriters of all time. He spent a lifetime researching the most effective methods of advertising. His direct approach for writing headlines cut through the clutter and grabbed the readers, pulling them into the ad. Caples penned one of the most famous headlines ever written: "They laughed when I sat down at the piano, but when I started to play!"

Howard Draft

Howard Draft was CEO of the 10th largest agency in the United States, Draftfcb. His rise to the top began at a 13-person Chicago shop that specialized in direct response advertising. When that agency partnered with the much larger Ted Bates Worldwide, Draft moved to New York and set up a direct marketing branch that was soon billing more than his old shop. By the mid-1990s, Draft owned the agency, now called Draft Direct, which grew to $600 million in billings. In 2003, he merged with FCB, one of the best known agencies in the world, to form Draftfcb.[24]

Danielle DeLauro

As senior VP of sales and marketing for the Cabletelevision Advertising Bureau, DeLauro spends every day advocating the value of cable TV to media agencies and advertisers. DeLauro has been at the forefront of presenting cable as a complete video offering, rather than as just a one-dimensional sell. And she knows what agencies and their clients are looking for, having spent nearly a decade on the agency side. As VP associate media director at Universal McCann, DeLauro managed 12 brands, including Maytag and Lowe's, with budgets totaling $100 million. Prior to Universal McCann, DeLauro was a media manager at Media.com, and spent time at DDB Worldwide, where she was a senior media planner for Universal Pictures.[23]

Banking on Millennials

ABC Bank is one of the ten largest banks in the United States, with over 3,000 banking offices and more than 5,000 ATMs in over 20 states. The bank provides regional consumer and business banking and wealth management services, as well as global payment services. For many years, the bank has been a provider of credit card services to a major U.S. airline. Due to an increasingly competitive market in the banking industry and a recent airline merger, the bank will lose the airline as a credit card client. The regional business banking is going reasonably well, but the consumer business side is becoming less profitable in the area of consumer checking accounts. Additionally, the bank has discovered through research that young Americans do not seem to be knowledgeable in the area of "budgeting" and seem to be unaware of the concepts of "expenditures" and "saving money."

ABC Bank has been working with a regional advertising agency and a public relations agency on branding, product advertising, and general publicity, which has helped position the bank as a regional leader in the banking industry. Most recently, ABC Bank explored some digital venues and experimented with applications for smart phones and tablets that allow customers to use augmented reality to search for and identify local ATMs.

Since the augmented reality application has become (out)dated quite quickly, the vice president of innovation and payment systems is asking you to explore new opportunities for how augmented reality could be used for the bank and its customers, specifically their younger Millennial consumers, and to develop a new smartphone application.

1 How do you assess the bank's situation and the VP's assignment to develop a new application?

2 What do you think about augmented reality in the context of financial services and ABC Bank, and how could you envision an application that helps promote the bank's services?

3 How could you develop a new value proposition, service, and/or application that takes into consideration the aforementioned information and could add value to the bank's existing as well as new customers?

4 What would be the advantage of an augmented reality application versus a new banking service that helps customers and potential customers with topics like savings, purchases, and budgeting in their daily lives? What could such a service look like?

Thomas Vogel, associate professor, Emerson College

1. Right Cause, Right Brand

(Contributed by Kwangmi Ko Kim, PhD, associate professor, Towson University.)

The focus of this exercise is to help you understand the importance of using the "right" cause to appeal to the "right" target market in cause-related marketing. In short, how to link the right cause to the right brand.

- Find one or two brands popular among certain demographic groups (maybe through brief interviews with groups ages 18–24, 25–34, 35–44, 45–54, and 55+).

- While interviewing them, you need to also ask each demographic group what causes are important to them. Narrow down their responses into two major causes.

- Study the cause-related marketing practices used by the brands identified in the first step.

- Now compare whether there is any congruence between the causes identified by each demographic group and the causes affiliated with their favorite brands or if there are any perfect partnerships waiting to happen.

2. Visual Word Associations

This exercise is designed to demonstrate the visual power of word associations.

- Think of a brand. Let's say: FedEx. Generate a benefits list.

- Pick the top three benefits and find the keywords for each.

- Now go to visualthesaurus.com and type in each keyword. (It's free the first time, and then it will cost you, but not much. We think it's worth it.) You will see a graphic clustering of associated words. Talk about proximity! For example, with *dependable* the clusters are (a) *good, safe,* and *secure;* (b) *honest, reliable,* and *true;* and (c) *steady-going* and *rock-steady.* (You can also click on each word and go deeper.)

- Now you have three concepting approaches. Generate three layouts that visually express each of the three clusters. Have each layout focus on a different direct tactic.

- We think visualthesaurus.com is a very cool site. It's great for headline generation too.

3. Passionate for a Cause

Letting your passion show is a great way to engage the target audience, and with direct marketing, engagement is paramount.

- Choose a nonprofit or social cause you are passionate about, such as the American Red Cross, Greenpeace, Big Brothers Big Sisters, breast cancer awareness, or a host of other great causes.

- Then create a print ad with headline, body copy, visual, and tagline. As this is part of a direct campaign, be sure to pay special attention to your Call to Action.

- Now, consider the strategically ideal direct medium in order to reach your target audience. Then execute your direct tactic.

- Present your direct tactic and your print ad and sell the class on why your two-part campaign has the potential to be extended—why it has legs. But, also give a rationale for why, even with just these two tactics, your Call to Action will be heard and responded to. Sell the class on strategy. After all, this is a cause you are passionate about.

Review chapter content and study for exams. http://study.sagepub.com/altstiel4e.

- Interactive practice quizzes
- Mobile-friendly eFlashcards
- Carefully selected chapter-by-chapter video and multimedia content

Chapter 15

Business-to-Business
Selling Along the Supply Chain

Some beginning copywriters dread business-to-business (B2B) assignments. The products aren't fun. The target audience is deadly serious. Many creative directors tell their team, "There are no boring products, only boring advertising." They might also add that some clients won't consider new technology to reach their target audience, so writers may be stuck with print ads and collateral.

Students typically struggle with B2B assignments. They usually rely on clichés, broad generalities, cute puns, and all the other creative crutches that demonstrate they don't understand the product or the market. You have to know something about your subject as well as the customer when you're creating business advertising. The secret is still finding that One Thing and keeping in mind that companies don't buy things, people do. And even if they are business customers, they have their own wants and needs.

Why B2B Is Different

While creating good B2B concepts can be a challenge, it also presents a great opportunity, especially for entry-level creatives. Rather than being stuck with a small piece of the account, you're more likely to work on a whole campaign. You might be able to work out a whole integrated plan that uses a lot of fun promotional and web components in addition to print ads and collateral. You might even work in some cool guerrilla marketing ideas to use at a trade show. Some clients love that, since they think they're getting more for their money. In *Hey Whipple, Squeeze This!* Luke Sullivan praises B2B: "Trade ads are just as important to your client's economy as its consumer work, and they're usually a better gig than a consumer campaign."[1] Here are a few reasons why B2B is different.

- The customer is buying products with his or her company's money.
- Traditionally, the copy has been more factual and less emotional than what's usually found in consumer advertising.
- In general, the emphasis is on generating immediate response rather than on long-term brand building.
- Ad budgets are usually much smaller than with mass-appeal consumer products, restricting many creative options.
- Most business products are not sold retail, which means they are either sold direct to buyers or through dealers or distributors.

Why B2B Is the Same

- Business customers still have wants and needs—saving money, success, and self-esteem. Sure, they want facts, but ultimately it's about making more money and feeling good about it.
- The copy and design principles discussed in previous chapters apply to business readers, maybe even more than they do with some consumer products.
- The Internet is just as important, and in some cases even more important, as a communication source and as part of an integrated marketing communications campaign.
- Branding for business products and services is becoming hugely important, especially as companies merge and change affiliations. Sometimes the brand name is the only constant.
- Even though the numbers of business customers may be smaller, using traditional mass media such as television, radio, outdoor, and newspapers may be an effective way to reach them.
- Companies do not buy products and services. People do.

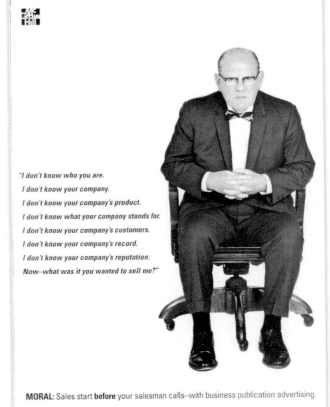

"I don't know who you are.
I don't know your company.
I don't know your company's product.
I don't know what your company stands for.
I don't know your company's customers.
I don't know your company's record.
I don't know your company's reputation.
Now—what was it you wanted to sell me?"

MORAL: Sales start **before** your salesman calls—with business publication advertising.

McGRAW-HILL MAGAZINES
BUSINESS•PROFESSIONAL•TECHNICAL

© McGraw-Hill

Many years ago, magazine publisher McGraw-Hill made the case for B2B advertising. The grumpy little man in the chair may not represent typical buyers today, but they still want answers to these questions.

Don't Forget Those Wants and Needs

Business buyers are human. They may use economic rationales, but they still have wants and needs similar to those of other consumers. For example:

- An office manager responds to a direct mailer from an office supply store that offers free delivery. This saves her time, so she can get more work done; she can save her company money, which makes her look good to the boss, which might mean she gets a raise. All of which satisfies her needs.

- A factory manager sees an ad for a robot that stacks boxes on pallets in minutes, saving valuable time and labor. This will save his company a lot of money, making him look good, which may mean a promotion and more money. (Starting to see a pattern?)

- A doctor reads a brochure, sees a medical journal ad, and checks a website for a new blood-thinning drug. She gets more information from a sales rep, including research reports. She prescribes the drug, not because she'll make more money, but because her need is to help her patients. Sometimes business is about more than making money.

Most of this chapter will deal with trade advertising generally aimed at businesspeople who buy products or services sold direct or through dealers, wholesalers, or retailers. For example, sump pumps sold to plumbers, lumber for housing contractors, engines for jet planes, and a million other products we all take for granted. Besides trade, there are several other B2B specialties:

Visual metaphors work for business ads too, especially when you're trying to simplify a complicated subject like data processing speed.

Pork producers know healthy hogs are happy hogs and more profitable. While warm and fuzzy approaches like this may attract some readers, most agricultural ads deal with the cold hard facts about a cruel and environmentally devastating industry.

B2B Special Categories

Businesses are defined by Standard Industrial Classification codes, and there are thousands of them. We'd like to cover a few large areas of business marketing that have unique wants and needs: agricultural, professional, and government.

Agricultural Advertising: It's Another Animal

Agricultural advertising requires a special approach. Farmers are consumers who buy industrial products—tractors, buildings, seed, chemicals, and the like. They ride boom-and-bust cycles that would make the most daring stockbrokers nauseous. When you talk to a typical farmer, he will always complain about the weather, the government, the markets, and whatever else is bugging him today. But for the most part he wouldn't trade his career choice for any city job. Forget about Old McDonald. Most modern dairy, poultry egg, and livestock farms are factories that sometimes subject animals to inhumane housing and load them with hormones and antibiotics. Crop farmers tap precious aquifers and rivers and often pollute the water table with pesticides. When confronted with the facts, agribusiness marketers will talk about feeding the world and claim that farming is still a noble profession. Just to prove that ethics don't get in the way of good business, some of the hottest creative shops have taken on ag clients and have won a ton of awards.

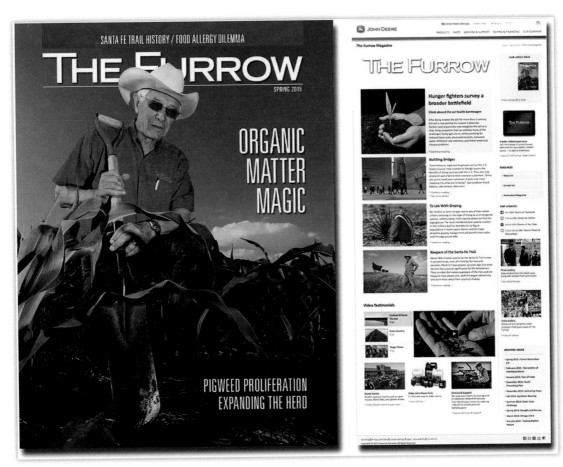

© The Furrow

John Deere has reached its dealers and customers for decades through *The Furrow* magazine. More recently this staple of agricultural journalism has gone digital, like so many other farm pubs.

Progressive must believe the fleet owner wants to see a cute concept featuring their spokesperson Flo more than their need for details.

Legal matters are serious business. So most law firms that advertise to businesses have to balance the need for getting attention with a straightforward message. In this ad, the headline reads, "It's not a tie. It's tiny cape worn backwards."

AHA Solutions used this multipart direct mail campaign to inform hospitals about the compensation and benefit solutions for doctors and nurses.

Someday you might work on an ag account. If so, you may have to hold your nose and keep these tips in mind:

- Many successful farmers are college-educated businesspeople and should be treated as such, not as bib-overall-wearing hicks. Appeal to their business sense, not to the nostalgia of a small family farm that disappeared years ago.

- Farmers are extremely sensitive to detail and very concerned about being up to date. Show a 10-year-old tractor, a CRT computer monitor, or an out-of-date satellite dish in your ad, and you've killed your sales message.

- You can have fun with the product, but never mock the farmer's country, family, profession, or lifestyle.

- Be careful with claims. If anyone recognizes BS, it's a farmer.

Professional Advertising

Not that we don't think other businesspeople are pros at what they do, but in this context *professional* applies to teachers, engineers, lawyers, accountants, doctors, dentists, architects, and other people who have specialized careers that usually require advanced education and training. Professionals read journals that are often the official publications of their professions, such as the *Journal of the American Medical Association*. Professionals operate under codes of ethics, so journals that allow advertising frown on wild, unsubstantiated ad claims; unauthorized use of a product; or any image that would denigrate their field. That's why so many professional journal ads play it safe and don't risk offending their readers. Other publications that appeal to professionals may be given a little more creative latitude, but remember, these professionals worked hard to get where they are, and it's not something to trivialize with silly advertising.

While professional journals are still respected sources of information, professionals go online first, just like every other businessperson. Content marketing in websites is especially critical to make a connection. Professionals want information, not hype. Direct marketing can also be effective, as long as it's informative. Medical marketing blogger Deanna Pogorelc advises, "Here's some advice for companies trying to get new medical products in front of the eyes of physicians: Aim to educate them rather than try to sell them, and do it via email or direct mail. Pharmaceutical and medical device companies, who are dealing with shrinking sales forces of their own, are moving away from traditional direct sales and trying different ways of marketing their products. The good news is that busy doctors still want new information about drugs and medical devices as long as it's relevant and useful."[4]

B2G: Your Tax Dollars at Work

Business-to-government (B2G) marketing is a specialized kind of B2B that's sometimes called public sector marketing. It involves marketing goods and services to all levels of government—local, state, and federal. B2G can include all the marketing communication tools used for traditional B2B, but government buyers have much stricter guidelines and usually have prenegotiated standing contracts and set prices. Nevertheless, through traditional and social networks, B2G marketers can influence a sale. For example, Xerox helps the federal government streamline its print service management, electronic collection, and Medicaid claims processing. With the new social media tools available, Xerox can provide much more information to their federal government customers. Edward Gala, vice president of marketing, explains, "When you get a message from Xerox, it comes with links to videos on YouTube. It comes with links to whitepapers and analyst reports that are accessible online. It comes with invitations to webinars where you can learn from thought leaders on a particular topic, whether it be security or sustainability or cost reduction."[5]

Integrated B2B Campaigns

Even the most traditional B2B marketers understand that business magazines are no longer the most effective way to reach their customers. Using integrated marketing communications (IMC) for

The long-running B2B campaign for Target featured their iconic mascot to tie in the broader consumer branding campaigns. This ad touts the benefits of using the Target gift card as an employee incentive.

B2B makes sense because most customers are easier to define and locate than consumers. All the IMC components listed in previous chapters apply to B2B. Because the number of key customers is sometimes very small, you may be able to create high-impact communication tools that generate higher response rates. As with consumer advertising, you need to think of how many different ways you can reach a customer. Do you go for a few high-impact rifle shots or use a lot of different marketing tools? Before you start developing tactics, consider the whole supply chain and that means understand how to push products into the pipeline and pull them through all the way to the consumer.

In Chapter 13 we looked at trade promotions that move products from the manufacturers to the distributors or wholesalers then to the retailers. Education and incentive need to be used every step of the way to encourage movement along the supply chain. Companies such as Heinz develop comprehensive themes that begin with their customers and carry through to consumers. Many times, manufacturers consider the distributor as the customer, and don't even try to reach the end user. Without a total plan, such an approach can create a very disjointed brand image, especially when most distributors or wholesalers don't have the resources or communication skills to develop a cohesive campaign.

Volkswagen developed an innovative campaign to encourage their dealers and customers to use genuine VW parts. The direct mail puzzle kit included one piece that changed everything. In this case, a pin instead of a contact lens. The completed puzzle can then be framed and displayed to make the point.

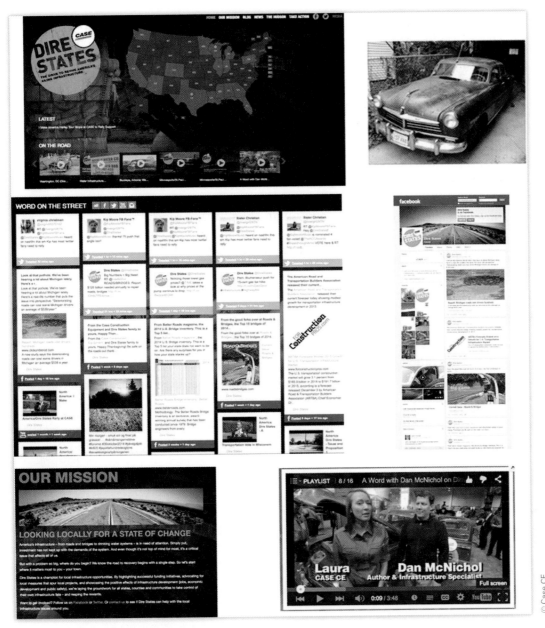

CASE construction equipment developed a coast-to-coast public advocacy campaign to draw attention to infrastructure problems. Using a very robust website, public meetings, trade show appearances, earned media coverage, and social media, the award-winning "Dire States" campaign not only raised awareness of the problem, but also created a lot of good will for the CASE brand.

Digital Tools for B2B

Many B2B clients adopted the Internet long before consumer brands. Email, banner ads, and text links encourage customers to respond. Incentives, special offers, discounts, and other sales promotion tools facilitate the pulling through the next stage of the pipeline. Whether it's used strictly for information or for direct selling, the Internet provides B2B marketers with tremendous advantages over "traditional" media, including the following:

- Provides more detailed information that you can't fit into an ad.

- Shows streaming video, animation, and interactive media.

- When used as part of an integrated personalized direct mail program using PURLs, it can build customer relationships faster than with traditional methods.

- Includes links to co-op partners and/or affiliated companies.

- Provides updated product information such as spec sheets, catalogs, parts forms, and troubleshooting guides that can be downloaded.

- Delivers company news; announces new promotions and special offers.

- Sets up merchant accounts for direct sales.

- Identifies dealers, shows their locations, and provides links to their sites.

- Tracks inquiries, builds databases, and establishes customer relationship management (CRM) programs.

B2B specialist Holger Schulze compared traditional marketing practices with the new world of marketing communications today. We've adapted some of his thoughts in Table 15.1.

The table shows a direction, not a destination, for B2B marketers. While few companies embrace all these trends, we are moving away from the old "spray and pray" approach—throw as much stuff out there as we can afford and hope someone gets the message. Marketers who take advantage of new technology will forge stronger, more personal relationships with customers with measureable results.

When building a B2B site, don't forget the three things you need to accomplish—get them to come, get them to stay, and get them to come back. When you want to drive customers to your site, trade ads,

How do you make ketchup green? A few years ago, Heinz announced that they were changing from plastic to plant-based packaging. They wanted restaurants to plant the new bottles on the tables. Then they asked consumers to check out the new packaging with an online contest to win a Prius.

Tradespeople are only as good as their tools, including the trucks that carry those tools.

direct mail, articles in trade publications, banner ads on other sites, and all the other tactics used in business-to-consumer (B2C) marketing apply. As far as keeping them there, the focus should be on education, motivation, and generating action, not entertainment. Even if viewers feel like playing games, watching videos, and reading blogs, chances are their bosses would rather see them downloading specs, comparing prices, and saving time on the web. When you want to get them to come back, it's the same as with consumer sites—keep the content fresh and let them know you have a new product or service worth checking out. Businesspeople are looking for updated sites that offer a wide range of web-based tools for sales leads, direct mail marketing, telemarketing, and CRM.

Online Events

Online events, sometimes called virtual events or online trade shows, allow companies to produce and host highly interactive experiences. Online events targeted to a specific audience provide an excellent opportunity to showcase a product line, build brand reputation, provide content, and connect with prospects and customers. For example, a company that provides continuing medical education can provide online courses and testing programs. A manufacturer with a new plant in Mexico can't bring customers to their facility, but they can provide a virtual plant tour online. Another company can do a podcast of speeches at their annual shareholder meeting. The possibilities are limited only by bandwidth and imagination.

B2B and Social Media

Many B2B clients were slow to embrace social media, and too many still consider it a sideline activity. As with B2C marketers, the biggest challenges are (a) understanding the potential of social media for business and (b) committing the personnel and time to make it work.

	Traditional Marketing	Marketing Today and Tomorrow
Balance of Power	Vendor	Buyer
Engagement Model	Vendor push (outbound)	Buyer pull (inbound)
Audience Focus	Broad	Focused (personalized)
Message Focus	Product (features)	Solutions delivering value
Presence	Physical (trade show, mail, ads)	Digital (web, social, email)
Management Focus	Activity/ budget impact (anecdotal)	Outcome/revenue impact (metrics)
Marketing Skill Focus	Creative	Analytical
Planning Horizon	Long term, rigid	Short term, flexible
Process Execution	Manual	Automated

Table 15.1 Traditional Versus Current and Future B2B Marketing Communications

Source: "B2B Marketing 2.0."[6] Courtesy of Temo Xopin

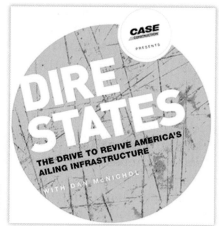
© Case CE

CASE is one of the world's leading manufacturers of construction equipment—excavators, dozers, motor graders, skid steers, wheel loaders—just about everything used to build and repair roads, bridges, and water utilities. CASE has a long-standing history of customer advocacy in the market and understands what really drives our customers' business. However, as a soft-spoken and modest Midwest brand, our actions speak louder than we do. We weren't getting any visibility to that investment and sweat equity, so we designed a program around what we inherently do anyway. We called it Dire States.

America's infrastructure is in terrible shape. Roads, bridges, and water systems from coast to coast are failing. We developed Dire States to shine a light on the problem. The program hit the road with noted author and infrastructure advocate Dan McNichol, who drove around the country in "Mrs. Martin," a rather dilapidated 1949 Hudson, to dramatize the deterioration of our infrastructure.

What began as an awareness campaign quickly shifted to advocacy as CASE/Dire States became actively involved in supporting local- and state-level infrastructure initiatives. This included a constitutional amendment in Wisconsin (passed by a margin of 80% to 20%), as well as a support and analysis of transportation funding in Pennsylvania. In Texas, CASE along with a local equipment dealer and advocacy groups promoted a statewide ballot initiative to fund road and bridge projects without raising taxes. It was approved by 80% of the voters.

The Texas program alone used the following integrated marketing communication tools:

- Articles published online on the *Wall Street Journal*, Politico, and Yahoo Finance sites.

- Electronic billboards in Times Square in New York City.

- Releases published by wire to more than 500 sites, generating over 200 million impressions.

- Ads in Dallas and Houston newspapers and trade publications. Ads featured the local equipment dealer and had QR codes to direct readers to specific Dire States content.

- More than 60 confirmed placements in critical trade publications and local media outlets.

- An op-ed piece in a prominent trade publication.

- Continuous support through social media channels, including a video published online and shared with media outlets.

- Web banner brand ads to congratulate the state for passing the proposition.

Dire States has proved to be a win-win proposition for all concerned. We've helped influence voters to upgrade infrastructure in their states and created a significant boost in brand consideration for CASE. But what good is that coverage—and why would an equipment manufacturer participate in thought leadership activities? The ultimate answer is sales. Within weeks of the initiative passing in Texas, our dealer sold three pieces of CASE equipment to a contractor whose relationship with the dealer was bolstered by the Dire States activities. Additional rental contracts and equipment quotes came in and, as the full effect of the legislation came into effect, CASE stands to benefit from the increased amount of roadwork performed. Altogether, based on current sales and rental contracts, the program in Texas has more than paid for itself and has established CASE as the thought leader in infrastructure discussions nationwide.

The Dire States campaign not only achieved success in thought leadership and sales, but also won the top PR campaign award from the Business Marketing Association. We appreciate the recognition, but I wasn't out to win marketing awards. The objective was to give back to our community and build trust in the brand.[7]

Athena Campos, senior director of marketing, CASE Construction Equipment, Racine, Wisconsin

Many companies use social media as a means of handling customer complaints. As long as unhappy customers are willing to vent on Facebook or Twitter, the companies feel they need to address the problem, calm down the complainers, and let the rest of the world know they are concerned. To do that effectively, a company needs to react quickly and take the right tone. That kind of instant, online customer service is certainly important, but it barely scratches the surface of social media's potential for B2B marketers. Content marketing is a perfect match for most B2B clients. Their customers are hungy for information, but not necessarily ready to read or hear a sales pitch. Some of the most common content in B2B landing pages, microsites, blogs, and social media marketing includes:

- Photos
- Videos
- Webinars
- Infographics
- Presentatipns
- White papers
- Case studies
- E-newsletters
- Research reports

The customer profile, product and content dictate which social networking platform to use. Table 15.2 summarizes the best way to use each one.

Companies are getting smarter about using social media as a proactive marketing tool to generate leads and build customer relationships. For example, American Express has been making a big push into the digital and social space, as they realized that the badge value of their card is disappearing in a swipeless world—even the Platinum and Centurion cards. OPEN, American Express's small business-focused division, partnered with Facebook to allow small business owners to use their Membership Rewards points to buy Facebook ads. Simple, social, very smart.

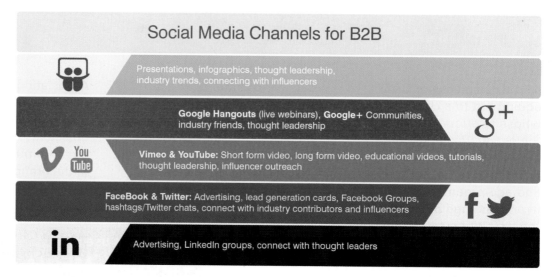

Table 15.2   Social Media Channels for B2B Marketing[8]

Source: Courtesy of Temo Xopin

© American Express

The American Express OPEN campaign encourages entrepreneurs to "Start Booming" in a partnership that offers free Facebook ads for Membership Rewards points. Amex also uses native advertising in a Mashable article about how small businesses can keep employees happy.

Cisco skipped the traditional launch plan and unveiled their ASR router entirely online. By leveraging social media, they could engage network engineers in a more interactive, fun way. Cisco met its audience where they were—in online venues and the gaming world. They unpacked the whole digital toolbox to include a Second Life virtual stage with musical groups and product information, a 3D game with prizes up to $10,000, a YouTube channel, video conferencing events, mobile apps, Facebook page, blogs, an online forum, and a social media widget to make it easier to share. Results: More than 9,000 people from 128 countries attended virtual launch events. That's 90 times more than past launches. Print advertising costs were replaced with nearly 3 times as many press articles and more than 1,000 blog posts and 40 million online impressions. Best of all, the whole launch cost one sixth of a similar launch using traditional methods, saving Cisco over $100,000.[9]

Advertising Creative

The Changing Face of B2B

Advertising Age interviewed leading marketers and agency execs to offer some predictions and challenges facing B2B marketers. Data and automated messaging are hot topics, but B2B marketers say their marketing must get more personal.[10] Here's a summary of some of the major trends they identified.

- **Less data, more emotions:** "We have found through our research . . . that decision-makers are increasingly looking to their gut instead of the data," said Christopher Becker, CEO and chief creative officer at B2B agency Gyro. "B-to-b marketing must become more humanly relevant."

- **Shareable content:** "Marketers are going to continue to lean into creating shareable content through digital and social channels," said John Kennedy, chief marketing officer (CMO) at Xerox. "Where teams are doing really great work is in creating really good video content that explains a complicated topic in a compelling way."

- **Holistic user experiences:** "Marketing will focus on the user experience. It will be a mission between marketing, the CIO and the CTO of the company, looking holistically at the user experience," said Eduardo Conrado, senior VP of marketing and IT at Motorola Solutions.

- **Consumerization:** "We need to realize that b-to-b customers are people. They go home and watch 'American Idol' and they sit in traffic on the way to work," said Adam Kleinberg, CEO of online agency Traction. "They have the same humanity and cultural insights you see in consumer work."

- **Reprioritizing marketing:** "One of the biggest things is a reprioritization of marketing within companies, particularly in b-to-b industrial companies, as they realize the business pressures have changed, especially with digitization," said Kathy Button Bell, CMO at Emerson. "You have to set up both worlds—online and offline—completely in parallel. Ninety-seven percent of marketing people are doing new types of work."

- **Connecting technologies:** "Right now there are a lot of unconnected technologies—everything from data management to predictive analytics. The next big leap is for us to connect all the relevant technologies in the interest of the customer experience and the customer journey," said Tom Stein, CEO of B2B agency Stein IAS Americas.[11]

Business use of
SOCIAL MEDIA

Limitations to using social media for business:

 50% Difficulty proving ROI

 33% Lack of time

 32% Little strategy planning

 23% Poor understanding of social media

 21% Insufficient audience

Top sites for business:

f	89%	g+	59%
Twitter	89%	YouTube	52%
in	88%	Pinterest	41%
B	65%	Instagram	19%

Source: ber-art.nl, 2015

The lines between B2B and B2C continue to blur as original equipment manufacturers, dealers, and consumers have access to online content and social media. This campaign about Briggs & Stratton lawnmower engines engaged the companies that buy the engines for their products, the dealers that sell and service lawnmowers, and consumers who buy them. The sales promotion asked people to provide videos of their lawnmower impressions. The winner, selected on social media, received a lawnmower and $5,000.

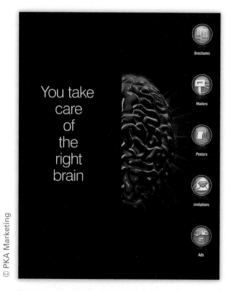

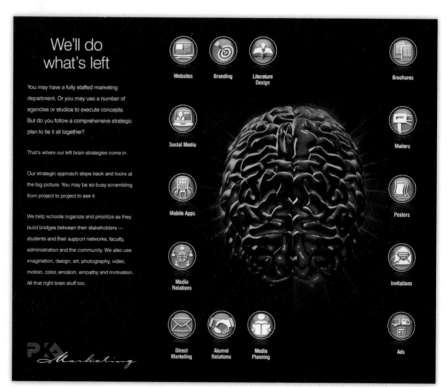

New business is the lifeblood of advertising agencies. This brochure was aimed at higher education institutions looking for added marketing horsepower for their in-house departments.

Courtesy of Peter Wagoner

I start every new business meeting the same way. Automotive, fashion, tech companies—they all hear the same thing. The title of "copywriter" is wrong. Because writing is only about 10% of what I do. Sometimes less.

My real job is to listen.

To find the truth of the brand—the stuff that keeps their most passionate advocates coming back—and make that truth relevant to a greater number of people.

That's really it. Find the brand truth. Find the human truth. Then find a way to connect the two. At my company there is an implied fourth step of "using a new technology." But that's lower on the totem pole.

Take Harley-Davidson, for example. I was talking to a rider when he mentioned that his bike had recently broken down on the side of the road. "Aw man, that sucks," I told him. And he said, "No, not really." He explained to me that a broken-down bike almost always leads to a great day. Because eventually someone will stop to help, and chances are, you're going to meet a really awesome person. Because—and I'll never forgot how he put this— "assholes don't stop."

That led to a real truth of the brand (for our particular segment). It's more about the people than about the bikes. Sure, we could have read that on a brief somewhere. But it wasn't until the biker was encouraged to go off topic that we saw the real passion behind the truth.

So it's a copywriter's job to be curious.

People like to think this mind-set only applies to fun, consumer-facing brands. Good! Let them think that. Don't correct them. This is how you're going to pass them: by realizing the person in the corner office is—and I know this is controversial—a person. A person who cares about things. A person who loves to be amazed by things. And a person with a unique set of goals, hopes, and dreams outside of the KPI spreadsheet saved on a desktop.

The moment you realize your B2B consumers are also B2C consumers, everything changes. Talk to them differently, and they'll respond differently. Find their truth and work backward from there.

I'm going to leave you with one last thought. If you want to succeed in advertising, become a professional at finding things interesting. The construction of your backpack, the joke your friend told, the crunch of your cereal. Find a reason to think everything around you is interesting. And once you find it—reverse engineer it. Figure out what made it so compelling, you can apply that same logic to your next project. It'll help you with your work. And it'll also make life a whole lot more, well, interesting.

Peter Wagoner, senior copywriter, SapientNitro

@peterjwagoner

Chapter 15 *Business-to-Business* 391

Chapter 15

Reid Hoffman

Reid Hoffman is best known as the founder of LinkedIn, a social network used primarily for business connections and job searching. Hoffman was instrumental in the creation of PayPal before he went on to found LinkedIn. He has cowritten *The Start-Up of You: Adapt to the Future, Invest in Yourself, and Transform Your Career*. He serves on the boards of Do Something (an organization for young people taking action), Mozilla (creator of Firefox), and Endeavor Global (an international nonprofit development organization that finds and supports high-impact entrepreneurs in emerging markets).

Harry Jacobs

Harry Jacobs exploded the myth that great advertising could only be done in New York. Under Jacobs's leadership, the Martin Agency in Charlotte, Virginia, became a creative powerhouse for consumer as well as agricultural and other B2B products. Today, the agency works on national and international accounts such as Coke, Hanes, Mercedes-Benz, Seiko, UPS, and Wrangler, to name a few. The Martin Agency has also been an incubator for the nation's top creative talent, developing creative directors who achieved acclaim at Wieden + Kennedy, Wells Rich Greene, Fallon, DDB, and Chiat\Day. Upon retirement from the Martin Agency, Jacobs was a founding board member of one of the top creative schools in the country, the Adcenter at Virginia Commonwealth University.

Asha Sharma

At only 26, Asha Sharma has risen to become the chief operating officer of Porch.com and was named one of *Forbes* magazine's "30 Under 30" for 2015. Asha helped build Porch from the ground up, working closely with CEO Matt Ehrlichman to develop the brand, build revenue streams, expand products, and recruit talent. She was the key player in financing a partnership with Lowe's.[12] Prior to joining Porch, Asha worked at Microsoft, Deloitte Consulting, Cargill, and SC Johnson & Son. Along the way Asha founded two companies, one recognized by President Obama in 2012. Asha attributes her success to learning from the talented people and being a relentless but realistic leader.[13]

Lawdan Shojaee

Shojaee, CEO of Axosoft, launched the "It Was Never a Dress" campaign to shift perceptions and assumptions about women; to show the sensitive and powerful gestures women make every day; and to invite women into places where they are often overlooked, or dismissed. Since the campaign launched, Axosoft's hashtag #itwasneveradress has received nearly 18 million impressions. Shojaee also connected her launch directly to the Girls in Tech conference. Ultimately, the "It Was Never a Dress" campaign could drive software sales for Axosoft. But Shojaee is banking on the next generation, who feel empowered by this campaign, to reach out to Axosoft the next time they need a project management tool.[14]

Saving the Advertising Account

For the past ten years, MKE Advertising had a long-standing and strong relationship with Winning Sports Retail Centers. Winning Sports is a regional goods retailer based in Chicago, with over 150 corporate-owned locations across the Midwest. Winning Sports started with a single location in a Chicago suburb in 1976 and within five years expanded to ten locations across Illinois and Wisconsin. From 1981 to 2008, Winning Sports added several locations each year and expanded their geographic footprint to include Minnesota, Iowa, Michigan, Indiana, Ohio, and Missouri.

Winning Sports is one of MKE's largest fully integrated accounts and a marquee client that helped them attract new clients over the years. Winning Sports' total advertising spend is $20 million per year, which includes traditional advertising (TV, radio, and print), digital advertising, social media, brand planning, research, point-of-purchase (POP), media planning, and buying. Sales at Winning Sports have been flat the past few years due to the economy and competition.

MKE Advertising received a call they were not expecting—a new chief marketing officer (CMO) had been hired at Winning Sports, and the account was put up for review. MKE Advertising has been invited to participate in the review, along with three top advertising competitors, all with retail marketing and advertising experience. The CMO cited that while MKE Advertising has been a great partner over the years, they are looking for fresh ideas to drive growth and expand the Winning Sports strategic footprint. The CMO also indicated that Winning Sports has lost touch with their customers and wants to relaunch their brand to attract new customers.

Winning Sports has given all agencies only four weeks to conduct research, develop their strategy,

Ryan Zaar, vice president, marketing program manager, HSA Bank, a Division of Webster Bank, N.A.

and present a fully integrated print, digital, and POP plan. MKE Advertising has their work cut out for them; while they have had the business for ten years, they now need to reevaluate their existing strategy, conduct research at their expense, and present a fully integrated plan in only a month. MKE also knows that when an advertising account is put up for review, only 25% of agencies retain the business, and clients often want a new agency to bring a fresh perspective.

1 As the incumbent advertising agency, you have a decision to either participate in the review or decline participating. What are the pros and cons of both decisions?

2 Conducting research is vital to better understanding the brand, competition, and customers. What are qualitative and quantitative research methods that you would recommend conducting? Provide a few examples of the research you would conduct.

3 MKE Advertising needs to conduct a competitive audit of the top competitors of Winning Sports. There are three main competitors; what type of information would you need to collect in order to better understand the competitive landscape and how to better position Winning Sports?

4 Winning Sports is looking for fresh ideas beyond traditional advertising, and they do a poor job with their Facebook and Twitter accounts. As the agency, what are possible ways that social media could be used for research, but more important, as part of the overall strategy to reposition the brand and add customers?

1. Spinning B2C to B2B

This exercise is all about finding the One Thing and linking B2C to B2B strategy.

- Find several campaigns for major consumer packaged good or service brands with at least three ads. Online options, such as adsoftheworld.com, are great because you can download the ads.

- As a class, select one campaign for which the brand would have strong B2B opportunities.

- Write a Copy Platform or Creative Brief, based on the concept in the B2C ads. The trick is to make the strategy, evolving out of the B2C ads, equally relevant to B2B consumers. End with one sentence describing the overarching concept in the campaign—the One Thing.

- Now concept an ad that is consistent with the brand, but solves the problem of moving the brand through the B2B marketplace.

- Present your ad, sharing your rationale. It's great way to see a wide range of strategic interpretations.

2. Who's Your Target?

This is a great exercise to show how brand messaging shifts depending upon the audience.

- *Instructors:* Pick a classic service brand such as FedEx. Before class, write a Positioning Statement and provide a short list of features and services.

- *Instructors:* Before class, go to the library and pick up as many B2B publications as you have students. Get obscure pubs like *Pulp & Paper* or *Curator: The Museum Journal*. Pull from the broadest range possible. Slip each publication into its own envelope.

- *Instructors:* Introduce the brand and the strategic information. Tell the students that they will each be writing a print ad, with 150 to 200 words, to run in a B2B publication.

- *Students:* Randomly select an envelope. The publication inside represents the target audience you are to reach, pitching FedEx's services. The ad will run in the same magazine.

- *Students:* Once the ads are complete, execute one other strategically conceived tactic based on what you learned about that industry.

- *Students:* Once both pieces are complete, present your work. You will be amazed at how different each approach will be, thus demonstrating the importance of understanding your B2B audience—any audience for that matter.

3. Let's Talk Business

Every day, students are surrounded by B2C ads. But what do you know about reaching the B2B target? Sometimes not enough. It's time to find out more about this demographic.

- Pick a national brand that is commonly carried at Walgreens, CVS, or another similar retailer.

- Do a SWOT (strengths, weaknesses, opportunities, threats) analysis of that brand. Then, as a class, and using your SWOTs, craft four questions that could help you understand the strengths, weaknesses, opportunities, and threats from the retailer's point of view.

- Next, go to the retail site and ask the manager the four questions.

- Bring the answers back to class and share them. As a class, look for patterns and insights.

- Taking what you have learned, create a promotion that will reignite retail engagement with the brand, while addressing the strengths, weaknesses, opportunities, and threats that you explored.

Review chapter content and study for exams. http://study.sagepub.com/altstiel4e.

- Interactive practice quizzes
- Mobile-friendly eFlashcards
- Carefully selected chapter-by-chapter video and multimedia content

Chapter 16

Survival Guide
Landing Your First Job and Thriving

We designed this book to help you develop better creative work. Now we'd like to share some of our personal insights about how to break into the business and thrive. We feature inspiring work by students and rising stars. We've also gathered some gems from some of the top names in our business, our fellow teachers, and creative recruiters to help you survive and thrive in the creative jungle. Gary Goldsmith, a former chief creative officer at Lowe New York, sums it up nicely: "They [students] are entering a business where the staffing is leaner and deadlines shorter than ever before. A business that has less and less time for the necessary teaching and mentoring that is required more than ever before."[1]

Three Ingredients for Success

Three ingredients are critical for a successful career in advertising creative. Talent. Persistence. Luck. Talent is essential. Persistence is crucial. Luck is the bonus you earn. So start laying the groundwork to get lucky and come out ahead of all the persistent people who are just as talented as you are. In the meantime, fake it till you are it.

Building Your Portfolio

The time to start preparing for this business is now. Take the advice of Joyce King Thomas, president and chief creative officer at McCann New York: "Show your book every 6 months and never stop working on it."[3] How many items should be in your portfolio? Every creative director may have a different answer. The bottom line—it's about turning insights into ideas and being able to walk someone through your work. The following is a compilation from dozens of creative professionals to help you craft a stellar portfolio—one that opens doors.

Inside a Junior Copywriter's Portfolio

- **Ideas. Ideas. Ideas.** This is the place to show that you can generate ideas that are transferable to brands, that are relevant to consumers, and which can live across multiple touchpoints.

- **Hard assignments** like consumer packaged goods where the only real difference is the quality of the advertising. As one creative director said, "Show me something I never would have thought of." Make yourself an asset that their agency can't live without.

- **Print ads** that clearly show concepting ability and always show a series. Demonstrate that you can extend your ideas. Have at least one or two ads for difficult categories, like life insurance or financial services.

- **Side projects:** Who are you outside of advertising? Show them what makes you tick. Be loud. Do something fun, crazy, and maybe even get famous in the process.

- **Billboards** or **posters** that demonstrate exceptional creative and strategic thinking.

- **Long-copy ads** or **brochures** that show you actually can write copy.

- **Radio:** It's a true copywriter's medium. (No art directors to mess it up!) If you can write good radio scripts, you can basically write anything. Have a couple of scripts that are strong conceptually, simple, and written to fit either a 30- or a 60-second format.

"Embrace your competitive advantage and believe in yourself. When someone asks you where you want to be in five years—reach for the stars, not the next level."[2]

Annette Fonte,
senior vice president, group
account director, Lapiz

Lapiz, a Hispanic agency in Chicago, uses posters to spur on their teams. Their message is wise. Remember it.

Breathe the fragrances of Catalonia

© Parés Baltà Winery

Pares Balta, a Spanish vineyard trying to break into the Italian market, was the perfect challenge for students in a cross-cultural summer creative program at Universitat Autònoma de Barcelona. Spanish creatives and a lone American teamed up to energize a group of Italian students. The result: great sensory-based advertising.

- **Websites** or **blogs** of substance. Show them you can write and maintain consistency across time and space. The design and content of your online portfolio is the best demonstration of your understanding of digital marketing.

- **Mobile** and **social** that show your ability to write tight. Demonstrate that you can think about how to reach consumers anytime and anyplace.

- **Complete campaigns** from multiple product categories with a combination of print and outdoor to show a snapshot of your thinking; nontraditional and social to demonstrate integration; TV and radio to show you can write; and websites and blogs to show that your writing transfers across media.

- *Overall*, demonstrate that you are **great** at concepts and trainable as a writer, and be ready to explain the strategy behind every piece in your book. You will not be hired for your expertise in English composition or your extensive vocabulary. In the end, it all comes back to ideas.

Inside a Junior Art Director's or Designer's Portfolio

- **Ideas. Ideas. Ideas.** In this sense art directors are no different from copywriters. As we said above, this is the place to show that you can generate ideas that are transferable to brands, that are relevant to consumers, and which can live across multiple touchpoints. Make yourself an asset that their agency can't live without.

- **Logos** and **brand identity projects**, including several examples across different product categories, from consumer packaged goods to service brands.

- **Print ads** that clearly show concepting ability and always show a series of at least three. The point here is to demonstrate that your ideas have legs.

- **Billboards** or **posters** that demonstrate exceptional creative and strategic thinking.

- **Nontraditional** to show that you can think conceptually and maximize every dollar. This is also a great place to show how far your creative thinking can go. Push the boundaries.

- **Websites, blogs,** and **apps**—anything that allows you to show that your ideas are transferable. Plus, these will demonstrate that you have command of a broad range of software. Your online portfolio is the best indication of your digital design expertise.

- **Brochures** or other **collateral** pieces that show that you actually can lay out different kinds of marketing tools. The ability to do collateral work will increase your value.

- **Complete campaigns** from multiple product categories with a combination of print and outdoor to show a snapshot of your conceptual thinking; nontraditional and social to demonstrate you understand integration; and websites and blogs to show that your design concepts transfers across media.

- *Overall*, demonstrate that you have **good design sense** and superior concepting ability, you know design software, and you can be trained to create great-looking stuff. It all comes back to ideas.

What Not to Put in Your Portfolio

- **Anything that is predictable**, such as ads for hot sauce, condoms, and animal shelters. If the product calls for an obvious approach, don't bother putting it in your book.

- **Traditional public service ads.** We all know the dangers of texting while driving, drunk driving, smoking, breast cancer, gambling, pollution, and drug addiction. It's all been done before and probably better than anything you can think of.

"If your book is terrible, you won't get much criticism. Most people just don't have the stomach to tell a bright-eyed young thing to get into a different line of work."[5]

Maxine Paetro,
copywriter and
best-selling author

© Peter Wagoner

It's amazing how rich a portfolio can become after a few years on the job. This one showcases the best current work and includes some "Big Weird Ideas" that might never get produced; and for old time's sake, an infographic résumé that helped him land his current job.

- **Brands with well-known advertising.** Do you really think you can do better creative than RG/A and its Clio Award–winning work for Converse; or Wieden + Kennedy and its killer Nike or Coca-Cola work; or Droga5 and its powerful public awareness campaigns for UNICEF's Tap Project? Use this work to inspire your work, not to tank your interview.

- **Go light on radio**, and probably skip TV. You don't be working on that for a while.

- **Creative Briefs**, Creative Strategy Statements, and Consumer Profiles. It's assumed you know this. That said, be ready to verbally demonstrate your strategic brilliance.

- **Sentimental favorites.** Don't include a sample just because your ad ran in the school paper or your ad club used your poster design, unless it's killer work. A good concept that never saw the light of day is a much better option.

- **Too much stuff.** Half a dozen great samples are better than 20 mediocre ones. Interviewers don't have a lot of time. Besides, they can spot great ideas instantly. The old adage "less is more" applies here.

Maxine Paetro has written the ultimate book on portfolios—How to Put Your Book Together and Get a Job in Advertising. It's chock full of great advice from the author and some of the top names in the creative field. One of her portfolio strategies is to build a "killer sandwich." We've taken that basic idea and come up with our own recipe for online and paper portfolios:

- First thing—the very best piece you've ever done. If you could put only one thing in the book, this would be it.

- Last thing—the second best thing you've ever done. Something so good it took a coin toss to move it to the back.

- Everything in between—first, think "campaigns" and be sure most of them have a nontraditional and digital executions. Then have examples across multiple product categories. You don't need a lot, but all of it needs to kick butt.

Why put the best at the beginning and end? Psychologists say people remember the first and last things they see.

© Emma Kolb

The student who created this billboard tweeted about it. That night she got a retweet from Rishi Tea. The next day Rishi asked to run it and offered her an internship. Liquid Zen, indeed.

6 steps to
PERSONAL BRANDING

1 **Do a personal SWOT analysis.**
You must be brutally honest.

You're 1 in a Million.
That means there are 7000 people in the world just like you.

2 **Get to work.**
Start building your ideas. Generate campaigns, creative ads, great content, and cool graphics. Do more than you think you'll ever need.

3 **Build your network.**
Not just your online networks. Join clubs. Leverage contacts. Arrange informational interviews. The more people you know, the stronger your personal brand.

5 **Develop your personal skills.**
Learn when to lead AND how to be a good team player. The "get along" factor is as important as your talent and expertise.

4 **Learn how to present.**
One-on-one, small groups, large groups. It builds confidence and separates you from the pack.

6 **Create an online presence.**
99% of your first impressions will be before anyone meets you. Your talent, skills and personality should build your brand.

99%

Source: TbA Marketing Group

Formatting Your Book

If you can actually show your work in a one-on-one meeting, a small minibook might be impressive, and you can leave it behind. You can also customize it for each interview. You can easily have this printed and bound at an office supply store or through an online service like Shutterfly or Vistaprint.

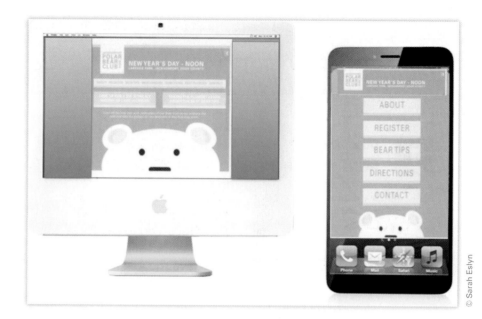

You simply won't get a job with just a print-based portfolio. This student's simple responsive desktop and mobile design shows she understands the importance of a strong idea and continuity across platforms.

However, most recruiters prefer electronic. Your online profile is your most valuable asset—the most important indication that you understand digital marketing. Start your blog or website at least two years before you intend to graduate, and keep it fresh. Make it a showcase for your best pieces and use it as a platform to demonstrate your personality and your creative thinking. You can also post your work on sites dedicated to showing student work. Remember, they are not only hiring based on your work, but they also want to know if you'll fit in. If you can segment your work into categories, you have the opportunity to show more variety—for example, your best six print ads, brochures, billboards, social, guerrilla concepts, at least two complete campaigns. If you want to really show capability, include business-to-business and something other than the typical public service clients. Campaigns with a Corporate Social Responsibility (CSR) twist are hot right now, especially with brands that you would not expect to use CSR tactics. And, that angle is winning a lot of Lions as Cannes. Keep mixing it up to bring in new stuff and weed out older and less than perfect work.

You can also email samples of your work by attaching JPEGs or building an instant-loading HTML email page. But we don't recommend this unless the recruiter or human resources people request it. Chances are it will end up in the junk mail folder.

Everything you've ever posted professionally or personally lives forever. So if there's anything online that you wouldn't want your grandmother to see, you might have a problem. Grandma may forgive you, but future employers won't. So keep your social media identity creative, but clean. Every word that flies off your fingertips and every image you post really does matter.

Now that we've spent some time on the nuts and bolts of your portfolio, we'd like to introduce you to the human aspects of the job hunt—your cover letter, résumé, and references.

Reaching Out

Crafting Your Résumé

Most creative directors or others who hire creative people demand résumés from applicants. Too many aspiring creatives assume that this is the time to demonstrate all the creativity they can muster.

Starting Human

© Lauren Habermehl

"When I was 7 years old, I fell out of a tree house and knocked out most of my top teeth. I've cycled through Africa top to bottom—more than once. I shook hands with Leonard Cohen." The letter went on for two more pages, beautifully written, skillfully typeset, ending with the words "Here's where you can find me." And a phone number. I called immediately.

This is one of the most memorable job applications I've ever received. It was from a very experienced art director looking for a new gig. I'd never met him, but I felt like I knew him. It's impossible to put a price on that.

Most job-hunting ad people send portfolios or links and think that's all they have to do—that the work is enough. But there's an entire zombie apocalypse worth of student talent in the world competing for creative director attention, so distinguishing

yourself can require more than a letter of recommendation from your teacher and a bunch of clever ideas. To this end, I've received charmingly packaged baked goods, boxes of candy, a Japanese bowl, even a bar of Dove soap with the word *Dove* recarved to say Dave, but the ones that stuck were those that gave me insight into the creators. Like the writer whose book wasn't ready when we needed to see it, so he filled the blank spaces with highly entertaining yellow Post-it notes telling us about the campaigns that would've been included if we'd given him more time. Or the young art director who designed a beautiful broadsheet with 12 images and 12 three-line stories about himself, including that he'd run away from home at 15 to compete in the World Roller Blading Championships. Or the girl just out of school who wrote Nancy and me a song, sat on a tall stool in her driveway, and had her Dad film her playing the guitar, singing it. Could've been utterly cringe-worthy, but it was funny, quirky, clever, and authentically her. We hired each of these people. Their books were very good, but we saw a lot of good books. What we seldom saw was real people who made themselves unforgettable.

So what can you do to make sure you exist for those bosses-to-be? First off, it's tough to know what creative directors are looking for these days, so I'll share what some of them

have told me: writers who edit, do layouts, understand type, and shoot film; art directors who write, shoot, and design; both of whom understand digital and social; digital people who write headlines, get brands, and know social; social people who . . . well, you get my drift. Oh, and who can take advantage of what each platform offers and know how it all works together. Oh, and who are passionate, flexible, open-minded, and experimental. Oh, and . . . and . . . and . . . . Oh, and they're more likely to roll the dice on someone who gets under their skin. That last wasn't a throwaway line. In all the pressure to build the book that outshines every other, it's easy to forget that people hire people, not merely "talent."

The key to the job you want might be . . . you. Yes, you. So, don't come in as just an "ad person." Are you a filmmaker? A stand-up comic? A knitter, blogger, fire-eater? All of the above? Bring it. Give them a reason to know you, not just your work. Human wins in the digital world.[6]

Janet Kestin, partner and cofounder of Swim, a creative leadership lab, along with Nancy Vonk. She and Nancy were the longtime chief creative officers at Ogilvy & Mather, Toronto.

So they put their names on bowling balls, bananas, toilet paper rolls, and other useless objects, in the hope that their unique résumé packages will pull them out of the pack. The truth is, no one wants to file a bowling ball, keep a banana in a drawer, or forward toilet paper to human resources. As cute as these gimmicks are, they usually won't help and, in most cases, will put you at the bottom of the pile. Write a rock star cover letter, provide a clean résumé, and let your creative work speak for itself.

Here's what the vast majority of creative executives who hire entry-level writers and art directors are looking for in a résumé. And remember, your LinkedIn profile is your public résumé.

- Keep it clean, easy to read, and simply designed. Remember, the résumé is for identifying you. The portfolio and cover letter are where you can leap to the head of the line.

- Your name, address, phone number(s), and email address are always at the top.

- Include your education, where you went to school, your major, software skills, relevant courses, or special programs such as study abroad. Your GPA doesn't matter—really.

- Sorry to tell you, but fraternity or sorority membership and athletic achievements aren't likely to wow them. So only add them if you have room on one page.

- What will wow them, beyond internships, is community service that leveraged your talents, along with funky ways you used creativity to give back to your community or advance causes.

- No selfies. No typos. No poor grammar. No references.

- Demonstrating that you have insight is key. Don't give a laundry list of tasks. Show them what you've learned. Here are a few examples from students who turned boring tasks into passionate *insights*—and landed jobs.

University Tour Guide

- Brand ambassador for Marquette University (task).
- *Learned how to read people* (insight).

Art Club Executive Director

- Organized and promoted Student Fine Art Night at the Haggerty Art Museum (task).
- *Recognized that creativity takes courage* (insight).

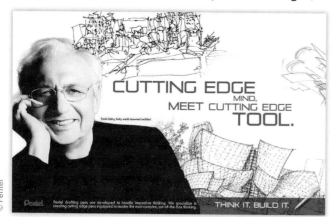

This aspiring art director used great creative thinkers from across the globe as the link between Pentel and consumers. She's now at Miami Ad School building a killer portfolio.

Art Museum Media Relations Intern

- Compiled media lists, wrote press releases, tracked publicity, and pitched exhibitions (tasks).
- *Fell in love with Chihuly, Picasso, Kandinsky and Calatrava on lunch breaks* (insight).

Writing Your Cover Letter

Your résumé tells the basic facts of your academic and work career and, as we mentioned, probably should not be the place for wild flights of fancy.

ICY HOT Out of Home
Ointment and Patch Dispensers

Hardware Stores

Fitness Centers

Creating pretty ads is one thing. But taking the brand message to the consumer shows strategic thinking. This student suggested placing dispensers of Icy Hot in home improvement stores and gyms, where people would be thinking about sore muscles.

However, your cover letter can be the one place to demonstrate your writing ability, your creativity, and your willingness to take risks or see the world differently. As with a cover letter for a product or service, you can follow the basic structure we described in Chapter 14. Except *you* are the product. What can you say about yourself that will get attention, stimulate interest, create a desire to know more about you, and ultimately generate action—an interview? One letter for an applicant started with, "I knew I'd be the right person for this job when the toilet fell on my head." That got our attention! The letter went on to describe how an accident at Home Depot convinced the applicant that he should pursue a career in advertising instead of in a big-box store. You can find hundreds of websites that will help you craft a cover letter. Your college career office will also help you with this. Most of them give you a formula for a pure vanilla letter. (Ignore vanilla.) So before you take the easy way out, think about the wants and needs of the customer—your potential employer, likely someone with a creative spirit or at least someone who wants to hire a creative spirit. How do you meet those wants and needs? What do you bring to the table? Then figure out a creative yet professional way to present the features and benefits of the world's most unique product—you.

Landing Your First Job

Agencies are looking for creative, flexible, dedicated people. We gathered a few of our best creative friends together and came up with this a list of core competencies and creative attributes. See how you measure up.

Core Competencies

- Understand agency culture, then nourish it.
- Create value for brands, consumers, and clients alike.
- Be a great listener who is generous and personable with colleagues and clients alike
- Be a student of culture and learn how to find and organize information. Make best friends with an awesome planner.
- Know the software. For art directors it's the Adobe Suite. For copywriters it's Word and Pages. It's Acrobat and Keynote for everyone.

I wrote on everything when I was a kid. Whether it was the bathroom wall or a notebook. Writing is just something I did. After taking a minor detour as a finance major, it's no surprise I ultimately ended up as a copywriter.

After college, I went to the VCU Brandcenter. I spent two years sharpening my pencil and my tongue, pulled countless all-nighters, and ate even more vending machine dinners. Well worth it, though. After graduation I landed a job at Publicis (now Publicis Kaplan Thaler) in New York City.

My first client at Publicis was a financial account with a lot of money and a lot of opportunity. By the end of my three years there, I had written everything from radio to websites. I worked on projects with sponsorships like the Olympics and the New York Mets. And even one with Beyoncé herself.

After Publicis, I went to Code and Theory. It was the polar opposite of Publicis. A small, independent, digital agency. There, I ran several social media accounts and digital campaigns for the likes of Snapple, Crush Soda, Mott's, 7UP, Clarisonic, Essie nail polish, and Maybelline. Being in that world helped me think like a social ninja and made me realize that consumers are now willing to buy brands solely based on their social presence.

My current home is next to the cornhole boards at Cramer Krasselt in Chicago. It's surreal to be working at one of the agencies I idolized when I was in school. Five years in this industry isn't a lot, but it's just as crazy, weird, and awesome as when I started.

Jen Stopka, senior copywriter, Cramer Krasselt (Remember the pile of journals? Thank you, Jen!)

@jenstopka

- Learn basic marketing principles, key advertising terms, and elementary financial literacy.
- Have clear ethical boundaries that you are willing to stand up for.
- Be nice: have confidence without being arrogant.
- Be a team player, and leadership skills will follow.
- Cultivate a strong work ethic.

Creative Attributes

- Be a great storyteller: people are interested in human truths.
- Be innovative: create ideas that live across multiple touchpoints.
- Learn how to marry headlines and graphics to form a single idea.
- Live and work with a digital mind-set, telling stories that cross platforms.
- Create campaigns with elements that work independently and collectively.
- Be able to sell your ideas as a team. Never say "I." Always say "We."

- Be able to come up with big ideas on small budgets.
- Accept criticism and use it to improve.
- Think beyond advertising.
- Never stop learning.

Surviving as a Junior Creative

Okay, you're in. Now the hard part starts. If you're lucky, you've had a few internships. If you're really lucky, you were a sponge and picked up survival tips along the way. Keep in mind that very few advertising new hires get their dream jobs. Dream jobs are earned. Once your find that dream job, remember, 100 other people want it too. You have to keep earning it. Top creatives across the world have a lot to say. Here's some of what we've learned[7]:

Survival Tips for Everyone

- Be brave.
- Be a sponge.
- Have a sense of humor.
- Be a squeaky wheel. Speak up.
- Nothing matters but the quality of your work.
- Be nice to everyone. Advertising's a small industry.
- Don't be arrogant. And don't have an attitude unless it's a good one.

"Each of us must be in continual beta in reinventing ourselves, our skills and approaches."[8]

Donna Speciale,
president, MediaVest

© Annie Pryatel and Donna Chen

This work by students at Brandcenter lays it on the line. Talk about the marriage of copy and visual.

- Do more than you're asked to do. And don't say no to any assignment.
- Keep your eyes on the prize, and you'll always be in demand.
- Be yourself. Don't try to sound like everyone else.
- Ask questions and observe your environment.
- Keep your head down and get the work done.
- Let your work be the great equalizer.
- Learn to present your work.
- Find a mentor.

Selling Your Work

In Chapter 1, we said that one role of a creative is selling ideas. You could opt to just slide your ideas under the client's, or your creative director's, door and run away, hoping he or she will like them. However, in selling your ideas, you're also selling yourself, ensuring gainful employment, and building some very valuable self-esteem. It seems like most people learn to fear public speaking while in kindergarten. Most people, even gifted public speakers, never get over that naked fear of standing in front of an audience. The difference is that gifted public speakers have the ability to channel that fear into positive energy.

At the risk of sounding like an ad for Toastmasters: The ability to present your ideas in public is a skill you'll use all your life, whether you're an advertising executive or just offering a toast at a wedding. While you may dread presenting your work to your peers, your creative director, or the client without solid presentation skills, your best idea will die before it even gets past your creative director.

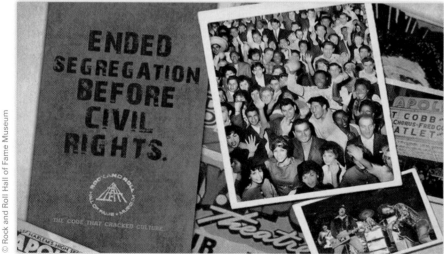

This student work rocks! It challenges us to think about our social and cultural history, while extending the authority of the Rock and Roll Hall of Fame and Museum far beyond its physical local in Cleveland, Ohio.

The germ of an idea can lead to a great concept, as demonstrated this copywriting student.

Here are 10 tips offered to students competing in the National Student Advertising Competition, sponsored each year by the American Advertising Federation. While they apply to a high-level formal new-business pitch, most of the tips work for informal presentations as well.

1. **Start with an idea.** Tell how your idea relates to your strategy and tactical recommendations. Keep using your idea throughout your presentation, and come back to it at the end. Hold onto it and sell it all the way through.

2. **If you have a theme, use it early and often.** Weave it through your presentation. If you use a stunt or a gimmick, make sure it fits. It should complement your theme and recommendations. Don't use a gimmick just to be different; rather, focus on the theme.

3. **Remember, the first minutes of your presentation are critical.** This is when you set the tone of your presentation. The introduction grabs attention. It should instantly engage the audience.

4. **Your insight of the target audience will drive your presentation.** It's very straightforward—who are you talking to, what will you tell them, how will you deliver the message, and how do you know it will work?

5. **Don't memorize.** Know your material and speak from the heart, not from memory. And above all, don't read from note cards. If you need note cards, sneak a peek before you begin speaking. Then trust yourself.

6. **Eye contact is important.** Use "eye bursts," where you look at an individual audience member for two to three seconds at a time. Find the "head nodders" — people who are listening and agreeing with you. (These should be your nonpresenting teammates.) They'll give you confidence.

7. **Aim for a tone that's confident but humble.** In other words, be confident and enthusiastic but also self-effacing when necessary. Don't come across as a know-it-all. Refer to your research as the basis for your opinions rather than your superior intelligence. Don't be afraid to use a little humor. Don't be deadly earnest or too flippant.

8. **Don't be a slave to your graphics or technology.** PowerPoint, Prezi, or Keynote should highlight the key concepts in your verbal presentation, but you still need to actually present the information. Don't read from your slides, and keep them simple. If you have a lot to say, use more slides.

"At the end of a presentation, it's not your brilliant strategy or clever ideas that win the business. It really depends on whether the client thinks you're the kind of people they want to hang around with."[10]

John Melamed, executive vice president, Cramer-Krasselt

9. **Get technical help.** If you're not confident of your technical ability, make sure you have someone who is an expert at setting up the equipment. Never apologize for poor-quality visuals, video, or audio. All anyone will hear is that you didn't care enough to give it your best effort.

10. **Ask for the business.** You're not there to just entertain them. You're there to land the business—or win the competition.

Making It Memorable

You have to find the right blend of entertainment and serious business information. Here are some methods others have used to open up their presentations:

- **Tell a story.** Every brand has a story. Every consumer has a profile. Every marketer needs an inspiration. Discover the story behind the product and the people who buy it—or need to buy it—and use it to open your presentation.

- **Ask a question.** One winning presentation opened with "Your house is burning down. Your family is safe, but you only have time to get one possession from your house. What would it be?" Or more generically, "What's the most important thing in your life?"

- **Start with a video.** If you use a video, it should be short and crisply edited, with a clear message. Remember, this sets the tone for the whole presentation.

- **Make a series of statements.** Each team member states an opinion or a misconception about the client or their products. Follow with "That's what people told us . . . and this is how we plan to change their minds."

- **Bring your target audience to life.** A day in the life. "Let me introduce you to . . . [names of people]." Or some other compelling way to draw the audience in.

Handling Questions

Sometimes the outcome of a presentation depends more on how you defend your work than on the quality of the work itself. Here are a few tips for dealing with questions. Remember, how you answer is just as important as what you say. Here are a few tips for dealing with questions:

- **Each question is an opportunity.** Don't take it as a criticism of your effort. Sometimes reviewers just want to see how you defend your work. If you get too defensive, vague, or impatient, your attitude may turn them off.

- **Answer the question!** You should be able to explain calmly and confidently why you did what you did. Prepare for them. Try to come up with the toughest possible questions.

- **Pay attention to your tone of voice.** Just like your physical motions, your tone of voice says a lot about you. Be sure to answer questions in a strong, consistent tone. Don't act offended, impatient, or flustered.

- **Avoid wavering.** Talking too softly, mumbling, or speaking too quickly won't win them over. Make eye contact and project confidence.

- **Put yourself in the questioner's shoes.** You are too close to your work. That's why it's hard for you to understand why someone doesn't get it. Think about the early phases of your planning. What questions did you ask yourself? Why did you do things that way? Those are some of the questions others will also have.

- **Get an outsider's opinion.** Have them review your work and presentation and invite their questions and comments. Don't be surprised if people are not as crazy about your ideas as you are. Encourage constructive criticism. It's good practice for handling your boss, clients, or competition reviewers.

"The secret is to keep listening to that wee, small voice—and don't ever be afraid of getting your hands dirty."[12]

Leo Burnett,
founder, Leo Burnett

Thinking on Your Feet

No matter how much you prepare for questions, you're going to get at least one that's a total surprise. Here are a few tips to handle that situation.

- **Take a deep breath.** Think for a second and then begin to answer. This will help calm your nerves and will give you the opportunity to "look before you leap" when it comes to answering important questions.

- **Repeat the question.** You can always ask the questioner to clarify a part of it. This gives you more time to think about an answer.

- **Finish your answer.** Don't taper off and leave a question unanswered. If you're in a group, your teammates will instinctively finish your sentence, making you look helpless. If you're by yourself, you'll seem indecisive.

- **Don't act surprised.** Retain your composure. For example, if someone asks you why you didn't do something, you could say, "We looked into that, but our research indicated that some other approaches would work better," or "We studied a lot of ways to do this and found this was the most cost-efficient way to achieve our objectives."

- **Forget "That's a good question."** That's code for "We never thought of that and don't have the answer."

- **Don't change the subject.** Think for a second and then answer the question to the best of your ability. If you sense the questioner is not satisfied, simply ask, "Did I answer your question?"

- **Don't argue.** Don't cave in. You had reasons for making these decisions. The questioners don't necessarily disagree, but they want to see how you defend your work.

Breaking Down Barriers to Success

We've talked a lot about making it in creative, from core competencies to résumés, portfolios, and selling yourself. One thing we didn't talk about is breaking down some of the invisible barriers you are likely to encounter. So, here's some plain talk about things to consider when you bump into generational, gender, and/or racial bias. We end with some killer resources for every aspiring creative.

What Every Millennial Creative Needs to Know

Millennials think differently than older generations, and they have now reached a critical mass in the workplace. With that, Millennials herald one of the biggest culture clashes our industry has seen in decades. First the bad news—Boomer and Gen X bosses don't understand you. Here are the biggest criticisms about your generation:

- They don't understand history and the significance of advertising pioneers. (That's a big loss.)
- They arrive without knowledge of how the business works, how clients make money, how agencies make money, and how everyone gets paid.
- They emphasize tactics over strategy, especially when it comes to digital. That can lead to amazingly cool ideas. But it also can leads to tactics that aren't integrated into sustainable campaigns.
- They struggle with the long view—whether it comes to campaign strategy or their own careers. (Sometimes gratification takes time.)
- They want it all. (Just like Boomers did and Gen Xers do.) They're not keen on loyalty when they've seen where it's left many of their parents.
- They don't understand the importance of details like punctuality, spelling, punctuation, grammar, and basic common courtesies.

Now for some good news: Millennials also bring a ton of great stuff. Stuff that may disturb a lot of Boomers and Gen Xers. Keep in mind, we are all working within a fairly inflexible system, and Millennials are primed to push back. So, here are Millennials' biggest assets:

- They bring unbridled enthusiasm and don't live in silos. They're willing to try new things over and over and . . . . They are the great disrupters.
- They are tech savvy and fearless when it comes to the digital space. (That fearlessness sometimes trips them up.)
- They grew up multitasking, and that means they are comfortable across disciplines and geographies.
- They are more open to diversity than previous generations. For Millennials, differences are both normal and something to be celebrated. (We know—it's a paradox.)
- They are irreverent and expect that their irreverence will be tolerated. (It will be if it leads to creative business solutions that drive return on investment.)
- Equity and a work-life balance are in their bones. Millennials are not willing to sell their souls to the company store (like many think their parents did).
- Social consciousness is in their DNA. They generally aren't willing to buy or promote crap they don't believe in (no matter how much you offer to pay them or what new title you offer).

So you see, it goes both ways. The trick is to understand how the people who will hire and promote you will view you. Then you need to understand your assets and how to leverage them. But—and this is a big but—be willing to earn your place on the team. It's called paying your dues. We've all done it and so will you.

What Every Junior Creative Woman Needs to Know

There are a lot more men than women in creative departments—a lot. As we mentioned earlier, women make up just 20% of all creatives and only 14% of all creative directors around the world.[14] It's a bit better in the United States, where 27% of all creatives are women and 25% of all creative directors are women.[15] The irony is that women make 80% to 85% of all consumption choices.[16] We also mean for cars, insurance, and home purchases. In fact women drive more of the purchase decisions in these categories than men, though the advertising you see often doesn't always reflect that. The reality is, there simply aren't a lot of women in creative departments.

So here's the rub—in schools, women make up the majority of advertising students, including those pursuing a creative track. Take a look around the room. Again, it raises the question: Why do men outnumber women by such wide margins in creative departments? We can't give you a definitive answer. Mostly it seems to reflect an unconsciousness around gender issues in creative departments. To help junior women, we decided to take a look at what some of today's top creative women are saying about surviving and thriving in creative. Our "Junior Women's Survival Guide" is a compilation of insights from female creative directors to CEOs.[17] Here's to "making yourself known."

Junior Women's Survival Guide

- Take risks.
- Don't be a girly girl.
- Don't let others talk over you.
- Learn from men and don't resent them.
- When you get a compliment, learn to simply say, "Thank you."
- Don't get pigeonholed in the "Pink Ghetto" on women's products.
- Don't ignore sexism if it exists. Confront it. It won't go away on its own.
- Don't be afraid to take a promotion, even when you think you're not ready.
- Look for mentors and network, especially with other women.
- Don't let yourself be intimidated. Hang in there.
- Use your instincts about women as consumers.
- Work really hard while you don't have kids.[18]

"Working together, we are a big number of the population and therefore a real power, a real change. If women help others, we can change the power structure of our world and expand opportunities for all."[13]

Lucille Gratacos,
account supervisor, Lapiz

You can go online and find good entry-level portfolios. But we doubt you'll ever find this treasure trove of ideas generated in these creative journals. Start writing. And don't stop.

© Jen Stopka

What Every Junior Multicultural Creative Needs to Know

America is becoming more and more diverse, as we talked about in Chapter 4. At the same time, brands live in an ever more global marketplace, which we discussed in Chapter 5. Yet, sadly, the advertising industry does not reflect this diversity. Historically the solution has been multicultural agencies. The logic goes this way: if you want to reach Black people, go to an African American agency. It's the same for Hispanics and Asian Americans. The cultural nuances, especially linguistically, are complex. Multicultural agencies certainly have deep cultural expertise, which means they have a lot to offer clients who want to reach multicultural audiences. And so, this is where you'll find most multicultural people employed. The truth is, in most general market agencies, minority employment is low, really low, as we talked about in Chapter 3. The reasons are far too complex to address in this book. However, we feel an obligation to suggest ways for bright, talented multicultural creatives to break into advertising creative and thrive. In spring 2015, at the American Academy of Advertising, a panel discussion was held on the topic of preparing women and minorities for success and leadership in creative. We thought we'd share their wisdom.

Multicultural Juniors' Survival Guide

- Self-awareness is key.
- Learn how to negotiate.
- Embrace your heritage. It is your point of differentiation.
- Find sponsors who are willing to advance your career. Do this from day one.
- Your standard of work and of self-presentation needs to be higher than that of other people.
- Speak often and speak loud. Your opinions come with a different perspective, and they may be undermined because of prejudice. Speak anyway.
- Multicultural shops may be a good fit, but don't let general market agencies intimidate you.
- Find a boss who is willing to lose business by standing up for the right thing.
- It you don't see yourself at the top, it may not be the right place for you.
- Work hard and be sure people see how hard you work.
- Use your instincts to create insightful work.
- Stand up for what you believe in.
- Be a team player.

As we've mentioned many times, networking is critical. Below, we also suggest a few resources that might help multicultural advertising professionals get a foot in the door. While the list below tends to follow the multicultural agency pattern, we nonetheless hope you find these resources of value as you strive for success in advertising.

Multicultural Juniors' Resources

- American Advertising Federation Mosaic Center at aaf.org
- The Association of Hispanic Advertising Agencies at ahaa.org
- The Asian American Advertising Federation at 3af.org
- African American Advertising Association on LinkedIn
- Hispanic Advertising Professionals on LinkedIn
- Asian American Mobile Marketing Group on LinkedIn
- Black Creatives: The Premier Network for Multicultural Talent on LinkedIn

We'd like to share some thoughts from Charles Hall, an African American copywriter who early in his career worked for Nike and later taught at VCU Brandcenter. While he wrote it with multicultural people in mind, we think it's good advice for everyone.

> to the blacks browns reds and yellows periwinkles teals and fuchsias
>
> if you want to be in advertising, there is one thing to remember.
>
> don't be afraid.
>
> of hard work, rejection, racism, responsibility, sexism.
>
> don't be afraid of being the only one in the room.
>
> don't be afraid to ask questions. find answers. listen. hear. trust . . . .
>
> don't be afraid to ask for help.
>
> don't be afraid to be smart. clever. witty. clever. funky. hard. street. elegant. beautiful. you . . . .
>
> don't be afraid to remind them that right after the black jokes come the jewish jokes, the polish jokes and the fat jokes . . . .

This game app was designed by four portfolio school students (two copywriters and two art directors) to play at parties while they were in the dark. It won a D&AD Award and a lot of thumbs-ups from the general public. This is the kind of creative thinking and collaboration that pulls aspiring creatives out of the pack.

don't be afraid when they don't understand your accent, dialect, or slang. your heroes, your sex symbols. your style. your music. your people. your culture. your you.

don't be afraid to take criticism . . . .

don't be afraid to have a personality. an opinion. a point of view. a perspective. an objective. a positive attitude.

don't be afraid of those who are threatened by your presence. or feel you don't belong. or those who need you to fail for them to succeed.

don't be afraid to understand the difference between racism and insecurity. between racism and power. between sexism and chauvinism.

don't be afraid to forgive. to apologize. to be humble . . . .

don't be afraid of titles, awards. salaries. egos. offices. windows. ponytails. clothes. jewelry. degrees, backgrounds. lifestyles. cars. beach houses . . . .

don't be afraid of not being popular . . . .

don't be afraid to work twice as hard. twice as long. twice as good . . . .

p.s. and under no circumstances whatsoever are you to be intimidated. because some will try.[19]

Getting That Next Great Job

Young creative people often ask about job-hopping. They're worried that changing jobs too many times will limit their future employability. In many industries that's a concern. But in the ad business, jumping from agency to agency is the norm. However, honor any commitments you've made, and try to stay at least one or two years before jumping again. And don't burn any bridges when you leave.

This concept-driven ad from an art direction student at Miami Ad School helped land her a job at Mother in New York.

©Teo Bazgu

You might have the opportunity to come back to a former employer a few years later for even more money. Advertising is a small world, and the "get along" factor is almost as important as talent. In the end, you will be judged on how well coworkers, bosses, and especially clients like you. That may very well determine how much you're really worth. And remember—never stop working on your portfolio.

Resources to Inspire

To wrap it up, we've compiled a list of resources: killer sites, indispensable social connection, must-read books, and essential news sources. We didn't do this alone. We reached out to a handful of creatives we admire from here and abroad, juniors as well as folks at the top.

Killer Sites

There are bazillions to choose from. Here's what the who's who of the creative world are viewing. We hope they inspire you too.

3percentconf.com	mcsweeneys.net
adverbox.com	millwardbrown.com
agencyspy.com	moderncopywriter.com
brandtags.com	seejane.org
changethis.com	sethgodin.com
creativity-online.com	ted.com
ffffound.com	theegotistnetwork.com
mademovement.com	therepresentationproject.org
mashable.com	visualthesaurus.com

University of Texas.edu

In the postdigital era, the digital and analog worlds blend seamlessly. This student's campaign for a record label includes streaming music, social media, experiential displays, guerrilla, and even vinyl record inserts.

Essential Social Connections

Here are who some of the wisest advertising people we know are following. Then again, Christina Knight, from INGO Stockholm said, "I follow ordinary people in social media. It's the only way to stay sane."[20] We're guessing she learns a lot from them too.

@3PercentConf	@heywhipple
@AdWomen	@InspirationRoom
@AgencySpy	@leeclowsbeard
@copymatt	@Mediabistro
@copyranter	@MediaPost
@creativitymag	@motherlondon
@droga 5	@sallyhogshead
@edwardboches	@trendwatching
@FastCompany	@tmontague
@GOOD	@WiedenKennedy
@GuyKawasaki	@WIRED

Must-Read Books

Good writers read. A lot. We know it's old-fashioned. Here's to making reading the (almost) new postmodern trend.

- *Under the Radar: Talking to Today's Cynical Consumer* by Jonathan Bond and Richard Kirshenbaum
- *The Art of the Pitch: Persuasion and Presentation Skills That Win Business* by Peter Coughter
- *Outliers: The Story of Success* by Malcolm Gladwell
- *I Can See You Naked* by Ron Hoff
- *Radical Careering: 100 Truths to Jumpstart Your Job, Your Career, and Your Life* by Sally Hogshead
- ~~*Darling, You Can't Do Both:*~~ *And Other Noise to Ignore on Your Way Up* by Janet Kestin and Nancy Vonk
- *Mad Women: A Herstory of Advertising* by Christina Knight
- *Brand Sense: Sensory Secrets Behind the Stuff We Buy* by Martin Lindstrom
- *The Brand Gap: How to Bridge the Distance Between Business Strategy and Design* by Marty Neumeier
- *Panati's Extraordinary Origins of Everyday Things* by Charles Panati
- *A Whole New Mind: Why Right-Brainers Will Rule the Future* by Daniel Pink
- *Paradox of Choice: Why Less Is More* by Barry Schwartz
- *How to Be an Explorer of the World: Portable Life Museum* by Keri Smith
- *Hey Whipple, Squeeze This! A Guide to Creating Great Advertising* by Luke Sullivan
- *Eats, Shoots & Leaves: The Zero Tolerance Approach to Punctuation* by Lynne Truss

Good Old-Fashioned News

Being informed about current events and industry trends is actually part of your job. Start (or keep) reading these and never stop.

- *Advertising Age*—If you read one magazine about advertising, this is it.
- *Adweek*—Edited for ad agency executives with the inside stories on creativity and successful global advertising strategies.
- BBC—This is one-stop shopping for global news that is well reported.
- *Communication Arts*—CA calls itself the world's most inspiring magazine. Who can argue?
- *New York Times*—Breaking news across America and the world and in-depth reporting on issues that matter with smart editorials.
- *Wall Street Journal*—When it comes to business, there is no better source.
- *WIRED*—The magazine that brings the digital world together with business imperatives.

Here's to a great life in advertising!

Chapter 16

WHO'S WHO?

Susan McManama Gianinno

In her role as chairman, Gianinno oversees all Publicis North America operations, including Publicis, Publicis Kaplan Thaler, Publicis Hawkeye, Publicis Modem and Riney. She is a member of the Publicis Worldwide Executive Committee (COMEX) and the Publicis Groupe Strategic Leadership Team. She is also a 2014 Advanced Leadership Fellow at Harvard University. The recipient of numerous industry honors, Susan is a member of the YWCA's Academy of Women Achievers and was selected by *Advertising Age* as one of the best and brightest "women to watch." She was honored with the MATRIX Award for Women in Communications and has recently been recognized by *Advertising Age* as one of the "100 Most Influential Women in Advertising."[21]

Omar Sotomayor and Gastón Soto Denegri

Omar Sotomayor and Gastón Soto Denegri are two young Peruvian creatives skyrocketing to the top. Copywriter Sotomayor and art director Soto Denegri won the Young Lions Competition at Cannes two years in a row. In 2010 they won a Young Lion for their work for a nonprofit charity dedicated to helping raise girls out of poverty. You saw their work earlier in the chapter. Back then they were working at Circus in Lima, Peru. In 2011 they won their second Young Lion with a TV spot they concepted and created in 24 hours. Today the creative duo is in Chicago creating great work at Lapiz, Leo Burnett's Hispanic advertising agency.[22]

Donna Speciale

Donna Speciale is regarded as one of the most outstanding thinkers in the media agency space. As president of investment and activation and agency operations at MediaVest, Speciale counted Coca-Cola, Kraft, Mars, Procter & Gamble, and Walmart among her clients and was named Advertising Women of New York's 2010 Advertising Woman of the Year. In 2012, she took the top ad sales post at Turner Broadcasting System's entertainment division. She exemplifies her own philosophy: "Those with the most agility and fearlessness win in the industry today."[23]

Sheryl Sandberg

In 2008 Mark Zuckerberg hired Sheryl Sandberg away from her position as global online sales for Google and made her chief operating officer of Facebook. After joining Facebook, Sandberg quickly began trying to figure out how to make Facebook profitable. She was named one of the 100 most influential people in the world according to *Time* magazine. Sheryl Sandberg coauthored her first book, *Lean In: Women, Work, and the Will to Lead*, a guide for professional women to help them achieve their career goals and for men who want to contribute to a more equitable society. In March 2014 Sandberg and Lean In sponsored the Ban Bossy campaign, a television and social media censorship advocacy campaign designed to ban the word *bossy* from general use due to its perceived harmful effect on young girls.

Buying Happiness

Sarah has just been turned down for a promotion at work. The promotion would have given her the title of "Director." Sarah feels disappointed in general and feels that her current job lacks status. She is feeling discouraged and that she will never be successful and especially to others without the title of "Director" to show her worth.

On the drive home Sarah hears one of the new commercials for the main shopping mall in town. The commercial has lively, fun-sounding music in the background and a male announcer discussing reasons to visit the mall.

We have everything you need, from dinner on the fly, to movie theaters, to stores that fulfill all of your shopping needs. So whatever you may be looking for, from that special gift or escape from your regular life, the perfect scent for your partner, or maybe celebrate a promotion or simply buy your way to happiness, we have it all in one-stop shopping and fun at Festival Mall. Check us out tonight!

Upon hearing the ad, Sarah decides to stop at the mall on the way home. As she walks around, an expensive luxury brand-name purse catches her eye. She really cannot afford this type of purse but thinks this could help boost her status among coworkers and friends. Recognizing that the purse seems to make her mood take a turn for the better, she impulsively buys the purse.

The next day, Sarah shows up at work with her new purse and is feeling like a million bucks. One of her close colleagues mentions how sorry she was to hear that Sarah did not get the promotion, but also mentions how much she likes Sarah's purse. At lunch, Sarah meets up with her sister, who also notices the purse but asks Sarah where she got the money to pay for it. Sarah said she charged it on her credit card. They further get into a discussion about the mall and the new advertisements for the mall, which are receiving some negative reactions from a few consumer and parent groups in the town.

1 If you were a critic of advertising and consumer culture, how would you use this scenario to develop a persuasive argument against advertising? Be sure to support your points and possibly even integrate a theory to help explain the underlying process of how advertising can influence people and Sarah specifically.

2 How could you change the commercial for the mall to avoid some of the current negative reactions in town? Make at least three recommendations and support your points.

3 Do you think Sarah's purchase was good for Sarah? Why or why not? Support your answer with at least three points and using case facts.

Carrie La Ferle, professor, Temerlin Advertising Institute, Southern Methodist University

CHAPTER 16

Okay, we admit it. These final exercises are not really exercises. Think of them as experiences that, once they become habitual, will sustain you on your professional journey.

1. Creative Think Tank

This is designed to keep your creative juices flowing. Find some creative friends and get going.

- Find a group of fellow creatives and have a dedicated meeting time every week.

- Carve out two or three hours each week dedicated to going on a creative hunting expedition. Be committed to coming away with at least three new creative concepts, ideas, or campaigns that rock your world.

- Now use your weekly meeting as a creative think tank. Share the new ideas you find and critique each other's work. And if you can find a place dedicated to this process, leave things behind. Create an artifact room.

- Chances are you'll become friends and allies for life.

2. Improving on Schedule

Making it in advertising can be a long journey. Here's one way to begin.

- Find an industry mentor, someone you trust and who will be brutally honest.

- Make a commitment to seeing them regularly. No excuses.

- Show them new and revised work every time you meet. Listen to them. Trust them.

- One day, return the favor.

3. Do Nothing

That's right, do nothing. And watch your work improve.

- Do nothing related to advertising for an entire day.

- Do this with regularity, even if infrequently.

- Rest and replenish your creative spirit.

Review chapter content and study for exams. http://study.sagepub.com/altstiel4e.

- Interactive practice quizzes
- Mobile-friendly eFlashcards
- Carefully selected chapter-by-chapter video and multimedia content

Appendix

Copy Platform (Creative Strategy Statement)

Product (Service) _____

The Product (or Service)

A. Primary features/benefits in order of importance (remember "So Whats")

Feature	Benefit
1. _____	1. _____
2. _____	2. _____
3. _____	3. _____
4. _____	4. _____

B. Exclusive or unique product (service) attributes: _____

_____

C. Can product claims be substantiated? _____

D. Parent company name important? _____ Why? _____

E. Brand value: High status _____ Low status _____ No brand image _____

The Consumer

A. Demographics (age, sex, education, income, occupation, geographic distribution) _____

_____

B. Psychographics (lifestyle, attitude, personality traits, buying patterns) _____

_____

C. Needs fulfilled by buying this product or service _____

_____

_____

The Marketplace

A. Major competitors/rank in market/market share

_____ / _____ / _____

_____ / _____ / _____

_____ / _____ / _____

B. Competitive advantage/disadvantage of product (service)

Competitor   Our advantage (disadvantage)

_____   _____

_____   _____

_____   _____

C. Position of product (service in market)

Parity product (no perceived competitive advantage) _____

New product category (first of its kind) _____

Significant improvement over similar products _____

D. Pricing position (compared to competition)

Premium priced _____ Comparably priced _____ Low priced _____

Creative Strategy

A.
The "One Thing": If you could say one thing about this product or service:

B. Significant facts or statistics about product, consumer, or market

_____

_____

_____

_____

_____

_____

_____

Copyediting and Proofreading Marks

Begin paragraph	¶ I'm going to make him an offer he can't refuse.
Set in italics	Go ahead. Make my day. (ital)
Set in caps	toto. I've got a feeling we're not in kansas anymore. (cap)
Set in lowercase	Say hello to My Little Friend!
Insert period, comma	No, Mr Bond I expect you to die. ∧ / ∧
Insert question mark	Do I feel lucky Well, do ya, punk ∧?
Insert apostrophe	Ill be back. ∨
Insert hyphen	Yippee ki yay, mother _____ . =
Insert quotes	I am serious...and don't call me Shirley. ∨ / ∨
Put in space	You're going to need a biggerboat. #
Close up	I'll have what she's having.
Set in boldface	Luke. I am your father. (bf)
Insert word	Houston, we have problem. ∧ a
Delete word	You can't handle the the truth.
Delete and close up	I love the smell of na palm when it's in the morning.
Leave as it was	Frankly, my dear, I don't give a damn. STET
Transpose	I see people dead
Spell out word	Who does number 2 work for? (sp)
Copy on next page	more
End of copy	### or _ 30 _ _____ Page Break _____

Additional Radio Terms

AFTRA	American Federation of Television and Radio Artists, one of the two main unions for voice talent
ANNCR	Announcer
Boom mike	Microphone on long extension, over announcer's head
Buyout	Total payment to talent for one-time use, as opposed to residual payments
Cans	Slang for announcer's headphones
Compression	Electronically removing dead air between words
Dead air	No sound between words or sound effects
Demo	Demonstration recording for reviewing or auditioning, not meant for airing
Donut	Nonvocal segment of musical segment or sound effect that allows an announcer to read copy over it
Double donut	Usually a commercial with a musical intro, announcer segment, musical middle, announcer segment, and musical close
Flight	Time frame that commercial runs
Phone patch	Review recording over phone lines instead of in the studio
PD	Public domain (music with no royalty fees, as in classical music)
Punch in	Insert re-recorded segment into commercial to replace a segment
P & W	Pension and Welfare, additional payments made to SAG/AFTRA talent
Residual	Payments made to talent after the initial run of the commercial
Reverb	Reverberation, an echo-like effect
SAG	Screen Actors Guild, one of the two main unions for voice talent
Sample	Digital recording and recreation of music or sound effect
Segue	Gradually lead into a new segment of a commercial
SFX	Sound effects
Slice of life	Simulated real-world situation, usually using dialogue
Spot	Commercial
Stage whisper	Whisper that's loud enough to be easily heard and understood
Stinger	Musical effect to provide emphasis, usually at the end of a jingle
Tag	End of a commercial, usually with the name of store locations, hours, or other information
Talent	Announcer, singers, or musicians in a commercial
Take	Reading of a segment of copy at one time; each reading is a take. Most commercials involve several takes.
Under	Reduce the volume of music or an effect so you can hear the announcer
Up	Raise the volume of music or an effect

Voice of God   Conversion with someone "off camera," usually with an effect such as an echo

White noise   Undefined noise such as static

Additional Television Terms

Accelerated montage	A sequence edited into progressively shorter shots to create a mood of tension and excitement.
Ambient light	The natural light surrounding the subject, usually understood to be soft.
Aspect ratio	The ratio of the width to the height of the film or television image. The formerly standard Academy aperture is 1.33:1. Widescreen ratios vary. In Europe 1.66:1 is most common; in the United States, 1.85:1. Anamorphic processes such as Cinemascope and Panavision are even wider, at 2.00:1 to 2.55:1.
Asynchronous sound	Sound that does not operate in unison with the image. Sound belonging to a particular scene that is heard while the images of the previous scene are still on screen, or which continue over a following scene. Also diegetic sound whose source cannot be seen on screen or sound unintentionally out of sync with the image track.
Backlighting	The main source of light is behind the subject, silhouetting it, and directed toward the camera
Bird's-eye shot	Same as **overhead shot**.
Blue screen (also called **green screen** or **chroma key**)	Shooting a subject in front of a blue or green background so that image can be superimposed over another background. The camera can be adjusted not to pick up blue or green, so in effect, you have a blocked-out image on a clear background.
Boom	A traveling arm for suspending a microphone above the actors and outside the frame. See also **crane**.
Bridge	A passage linking two scenes either by continuing music across the transition or by beginning the sound (including dialogue or music) of the next scene over images of the previous scene (aka "sound advance") a very common phenomenon in contemporary cinema.
Continuity editing	Technique whereby shots are arranged in sequence to create the illusion of a credible chronological narrative. Often contrasted with **montage** editing.
Crane	A mechanical arm-like trolley used to move a camera through space above the ground or to position it at a place in the air. A **crane shot** allows the camera to vary distance, angle, and height during the shot (aka **boom** shot).
Cross cutting	Intermingling the shots of two or more scenes to suggest **parallel action**.
Cutaway	A shot inserted in a scene to show action at another location, usually brief, and most often used to cover breaks in the main take, as in television and documentary interviews. Also used to provide comment on the action, for example by cutting away from scenes of explicit sex or extreme violence.

Depth of field	The range of distances from the camera at which the subject is acceptably sharp
Detail shot	Usually more magnified than a close-up. A shot of a hand, an eye, a mouth, or a subject of similar detail
Drive-by shot	View of person, object, or place from a camera located on a moving vehicle as it passes by
Establishing shot	Generally a long shot that shows the audience the general location of the scene that follows, often providing essential information and orienting the viewer
Fast motion	Also called *accelerated motion*. The film is shot at less than 24 frames per second, so that when it is projected at the normal speed, actions appear to move much faster. The camera is undercranked. Often useful for comic effect.
Flashback	A scene or sequence (sometimes an entire film) that is inserted into a scene in "present" time and that deals with the past. The flashback is the past tense of film.
Flash forward	On the model of **flashback**, scenes or shots of future time; the future tense of film.
Flash frame	A shot of only a few frames in duration, sometimes a single frame, which can just barely be perceived by the audience
Focus pull	To pull focus during a shot in order to follow a subject as it moves away from or toward the camera
Follow focus	To pull focus during a shot in order to follow a subject as it moves away from or toward the camera
Follow shot	A tracking shot or zoom, which follows the subject as it moves
Frame	(1) Any single image on the film. (2) The size and shape of the image on the film, or on the screen when projected. (3) The compositional unit of film design
Freeze frame	A freeze shot, which is achieved by printing a single frame many times in succession to give the illusion of a still photograph when projected
FX	Normal abbreviation of "effects." See **SFX**.
Gaffer	Chief electrician, responsible to the director of photography, is responsible for all major electrical installations on the set, including lighting and power.
High key	A type of lighting arrangement in which the **key light** is very bright, often producing shadows
Intercutting	Same as **parallel editing**, that is, the cutting between different narrative strands of a film intended to be taken as happening simultaneously
Key light	The main light on a subject. Usually placed at a 45° angle to the camera-subject axis
Mask	Shield placed in front of the camera lens to change the shape of the image. Often used as POV (point-of-view) shots, for example, looking through binoculars or a keyhole
Master shot	A long take of an entire scene, generally a relatively long shot that facilitates the assembly of component closer shots and details. The editor can always fall back on the master shot; consequently it is also called a *cover shot*.

Match cut	A cut in which the two shots joined are linked by visual, aural, or metaphorical parallelism. Famous example at the end of *North by Northwest*, Cary Grant is pulling Eva Marie-Saint up the cliff of Mt. Rushmore; match cut to Grant pulling her up to a Pullman bunk. Do not confuse with jump cut.
Montage editing	Technique of arranging shots in sequence to create connotations and associations (see **montage**) rather than a standard chronologically unfolding narrative (see **continuity editing**)
Parallel action	A device of narrative in which two scenes are observed in parallel by **cross cutting**. Also called *parallel montage*
Parallel editing	Narrative construction **cross cutting** between two or more lines of action supposed to be occurring simultaneously. Usually restricted to particular sequences in a film, **cross cutting** can also occur between lines of action that are thematically related rather than simultaneous.
Postproduction	The increasingly complex stage in the production of a film that takes place after shooting has been completed and involving editing, the addition of titles, the creation of special effects, and the final soundtrack, including dubbing and mixing
Preproduction	Phase of film production following the securing of financial backing but preceding shooting. It includes work on the script, casting, hiring crews, finding locations, constructing sets, drawing up schedules, arranging catering, and so on.
Reaction shot	A shot that cuts away from the main scene or speaker in order to show a character's reaction to it
Rough cut	The first assembly of a film, prepared by the editor from the selected takes, which are joined in the order planned in the script. Finer points of timing and montage are left to a later stage.
Shooting ratio	The ratio between film actually exposed in the camera during shooting to film used in the final cut. A shooting ratio of ten to one or more is not uncommon.
Soft focus	Filters, Vaseline, or specially constructed lenses soften the delineation of lines and points, usually to create a romantic effect.
Subjective camera	A style that allows the viewer to observe events from the point of view of either a character or the persona of the author.
Swish pan	Also called flick pan, zip pan, whip pan. A pan in which the intervening scene moves past too quickly to be observed. It approximates psychologically the action of the human eye as it moves from one subject to another.
Sweep in/out	Frame-by-frame revelation from blackout of complete image. More commonly called **wipe in**. Sweep out is the opposite of sweep in.
Synchronous sound	Sound whose source is visible in the frame of the image or whose source is understandable from the context of the image, for example, source music
Tracking shot	Generally, any shot in which the camera moves from one point to another either sideways, in, or out. The camera can be mounted on a set of wheels that move on tracks or on a rubber-tired dolly, or it can be handheld. Also called **traveling shot**
Wild sound	Sound recorded separately from images

Additional Digital Terms

Above the fold	Refers to information placed at the top of an email or webpage, so that visitors see it first, without scrolling
Ad tracking	Checks how many hits or clicks an ad receives. It is a useful tool for discovering where the most revenue comes from, and how to better personalize ads to reach more customers, and encourage more new customers.
Affiliate program	A program where other people known as affiliates agree to advertise for the sponsor's site. In return, they receive commissions or residual payments.
Application programming interface (API)	Documented interface that allows one software application to interact with another. For example, Twitter API
Black-hat SEO	Tactics that attempt to gain higher search engine rankings for a particular website through unethical means
Churn rate	A measure of customer attrition, defined as the number of customers who cease being customers over a specified time period divided by the average total number of customers over that same time period
Click-through rate (CTR)	A measure of the success of online advertising achieved by dividing the number of clicks on a webpage or online ad by the number of appearances of that webpage/online ad (i.e., number of impressions)
Collective intelligence	Information shared that emerges from the collaboration and competitions of many individuals and appears in consensus decision making in social networks
Conversion	The percentage of people whose activity can be tracked from clicking on an ad or visiting a website to actually purchasing a product or service. A high conversion rate indicates that the link, ad, or site was successful.
Content management system (CMS)	A format to design and populate websites that allows creation of content without extensive knowledge of programming language. CMS can range from very simple to quite complex and from free open-source programs to very costly, depending on their capabilities.
CSS (Cascading Style Sheets)	A flexible system of rules that govern the appearance of content on a webpage. Most modern websites separate content from style to simplify making revisions.
Dynamic content	Information in webpages, Flash movies, email, e-newsletters, and so on, that changes automatically based on database or user information. When used effectively, this content targets users' specific needs, providing what they are looking for, when they are looking for it, and in the format they have asked for.
Engagement	The point in the buying cycle or sales cycle after the potential buyer has identified potential vendors and solutions and begins a dialogue with the organization (or salesperson)
Hits	A poor measurement of activity used in web analytics, a hit is defined as any request for a file from a web server.
Impression	The exposure of a clickable ad on a website to one individual person

Inbound marketing	Focuses on getting found by customers. Related to **relationship marketing** and **permission marketing**, wherein customers seek out information rather than being contacted by an advertiser
Keywords	Words or phrases used by a prospect when performing a search. Marketers optimize their websites according to the search volumes of keywords related to their industry, product, or service. Marketers can also create ads related to keywords that appear in paid search listings.
Link building	An aspect of search engine optimization where website owners cooperate to add links to their sites from other sites to improve their search engine ranking. Blogging is a popular method of link building.
Mashup	Multiple layers of media from preexisting sources to create a new work.
News aggregator	A web-based tool or desktop application that collects syndicated content.
Newsreader	A newsreader gathers the news from multiple blogs or news sites via RSS, allowing readers to access all their news from a single website or program
Open rate	A measure of email effectiveness, the open rate indicates how many emails have been viewed.
Opt-in	Choice that customers make to willingly sign up for emails or services online
Opt-out	Another term for *unsubscribe*
Organic search	Results are listings in search engine results pages that appear because of their relevance to the search terms, as opposed to their being advertisements.
Outbound link	A link that leads people to a different website from the one they are visiting
Pay-per-click	Online advertising where an advertiser pays a pre-agreed price each time a user clicks on their advertisement. The cost for the click is often negotiated via an auction, with ad placement determined by the relative size of the bid, as well as other factors.
Pay-per-inclusion	Marketing programs that guarantee website listings for specific keyword search terms for a fee.
Pay-per-sale	Often associated with affiliate programs, a pay-per-sale program gives people a small percentage of the sales they receive on each item based on a referral.
Search engine optimzation	The process of improving the volume or quality of traffic to a website from search engines via unpaid or organic search traffic
Short Message Service (SMS)	A service for sending short messages to mobile devices
Sidebar	A column (or multiple columns) along either or both sides of a blog site's main content area that often includes contact information of the author, the blog's purpose and categories, links to archives, honors, and other widgets
Skyscraper	Online ad format that is tall and narrow. Skyscraper ads are typically run along the right or left margin of a webpage.

SMO	Social media optimization
Social affinity marketing (SAM)	Identifies and predisposes important decision makers and customer audiences, so that a company can assume an authority leadership position on critical issues that enhance brands and strengthen strategic selling proposition.
Tag Cloud	Visual depiction of user-generated tags typically used to describe the content of websites
TweetDeck	An application that connects users with contacts across Twitter, Facebook, MySpace, LinkedIn, and more.
Unique visitor	Website measurement that records unique IP addresses as individual visitors
Web analytics	Measurement, collection, analysis, and reporting of Internet data to aid understanding and optimization
Webinar	Live meetings, training, or presentations on the Internet

Content Curation Websites

- **Feedly:** Offers a one-stop shop to stay on top of customer blogs, follow influential media, or discover new industry experts. Check out the hashtag search for specific topics of interest.

- **LinkedIn:** Lets you gather information through your connections, monitor industry news and trends via Pulse, or follow Influencers.

- **Twitter lists:** Offers an easy way to categorize groups of Twitter users and then view their tweets in a separate timeline.

- **Prismatic:** Operates much like Feedly to follow topics of interest and discover new content on your mobile device. It's also integrated with Facebook and Twitter.

- **Newsle:** A web app that tracks people in the news so you never miss an important story about a customer, prospect, or person you care about.

- **Mention:** A solid alternative to Google Alerts, especially for those of us who tend to lose track of email alerts.

- **Flipboard:** A powerful content discovery engine that folded in the mobile news reading app from Zite, a former competitor. Flipboard brings you news catered to your interests and also learns your reading habits using algorithms.

- **inPowered:** A content discovery and amplification platform that provides credible third-party validation.

- **Medium:** A blog publishing platform with a collection search feature so you can quickly sift through posts to find stories related a specific subject.

- **Quibb:** Available by invite only. Once you're connected you'll find a community of people from your field sharing links and articles.[1]

The Whole Book in One Page

- Writing well matters. It gives you a real competitive advantage.

- Discover the "One Thing" you can communicate. Look for that single adjective that defines a brand.

- Don't write to the masses. Talk to an individual.

- Write hot. Edit cold. In other words, write with enthusiasm and let the words flow. Later, go back and edit ruthlessly.

- Learn to write theme lines. Really good taglines or slogans can make a product.

- Learn teamwork. Not just with art directors, but also account people and the client.

- Become valuable to the client and you become valuable to your current employer and your next employer.

- Think visually. Look for the visual-verbal connection. They work together—one should not describe the other.

- Understand the principles of design for print and online. Know what works and why.

- Keep it simple. That applies to copy and design. When you emphasize everything, you emphasize nothing.

- Think campaigns. Different elements that work individually and cumulatively to convey the message.

- Learn everything you can about digital marketing and social media, but never forget return on investment.

- Look around. Not everyone looks like you or thinks like you. Understand that diversity makes companies stronger and feeds creativity.

- As a Millennial, you bring technical expertise, an open mind, tolerance, and can-do enthusiasm to the workplace. But you still have a lot to learn.

- Think globally. Understanding of different cultures and customs is critical to creating advertising messages that resonate. This applies to your local community too.

- Get involved in outside activities. Take an interest in life outside of advertising.

- Learn how to present. Be confident, persuasive, and logical. Defend your opinions, but know when to back down.

- Continually upgrade your portfolio. Weed out anything less than wonderful.

- Accept criticism and use it to improve. Throw a tantrum and you won't sell the *next* idea either.

- Never forsake your own moral compass. Do the right thing, even if no one makes you.

- We'll end where we started—never stop learning!

Notes

Chapter 1

1. William Bernbach, *Bill Bernbach Said . . .* (New York: Doyle Dane Bernbach, 1989), p. 3.
2. https://www.youtube.com/watch?v=CkCzGBK3aWY (accessed November 28, 2014).
3. Walter Isaacson, *Steve Jobs* (New York: Simon & Schuster, 2011), p. 56.
4. Tom Altstiel and Jean Grow, *Advertising Creative: Strategy, Copy, Design*, 3rd ed. (Thousand Oaks, CA: Sage, 2013), p. 8.
5. Wayne Weiten, *Psychology Themes and Variations* (Belmont, CA: Thomson Wadsworth, 2005), pp. 255–56.
6. Mihaly Csikszentmihalyi, "Implications for a Systems Perspective for the Study of Creativity," in *Handbook of Creativity*, ed. Robert Sternberg (Cambridge, MA: Cambridge University Press, 1999), p. 314.
7. Mark Runco, "Creativity," *Annual Review of Psychology* (2004), p. 55.
8. Runco, "Creativity," p. 658.
9. Daniel Pink, *A Whole New Mind: Why Right-Brainers Will Rule the Future* (New York: Penguin, 2006), p. 3.
10. Isaacson, *Steve Jobs*, p. ix.
11. See "Maslow, Abraham Harold," in *Microsoft Encarta Online Encyclopedia* (2005), http://www.encarta.com (accessed May 19, 2005).
12. Leo Burnett, *100 Leos: Wit and Wisdom From Leo Burnett* (Chicago: NTC Business Press, 1995), p. 47.
13. Isaacson, *Steve Jobs*, p. xxi.

Chapter 2

1. Angela Partington, ed., *The Oxford Dictionary of Quotations* (New York: Oxford University Press, 1992), p. 501.
2. Michael Jackman, ed., *Crown's Book of Political Quotations* (New York: Crown, 1982), p. 2.
3. "Will Rogers Quotes," BrainyQuote, http://www.brainyquote.com/quotes/quotes/w/willrogers141123.html (accessed November 28, 2014).
4. Jef I. Richards quotes, BrainyQuote, http://www.brainyquote.com/quotes/authors/j/jef_i_richards.html (accessed August 28, 2015).
5. "David Ogilvy Quotes," BrainyQuote, http://www.brainyquote.com/quotes/authors/d/david_ogilvy.html (accessed November 29, 2014).
6. Randall Rothenberg, "The Definition of Advertising Has Never Been More Unclear: Source of Both Opportunity and Crisis," *Adweek*, September 16, 2013, http://www.adweek.com/news/advertising-branding/definition-advertising-has-never-been-more-unclear-152434 (accessed September 17, 2013).
7. Bill McCaffrey, "Hook, Line, and Sinker: 7 Tips for a Killer Call-to-Action," October 9, 2014, http://www.wordstream.com/blog/ws/2014/10/09/call-to-action (accessed May 12, 2015).
8. Tom Altstiel and Jean Grow, *Advertising Creative: Strategy, Copy, Design*, 3rd ed. (Thousand Oaks, CA: Sage, 2013), p. 21.
9. "Mary Wells Lawrence," *Vogue*, February 15, 1972.
10. Glenn Griffin and Deborah Morrison, *The Creative Process Illustrated: How Advertising's Big Ideas Are Born* (Cincinnati, OH: How, 2010), p. 24.
11. Griffin and Morrison, *The Creative Process Illustrated*, p. 117.
12. Luke Sullivan, *Hey Whipple, Squeeze This: A Guide to Creating Great Ads* (New York: John Wiley, 1998), p. 35.
13. Griffin and Morrison, *The Creative Process Illustrated*, p. 47.
14. Bruce Bendinger, *The Copy Workbook* (Chicago: The Copy Workshop, 2002), p. 105.
15. Meghan Casserly, "The World's Happiest Brands," Forbes.com, November 11, 2011, http://money.msn.com/how-to-invest/the-worlds-happiest-brands (accessed December 20, 2011).
16. Ibid.

17. George Felton, *Advertising: Concept and Copy* (Englewood Cliffs, NJ: Prentice Hall, 1994), p. 60.
18. Judith Aquino, "The 10 Most Successful Rebranding Campaigns Ever," BusinessInsider.com, February 10, 2011, http://www.businessinsider.com/10-most-successful-rebranding-campaigns-2011-2 (accessed February 6, 2015).
19. Quoted in money.cnn.com/2015/01/14/investing/burberry-sales-hong-kong-protests/index.html (accessed February 6, 2015).
20. Aquino, "The 10 Most Successful Rebranding Campaigns Ever."
21. Sullivan, *Hey Whipple, Squeeze This*, p. 28.
22. Ibid.
23. Alain Thys, "The Ten Truths of Branded Storytelling," Future Lab, July 26, 2006, http://www.futurelab.net/blog/2006/07/ten-truths-branded-storytelling (accessed December 9, 2008).
24. "Brand Story: What's the Story? The Legend of Your Brand," Mark Di Somma Workshops, 2006, http://www.markdisomma.com/workshop.asp?ID=3 (accessed January 2, 2012).
25. Tim Nudd, "Not Just a Tech Genius," *Adweek*, October 10, 2011, p. 37.
26. Laurence Vincent, *Legendary Brands: Unleashing the Power of Storytelling to Create a Winning Market Strategy* (Chicago: Dearborn, 2002), p. 70.
27. Brad VanAuken, "The Brand Management Checklist—Advanced," *Branding Strategy Insider*, July 15, 2007, http://www.brandingstrategyinsider.com/2007/07/the-brand-manag.html#.VcvIGTHF98E (accessed December 8, 2008).
28. Stefan Stroe, "Best & Worst Brand US Extensions . . . but What About the Romanian Ones?" May 7, 2007, http://www.stefanstroe.ro/2007/03/07/best-worst-brand-US-extensions-but-what-about-romanian-ones/ (accessed December 8, 2008).
29. Ellen Wagner, "King of the Bounce," May 2015.
30. Yisha Zhang, "It's Just Like Swimming," May 2015.
31. http://christinebronstein.com/post698858138/why-a-brand-of-wives (accessed April 19, 2012).
32. "Adweek's 2011 Brand Genius Awards," *Adweek*, October 24, 2011, p. 22.

Chapter 3

1. Diego Figueroa, personal communication, April 13, 2015.
2. Jean M. Grow and Tao Deng, "Sex Segregation in Advertising Creative Departments Across the Globe," *Advertising & Society Review*, 14/4, 2014.
3. "Big Pharma," Drugwatch.com, http://www.drugwatch.com/manufacturer/ (accessed February 15, 2015).
4. Megan Orciari, "Fast Food Companies Still Target Kids with Marketing for Unhealthy Products," YaleNews, November 4, 2013, http://news.yale.edu/2013/11/04/fast-food-companies-still-target-kids-marketing-unhealthy-products (accessed February 15, 2015).
5. Andrew Pollack, "F.D.A. Approves Addyi, a Libido Pill for Women," *The New York Times*, August 18, 2015, http://www.nytimes.com/2015/08/19/business/fda-approval-addyi-female-viagra.html?_r=0 (accessed August 28, 2015).
6. "Big Pharma," Drugwatch.com.
7. "Outside Spending," OpenSecrets.org, https://www.opensecrets.org/outsidespending/summ.php?chrt=V&type=S (Accessed February 15, 2014).
8. Tami Anderson, Elizabeth Howland, and How Marketing, "7 Powerful Insights for Marketing to Women," http://www.startupnation.com/business-articles/1220/1/AT_Powerful-Insights-Marketing-Women.asp (accessed February 23, 2012).
9. John Ourand, "In Wake of Ray Rice Controversy, More Women Are Watching NFL Games," *Sports Business Journal*, November 19, 2014, http://www.bizjournals.com/baltimore/news/2014/11/19/in-wake-of-ray-rice-controversy-more-women-are.html?page=all (accessed January 23, 2015).
10. Lisa Bertagnoli, "McDonald's Has a New Generational Problem: Kids," *Crain's Chicago Business*, September 6, 2014, http://www.chicagobusiness.com/article/20140906/ISSUE01/309069980/mcdonalds-has-a-new-generational-problem-kids (accessed January 23, 2015).
11. Susan Krashinsky, "Why Seniors Tend to Give Marketers the Benefit of the Doubt," *The Globe and Mail*, August 27, 2012, http://www.theglobeandmail.com/report-on-business/industry-news/marketing/why-seniors-tend-to-give-marketers-the-benefit-of-the-doubt/article4495844/ (accessed February 15, 2015).
12. Ibid.

13. Ibid.

14. Kelly Brownell, "Marketing of Sugary Drinks to Kids and Teens: As Strong as Ever," *The Atlantic*, October 31, 2011, http://www.theatlantic.com/health/archive/2011/10/marketing-of-sugary-drinks-to-kids-and-teens-as-strong-as-ever/247580/ (accessed February 18, 2012).

15. See the 4A's website at http://www.aaaa.org.

16. AMA Publishing, "Statement of Ethics," http://www.marketingpowr.com/AboutAMA/Pages/StatementofEthics.aspx (accessed November 12, 2011).

17. Chris Moore, "Ethics in Advertising," Advertising Education Foundation, 2004 http://www.aef.com/on_campus/classroom/speaker_pres/data/3001 (accessed February 14, 2015).

18. Ondřej Gottwald, "Driving Responsibly, Czech Style," May 2015.

19. "Quotes," www.DizzyDean.com, http://www.dizzydean.com/quotes.htm (accessed January 5, 2012).

20. Diane Richard, "Local Advertisers Turn to Arbitration to Resolve Disputes over Ads," *Minneapolis-St. Paul City Business*, Vol. 15, No. 9 (August 1, 2007), p. 1.

21. Katy Bachman, "Skechers Settles Deceptive Ad Cases with FTC for $40M: Reminiscent of Reebok Suit, Settlement Is Commission's Largest." *Adweek*, May 16, 2012, http://www.adweek.com/news/advertising-branding/skechers-settles-deceptive-ad-case-ftc-40m-140577 (accessed February 15, 2015).

22. Laura O'Reilly, "Red Bull Will Pay $10 to Customers Disappointed the Drink Didn't Actually Give them 'Wings,'" BusinessInsider.com, October 8, 2014, http://www.businessinsider.com/red-bull-settles-false-advertising-lawsuit-for-13-million-2014-10 (accessed February 15, 2015).

23. Jon McDonald, "Finding an Agency That's 'Just Right,'" May 2015.

24. "Law Quotes," BrainyQuote, http://www.brainyquotes.com/quotes/keywords/law.html (accessed January 6, 2012).

25. Robert Brauneis, "Copyrights and the World's Most Popular Song," October 24, 2010, http://papers.ssrn.com/so13/papers.cfn?abstract_id=1111624 (accessed January 4, 2012).

26. Kim Hooper, "Writing by Day," http://day.kimhooperwrites.com/2011/09/12/from-the-experts-jim-durfee/ (accessed February 13, 2012).

27. David A. Weinstein, "Overlooking or Forgoing Federal Registration of a Trademark Can Be a Costly Mistake," *Advertising & Marketing Review*, November, 1, 2001, p. 5.

28. Walter Isaacson, *Steve Jobs* (New York: Simon & Schuster, 2011), pp. 419–20.

29. William Arens, Michael Weigold, and Christian Arens, *Contemporary Advertising*, 12th ed. (New York: McGraw-Hill Irwin, 2009), p. 132.

Chapter 4

1. Stuart Elliott, "The Top 5 Changes in Madison Ave. Over the Last 25 Years," *The New York Times*, December 19, 2014, http://www.nytimes.com/2014/12/19/business/media/the-top-5-changes-on-madison-ave-over-the-last-25-years.html?_r=1 (accessed January 15, 2015).

2. U.S. Census Bureau, http://www.census.gov (accessed February 21, 2012).

3. Rich Miller, "Is Everybody Single? More Than Half the U.S. Now, Up for 37% in '76," Bloomberg.com, September 8, 2014, http://www.bloomberg.com/news/2014-09-09/single-americans-now-comprise-more-than-half-the-u-s-population.html (accessed January 8, 2015).

4. Eric Klinenberg, "The Solo Economy," *Fortune*, February 6, 2012, pp. 130–32.

5. Kimberly Gedeon, "All about the Swirly, Baby! Interracial Couples in the States . . . by the Numbers," *Madame Noire*, June 20, 2014, http://madamenoire.com/432922/swirl-interracial-couples-america-numbers/.

6. Ibid.

7. Marti Barletta, "Maddened by 'Mad Men': Decades Later, Markets Are Finally Coming to Understand Women's Buying Power," *Advertising Age*, July 28, 2008.

8. Teresa Cuevas, personal communication, April 13, 2015.

9. "In Plain Sight: The Black Consumer Opportunity," *Advertising Age* supplement, April 23, 2012, http://brandedcontent.adage.com/pdf/CABblack consumer.pdf (accessed January 5, 2015).

10. Stone Brown, "African Americans Aren't Dark-Skinned Whites," http://www.diversityinc.com (accessed December 6, 2004).

11. "In Plain Sight."
12. Brown, "African Americans Aren't Dark-Skinned Whites."
13. "In Plain Sight."
14. Ibid., p. 25.
15. Ibid., p. 26.
16. Ibid.
17. "In Plain Sight."
18. Catriona Davies, "Inside Beyonce's Business Empire: How She Became a Global Brand," CNN International, May 8, 2013, http://edition.cnn.com/2013/05/02/business/beyonce-business-global-brand/ (accessed January 7, 2015).
19. "In Plain Sight," p. 14.
20. Ibid, p. 8.
21. Stephen Donadio, ed., *The New York Public Library Book of Twentieth-Century American Quotations* (New York: Stonesong, 1992), p. 70.
22. "In Plain Sight," p. 12.
23. Keith Jamerson, "Finding a Seat at the Table," May 2015.
24. "Hispanic Fact Pack," *Advertising Age*, July 28, 2014, http://adage.com/article/hispanic-marketing/ad-age-s-2014-hispanic-fact-pack/294335/, p. 36 (accessed January 4, 2015).
25. Ibid., p. 14.
26. Leo Olper, personal interview, New York, January 5, 2015.
27. Ileana Alémán-Rickenbach, personal communication, July 13, 2004.
28. Ibid.
29. Ibid.
30. Ibid.
31. U.S. Census Bureau, http://www.census.gov (accessed February 15, 2012).
32. Ibid.
33. Ibid.
34. http://css.edu/user/dswenson, October 8, 2001 (accessed June 1, 2005).
35. Hispania Accent, "Market Facts," http://www.hispania-accent.com/?page_id=25 (accessed March 4, 2012).
36. "Hispanic Fact Pack," p. 36.
37. Ibid., p. 3.
38. Stuart Feil, "The Best of Both Worlds," *Adweek*, March 12, 2012, p. H12.
39. Ibid.
40. "Hispanic Fact Pack," p. 39.
41. Ibid., p. 30.
42. Peter Ortiz, "Calling the Shots—in Spanish," *DiversityInc*, December 13, 2004.
43. "Sports and Hispanic Males in the United States," TNT Media Services, http://www.thecab.tv/main/bm~doc/sports-and-hispanic-males.pdf (accessed January 11, 2015).
44. "Hispanic Fact Pack," p. 8.
45. "Significant, Sophisticated, and Savvy: The Asian American Consumer 2013 Report," Nielsen, February 2014, p. 31.
46. Ibid., p. 2.
47. "The Rise of Asian Americans," The Pew Research Center, April 4, 2013.
48. Ibid.
49. "Significant, Sophisticated, and Savvy," p. 29.
50. Anya Kamenetz, "Study: 2 In 5 Americans Earning Degrees After High School," http://www.npr.org/sections/thetwo-way/2014/04/22/304577740/study-2-in-5-americans-earning-degrees-after-high-school (accessed May 21, 2015).
51. Ibid.
52. Ibid., p. 4.
53. Ibid., p. 24.
54. Ibid.
55. "Significant, Sophisticated, and Savvy," p. 19.
56. Ibid.

57. Ibid., p. 21.
58. Ibid., pp. 18, 25.
59. Witeck-Combs Communications and Harris Interactive, "Gay Consumers' Brand Loyalty Linked to Corporate Philanthropy and Advertising," http://www.prnewswire.com/news-releases/gay-consumers-brand-loyalty-linked-to-corporate-philanthropy-and-advertising-76326382.html (accessed August 14, 2015).
60. Elliott, "The Top 5 Changes in Madison Ave.."
61. Jean Grow, "The Gender of Branding: Early Nike Women's Advertising as a Feminist Antenarrative," *Women's Studies in Communication*, Vol. 31, No. 3 (2008), pp. 310–43.
62. "How to Appeal to Facebook's Fastest Growing Demographic: Seniors," All Facebook, http://allfacebook.com/facebook-seniors_b61114 (accessed January 4, 2015).
63. Ibid.
64. Ibid.
65. Beth Snyder Bulik, "Boomers—Yes, Boomers—Spent the Most on Tech," *Advertising Age*, October 11, 2010.
66. "1 in 3 Elderly Americans Use Social Media, Technical.ly Philly, April 16, 2013, http://technical.ly/philly/2013/04/16/1-in-3-elderly-americans-use-social-media/ (accessed January 5, 2015).
67. Ibid.
68. Jay Ehert, "Marketing to Generation X," The Marketing Blog, June 27, 2011, http://themarketingspot.com/2011/06/marketing-to-generation-x.html (accessed January 27, 2015).
69. Ibid.
70. Ibid.
71. Ibid.
72. Bruce Drake, "6 New Findings About Millennials," The Pew Center, March 7, 2014, http://www.pewresearch.org/fact-tank/2014/03/07/6-new-findings-about-millennials/ (accessed January 10, 2015).
73. "Millennials in Adulthood: Detaching for Institutions, Networked With Friends," The Pew Center, March 7, 2014, http://www.pewsocialtrends.org/2014/03/07/millennials-in-adulthood/ (accessed January 10, 2015).
74. S. L. Calvert, "Children as Consumers: Advertising and Marketing," *The Future of Children*, Vol. 18, No. 1, pp. 205–34.
75. Anna R. McAlister and T. Bettina Cornwell, "Children's Brand Symbolism Understanding: Links to Theory of Mind and Executive Functioning," *Psychology & Marketing*, Vol. 27, No. 3, pp. 203–28.
76. Kelly Brownell, "Marketing of Sugary Drinks to Kids and Teens: As Strong as Ever," *The Atlantic*, http://www.theatlantic.com/health/archive/2011/10/marketing-of-sugary-drinks-to-kids-and-teens-as-strong-as-ever/247580/ (accessed August 14, 2015).
77. Amanda Stevens and Thomas Jordan, *PurseStrings: New Proven Ways of Reaching the Hearts and Minds of Female Consumers* (HY Connect, 2011), p. 204.
78. Ibid.
79. Bridget Brennan, "Marketing to Women: Trend to Watch in 2015, *Forbes*, December 30, 2014, http://www.forbes.com/sites/bridgetbrennan/2014/12/30/marketing-to-women-trends-to-watch-in-2015/ (accessed May 23, 2015).
80. Dawn L. Billings, "The Purchasing Power of Women," http://she-conomy.com/2012/02/19/the-purchasing-power-of-women-infographic/ (accessed February 23, 2012).
81. Ibid.
82. Cheryl C. Berman, Diane Fedewa, and Jeanie Caggiano, "Still Miss Understood: She's Not Buying Your Ads," *Advertising & Society Review*, Vol. 7, No. 2 (2006), muse.jhu.edu.
83. Stevens and Jordan, *PurseStrings*, p. 46.
84. Ibid., pp. 186–201.
85. Michael Hastings-Black, "Marketing Must Engage the Muslim Consumer," *Advertising Age*, November 10, 2008.
86. John Kuraoka, "How to Write Better Ads," http://www.kuraoka.com/how-to-write-better-ads.html (accessed May 25, 2005).
87. Ibid.
88. The Editors of *Advertising Age, Advertising Age: Top Ad Campaigns*, January 12, 2015, http://adage.com/lp/top15/#ebook.
89. Ibid.
90. Anthony Vagnoni, "'Role Model' Jones, 59, Dies," *Advertising Age*, July 16, 2001, http://adage.com/article/news/role-model-jones-59-dies/54271/ (accessed January 18, 2012).
91. The Editors of *Advertising Age, Advertising Age: Top Ad Campaigns*.

Chapter 5

1   Joan Voight, "Unilever's Keith Weed: Saving the World at Scale," *Ad Week*, March 23, 2015, p. 27.

2. Ibid.

3. Ibid.

4. Gillian Tan, "Oasis Beverages, TSG Reach Deal to By Pabst Brewing Co.," *The Wall Street Journal*, September 18, 2014, http://www.wsj.com/articles/oasis-beverages-tsg-reach-deal-to-buy-pabst-brewing-co-1411064900 (accessed April 9, 2015).

5. Geert Hofstede, The Hofstede Centre, http://geert-hofstede.com.

6. Ibid.

7. Shankar Gupta-Harrison, "Four Ways to be Globally Relevant," *Adweek*, March 23, 2015, p. 17.

8. Millward Brown, *BrandZ Top 100 Most Valuable Global Brands for 2014*, http://www.millwardbrown.com/mb-global/brand-strategy/brand-equity/brandz/top-global-brands/regions (accessed August 15, 2015).

9. Ibid.

10. Ibid.

11. Ibid.

12. Jack Neff, "K-C: 'We Don't Believe in Digital Marketing . . . [but] Marketing in a Digital World,'" *Advertising Age*, March 21, 2012, p. 48, http://adage.com/article/cmo-strategy/kimberly-clark-elevates-clive-sirkin-top-marketing-post/233451/?utm_source=daily_email&utm_medium=newsletter&utm_campaign=adage (accessed June 12, 2012).

13. Mhairi McEwan, "It's Not Just Samba and Carnival: Media and Marketing in Brazil," *The Guardian*, June 12, 2014, http://www.theguardian.com/media-network/media-network-blog/2014/apr/11/brazil-marketing-world-cup (accessed March 21, 2015).

14. Ibid.

15. Ibid.

16. Chris Smith, "The Biggest Sponsors of Brazil's 2014 World Cup Spend Big to Engage With Fans," *Forbes*, June 6, 2014, http://www.forbes.com/sites/chrissmith/2014/06/12/the-biggest-sponsors-of-brazils-2014-world-cup/ (accessed April 18, 2015).

17. Millward Brown, *BrandZ Top 100 Most Valuable Global Brands*.

18. Terri Morrison and Wayne A. Conaway, *Kiss, Bow, or Shake Hands: Sales and Marketing* (New York: McGraw-Hill, 2012), p. 34.

19. Bradley Johnson, "Where's the Growth in Marketing? Follow the BRIC Road," *Advertising Age*, http://adage.com/article/global-news/growth-marketing-follow-bric-road/231359/ (accessed August 15, 2015).

20. Morrison and Conaway, *Kiss, Bow, or Shake Hands*, p. 31.

21. Christine Moorman, "The Riddle of Marketing in Russia," *Forbes*, February 2, 2014, http://www.forbes.com/sites/christinemoorman/2014/02/18/the-riddle-of-marketing-in-russia/ (accessed April 15, 2015).

22. Steven Davy and Daniel Gross, "Russia's Political War on Imported Food, Flower—and Wine," PRI's The World, August 18, 2015, http://www.pri.org/stories/2015-08-18/russia-starts-flower-war-destroying-dutch-imports-over-malaysian-airlines (accessed August 28, 2015).

23. Pavel Marceux, "Russian Advertising Market to Slow Down in 2015, but Online Remains a Growth Area," *East-West Digital News*, February 4, 2015, http://www.ewdn.com/2015/02/04/russian-advertising-market-to-slowdown-in-2015-but-online-remains-a-growth-area/ (accessed April 15, 2015).

24. Millward Brown, *BrandZ Top 100 Most Valuable Global Brands*.

25. Morrison and Conaway, *Kiss, Bow, or Shake Hands*, p. 158.

26. Moorman, "The Riddle of Marketing in Russia."

27. Millward Brown, *BrandZ Top 100 Most Valuable Global Brands*.

28. Simon Hay, "How India Could Change Retail Marketing as We Know It," *Forbes*, January 27, 2014, http://www.forbes.com/sites/onmarketing/2014/01/27/how-india-could-change-retail-marketing-as-we-know-it/ (accessed April 15, 2015).

29. Morrison and Conaway, *Kiss, Bow, or Shake Hands*, p. 93.

30. Neil Munshi, "Spain's Starring Role in Bollywood Movie a Boon to Tourism," *Advertising Age*, February 6, 2012, p. 6.

31. Johnson, "Where's the Growth in Marketing?"

32. Ibid.

33. Ibid.

34. Ibid.

35. Greg Paull, "The Biggest Mistakes Most U.S. Marketers Make in China—and How Some Are Learning From Them," *Forbes*, March 4, 2013, http://www.forbes.com/sites/onmarketing/2013/03/04/the-biggest-mistakes-most-u-s-marketers-make-in-china-and-how-some-are-learning-from-them/ (accessed April 15, 2015).

36. Johnson, "Where's the Growth in Marketing?"

37. Ibid.

38. Latin American Multichannel Advertising Council, "The Advertising Industry in Mexico Deserves to Know the Truth," October 12, 2011, http://www.lamac.org/america-latina-ingles/releases/the-advertising-industry-in-mexico-deserves-to-know-the-truth (accessed June 12, 2001).

39. Fernando Alvarez Kuri, "Mexico: Dynamism in the Making," Millward Brown, http://www.millwardbrown.com/mb-global/brand-strategy/brand-equity/brandz/top-latin-american-brands/mexico/local-market-overview (accessed April 15, 2015).

40. Ibid.

41. Morrison and Conaway, *Kiss, Bow, or Shake Hands*, p. 151.

42. Alvaro Carvajal, "Mexico," *Advertising Age*, October 17, 2011, p. 8.

43. Stephan Mangham, "Indonesia," *Advertising Age*, October 17, 2011, p. 8.

44. Neff, "K-C: 'We Don't Believe in Digital Marketing . . . [but] Marketing in a Digital World.'"

45. Ibid.

46. Rohit Razdan, Mohit Das, and Ajay Sohoni, "The Evolving Indonesian Consumer," McKinsey 7 Company, January 2014, http://www.mckinseyonmarketingandsales.com/evolving-indonesian-consumer (accessed April 15, 2015).

47. Buz Sawyer, "South Korea," *Advertising Age*, October 17, 2011, p. 8.

48. Ibid.

49. Toygun Yilmazer, "Turkey," *Advertising Age*, October 17, 2011, p. 8.

50. Ibid.

51. Ibid.

52. Ibid.

53. Aysenur Guven, "Marketing in Turkey," IDG Connect, January 20, 2014, http://www.idgconnectmarketers.com/blog-abstract/7440/interview-insight-marketing-turkey (accessed April 15, 2015).

54. Morrison and Conaway, *Kiss, Bow, or Shake Hands*, p. 223.

55. Ibid., p. 8.

56. Millward Brown, *BrandZ Top 100 Most Valuable Global Brands*.

57. Matt Wisla, "Brand Positioning and Sacrifice in China," May 2015.

58. Marieke de Mooij, *Global Marketing and Advertising: Understanding Cultural Paradoxes* (Thousand Oaks, CA: Sage, 2010), p. 29.

59. "Advertising: The Year's 10 Most Killer Pieces of Creative," *Advertising Age*, December 11, 2011, http://adage.com/results?endeca=1&searchprop=AdAgeAll&return=endeca&search_offset=0&search_order_by=score&search_phrase=10+most+killer+peices+of+creative (accessed February 12, 2012).

60. Ibid.

61. "The Five Best Global Ideas," *Advertising Age*, February 6, 2012, p. 6.

62. Ibid.

63. Kate MacArthur, "Kraft's Name Brings New Meaning to Snacking in Russia," *Advertising Age*, March 22, 2012, http://adage.com/article/global-news/kraft-s-close-russian-translation-oral-sex/233459/ (accessed February 20, 2012).

64. Laurel Wentz, "Brazilian Creative Renata Florio Joins U.S. Hispanic Shop Wing," *Advertising Age*, September 8, 2011, http://adage.com/article/hispanic-marketing/brazil-creative-renata-florio-joins-u-s-hispanic-shop-wing/229669/ (accessed March 28, 2012).

65. "40 Under 40," *Advertising Age*, January 21, 2013, http://adage.com/article/news/ad-age-s-40-40-marketing-agencies-media/239173/#Bond (accessed January 19, 2015).

66. "The Brand Union Names Juan Tan Creative Director, China," press release, The Brand Union, June 28, 2011, http://www.thebrandunion.com/news/news_posts/2011/06/the-brand-union-names-juan-tan-as-creative-director-china/#news/news/posts/2011/06/the-brand-union-names-juan-tan-as-creative-director-china (accessed March 25, 2012).

Chapter 6

1. Quote from the Clio Awards website, 1996, http://www.clioawards.com/html/wsj/spivak.html (accessed January 10, 2005).
2. "Famous Quotes on Advertising," Zag Studios, http://www.zagstudios.com/ZagStudios/famous_quotes_on_advertising.htm (accessed January 5, 2015).
3. Daniel Pink, *A Whole New Mind: Why Right-Brainers Will Rule the Future* (New York: Riverhead, 2005), p. 50.
4. Daniel Pink, *A Whole New Mind*, p. 50.
5. Morris Hite, *Adman: Morris Hite's Methods for Winning the Ad Game* (Dallas: E-Heart Press, 1988), p. 165.
6. Paul Arden, *It's Not How Good You Are, It's How Good You Want to Be* (London: Phaidon, 2003), p. 80.
7. Maureen Shirreff, interviewed by authors, February 2009.
8. "Famous Quotes on Advertising," Zag Studios, http://www.zagstudios.com/ZagStudios/famous_quotes_on_advertising.htm (accessed January 5, 2015).
9. Leo Burnett, *100 LEO's: Wit & Wisdom From Leo Burnett* (Chicago: NTC Business Press, 1995), p. 7.
10. Arden, *It's Not How Good You Are*, p. 78.
11. Robin Williams, *The Non-Designer's Design Book: Design and Typographic Principles for the Visual Novice* (Berkeley, CA: Peachpit, 2004), p. 15.
12. Quote from the Clio Awards website, http://www.clioawards.com/html/wsj/krone.html (accessed December 20, 2004).
13. Williams, *The Non-Designer's Design Book*, p. 35.
14. Quote from the Clio Awards website, http://www.cliowards.com/html/wsj/spivak.html (accessed December 20, 2004).
15. Adapted from "The Psychology of Color in Advertising," November 13, 2013, http://jpmktg.com/2013/11/the-psychology-of-color-in-advertising/ (accessed February 12, 2015).
16. Margaret Johnson, "A History Lesson With Häagen-Dazs," May 2015.
17. Williams, *The Non-Designer's Design Book*, p. 71.
18. Woody Pirtle, contribution to *Graphic Design: Inspirations and Innovations*, ed. Diana Martin (Cincinnati, OH: North Light, 1998), p. 50.
19. Kim Hooper, http://day.kimhooperwrites.com/2011/09/12/from-the-experts-jim-durfee (accessed June 15, 2012).
20. "40 Under 40," *Advertising Age*, January 21, 2013, http://adage.com/article/news/ad-age-s-40-40-marketing-agencies-media/239173/#Bond (accessed January 19, 2015).
21. "Top 100 People of the Century," *Advertising Age*, March 29. 1999, http://www.adage.com/century/people.html (accessed June 3, 2005).
22. Ibid.

Chapter 7

1. Thomas O'Guinn, Chris Allen, and Richard Semenik, *Advertising and Integrated Brand Promotion* (Mason, OH: SouthWestern, 2003), p. 50.
2. Quote from the Clio Award website, http://www.clioawards.com/html/wsj/dupuy.htm, 1996 (accessed December 20, 2004).
3. Jim Albright, *Creating the Advertising Message* (Mountain View, CA: Mayfield, 1992), p. 49.
4. "Steve Jobs Quotes," BrainyQuote, http://www.brainyquote.com/quotes/authors/s/steve_jobs.html (accessed January 6, 2012).
5. Nancy Gardner, "Celebrity Voice-Overs: That Not-Too Familiar Voice Could Be Selling You Something," Foster School of Business News Website, December 20, 2005, http://bschool.washington.edu/new/full_stories//voice-overs.html (accessed December 10, 2008).
6. Marc Bain, "Why Doesn't Serenca Williams Have More Sponsorship Deals?" The Atlantic, August 31, 2015, online.
7. Tom Monahan, "When an Ad Is Not a Campaign," *Communication Arts*, May/June 2000, http://ww.comarts.com/ca/colad/tomM_.31.html (accessed May 27, 2005).
8. Bob Garfield, "Top 100 Advertising Campaigns of the Century," *Advertising Age*, March 29, 1999, http://www.adage.com/century/campaigns.html (accessed May 27, 2005).

9. Albright, *Creating the Advertising Message*, p. 49.
10. "21st Century Ad Campaigns," *Advertising Age*, 2015, http://www.adage.com/lp/top15/ (accessed January 15. 2015).
11. Ibid.
12. Adstars 2015, "Preliminary Judges," http://www.adstars.org/judges/judges_view.asp?s=Cha&idx=730&j=1 (accessed January 2, 2015).

Chapter 8

1 David Ogilvy, *Confessions of an Advertising Man* (New York: Ballantine Books, 1971), p. 92.
2. Morris Hite, *Adman: Morris Hite's Methods for Winning the Ad Game* (Dallas: E-Heart Press, 1998), p. 33.
3. Phillip Ward Burton, *Advertising Copywriting* (Lincolnwood, IL: NTC Business, 1991), p. 54.
4. Glenn Griffin and Deborah Morrison, *The Creative Process Illustrated: How Advertising's Big Ideas Are Born* (Cincinnati: How, 2010), p. 128.
5. George Felton, *Advertising: Concept and Copy* (Englewood Cliffs, NJ: Prentice Hall, 1993), p. 93.
6. Kat Gordon, "Crash Landing" May 2015.
7. Denis Higgins, *The Art of Writing Advertising: Conversations With Masters of the Craft: William Bernbach, George Gribbin, David Ogilvy, Leo Burnett, Rosser Reeves* (New York: McGraw-Hill, 2003), p. 92.
8. Kim Hooper, "Writing by Day," http://day.kimhooperwrites.com/2011/09/12/from-the-experts-jim-durfee/ (accessed February 10, 2012).
9. Felton, *Advertising Copywriting*, p. 99.
10. Designers and Art Directors Association of the United Kingdom, *The Copy Book* (Hove, UK: RotoVision SA, 2001), p. 120.
11. John Caples, *Wall Street Journal* ad, 1978.
12. Alex Lahr, "On Being a Sponge," May, 2015.
13. Seth Godin, *All Marketers Are Liars* (New York: Penguin, 2005), p. 9.
14. Ibid., p. 810.
15. Ibid., p. 122.
16. Ibid., p. 89.
17. Higgins, *The Art of Writing Advertising*, p. 118.
18. Caples, *Wall Street Journal* ad, 1978.
19. Zag Studies website, http://www.zagstudios.com/ZagStudios/famous_quotes_on_advertising.html (accessed January 5, 2015).
20. "David Ogilvy Quotes," BrainyQuote, http://www.brainyquotes.com/quotes/keywords/advertising.html (accessed January 6, 2012).
21. Hooper, "Writing by Day."
22. MacMillan Speaker Series, bio, www.macmilliamspeakers.com/janemaas (accessed April 19, 2012).
23. Randall Rothernberg, "The Advertising Century," *Advertising Age*, March 29, 1999, http://www.adage.com/century/Rothenberg.html (accessed June 27, 2005).
24. "TV Ratings: Puppy Bowl X Fetches 13.5 Million Viewers on Super Bowl Sunday," Hollywood Reporter, http://www.hollywoodreporter.com/live-feed/tv-ratings-puppy-bowl-x-677011 (accessed August 19, 2015).
25. Outdoor Advertising Association of America, "Out of Home Advertising: Take Your Message Further," https://www.oaaa.org/OutofHomeAdvertising/OutofHomeAdvertising.aspx (accessed August 19, 2015).

Chapter 9

1 Quote from the Clio Awards website, http://www.cliowards.com/html/wsj.spivak.html (accessed January 10, 2005).
2. Quote from the Clio Awards website, http://www.cliowards.com/html/wsj.riney.html (accessed December 20, 2004).

3. "Advertising & PIB: Kelly Awards," Magazine Publishers of America, http://www.magazine.org/advertising_and_pib/kelly_awards/winners_and_finalists (accessed June 28, 2005).

4. Quote from the Clio Awards website, http://www.cliowards.com/html/wsj.spivak.html (accessed January 10, 2005).

5. "Famous Quotes on Advertising and Copywriting," Zag Studios, http://www.zagstudios.com/ZagStudios/famous_quotes_on_advertising.html (accessed January 5, 2015).

6. Quote from the Clio Awards website, http://www.cliowards.com/html/wsj.mcelligott.html (accessed December 20, 2004).

7. Allstate LGBT community quantitative study, August 2011, and on-the-street qualitative interviews, 2011.

8. CMI's 8th Annual LGBT Community Survey. Community Marketing Inc., 2014.

9. Christopher Warmamen, "Out Holding Hands," May 2015.

10. Brenda Martinez, "Following a Gut Feeling," May 2015.

11. The Editors of *Advertising Age*, "Advertising Age: Top Ad Campaigns," January 12, 2015, http://adage.com/lp/top15/#ebook.

12. Ibid.

Chapter 10

1 Randall Rothenberg, "TV, the Darwinian Darling of Media," *Adweek*, April 27, 2015, p. 22.

2. Luke Sullivan, *Hey Whipple, Squeeze This! A Guide to Creating Great Ads* (New York: John Wiley, 1998), p. 132.

3. "Carol Burnett Quotes," BrainyQuote, http://www.brainygquote.com/quotes/authors/c/carol_burnett.html (accessed January 1, 2015).

4. "Jeff Goodby's Creative Rules," *Advertising Age*, January 29, 2001, Center for Interactive Advertising, http://www.ciadvertising.org/student_account/spring_02/adv382jeoff/ultimategoodby/creative.html (accessed July 6, 2005).

5. A. J. Jewler and B. L. Drewiany, *Creative Strategy in Advertising*, 7th ed. (Belmont, CA: Wadsworth, 2001), p. 160.

6. Paul Townsend, "Why the Future of TV Advertising Is Hazy," November 25, 2014, http://blog.flite.com/home/2014/11/15/why-the-future-of-tv-advertising-is-hazy (accessed December 30, 2014).

7. Christina Knight, "The Real Heroes," May 2015.

8. "How Much Do Television Ads Cost?" December 26, 2014, www.gaebler.com/Television-Advertsing-Costs.htm (accessed December 30, 2014).

9. "Rod Serling Quotes," BrainyQuote, http://www.brainyquote.com/quotes/quotes/r/rodserling102084.html?src=t_television (accessed January 1, 2015).

10. Peter Daboll, "Should CEOs Be in TV Ads?" March 13, 2012, http://www.forbes.com/sites/onmarketing/2012/03/13/should-ceos-be-in-tv-ads/ (accessed December 30, 2014).

11. Derrick Harmon, "Lyrics to Go," May 2015.

12. Mike McAvoy, "From Print to Digital," speech at 2015 Digital Advertising Summit, Marquette University, March 18, 2015.

13. Sullivan, *Hey Whipple*, p. 56.

14. David Ogilvy, *Confessions of an Advertising Man* (New York: Ballantine, 1971), p. 70.

15. Phillip Ward Burton, *Advertising Copywriting* (Lincolnwood, IL: NTC Business, 1991), p. 258.

16. Rothenberg, "TV, the Darwinian Darling of Media."

17. Ibid.

18. Ibid.

19. E. J. Schultz, "Coke Did Not Pay for its 'Mad Men' Role, Says Company," *Advertising Age*, May 18, 2015, http://adage.com/article/cmo-strategy/coke-played-limited-role-mad-men-finale/298668/ (accessed May 19, 2015).

20. "In Pursuit of the Perfect Programmatic Video Strategy," *Adweek*, November 3, 2014, p. T1.

21. Ibid.

22. Karen Lee, "The Lowdown on Lee Clow: Advertising's Chief Creative Maven of the Last Quarter Century," Center for Interactive Advertising, 2000, http://www.ciadvertising.org/student_account/fall_00/adv382j/klee/Lee_Clow.htm (accessed July 6, 2005).

23. "40 Under 40," *Advertising Age*, January 21, 2013, http://adage.com/article/news/ad-age-s-40-40-marketing-agencies-media/239173/#Bond (accessed January 19, 2015).
24. The Editors of *Advertising Age*, *Advertising Age: Top Ad Campaigns*, January 12, 2015, http://adage.com/lp/top15/#ebook.
25. The Editors of *Advertising Age*, *Advertising Age: Top Ad Campaigns*, January 12, 2015, http://adage.com/lp/top15/#ebook.

Chapter 11

1. Keith Reinhard, "Tools Change, Craft Is Forever," *Adweek*, February 16, 2015, p. 14.
2. Danielle Sacks, "The Future of Advertising," *Fast Company*, November 17, 2010, http://www.fastcompany.com/magazine/151/mayhem-on-madison-avenue.html (accessed February 13, 2012).
3. Reinhard, "Tools Change, Craft Is Forever," p. 14.
4. Armen Ghazarian, "5 UX KPIs You Need to Track," Designmodo, May 17, 2014, http://designmodo.com/ux-kpi/html (accessed February 20, 2015).
5. Tim Cadogan, "Single to Sequential Storytelling," Advertising Week Social Club, September 20, 2013, http://www.theawsc.com/2013/09/20/single-to-sequential-storytelling/html (accessed February 20, 2015).
6. Kirk Strong, "Proven Web and Social Media Strategies," speech at Marquette University, October 13, 2013.
7. "Keyword Research," Moz.com, January 2015, http://www.moz.com/beginners-guide-to-seo/keyword-research.html (accessed February 28, 2015).
8. Ibid.
9. Randall Rothenberg, "From Big Data to Big Content," *Adweek*, February 9, 2015, p. 21.
10. Alik Brundrett Marketing + Design, home page, http:/www.alikbundrett.com (accessed August 21, 2015).
11. Nicollete Beard, "Content Marketing With Microsites: Pros, Cons, Examples & Best Practices," Top Rank Online Marketing blog, November 2013, http://www.toprankblog.com/2013/11/microsite-content-best-practices/html (accessed February 17, 2015).
12. Ibid.
13. Danielle Sachs, "The Future of Advertising," *Fast Company*, November 17, 2010, http://www.fastcompany.com/magazine/151/mayhem-on-madison-avenue.html (accessed February 13, 2012.)
14. Freddie Chavda, "Falling Into Advertising," May 2015.
15. http://www.3percentconf.com/index.php/rebecca-rivera (accessed April 19, 2012).
16. "First Mover: Simon Fleming-Wood," *Adweek*, February 6, 2012, p. 12.

Chapter 12

1. Robert Klara, "Catering to Your Mobile Life," *Adweek*, March 2, 2015, p. 26.
2. Marisa D'Amelio, "Digital and the Reimagination of Everything," speech at the 2015 Digital Advertising Summit, Marquette University, March 18, 2015.
3. Pat Chambers, "Content and the Consumer in the Social Age: An In-Depth Look at How BuzzFeed Is Leading the Industry's Trends in Social, Mobile and Video," speech at the 2015 Digital Advertising Summit, Marquette University, March 18, 2015.
4. Jake Rocheleau, "Web Design: 20 Hottest Trends to Watch for in 2014," http://www.hongkiat.com/blog/web-design-trends-2014/ (accessed February 17, 2015).
5. Ki Mae Heussner, "Do Mobile Ads Still Suck?" *Adweek*, February 13, 2012, p. 30.
6. Melissa Hoffmann, "Data Points: Mobile Ads' Big Challenge," *Adweek*, October 27, 2014, p. 14.
7. Don McNeill, "How to Help Create Content That Doesn't Suck," speech at the 2015 Digital Advertising Summit, Marquette University, March 18, 2015.
8. Dave Evans, *Social Media Marketing: The Next Generation of Business Engagement* (Somerset, NJ: John Wiley, 2013). p. 15.
9. "Shazam Update Features a Great New TV Experience, Music Content and an Innovative Facebook Integration," news release, May 15, 2014.

10. eMarketer, http://www.emarketer.com/Article/Mobile-Gaming-Revenues-Lag-Behind-Other-Channels/1010328#IasLgc20VW98jBx0.99 (accessed February 15, 2015).

11. Katy Lynch, "The Social Media Landscape in 2015," speech at the 2015 Digital Advertising Summit, Marquette University, March 18, 2015.

12. Adapted from "Which Platform Is Best," white paper by DMI Mobile Enterprise Solutions, 2013, and Tilo Mitra, "Developing a Web App vs. a Native App," May 9, 2013.

13. Ibid.

14. "Mobile Mistrust," *Adweek*, March 2, 2015, p. 15.

15. "5 Trends Impacting Mobile," *Adweek*, January 5, 2015, p. M1.

16. Augie Ray, "Stop Social Media Marketing," Experience: The Blog, October 7, 2014, http://www.experiencetheblog.com/2014/stop-social-media-marketing.html (accessed January 26, 2015).

17. Don Mathis, "What Facebook's Atlas Means for Brands and Agencies," *Advertising Age*, October 8, 2014, http://adage.com/article/digitalnext/facebook-s-atlas-means-brands-agencies/295293/ (accessed March 20, 2015).

18. Michelle Castillo, "Does Facebook Want to Eat YouTube's Lunch?" *Adweek*, April 20, 2015, p. 12.

19. Compiled from Ketchem.com website, http://www.ketchem.com/wendy%E1%80%99s-pretzel-bacon-cheeseburger (accessed March 28, 2015), and https://www.thinkwithgoogle.com/campaigns/wendys-pretzel-bacon-cheeseburger-love-songs.html (accessed March 28, 2015).

20. Kim Lachance Shandrow, "5 Worst Twitter Marketing Fails of 2014," Entrepreneur.com website, December 18, 2014 http://www.entrepreneur.com/article/240696 (accessed April 1, 2015).

21. Lauren Johnson, "Brands Hitch to YouTube Stars," *Adweek*, April 27, 2015, p. 8.

22. Michael Estrin, "10 Huge Marketing Wins on Instagram," iMedia Connections, May 6, 2014, http://www.imediaconnection.com/content/36444.asp#multiview (accessed March 10, 2015).

23. Gabriel Beltrone, "Instagrammers in Demand by Major Brands," *Adweek*, May 26, 2012, p. 19.

24. "Social Media Visual," *Adweek*, October 21, 2013, pp. S1–S3.

25. Lynch, "The Social Media Landscape in 2015."

26. Emma Bazllian, "Instagram Lags Among Brands," *Adweek*, April 29, 2015, p. 6.

27. Lynch, "The Social Media Landscape in 2015."

28. "Social Media Visual."

29. D'Amelio, "Digital and the Reimagination of Everything."

30. "Pinterest Directory & Stats," Repinly.com (accessed April 10, 2012).

31. Paul Ausick, "Facebook's Instagram Now Claims More Users Than Twitter," 24/7 Wall St. blog, December 10, 2014, http://247wallst.com/apps-software/2014/12/10/facebooks-instagram-now-claims-more-users-than-twitter.html/ (accessed December 14, 2014).

32. Garett Sloane, "Snapchat's Vertical Challenge," *Adweek*, April 27, 2015, p. 20.

33. Lynch, "The Social Media Landscape in 2015."

34. *2015 CMO's Guide to the Social Landscape*, CMO.com, March 9, 2015, http://www.cmo.com/articles/2015/3/4/cmos_guide_2015_social_landscape.html (accessed July 30, 2015), and *2014 CMO's Guide to the Social Landscape*, CMO.com, March 13, 2014, http://www.cmo.com/articles/2014/3/13/_2014_social_intro.html (accessed July 30, 2015).

35. Evans, *Social Media Marketing*.

36. Neal Schaffer, *Maximize Your Social: A One-Stop Guide to Building a Social Media Strategy for Marketing and Business Success* (Somerset, NJ: John Wiley, 2013).

37. Ray, "Stop Social Media Marketing."

38. Kristina Monillos, "Because They're Happy," *Adweek*, March 2, 2015, p. 8.

39. Ray, "Stop Social Media Marketing."

40. Ibid.

41. Ibid.

42. Jeff Koyen, "Mouth Meets Mouse," *Adweek*, November 21, 2011, pp. W1–W9.

43. Lisa Mahapatra, "Social Media Marketing: How Do Top Brands Use Social Platforms?" *International Business Times*, August 9, 2013, http://www.ibtimes.com/social-media-marketing-how-do-top-brands-use-social-platforms-charts-1379457 (accessed April 1, 2015).

44. Paul Maccabee, "Was Ellen's Oscar Selfie Worth $1 Billion to Samsung?" Maccabee blog, May 14, 2014, http://info.maccabee.com/blog/was-ellen's-oscar-selfi-worth-1-billion-to-samsung (accessed March 28, 2015).

45. Suzanne Vranica, "Behind the Preplanned Oscar Selfie: Samsung's Ad Strategy," *Wall Street Journal Online*, March 3, 2014, http://www.wsj./com/articles/SB10001424052702304585004579417533278962674/ (accessed March 28, 2015).

46. Jon Yokogawa, "Rethinking Possible," May 2015.

47. Tim Kirberg, "Rampant Curiosity," April 2015.

48. Anson Alexander, "Top 20 Social Media Quotes of All Time," http://ansonalex.com/technology/top-20-social-media-quotes-of-all-time/ (accessed August 22, 2015).

49. Katy Lynch, "The Social Media Landscape in 2015."

50. Ibid.

51. "40 Under 40," *Advertising Age*, January 21, 2013, http://adage.com/article/news/ad-age-s-40-40-marketing-agencies-media/239173/#Bond (accessed January 19, 2015).

52. "Q & A: Jessica Rodriguez," *Adweek*, April 20, 2015, p. 20.

53. "TR35 Young Innovator," Technology Review (Massachusetts Institute of Technology), 2008, http://www.technologyreview.com/tr35/Profile.aspx?Cand=T&TRID=700 (accessed November 5, 2008).

Chapter 13

1. The Editors of *MediaLife*, "Five Big Coming Trends in Out of Home," *MediaLife*, June 27, 2014, http://www.medialifemagazine.com/five-big-coming-trends-home/ (accessed December 15, 2014).

2. Zag Studios, "Famous Quotes on Advertising & Copywriting," http://www.zagstudios.com/ZagStudios/famous_quotes_on_advertising.html (accessed December 21, 2014).

3. Ibid.

4. Luke Sullivan, *Hey Whipple, Squeeze This! A Guide to Creating Great Ads* (New York: John Wiley, 1998), p. 82.

5. Courtney Scharf, "3 Examples of Exceptional Out-of-Home Advertising Strategies," TrendReports.com, June 26, 2013, http://www.trendreports.com/article/out-of-home-advertising (accessed January 10, 2015).

6. Jay Conrad Levinson, *Guerilla Marketing Attack* (Boston: Houghton Mifflin, 1989), p. 109.

7. Lucia Moses, "The Roadblocks of Native Advertising," *Adweek*, October 13, 2013, p. 14.

8. Ben Lovejoy, "Apple Product Placements Reaches New Heights in Netflix Show 'House of Cards,'" February 5, 2013, http://www.macrumors.com/2013/02/05/apple-product-placement-reaches-new-heights-in-netflix-show-house-of-cards/ (accessed January 17, 2015).

9. FIND/SVP & MediaPost.com (accessed December 15, 2008).

10. Ibid.

11. Will Rust, "East Meets West," May 2015.

12. Adapted from Michael Gerard, "Content Marketing and Native Advertising: What's the Difference?," *Target Marketing Magazine*, January 8, 2014, http://www.targetmarketingmag.com/article/content-marketing-native-advertising-whats-difference/1 (accessed January 16, 2015).

13. George E. Belch and Michael A. Belch, "Sales Promotion," in *Advertising and Promotion: An Integrated Marketing Perspective*, 6th ed. (New York: McGraw-Hill, 2003), pp. 510–561.

14. Amanda Eggert, "Roll Up Your Sleeves," May 2015.

15. George E. Belch and Michael A. Belch, "Public Relations, Publicity, and Corporate Advertising," in *Advertising and Promotion: An Integrated Marketing Perspective*, 10th ed. (New York: McGraw-Hill, 2013), p. 601.

16. "Why Hillary Clinton Is Looking to Adland for Message Makers," *Advertising Age*, January 20, 2015, http://504939-app1.adage.com/article/news/hillary-adland-message-makers/296647.

17. "40 Under 40," *Advertising Age*, January 21, 2013, http://adage.com/article/news/ad-age-s-40-40-marketing-agencies-media/239173/#Bond (accessed January 19, 2015).

18. The Editors of *Advertising Age*, *Advertising Age: Top Ad Campaigns*, January 12, 2015, http://adage.com/lp/top15/#ebook.

Chapter 14

1   Bob Stone and Ron Jacobs, *Successful Direct Marketing Methods*, 7th ed. (New York: McGraw-Hill, 2001), p. 5.

2. Carol Krol, "Marketer's Secret Weapon: Direct Mail," *Direct Marketing News*, February 2011, p. 23.

3. Ibid.

4. Connie O'Kane, "Direct Mail With Promotional Products, Imprint" (publication of the Advertising Specialty Institute), available on Printable Promotions website, http://www.printablepromotions.com/Articles/DirectMail.htm (accessed June 30, 2005).

5. Philip Ward-Burton, *Advertising Copywriting* (Lincolnwood, IL: NTC Business Books, 1991), p. 163.

6. Maxine Paetro, *How to Put Your Book Together and Get a Job in Advertising* (Chicago: The Copy Workshop, 2001), p. 189.

7. Grant Johnson, "Hey, (Your Name Here)! When Does Personalization Go Too Far?" *DIRECT*, February 2008, p. 20.

8. Ibid.

9. Drayton Bird, *Commonsense Direct Marketing*, 3rd ed. (Lincolnwood, IL: NTC Business Books, 1994).

10. "Top 5 Tips: Direct Mail Checklist for 2015," January 9, 2015, http://www.primenet.com/top-5-tips-direct-mail-checklist-fot-2015/ (accessed January 20, 2015).

11. Stuart Feil, "5 Trends Defining Email Today," *Adweek*, October 27, 2014, pp. E1–E2.

12. Ibid.

13. Ibid.

14. Ibid.

15. Ibid.

16. "Better Looking Emails Perform Better," *Adweek*, October 27, 2014, p. E3.

17. Feil, "5 Trends Defining Email Today."

18. Kenneth Clow and Donald Baack, *Integrated Advertising, Promotion and Marketing Communications*, 5th ed. (Upper Saddle River, NJ: Pearson Education, 2012), p. 248.

19. Adapted from "Mail and Email Research Report 2014," Royal Mail MarketReach, January 21, 2015, http://www.slideshare.net/MarketReach/mail-and-email-research-report-2014 (accessed January 23, 2015).

20. "Email Marketers Are Cross-Channel Leaders," *Adweek*, October 27, 2014, p. E5.

21. Sarah Whalen, "Starving for Work," May 2015.

22. Drayton Bird, Wikipedia, http://en.wikipedia.org/wiki/Drayton_Bird (accessed February 22, 2012).

23. "40 Under 40," *Advertising Age*, January 21, 2013, http://adage.com/article/news/ad-age-s-40-40-marketing-agencies-media/239173/ (accessed January 19, 2015).

24. William F. Arens, Michael F. Weigold, and Christian Arens, *Contemporary Advertising*, 10th ed. (Boston: McGraw-Hill, 2006), p. 584.

Chapter 15

1   Luke Sullivan, *Hey Whipple, Squeeze This! A Guide to Creating Great Ads* (New York: John Wiley, 1998), p. 83.

2. Ibid.

3. Seth Godin, *Purple Cow: Transform Your Business by Being Remarkable* (New York: Penguin, 2002), p. 87.

4. Deanna Pogorelc, "Marketing a Product to Physicians? Think Education and Email," July 22, 2013, http://medcitynews.com/2013/07/marketing-a-medical-product-to-physicians-think-education-and-email/ (accessed May 21, 2015).

5. Tim Peterson, "B-to-G Marketers Shift Focus to Digital and Social Channels," *DM News*, August 2011, p. 35.

6. "B2B Marketing 2.0," The Funnel website, June 29, 2010, amc3m.com/b2b-markting-today-and-yesterday (accessed January 11, 2015).

7. Athena Campos, "How Thought Leadership Translates Into Sales," May 2015.

8. Casey Hibbard, "How Social Media Helped Cisco Shave $100,000 Off a Product Launch," *Social Media Examiner*, August 30, 2010, http://www.socialmediaexaminer.com/cisco-social-media-product-launch (accessed February 20, 2012).

9. "American Express OPEN-Social Campaign," afghanistan bananastan, http://www.afghanistanbananastan.com/American-Express-OPEN-Social-Campaign (accessed January 11, 2015).

10. Kate Maddox, "Seven B-to-B Marketing Trends That Will Shape 2015," *Advertising Age*, January 13, 2015, http://adage.com/article/btob/b-b-marketing-trends-shape-2015/296518/ (accessed January 20, 2015).

11. Ibid.

12. Laura Dunn, "Women in Business Q&A: Asha Sharma, COO, Porch.com," Huffington Post, April 9, 2015, http://www.huffingtonpost.com/laura-dunn/women-in-business-qa-asha_b_6635676.html (accessed May 12, 2015).

13. Jennifer Rooney, "The 30 Under 30: Setting a New Standard in Marketing and Advertising," *Forbes*, January 5, 2015, http://www.forbes.com/sites/jenniferrooney/2015/01/05/the-30-under-30-setting-a-new-standard-in-marketing-and-advertising/ (accessed May 12, 2015).

14. Kate Maddox, "B-to-B Software Company Makes You Rethink Global Symbol for Women," *Advertising Age*, May 8, 2015, http://adage.com/article/btob/a-dress-campaign-empowering-women/298531/ (accessed May 12, 2015).

Chapter 16

1 Maxine Paetro, *How to Put Your Book Together and Get a Job in Advertising* (Chicago: Copy Workshop, 2002), p. 152.
2. Email, April 13, 2015.
3. Joyce King Thomas, interview by authors, June 2007.
4. Paul Arden, *It's Not How Good You Are, It's How Good You Want to Be* (London: Phaidon, 2003), p. 30.
5. Paetro, *How to Put Your Book Together*, pp. 185–86.
6. Janet Kestin, "Starting Human," May 2015.
7. Sheri J. Broyles and Jean M. Grow, "Creative Women in Advertising Agencies: Why So Few 'Babes in Boyland,'" *Journal of Consumer Marketing* 15, No. 1 (2008), pp. 4–6.
8. Chris Ellis, "The Power of Local," *Adweek*, October 19, 2011, p. C1.
9. Judy John, interview by authors, July 2007.
10. John Melamed, presentation, Marquette University, Milwaukee, WI, February 10, 2004.
11. Arden, *It's Not How Good You Are*, p. 68.
12. Leo Burnett, "Keep Listening to That Wee, Small Voice," talk to the Chicago Copywriters Club, October 4, 1960.
13. Email, April 13, 2015.
14. Jean Grow and Tony Deng, "Sex Segregation in Advertising Creative Departments Across the Globe," *Advertising & Society Review*, 14, No. 4 (2014), http://muse.jhu.edu/login?auth=0&type=summary&url=/journals/advertising_and_society_review/v014/14.4.grow_fig02.html (accessed March 10, 2015).
15. Ibid.
16. Broyles and Grow, "Creative Women in Advertising Agencies," pp. 4–6.
17. Interview series, April to June 2007.
18. Ibid.
19. Paetro, *How to Put Your Book Together*, p. 156.
20. Email, March 19, 2015.
21. "Women in Advertising: The Power Players," *Advertising Age*, September 24, 2012, http://adage.com/article/special-report-100-most-influential-women-in-advertising/women-advertising-power-players/237258/ (accessed March 14, 2015).
22. Marco, "Cannes Advertising Festival Starts With Young Lions Winners," *Fast Media*, June 21, 2010.
23. Ellis, "The Power of Local."

Appendix

1. Bernie Reeder, "11 Unique Places to Find Quality Content to Share With Prospects," Yesware, March 28, 2014, http://www.yesware.com/blog/2014/03/28/11-unique-places-youll-find-quality-content-share-prospects/ (accessed January 12, 2015).

Index

About the Authors

Tom Altstiel (MS, University of Illinois at Urbana-Champaign, B.A., Valparaiso University) is an owner/partner of Prom Krog Altstiel, Inc. (PKA Marketing), an integrated marketing communications service provider. Tom is responsible for developing creative strategy and tactics for digital, print, broadcast, video, and new business development. Tom has developed creative work for hundreds of consumer and business-to-business clients, including Toyota, Johnson Controls, Eaton, 3M, Evinrude, and Snap-On Tools. He has won over 250 local, regional, and national awards for creative excellence. Since 1999, Tom has been an adjunct instructor at Marquette University, teaching Copywriting, Advanced Copywriting, Campaigns, and Principles of Advertising. He received the Dean's Award for Outstanding Part Time Faculty at Marquette. Follow him on LinkedIn.

Jean Grow (PhD, University of Wisconsin–Madison; M.A., University of Wisconsin–Stevens Point; B.F.A., School of the Art Institute of Chicago) is an Associate Professor of Advertising and Director of the Fine Arts Program at Marquette University. Jean has won numerous fellowships and awards, including AEJMC's Institute for Diverse Leadership in Journalism and Communication Fellowship (2015–2016); a Visiting Professorship, University of Modena, Italy (2013); the Spanish Ministry of Science and Innovation Research Grant (2010–2013); and the Dean's Award for Teaching Excellence (2007). Her academic research appears in publications such as *Advertising & Society Review*, *Communication & Society*, and the *International Journal of Advertising*. Prior to joining the academy, Jean worked as an artists' representative with agency clients such as Leo Burnett, DDB, and JWT on brands including Coca-Cola, Kellogg's, and Zenith. Follow her @jeangrow or on one of her two blogs: ethicalaction.wordpress.com or growculturalgeography.wordpress.com.